Contextualization or Syncretism?

Evangelical Missiological Society Monograph Series

Anthony Casey, Allen Yeh, Mark Kreitzer, and Edward L. Smither
SERIES EDITORS

———————————

A Project of the Evangelical Missiological Society
www.emsweb.org

"Brotherson has crafted a classic exploration of issues that divide Evangelicals on the subject of how far is too far in contextualizing the gospel in ministry among Muslims. . . . He is concerned that the insider movement has inadequately exegeted a variety of Scripture passages. This work is the best I've seen by an experienced practitioner. I highly commend Brotherson's book."

—**Phil Parshall**, SIM, retired

"Brotherson's thorough study brings a much-needed voice to the ongoing discussion surrounding contextualization, particularly in Muslim contexts. . . . Through meticulous analyses of biblical texts and careful treatment of Muslim forms of worship, Brotherson has much to teach us about a 'theology of worship and forms.' This is a foundational study for any future research on contextualization and insider movements."

—**Ayman S. Ibrahim**, Director, Jenkins Center for the Christian Understanding of Islam, The Southern Baptist Theological Seminary

"Brotherson makes a vitally important contribution to debates surrounding the tension between contextualization and syncretism in mission. His consideration of arguments for and against insider movement (IM) methods is welcome. Much discussion of IM from both sides is polemical and undignified, involving far more heat than light. This book is the antithesis of that, being measured, without any agenda, irenic, and extremely helpful. Brotherson's research speaks into a great gap within today's church."

—**Peter G. Riddell**, Senior Research Fellow, Australian College of Theology

"This book is indispensable to any discussion on ministry—teaching, preaching, evangelism, and church planting—because all ministry is cross-cultural, whether we realize it or not. The book's real value is its careful sifting of relevant biblical texts to provide the exegetical warrant for its conclusions. *Contextualization or Syncretism?* is a knowledgeable guide as we navigate the delicate line between contextualization and syncretism."

—**Sam Chan**, author of *Evangelism in a Skeptical World*

"This is a remarkable achievement. Brotherson lucidly applies careful scriptural analysis informed by biblical theology and the missiological experience of a seasoned practitioner to the sensitive and hotly debated topic of insider movements. . . . *Contextualization or Syncretism?* also provides specific applications that aim to strengthen dependence on Christ and seek his glory. I hope it gets a wide reading!"

—**Alan J. Thompson**, Senior New Testament Lecturer, Sydney Missionary and Bible College

Contextualization or Syncretism?

The Use of Other-Faith Worship Forms in the Bible and in Insider Movements

Derek Brotherson

FOREWORD BY
A. Scott Moreau

◆PICKWICK *Publications* • Eugene, Oregon

CONTEXTUALIZATION OR SYNCRETISM?
The Use of Other-Faith Worship Forms in the Bible and in Insider Movements

Evangelical Missiological Society Monograph Series 10

Copyright © 2021 Derek Brotherson. All rights reserved. Except for brief quotations in critical publications or reviews, no part of this book may be reproduced in any manner without prior written permission from the publisher. Write: Permissions, Wipf and Stock Publishers, 199 W. 8th Ave., Suite 3, Eugene, OR 97401.

Pickwick Publications
An Imprint of Wipf and Stock Publishers
199 W. 8th Ave., Suite 3
Eugene, OR 97401

www.wipfandstock.com

PAPERBACK ISBN: 978-1-6667-0105-0
HARDCOVER ISBN: 978-1-6667-0106-7
EBOOK ISBN: 978-1-6667-0107-4

Cataloguing-in-Publication data:

Names: Brotherson, Derek, author. | Moreau, A. Scott, foreword.

Title: Contextualization or syncretism? : the use of other-faith worship forms in the Bible and in insider movements / by Derek Brotherson ; foreword by A. Scott Moreau.

Description: Eugene, OR: Pickwick Publications, 2021 | Evangelical Missiological Society Monograph Series 10 | Includes bibliographical references.

Identifiers: ISBN 978-1-6667-0105-0 (paperback) | ISBN 978-1-6667-0106-7 (hardcover) | ISBN 978-1-6667-0107-4 (ebook)

Subjects: LCSH: Insider movements—Biblical teaching. | Missions—Theory.

Classification: BR128.I57 B76 2021 (print) | BR128.I57 (ebook)

11/09/21

All Scripture quotations, unless otherwise indicated, are taken from the Holy Bible, New International Version®, NIV®. Copyright ©1973, 1978, 1984, 2011 by Biblica, Inc.® Used by permission of Zondervan. All rights reserved worldwide. www.zondervan.com The "NIV" and "New International Version" are trademarks registered in the United States Patent and Trademark Office by Biblica, Inc.®

However, where the Hebrew or Greek text is provided in parentheses, the translations are my own.

For Anna

Contents

Foreword by A. Scott Moreau | xi
Acknowledgments | xv
Abbreviations | xvii

1. **Introduction** | 1
   1. Introduction   1
   2. Statement of the problem   2
   3. Literature review   3
      a. A history of IM and the surrounding debate   4
      b. Contextualization and syncretism in missiological literature generally   18
      c. A key issue: the relationship between form and meaning   28
   4. Assumptions, research methodology, delimitations and definitions   35
      a. Assumptions   35
      b. Research methodology   37
      c. Delimitations   46
      d. Definitions   47
   5. Projected contribution to the field   50

2. **Old Testament Appropriation Texts** | 52
   1. Introduction   52
   2. Genesis 17 and circumcision   52
      a. The relevance of the text to the research problem   53
      b. The meaning of the text for the original audience   55
      c. The meaning of the text for Christians today   66
   3. Exodus 12-13 and the Passover   73
      a. The relevance of the text to the research problem   74

  b. The meaning of the text for the original audience   78
  c. The meaning of the text for Christians today   88
 4. First Chronicles 28 and the temple   92
  a. The relevance of the text to the research problem   93
  b. The meaning of the text for the original audience   95
  c. The meaning of the text for Christians today   105
 5. Conclusion   109

3. **Old Testament Resistance Texts** | 110
 1. Introduction   110
 2. Exodus 32-34   110
  a. The relevance of the text to the research problem   110
  b. The meaning of the text for the original audience   115
  c. The meaning of the text for Christians today   127
 3. Deuteronomy 12   132
  a. The relevance of the text to the research problem   132
  b. The meaning of the text for the original audience   134
  c. The meaning of the text for Christians today   148
 4. Hosea 8   154
  a. The relevance of the text to the research problem   155
  b. The meaning of the text for the original audience   157
  c. The meaning of the text for Christians today   169
 5. Conclusion   173

4. **New Testament Appropriation Texts** | 175
 1. Introduction   175
 2. Acts 2-7 and temple worship   175
  a. The relevance of the text to the research problem   176
  b. The meaning of the text for the original audience   180
  c. Other references to temple worship   191
  d. The implications of Acts 2-7 and related texts for the IM debate   198
 3. Acts 15   202
  a. The relevance of the text to the research problem   202
  b. The meaning of the text for the original audience   205
  c. Other NT references to circumcision, the law and the prohibitions   227
  d. The implications of Acts 15 and related texts for the IM debate   228

4. First Corinthians 8-10   234
5. Conclusion   234

5. **New Testament Resistance Texts | 236**
    1. Introduction   236
    2. Acts 15   236
    3. First Corinthians 8-10   236
        a. The relevance of the text to the research problem   237
        b. The meaning of the text for the original audience   238
        c. Other references to idol food in the NT   260
        d. The implications of 1 Corinthians 8-10 for the IM debate   261
    4. Colossians 2:6-23   270
        a. The relevance of the text to the research problem   271
        b. The meaning of the text for the original audience   274
        c. The implications of Colossians 2 for the IM debate   285
    5. Conclusion   288

6. **Conclusion | 289**
    1. Synthesis and implications   289
        a. The Bible neither permits outright nor prohibits outright the use of the forms of other faiths   289
        b. The Bible asserts a NT freedom to choose forms and equips believers to do so   290
        c. The most important factor in determining a form's usefulness is its impact on worship, *not* contextualization   291
        d. The biblical authors equip form-selectors to choose forms that facilitate worship through a theology of worship and forms   292
    2. How is contextualization to be distinguished from syncretism?   299
    3. A way forward?   300
        a. Poston: IM is syncretistic in its very essence   301
        b. Davis, Peterson and others: the biblical precedent argument   301
        c. Talman and others: the "biblical compatibility" test   303
        d. Kraft: the allegiance test   304
        e. A way forward: a focus on the impact of forms on worship   304
    4. Areas for further study   305

Appendix | 307

Bibliography | 313

Foreword

SINCE THE COINING OF the term in 1972, and the use of it by evangelicals shortly thereafter, contextualization has generated as much confusion and controversy as any other term used in missions today. In the fifty years since its introduction to the missiological world, it has come to be recognized as a reality that has undergirded and permeated the Church since God inaugurated that Body through Christ's reconciling sacrifice. We see it from Old to New Testament, and from the earliest stories of the church to the varieties of the Church seen around the globe today.

One of the challenges is that contextual faith is so close to us that we don't often even see it for what it is. In Wheaton, where I live, I attend a church in an environmentally controlled setting, seated in a comfortable chair, singing hymns and choruses that I'm comfortable with, listening to the pastoral prayer and the Word preached, giving (online these days!), and greeting my church neighbors. I'm so comfortable with it I don't think of it as contextual—it's just "the church service." I may not recognize that the practices, rituals, ethics, art, and social patterns of my church are deeply embedded in my cultural and social norms. For those who have never left their "native church" environment, it often takes believers from others church environments asking questions to which their answer devolves to, "That's just the way we do it."

On the opposite pole, however, contextualization becomes controversial and threatening when different (and, to me, strange) cultural norms are embedded in the church. This is particularly acute when these norms—and the ensuing forms—feel wrong to me because they appear to parallel (or are identical to) non-Christian religious practices. My tendencies to see "other" as "wrong" make this particularly vexing. All too often I am tempted to see your contextually embedded practices as syncretism (or even heresy), and you may well be tempted to see mine in the same way.

Take, for example, the word "Christian." What it has traditionally meant in the West has shifted. But rarely does it mean Crusader, drunkard, promiscuous, and blasphemer. Yet for many Muslims these are far more likely associations with the word "Christian" than charitable, forgiving, loving and merciful. Today I see some of my friends and colleagues shunning the word "evangelical"—in light of what that term means in the larger American landscape. Similarly, it should not surprise us if Muslims who come to faith in Christ do not self-identify as "Christians"—there is just too much baggage associated with the term.

This is but one glimmer of the challenge we see today in the contemporary discussion over "Insider Movements" in Islam. As the discussion and discord has been drawn out over the past several decades, lines have been drawn over the understanding of alleged biblical and historical precedents for movements of God staying within their own religious boundaries and not crossing over into overt "Christian" territory.

During that time, deep and challenging questions have arisen that continue to reverberate in every corner of the missiological world. Until Philip Jenkins popularized the massive and amazing growth of the global church in the early twenty-first century, however, the ideas framing contextualization were largely hidden in the eddies of missiological reflection, and not often seen in theological or exegetical discourses.

Unfortunately, one result has been that the ongoing and divisive debates over Insider Movements has not had the benefit of extended exegetical, theological and historical discourse. We've drawn from the well of anthropology and added limited (and often shallow) biblical discussions (and some prooftexting), but have not had the pleasure of gleaning from in-depth analysis by exegetes, theologians and historians to help guide our discussion.

I'm grateful, then, for Derek Brotherson's deep exegetical and theological dive into the most significant texts used by both sides of the Insider Movement debates. Brotherson clarifies for all of us significant biblical insights about appropriating or resisting forms of worship from other faiths.

I'm grateful that he refuses to draw a simple line either admitting or denying any and all Muslim forms of worship. Rather, on the foundation of significant and clear exegetical reflection, he posits that the biblical authors themselves demand we ask this question: What is the *impact* of using traditionally Muslim forms in Christian worship? He notes that we have freedom to use a variety of forms to worship God, but the biblical authors offer for us a "robust and profound theology of worship and forms." Ultimately, "if using a Muslim worship form compromises true worship in any way, then the use of the form could result in syncretism."

The question is not whether a particular form of worship is itself morally neutral, or whether it coheres with a biblical form, but rather what is the *outcome* of using that particular form on worship. This, he convincingly argues through the book, is what we see again and again in Scripture.

Turning to Insider Movements, rather than giving a blanket answer, he asks the form-givers (or form-adaptors or form-contextualizers) to posit the question themselves: Does using this form enable believers from Muslim backgrounds to truly worship God through Christ? Alternately: Does this form enhance the possibility of moving believers in the direction of false or syncretistic worship?

He conclusively demonstrates that to the biblical authors, form and meaning are not readily separated, and we need to pay clear attention to both. This is the type of discussion of biblical texts by a biblical/theological erudite scholar intimately familiar with the missiological questions that I have been hoping to see for the last 20 years. I will rely heavily on his excellent analysis and conclusions in the years to come.

A. Scott Moreau, DMiss

Dean, Wheaton College Graduate School
Professor of Intercultural Studies

Acknowledgments

I WOULD LIKE TO thank a number of people for their help during the writing of the thesis on which this book is based. I am deeply grateful to my principal supervisor, Dr. Alan Thompson. During my years as an MDiv student at Sydney Missionary and Bible College, I loved attending Alan's classes. His passion for a careful, biblical-theological reading of Scripture that results in the Lord Jesus Christ being known and glorified was infectious and made a lasting impression on me. As a doctoral supervisor, Alan has been kind, wise, and insightful. I have learned so much through my interactions with him.

I am also enormously grateful to my secondary supervisor, Dr. Richard Hibbert. Richard's profound commitment to helping the unreached know Christ, combined with his missiological expertise and experience, have made him a wonderful guide through this journey. Even when I presented ideas to him that differed from his own, he was always full of grace, gentleness, and a constructive mindset. In his journey with cancer, Richard has been a most valued role model, showing me and everyone around him how to face hardship with a joyful hope in Christ.

The research community at Sydney Missionary and Bible College has been a great encouragement and stimulation. It has been a pleasure to be able to participate in this community's regular colloquia via Skype. Particular thanks go to Dr. Kirk Patston and Dr. Alan Mugridge for their contributions as successive directors of postgraduate study, to postgraduate administrative assistant Jenny Rattray, and to the college librarians: Meredith Tsai, Jacqui Buckland, Katrina Traeger, and Janet Kirk. I have done my research from Southeast Asia, and the library staff have been generous and helpful by scanning and emailing material for me. As one who has only recently finished his PhD, Dr. Joshua Reeve has been a much-appreciated source of encouragement and practical advice.

A number of people have assisted by reading draft versions of part or all of the book, and making helpful suggestions. In this regard, I would like to thank Dr. Geoffrey Harper; Dr. Jerry Hwang; my wife, Anna; my parents, Lee and Bev; and a number of colleagues on the field who cannot be named for security reasons. All errors and shortcomings that remain are entirely my own.

I am very grateful to the wonderful people of my mission agency. I am thankful to the leadership for giving me permission to conduct this research while serving on the field. I am thankful to my colleagues, for their encouragement to persevere, and for their probing and stimulating interactions on the topic, sharing their (sometimes strongly-held!) convictions with me, all in the context of brother- and sisterhood in Christ.

I am also thankful to my students here in Southeast Asia, and the missionary community more generally (both local and expatriate), for sharing their insights and experiences. It has been especially helpful and enriching to hear the perspectives of former students who are now serving as evangelists and church planters.

Finally, my deepest thanks go to my wife, Anna, and our children, Liam, Jasmine, Juliet, and Amazon. They are all a profound source of joy and I am so thankful to God for them. Anna has made tremendous sacrifices, and has also been so encouraging and patient. Her commitment to Christ and his mission inspire me.

May God use this book for his glory.

Derek Brotherson

Southeast Asia
October, 2019

Abbreviations

ABCS	Asia Bible Commentary Series
ABD	*Anchor Bible Dictionary*. Edited by David Noel Freedman. 6 vols. New York: Doubleday, 1992.
ANE	Ancient Near East(ern)
AOTC	Abingdon Old Testament Commentaries
ApOTC	Apollos Old Testament Commentary
AYBC	Anchor Yale Bible Commentaries
BBR	*Bulletin for Biblical Research*
BECNT	Baker Exegetical Commentary on the New Testament
BMB	Believer(s) from a Muslim background
BNTC	Black's New Testament Commentaries
BT	Biblical Theology
CI	*Critical Inquiry*
CTJ	*Calvin Theological Journal*
CBQ	*Catholic Biblical Quarterly*
CSR	*Christian Scholar's Review*
DAC	*Dictionary of Asian Christianity*. Edited by Scott W. Sunquist. Grand Rapids: Eerdmans, 2001.
DLNT	*Dictionary of the Later New Testament and its Developments*. Edited by Ralph P. Martin and Peter H. Davids. Downers Grove: IVP, 1997.
DJG	*Dictionary of Jesus and the Gospels*, 2nd ed. Edited by Joel B. Green et al. Downers Grove: IVP Academic, 2013.
DOTHB	*Dictionary of the Old Testament: Historical Books*. Edited by Bill T. Arnold and Hugh G. M. Williamson. Downers Grove: IVP, 2005.

DOTP	*Dictionary of the Old Testament: Pentateuch.* Edited by T. Desmond Alexander and David W. Baker. Downers Grove: IVP, 2003.
DPL	*Dictionary of Paul and His Letters.* Edited by Gerald F. Hawthorne et al. Downers Grove: IVP, 1993.
EDT	*Evangelical Dictionary of Theology.* Edited by Walter Elwell. Grand Rapids: Baker, 1984.
EDWM	*Evangelical Dictionary of World Mission.* Edited by A. Scott Moreau. Grand Rapids: Baker, 2000.
EGGNT	Exegetical Guide to the Greek New Testament
EMQ	*Evangelical Missions Quarterly*
EQ	*Evangelical Quarterly*
ERE	*The Encyclopedia of Religion and Ethics.* Edited by James Hastings et al. Edinburgh: T & T Clark, 1994.
ERT	*Evangelical Review of Theology*
FOTL	Forms of the Old Testament Literature
GNTE	Guides to New Testament Exegesis
HCHCB	Hermeneia: A Critical & Historical Commentary on the Bible
HS	*Hebrew Studies*
HUCA	*Hebrew Union College Annual*
IBMR	*International Bulletin of Missionary Research*
ICC	International Critical Commentary
IJFM	*International Journal of Frontier Missiology*
IM	Insider Movements
IRM	*International Review of Mission*
ITC	International Theological Commentary
IVP	InterVarsity Press
IVPNTC	IVP New Testament Commentary
JAM	*Journal of Asian Mission*
JAOS	*Journal of the American Oriental Society*
JBR	*Journal of Bible and Religion*
JBL	*Journal of Biblical Literature*
JETS	*Journal of the Evangelical Theological Society*
JJS	*Journal of Jewish Studies*
JSNT	*Journal for the Study of the New Testament*

JSOT	*Journal for the Study of the Old Testament*
JSS	*Journal of Semitic Studies*
JTI	*Journal of Theological Interpretations*
JTS	*Journal of Theological Studies*
JPSTC	The JPS Torah Commentary
LXX	Septuagint (The Greek Old Testament)
MIR	*Missiology: An International Review*
MF	*Mission Frontiers*
MS	*Mission Studies*
MT	Masoretic Text
NAC	New American Commentary
NBD	*New Bible Dictionary*. Edited by D. R. Wood et al. 3rd ed. Downers Grove: IVP, 1996.
NCBC	New Cambridge Bible Commentary
NCentBC	New Century Bible Commentary
NDBT	*New Dictionary of Biblical Theology*. Edited by T. Desmond Alexander and Brian S. Rosner. Downers Grove: IVP, 2000.
NIBC	New International Biblical Commentary
NICNT	New International Commentary on the New Testament
NICOT	New International Commentary on the Old Testament
NIDNTTE	*New International Dictionary of New Testament Theology and Exegesis*. Edited by Moisés Silva. 5 vols. Grand Rapids: Zondervan, 2014.
NIDOTTE	*New International Dictionary of Old Testament Theology and Exegesis*. Edited by Willem A. VanGemeren. 5 vols. Grand Rapids: Zondervan, 1997.
NIGTC	The New International Greek Testament Commentary
NIV	New International Version
NIVAC	NIV Application Commentary
NT	New Testament
NTS	*New Testament Studies*
OT	Old Testament
OTL	Old Testament Library
PCS	Preacher's Commentary Series
PNTC	Pillar New Testament Commentary

RQ	*Restoration Quarterly*
RB	*Revue Biblique*
SBT	*Studia Biblica et Theologica*
ST	*Studia Theologica*
SJOT	*Scandinavian Journal of the Old Testament*
SHBC	Smyth & Helwys Bible Commentary
STR	*Southeastern Theological Review*
SFM	*St Francis Magazine*
THOTC	Two Horizons Old Testament Commentary
TJ	*Trinity Journal*
TNTC	Tyndale New Testament Commentaries
TOTC	Tyndale Old Testament Commentaries
TynBul	*Tyndale Bulletin*
UBCS	Understanding the Bible Commentary Series
VT	*Vestus Testamentum*
WBC	Word Biblical Commentary
WestBC	Westminster Bible Companion
ZAW	*Zeitschrift für die Alttestamentliche Wissenschaft*
ZECNT	Zondervan Exegetical Commentary on the New Testament
ZECOT	Zondervan Exegetical Commentary on the Old Testament

1

Introduction

1. Introduction

FOR CENTURIES, CHRISTIAN MISSIONARIES have expressed frustration and disappointment with their lack of success in bringing large numbers of Muslims to faith in Christ.[1] In recent decades, a range of contextualized methods have been used and championed as a means of catalyzing movements of Muslims turning to Christ. They are designed to enable Muslims to come to faith in Christ and yet remain inside their existing socio-religious community. The goal is that unnecessary barriers to conversion are removed, unnecessary "extraction" is avoided, and new believers are able to function as witnesses to Christ within their Muslim communities. These methods are commonly associated with Insider Movements (IM).

In order to retain an insider status, and in an attempt to avoid some of the negative connotations and misunderstandings associated with Christianity in much of the Muslim world, many believers from a Muslim background (BMBs) who are part of IM avoid self-identifying as "Christian." Instead, they retain their Muslim identity, or adopt a modified Muslim identity (for example, "Muslim follower of *Isa al Masih*").[2] An important debate is currently taking place concerning the question of the identity of insiders.[3] However, issues relating to identity will not be the direct focus of this book.

The focus will instead be on the IM approach to practices used by Muslims in their worship (hereafter, "Muslim forms"). There are in fact a variety of approaches to Muslim forms within IM, and not all insiders embrace all of the approaches described here.

---

1. Azumah, "Islam," 7.
2. Dutch, "Should Muslims," 68.
3. See Barnett, "Refusing to Choose"; Green, "Conversion"; Green, "Identity Issues"; Kraft, *Searching*; Greenlee, "Living Out"; Fletcher, "Insider Movements," 179–208; Greenham, "Communal Solidarity," 247–64; Miller, "Word Games," 283–98; Abdo, "BMB's Identity," 435–36.

Nevertheless, the following approaches to Muslim forms are commonly associated with IM, as reflected in the literature of IM proponents.[4] Insiders retain Muslim forms, but seek to invest them with new Christian meanings.[5] So, for example, some use a modified version of the Muslim *sholat* (or *salat*) ritual prayer routine, whereby traditional Muslim body postures are used when praying, but Bible quotations are substituted for Qur'anic ones.

> [These worshipers are] careful to do the necessary ablutions, and to pray with the head covered and feet unshod on a clean surface and to face in the direction of the Ka'ba in Mecca.[6]

Other Muslim worship forms that are "adopted and adapted"[7] to facilitate contextualized worship of Christ include those related to Muslim fasting, music, Scripture-chanting, and festivals.[8] For some insiders, mosque worship is also one of the forms that they retain. These insiders join with Muslims who are not followers of Christ in reciting the Qur'an and the *shahadah* (the Muslim confession of faith which affirms the prophethood of Muhammad), yet as they do so, they inwardly give new, Christian meanings to these practices.[9]

Missionaries seeking to catalyze IM who are not themselves from Muslim backgrounds (sometimes described as "alongsiders")[10] ordinarily use some of these Muslim forms, but not all (for example, most do not attend mosque worship).[11]

2. Statement of the problem

The use by insiders of Muslim forms has generated a lot of controversy.[12] Proponents describe this as good, biblical contextualization, while critics reject it

---

4. See further Farah, "Complexity."
5. Uddin, "Contextualized," 269.
6. Bill and Jane, "Pointing," 88.
7. Higgins, "Key," 156.
8. Parshall, *Muslim*, 171–234. Parshall does not advocate IM, but he does advocate using some Muslim forms.
9. Lewis, "Honoring," 16–18; Parshall, *Muslim*, 71; Farrokh, "Shahada."
10. Travis and Travis, "Roles."
11. Travis and Travis, "Roles"; Farah and Meeker, "W-Spectrum."
12. For summaries of the debate, see Bourne, "Summary"; William, "Inside/Outside."

as syncretistic.[13] The stakes are high. For proponents, IM methodology opens up exciting opportunities for movements to Christ in previously highly resistant areas. For critics, the methodology distorts the gospel, stunting the spiritual growth of insiders and threatening their very salvation.

The field problem that gives rise to this book, then, is the crucial need for BMBs and cross-cultural missionaries to be equipped to discern which of these practices can be embraced as good contextualization, and which would be better avoided because of the potential to produce syncretism.

The conceptual problem that lies behind this field problem is the need for the articulation of a biblically-grounded method for distinguishing contextualization from syncretism. Missiologists frequently acknowledge the difficulty of distinguishing the two concepts. As Van Rheenen notes, this is because they are interrelated:

> Syncretism cannot be defined without an understanding of contextualization since the two processes are interrelated. . . . What is considered authentic contextualization by some may be interpreted as syncretism by others.[14]

Poston suggests that the biblical imperative to contextualize on the one hand, and to avoid syncretism on the other, represents "two seemingly opposed principles."[15] Nevertheless, no consensus on IM can be reached until a biblically-grounded method for distinguishing the two concepts is articulated and agreed upon. For this reason, the basic question explored in this book is: *With regard to the use of forms from other faiths, how, according to the Bible, is contextualization to be distinguished from syncretism?*

3. Literature review

This literature review consists of three parts. First, an analysis of the IM debate; second, an analysis of missiological literature more generally as it relates to contextualization and syncretism; and third, an analysis of the missiological literature relating to the use of the forms of other faiths. At each stage, gaps in the literature and opportunities for further development will be noted. These will then become the basis for the rationale for this book.

---

13. William, "Inside/Outside," 59–64.
14. Van Rheenen, "Syncretism," 3.
15. Poston, "You Must Not," 243.

a. A history of IM and the surrounding debate

Missiologists seeking to describe the history of IM have pointed to a range of influences that contributed to its development. For example, Donald McGavran's writings on "extractionism," the "Homogenous Unit Principle" and "People Movements" are often cited as important influences.[16] However, in keeping with this book's more narrow focus on contextualized use of Muslim forms, the following history of IM will focus on developments related to those practices.

i. Obstacles faced by missionaries in the Muslim world

Before considering the contributions of key individuals to the development of IM methodology, it is helpful to describe the ministry challenges to which these individuals were responding. In the history of the modern missionary movement, there has long been frustration at the "meager number of Muslims coming to faith in Christ."[17] Even the heroes of Muslim ministry in the early twentieth century saw only small numbers of Muslims come to faith despite a lifetime of service. For example, Samuel Zwemer saw "less than a dozen," and William Miller, ten.[18]

A number of reasons have been offered for this. First, missionaries face strong theological resistance to Christianity. A range of foundational Christian doctrines are considered blasphemous or offensive according to the standards of orthodox Islamic theology.[19] Many Muslims are frequently warned to be wary of these teachings. For many Muslims, to believe the Christian doctrine of the Trinity and of Jesus' status as the Son of God is *shirk* (the unpardonable sin).[20]

---

16. Waterman, "Insider," 293; Coleman, *Theological Analysis*, 1; Wolfe, "Insider," 32, 34, 48, 95–96; Higgins, "Inside What?," 75. For McGavran's writings, see McGavran and Wagner, *Understanding*, 163; McGavran, *Bridges*. On other possible influences, see Nikides, "Building," 84–89.

17. Waterman, "Insider," 292. See also Azumah, "Islam," 7.

18. Waterman, "Insider," 292.

19. Islamic thought is diverse, and many prefer to speak of "Islamic theologies" rather than "orthodox Islamic theology": see Schmidtke, "Introduction," 1. Nevertheless, the primary texts of Islam (the Qur'an and Hadith) do contain a polemic against certain Christian doctrines (for example, see Surah 112). See further Thomas and Roggema, *Christian-Muslim Relations*.

20. Coleman, *Analysis*, 8; Corniche, "Allergic Reaction," 11–12.

Second, missionaries face strong cultural resistance. Religion and culture are fused in most parts of the Muslim world.[21] As such, Christianity is closely identified with Western culture and is strongly resisted out of a fear that it will bring with it many perceived Western evils. Missionaries in the Muslim world frequently describe their encounters with this mindset. For example, Travis describes,

> [The word "Christian"] connotes Western culture, war (the Crusades), colonialism and imperialism. . . . [Muslims] associate Christianity . . . [with] negative aspects of present day western culture like immodest dress, sexual promiscuity, disrespect of elders, indulgence in alcohol, Hollywood violence, narcotics and pornography.[22]

Thus resistance to missionaries is often motivated by resistance to values such as immodesty, individualism, personal liberty, consumerism, and greed, which are strongly associated with Western culture in the minds of many Muslims.

Third, missionaries face strong social resistance.[23] Group solidarity and conformity are highly valued in much of the Muslim world, and so there is strong community pressure to remain loyal to the community's faith, Islam.[24] In addition, religious identity is usually fused with ethnic, familial, historical and political identity. And so, for example, participation in Islamic traditions like fasting and ritual prayer is an expression of community solidarity, as well as religious duty.[25] As a result, conversion to Christianity is looked upon by the community not merely as a renunciation of Islam, but also as a rejection of the convert's family, ethnicity, cultural heritage and even nationality.[26] A convert's family or community may feel deeply ashamed of this betrayal, and even expel the convert in order to minimize this shame.[27] Other family and community sanctions imposed may include the confiscation of the convert's children and property, the revocation of inheritance and loss of employment.[28] The result is that Muslims may be reluctant even to listen to the claims of missionaries,

---

21. Wolfe, "Insider," 53; Corniche, "Allergic Reaction," 11–12.
22. Travis, "Messianic," 54. Cf. Massey, "His Ways," 191.
23. Massey, "Misunderstanding," 300–301; Coleman, *Analysis*, 9.
24. Corniche, "Allergic Reaction," 11–12.
25. Wolfe, "Insider," 24–25.
26. Woodberry, "To the Muslims," 25; Dutch, "Should Muslims," 16.
27. See further Frank, *Covered Glory*.
28. Wolfe, "Insider," 52–53.

for fear of the social consequences.²⁹ Thus community pressure functions as a significant obstacle.

It is important to recognize that IM methodology was formulated to address these considerable ministry challenges. According to IM proponents, the cultural and social barriers, more than the theological, have been the primary causes of Muslim resistance.³⁰ On the basis of this conviction, then, they developed contextualized practices designed to permit Muslims to come to Christ without breaking with their cultural heritage or leaving their communities.³¹ As one IM advocate puts it, the goal is to remove fear and "open the door for Muslims to listen to the Gospel with an open mind and heart."³²

ii. Kraft

It was against the background of these obstacles that, in 1974, Charles Kraft made a proposal that significantly shaped evangelical mission to Muslims in the subsequent decades. He called missionaries to "bend every effort toward stimulating a faith renewal movement within Islam."³³ Significantly, he proposed that Muslims coming to faith "maintain their Muslim cultural allegiance, worship forms and self respect."³⁴ In 2005, Kraft further elaborated on the idea:

> For religion is a facet of culture. And, just as the non-religious forms of a culture are available for the expression of Christian faith, so the religious forms of that culture can also be used—on condition that the Satanic power in them is broken and the meanings are Christian. Almost any cultural forms can be captured for Christ.³⁵

---

29. Rick Brown's response in Corwin, "Humble Appeal," 14.
30. McCurry, "Time," 14.
31. Moreau, *Mapping*, 161; Waterman, "Insider," 296.
32. Rick Brown in Corwin, "Humble Appeal," 14.
33. Kraft, "Stress Factors," 143.
34. Kraft, "Religious Barriers," 76.
35. Kraft, "Religion or Faith," 96.

iii. Parshall

Kraft's proposal "launched a wave of exploration in using the religious forms of various Islamic cultures."[36] In 1980, Phil Parshall, a former student of Kraft, published *New Paths in Muslim Evangelism*, in which he described his experiments in using Muslim forms in Bangladesh. This book was very influential.[37] It set out a comprehensive plan for the use of Muslim prayer forms, fasting, music, chanting, festivals and ceremonies.[38] It advocated praying with raised hands, using Islamic terms, wearing Islamic-style clothing, and avoiding pork, alcohol and owning dogs.[39]

During the 1980s, testimonies from BMBs began to emerge in which they embraced and defended the use of Islamic forms. For example, Rafique Uddin, a BMB from East Asia, wrote,

> To me and to many other first-generation believers in Christ it is a necessity that we continue the Islamic forms of worship but give Christian meanings to these forms. Growth in Christ is much easier if culture shocks can be mitigated through retaining as much as possible of the cultural forms of worship.[40]

iv. Woodberry

In 1989, Dudley Woodberry sought to demonstrate that, historically, "the so-called 'pillars of Islam' had for the most part been used before by Jews and Christians."[41] If contemporary Islamic forms were originally borrowed from Jews and Christians, then, reasoned Woodberry, "with some adjustments," they could be used again by believers today.[42] Woodberry's article emboldened some missionaries to an even more radical experimentation with the use of Islamic forms.[43]

---

36. Waterman, "Insider," 295.
37. Wolfe, "Insider," 68.
38. Parshall, *New*, 199–209.
39. Parshall, *New*, 159–219.
40. Uddin, "Contextualized," 269.
41. Woodberry, "Contextualization," 183.
42. Woodberry, "Contextualization," 183.
43. See, for example, Travis and Travis, "Appropriate," 398. See further Moreau, *Mapping*, 161.

v. Travis and the C-Spectrum

In 1998, John Travis classified different types of contextualized Muslim fellowships when he published what came to be known as the C-Spectrum.[44] The spectrum described six increasing levels of engagement with, and use of, Muslim language, forms, and identity.[45] At one end of the spectrum was C1, which referred to believers who use "foreign language and cultural forms." At the other was C5, in which believers "remain legally and socially Muslim," and C6, in which believers keep their faith secret due to fear of persecution.[46]

Travis's publication of the spectrum "lit a firestorm of controversy."[47] The appropriateness of C6 was not debated: because C6 describes a situation "where public confession of Christ is tantamount to imprisonment or martyrdom, "there was widespread agreement that "C-6 believers should be the subject of our prayers, not our analysis."[48] It was C5, rather, that became the focal point for the controversy. Whereas C4 described practices that had been advocated by Parshall eighteen years earlier and which had already gained significant acceptance in the evangelical missionary community, C5 broke new ground. Significantly, C5 believers were "viewed as Muslims by the Muslim community" and often observed all five pillars of the Muslim faith.[49] C5 believers thus used a wider range of Muslim forms and engaged in a more comprehensive reinterpreting of Islamic worship forms.[50] For example, whereas Parshall had encouraged BMBs to use Muslim ritual prayer forms (with modifications) outside *but not inside* the mosque,[51] many C5 believers participated in mosque worship. For some,[52] this included reciting the *shahadah* (the Muslim confession of faith). Whereas C4 believers had refused to do so on the grounds that it affirms the prophethood of Muhammad, C5 believers justified doing so by giving the *shahadah* a new meaning. Higgins explains,

---

44. Travis, "C1 to C6."
45. Woodberry, "To the Muslims," 23–24; Tennent, "Followers," 101.
46. Travis, "C1 to C6," 407–8.
47. William, "Inside/Outside," 58.
48. Tennent, "Followers," 102.
49. Tennent, "Followers," 408.
50. Wolfe, "Insider," 83–84.
51. Parshall, *New*, 202; Parshall, *Beyond*, 84.
52. The spectrum deals in generalizations, and there is considerable diversity within C5. Tennent, "Followers," 103.

Mosque attendance might be not only pragmatic, but could go deeper, becoming a meaningful worship form. Saying the *shahadah* is possible for some, though probably with a qualified meaning such as understanding it to mean that Muhammad had a prophetic role in his earlier, Meccan years.[53]

Thus C5 involved a more comprehensive and radical appropriation of Muslim worship forms, with even mosque worship being conceptualized as meaningful, Christ-centered worship for BMBs.

vi. Insider Movements

In the years that followed, C5 proponents began using the term IM to describe groups of C5 believers. The most frequently cited definition of IM is that of IM proponent Rebecca Lewis:

> An "insider movement" is any movement to faith in Christ where a) the gospel flows through pre-existing communities and social networks, and where b) believing families, as valid expressions of the Body of Christ, remain inside their socioreligious communities, retaining their identity as members of that community while living under the Lordship of Jesus Christ and the authority of the Bible.[54]

In describing IM, it is important to recognize that considerable variety in belief and practice exists amongst IM practitioners and theorists. Not all IM practices discussed in this book are necessarily advocated by any given IM proponent.[55] Yet a common and foundational conviction is that Muslims can live under the lordship of Jesus and the authority of the Bible without severing ties with their pre-conversion religious community.[56] For this to happen, a radical reinterpretation of Muslim forms is required.

For most participants in the debate, C5 and IM are synonymous, and are used interchangeably.[57] Importantly, regarding the use of Muslim forms, there is no significant difference between C5 and IM. Both advocate that Muslim forms be used and radically reinterpreted by believers.

---

53. Higgins, "Identity," 121.

54. Lewis, "Promoting," 75. For additional definitions, see Higgins, "Key," 156; Woodberry, "To the Muslims," 23–24; Smith, "Assessment," 23.

55. Coleman, *Analysis*, 6; Waterman, "Insider," 298–99; Farah, "Complexity," 89.

56. Coleman, *Analysis*, 8.

57. William, "Inside/Outside," 61. Rebecca Lewis is an exception here. See Lewis, "Promoting," 76.

And so, for example, the following description from Higgins of the IM approach to Muslim forms is no different from what had already been articulated as the C5 approach:

> Insider Movements, even as they continue to embrace old forms and expressions, also bring in radically new meanings and truths.[58]

Some IM proponents recommended that a "biblical compatibility" test be used to determine whether a given Muslim form is suitable for use by believers.[59] According to this test, BMBs "retain anything that is compatible with the Bible," reject those elements that are not, and "reinterpret those elements that can be redeemed."[60] Forms are rejected as "biblically incompatible" if they are intrinsically immoral or otherwise explicitly prohibited in the Bible. For Talman, biblically incompatible forms are those with a "dark, deceptive, destructive" character.[61] Lewis cites certain ethically abhorrent practices such as infanticide as examples of forms that are "incompatible with the Gospel and untransformable."[62]

Over time, IM proponents published articles advocating and defending a range of practices in which Islamic forms were used. These included participation in mosque worship (including Qur'an recitation and affirmation of the *shahadah*),[63] participation in the *hajj* (the annual Islamic pilgrimage to Mecca),[64] participation in *ramadan* (the Muslim fasting month),[65] and observance of *zakat* (Muslim alms-giving requirements).[66] It is important to remember that, for IM proponents, use of these Muslim forms involves infusing them with a Christ-centered meaning and function.[67] At the same time as proponents advocated and defended these practices, they also began to report

---

58. Higgins, "Key," 158.

59. See Higgins, "Key," 156; Talman, "Old Testament," 56; Brown, "Biblical Muslims," 70–73; Rebecca Lewis in Brogden, "Inside Out," 35.

60. Talman, "Old Testament," 56.

61. Talman, "Old Testament," 51.

62. Lewis in Brogden, "Inside Out," 35. See further, Brown, "Biblical Muslims," 70–73.

63. William, "Inside/Outside," 62–63.

64. Higgins, "Key," 162.

65. Talman, "Old Testament," 56.

66. Woodberry, "Contextualization," 179–80, 182–83.

67. Higgins, "Acts 15," 38; Woodberry, "To the Muslims," 27; Travis and Woodberry, "When God's Kingdom," 26.

large numbers of Muslims coming to Christ as part of IM, with estimates of believers in certain places being in the hundreds of thousands.[68]

vii. The debate: contextualization or syncretism?

IM methodology has triggered a significant missiological debate. The debate was initially confined to a handful of missiological journals (especially EMQ, IJFM and SFM), but in more recent times it has been taken up in missiological texts, books, monographs, and practitioner websites.[69] Similarly, while it began as a debate amongst missionaries in Muslim countries, it has now attracted the attention of the worldwide church.[70]

IM proponents offer a range of arguments in support of IM methodology. First, they advance a number of biblical arguments. Most commonly, they point to what they describe as a series of biblical precedents for IM methodology.[71] This biblical precedent argument is described in greater detail below (chapter 1, §3.c.iii.). Second, some advance a pragmatic argument, pointing to the significant obstacles faced by missionaries in the Muslim world (chapter 1, §3.a.i. above), and arguing that BMBs need to be able to remain inside their socio-religious communities. Brown, for example, suggests that C4 is "not a feasible way to foster church-planting movements" because C4 believers are usually driven out of the community.[72] Third, some advance an empirical argument, pointing to the existence of large IMs in various parts of the world as evidence that God is at work through IM methodology. For example, Woodberry writes,

---

68. Decker, "Christian," 8.

69. For monographs and books devoted to the topic, see Coleman, *Analysis*; Wolfe, "Insider"; Morton, *Insider*; Carson, *Son of God*; Lingel et al., *Chrislam*; Talman and Travis, *Understanding*; Hwang, *Toward*; Ibrahim and Greenham, *Critique*. For an example of the debate entering general missiological texts, see Moreau et al., *Introducing*, 298. For practitioner websites, see http://btdnetwork.org/, http://muslimministry.blogspot.com.au, http://biblicalmissiology.org/.

70. Some denominations have written position papers on IM. See, for example, PCA Study Committee on Insider Movements, "Report." A proponent of the "emergent church" movement in Western contexts has proposed that IM methodology be applied in the "post-Christian West": Frost and Hirsch, *Shaping*, 93.

71. See, for example, Woodberry, "To the Muslims," 25–27; Massey, "His Ways," 188–97; Higgins, "Key," 158; Brown, "Biblical Muslims," 70; Caldwell, "Jesus in Samaria," 25–31; Higgins, "Identity," 118–22; Lewis, "Integrity," 42.

72. Brown, "Contextualization," 133. See also Woodberry, "To the Muslims," 26; Wolfe, "Insider," 1–2; William, "Inside/Outside," 79–80; Massey, "His Ways," 195.

> There are now case studies of insider movements in a number of regions in Asia and Africa that . . . give clear evidence that God is working in them.[73]

Thus a range of arguments have been offered in support of IM. Underlying all of these is the conviction that IM methodology is an appropriate contextualization of the gospel in Muslim settings.[74]

Critics of IM, for their part, have raised a series of objections. Some argue that IM inappropriately seeks to avoid the persecution of believers, which Jesus predicted would occur.[75] Others claim that IM methodology is deceptive.[76] Others argue that IM takes an inappropriately and unacceptably positive view of the Quran and Muhammad.[77] Others object that Muslim-idiom translations promoted by some IM proponents obscure and compromise the message of Scripture.[78] Others argue that IM methodology stunts the discipleship process.[79] Still others complain that it bypasses the global body of Christ and existing local churches.[80]

However, possibly the most commonly raised objection is that IM methodology is syncretistic. Whereas some express their concern tentatively, speaking of "the danger of syncretism,"[81] or asking if IM has "crossed the line into syncretism,"[82] others are more forthright. Nikides describes IM as "unadulterated syncretism."[83] Poston writes, "This phenomenon is

---

73. Woodberry, "To the Muslims," 25. See also Travis and Travis, "Contextualization," 12; Brown, "Brother Jacob," 41–42.

74. Brown, "Contextualization," 133.

75. Ayub, "Observations," 28; Iskander, "Question Marks," 431–34.

76. Waterman, "Roots," 59; Corwin, "Humble Appeal," 11; Williams, "Aspects," 87; Patterson, "Essential," 365–73.

77. Ibrahim, "Critical Reflections," 139–57; Fadi, "Biblical Salvation," 159–77; Walker, "Why the Church," 105–21.

78. Carson, *Son of God*, ch. 3; Lowe, "Son of God," 299–326; Sanavi, "Insider Movement," 441–46; Harriman, "Epilogue," 455–500; Simnowitz, "Appendix," 501–23.

79. Kuhn, "*Tawḥīd*," 327–44; Barrett Fisher, "Practical Look," 345–62; Akin, "Insider Movement," 451–53.

80. Tennent, "Followers," 111; William, "Inside/Outside," 83; Poston, "You Must Not," 251.

81. Brogden, "Inside Out," 33.

82. Phil Parshall, "My Thirty Year Odyssey with Contextualization," unpublished article, quoted in Williams, "Aspects," 86.

83. Nikides, "Response," 100.

syncretistic in its very essence."[84] Morton asks, "Aren't we really seeing a frog in a suit? Isn't this syncretistic?"[85]

IM proponents have responded to the allegation of syncretism in a variety of ways. Some have conceded the danger, yet maintain their support for IM on the grounds that it is, on balance, the best and most effective approach.[86] However, most respond by arguing that IM is not syncretistic, but is instead a legitimate contextualization of the gospel.[87] Indeed, Rebecca Lewis turns the allegation of syncretism on the critics, suggesting that it is non-IM methodology that is syncretistic, since it requires the importing of foreign forms which distort the gospel.[88]

viii. An analysis of the debate

The debate has now been going for over 20 years, yet no consensus has been reached on the crucial question of whether IM methodology should be embraced as appropriate contextualization, or rejected as syncretistic.[89] William comments on this lack of progress:

> Strikingly, most of those writing in the current debate come from Western, evangelical backgrounds. . . . The disagreement, then, begs the question: if those disagreeing over appropriate contextualization come from largely common backgrounds, what are they disagreeing over and why do they disagree?[90]

What follows is an analysis of some key features of the debate. This analysis highlights gaps in the literature which this book seeks to address.

---

84. Poston, "You Must Not," 252.

85. Morton, *Insider*, ch. 11. See also Patterson, "Essential," 370; Sanavi, "Insider Movement," 445–46; Akin, "Insider Movement," 451.

86. Brown, "Contextualization," 132–33.

87. Travis and Travis, "Contextualization," 12–15; Woodberry, "Contextualization"; Woodberry, "To the Muslims"; Travis, "Must all Muslims"; Travis and Travis, "Appropriate," 397–414.

88. Lewis, "Integrity," 42.

89. Corwin, "Insider Movements," 10–11.

90. William, "Inside/Outside," 58–59.

1. A FOCUS ON A LIMITED AND UNREPRESENTATIVE SELECTION OF BIBLICAL TEXTS

In making the case that there is biblical support for IM practices, IM proponents frequently cite as "precedents" a series of biblical texts that appear to authorize the appropriation by God's people of the forms of other faiths (hereafter, "appropriation texts"). They point to a series of similarities between the worship forms used by Israel and those used by the surrounding nations in the OT era as evidence that borrowing of worship forms is valid.[91] In addition, Melchizidek,[92] Namaan,[93] the sailors in Jonah,[94] the Samaritans in John 4,[95] early Jewish believers,[96] and the Gentiles of Acts 15[97] are all presented as examples of people coming to faith in the true God but continuing to worship from within their pre-existing religious system, using the forms of that system.

Almost all of the debate concerning whether there is biblical support for IM practices focuses on these appropriation texts. However, the biblical data regarding the use by the people of God of the forms of other faiths is more diverse than this. As a minority of participants in the debate have acknowledged,[98] other texts exist that appear to prohibit such appropriations (hereafter, "resistance texts").[99] Most IM proponents do not discuss these texts.[100] In fact, most IM *critics* do not discuss them either. Instead,

---

91. Petersen, "Investigation," 117–29; Talman, "Old Testament," 49–51.

92. Higgins, "Inside What?," 85.

93. Higgins, "Key," 158; Higgins, "Inside What?," 90–91; Higgins, "Biblical Basis," 213–16; Travis, "Messianic," 55; Woodberry, "To the Muslims," 26.

94. Higgins, "Inside What?," 85.

95. Caldwell, "Jesus in Samaria," 25–31; Higgins, "Key," 158–59; Lewis, "Honoring," 17–18; Lewis, "Integrity," 42–43.

96. Brown, "Biblical Muslims," 70; Caldwell, "Jesus in Samaria," 30; Higgins, "Acts 15," 37–38; Higgins, "Inside What?," 77–80; Lewis, "Integrity," 42; Talman, "Islam," 12; Travis, "Messianic," 54.

97. Lewis, "Honoring," 18; Higgins, "Acts 15," 29–40; Woodberry, "To the Muslims," 25–27.

98. See Poston, "You Must Not," 245–52; Nikides, "Response," 100; Nikides, "Lost," ch. 2.1; Talman, "Old Testament," 51–52.

99. For example, Exod 23:23–33; 32:1–35; 34:10–16; Deut 7:25–26; 12:1–32; 16:21–22; 18:9–15; 1 Kgs 12:25–33; 2 Kgs 16:10–18; 17:6–23; 18:4; 23:4–7; Acts 8:9–24; 13:4–12; 15:20, 29; 19:19–20, 1 Cor 8:7–13; 10:14–22; 2 Cor 6:14–18; Col 2:6–22; Heb 8:1—10:39; Rev 2:20–29.

100. Nikides, "Lost," ch. 2.1.

they critique IM proponents' interpretation and application of appropriation texts.[101]

The result is that the IM debate lacks biblical balance. Resistance texts and their implications for IM methodology are rarely considered. As well, very few have considered both sets of texts (appropriation and resistance) alongside each other, in order to discover how they relate to one another and to provide a rationale for the Bible-writers' nuanced stance towards the forms of other faiths.[102] Thus to date, the debate has been based on a limited and unrepresentative selection of biblical texts.

2. An insensitivity to the salvation-historical setting of biblical texts

In advancing their biblical arguments for and against IM, some participants in the debate demonstrate an insensitivity to the salvation-historical setting of biblical texts. In claiming appropriation texts as precedents justifying the use of Muslim forms, IM proponents often fail to identify the stage of salvation history from which the relevant texts are taken, and consider whether any relevant developments have occurred since that time which might prevent the texts being applied as precedents.[103] Likewise, some IM critics have also demonstrated an insensitivity to the progressive nature of revelation.[104]

3. A resistance to input from "outsiders"

Another feature of the debate has been a resistance from some IM proponents to contributions from people who have not had first-hand field experience of IM. IM proponent Travis writes,

> The "validity" of a religious movement such as C5 can only rightly be understood through the interaction of Biblical/theological reflection *and* firsthand experience of what God is doing today in the Muslim world.[105]

---

101. See Tennent, "Followers."
102. Talman is an exception: Talman, "Old Testament," 51–52.
103. See, for example, Petersen, "Investigation," 117–29; Talman, "Old Testament," 49–51; Lewis, "Honoring," 18. See further Garner, "High Stakes."
104. See, for example, Poston, "You Must Not," 245, 252–53.
105. Travis et al., "Four responses," 124 (emphasis original).

IM proponent Massey likewise asserts that IM can only be evaluated by those with "actual ministry experience,"[106] and with personal knowledge of IM believers.[107] He dismisses the input of others on the grounds that they "don't have such relationships, and so base their objections on various biblical points of reference without having seen 'the Holy Spirit poured out upon them.'"[108] Likewise, Greer asks,

> What authority do outsiders actually have as they assess and evaluate what insider believing communities do? Where do outsider theological concerns cross the line and actually exemplify a form of theological imperialism—a *theolonialism?*[109]

IM proponents make an important point here: IM methodology is undoubtedly best understood by those with first-hand experience of the relevant contexts and challenges faced, and who are able to witness signs that God is at work amongst them. However, there is a danger that if the input of "outsiders" is ignored, IM methods will not be subjected to the "normal set of checks and balances that operates in the larger body of Christ."[110] For example, Corwin writes of his concern that IM advocates are "not engaging as broadly as needed with their peers in the larger mission community."[111] Likewise, Moreau writes of the need for participants in the IM debate to bring "into the discussion the resources and insights of those with appropriate expertise."[112] He adds,

> Perhaps most tragic is the appearance that evangelical church historians, religious scholars, theologians, and biblical scholars are not participating [in the debate].... An unfortunate result is that we lose valuable input from outstanding resources.[113]

Similarly, Brogden writes,

> The probing questions of theologians like John Piper have been dismissed because he does not live among Muslims.... To reject

---

106. Massey, "Misunderstanding," 298.
107. Massey, "Misunderstanding," 303.
108. Massey, "Misunderstanding," 303.
109. Greer, "Review," 206 (emphasis original).
110. Moreau, *Mapping*, 164.
111. Corwin, "Humble Appeal," 5.
112. Moreau, *Mapping*, 165.
113. Moreau, *Mapping*, 164–65.

the input of theologians just because they do not live among Muslims can be injudicious.[114]

To the extent that biblical arguments are offered both for and against IM, there is a great need for the input of specialists, particularly biblical scholars.

ix. Recent developments in the debate

There has been a series of developments in the IM debate in recent years. First, whereas the early debate was sometimes marked by a heated tone and even ungenerous characterizations of opponents,[115] increasingly, there have been attempts by practitioners with opposing views to engage in constructive dialogue. For example, "Bridging the Divide" is a network established to bring scholar-practitioners with a range of views together "into a context where personal relationships can be built, issues can be openly and respectfully aired, and differing views can be discussed, with 'iron sharpening iron.'"[116]

Second, whereas participants in the debate have long bemoaned the lack of published field research conducted into IM,[117] recently a series of studies has been published.[118]

Third, there have been developments relating to the terms and analytical tools used in the debate. The usefulness of the C-Spectrum as a descriptive or evaluative tool has been questioned on the grounds that it is "simplistic" and that it unhelpfully focuses the debate upon cultural engagement at the expense of important theological issues.[119] Some have sought alternative labels for different approaches to Muslim contextualization. Jaz and Waterman, for example, use the term CITO (Cultural Insider, Theological Outsider) to describe the approach which they advocate.[120] However, as with the C-Spectrum, CITO has also been criticized for blending together important distinctions and creating misunderstanding.[121] A related development is that Farah and Meeker, recognizing that

114. Brogden, "Inside Out," 36.

115. See Grafas, "View," 936; Massey, "Misunderstanding," 302–4; Dixon, "Moving," 4; Nikides, "Response," 93; Brogden, "Inside Out," 38.

116. Waterman, "Insider," 299. See further Owens, "Syncretism," 78–79; Higgins, "Biblical Basis," 211.

117. Dixon, "Moving," 7.

118. Three field studies are reported in Farrokh, "Umma," 69–80. See also Prenger, *Muslim*.

119. Dixon, "Moving," 8–10; Wolfe, "Insider," 66, 88–89.

120. Jaz, "Cultural Insider"; Waterman, "God's Kingdom."

121. Farah, "Complexity."

confusion has arisen because the categories of the C-Spectrum have sometimes been misapplied to cross-cultural missionaries (whereas they were intended to apply to BMBs), have developed the "W-Spectrum" to classify the different cross-cultural workers' approaches to contextualized Muslim ministry.[122] As well, confusion surrounding the term IM has also led some to adopt different terminology. Alternatives that have been proposed include "Movements to Jesus within Islam," "Kingdom Movements to Jesus," "the Kingdom Paradigm," and "Incarnational Movements."[123] However, the methodology is essentially the same. IM remains the most frequently used term, and so is used in this book.

While some of these developments are to be welcomed as signs that the debate is progressing and maturing, the fundamental tension underlying the debate—that is, confusion regarding how to distinguish contextualization from syncretism—remains unresolved. There is still no consensus on IM.

x. Conclusion: the gap in the literature on IM

The above analysis of the IM debate highlights an important gap in the literature relating to IM. The debate needs to be better informed by a study that considers both appropriation and resistance texts, and especially their relationship to one another. It also needs to draw upon the methods and insights of biblical scholars and the hermeneutical tools of biblical theology to ensure the soundness of interpretations given to key biblical texts, especially those from earlier stages in salvation history.

b. Contextualization and syncretism in missiological literature generally

The debate regarding whether IM can be embraced as good contextualization or rejected as syncretism has not occurred in a vacuum, but rather against the backdrop of developments in missiological literature generally regarding contextualization and syncretism. It is to these that we now turn.

---

122. Farah and Meeker, "W-Spectrum," 366–75.

123. Higgins, "Discipling," 26–27; Garner, "High Stakes," 249; Waterman, "Insider," 298–99.

i. Contextualization

An analysis of the history of contextualization in missiological literature and of the diversity of models that have been proposed is well beyond the scope of this book.[124] Indeed, as Flemming points out, because the term is used by thinkers from a wide range of philosophical and theological perspectives, contextualization is a "slippery" term which is used by different people to mean a range of different things.[125] Since the IM debate is a debate amongst evangelicals, the focus here is to identify commonly accepted evangelical definitions of the term as a platform for the discussion that follows.

Evangelicals typically define contextualization as the process of relating the message of Scripture to local cultures and contexts. Flemming, for example, defines it as "the dynamic and comprehensive process by which the gospel is incarnated within a concrete or historical situation."[126] Likewise, Hesselgrave and Rommen define it as follows:

> the attempt to communicate the message, person, works, Word and will of God in a way that is faithful to God's revelation . . . and that is meaningful to respondents in their respective cultural and existential contexts.[127]

A wide range of matters are described by missiologists as being subjected to the contextualizing process. For example, the literature on contextualization contains discussion of contextualized communication, patterns of relating, leadership, ritual forms, hermeneutics, and theology.[128] Contextualization refers not only to the communication of the gospel by evangelists, but also to its application and expression by believers in all areas of life.[129]

Unlike missiologists from some other traditions, evangelicals ordinarily affirm that Scripture must be given priority over the context into which it is applied.[130] Thus while elements of the context (such as images, metaphors, rituals, and words) might be used by evangelists to make Scripture understandable and impactful, or by believers generally to express

---

124. See Moreau, *Mapping*, 32–45; Keller, *Gospel Contextualization*, 12–15.

125. Flemming, *Contextualization*, 18–19.

126. Flemming, *Contextualization*, 19.

127. Hesselgrave and Rommen, *Contextualization*, 200.

128. Wolfe, "Insider," 19, 174; Keller, *Gospel Contextualization*, 25; Nicholls, *Contextualization*, 24; Carson, *Biblical Interpretation*.

129. Conn, *Eternal Word*, 182; Moreau, *Mapping*, 64–65; Whiteman, "Function," 53.

130. Moreau distinguishes translation models of contextualization which assign Scripture priority over context from existential models which do not: Moreau, "Adapted Message," 335–36.

their faith, evangelicals agree that these elements must not be allowed to distort the meaning of Scripture.[131] Of course, conflicts often arise regarding whether such distortion has occurred.[132] This brings us to a discussion of syncretism in missiological literature.

ii. Syncretism

Evangelicals define syncretism as the blending of biblical faith with non-Christian elements with the result that the integrity of the former is negatively impacted. For example, Moreau defines syncretism as "the replacement or dilution of the essential truths of the gospel through the incorporation of non-Christian elements."[133] Likewise, Van Rheenen suggests,

> [Syncretism is the] reshaping of Christian plausibility structures, beliefs and practices through cultural accommodation so that they reflect those of the dominant culture.[134]

Evangelical definitions of syncretism typically contain two basic elements: a process (aspects of Christian faith are blended with non-Christian elements) and an outcome (Christian faith is compromised). However, the simplicity of these definitions masks a range of difficulties which missiologists have faced in defining and identifying syncretism. It is important to survey these, since they help to explain the confusion and lack of consensus in the IM debate described above.

First, there has been some debate regarding what exactly is being mixed. Some, like Ringgren, limit syncretism to the mixing "of two or more religions."[135] But this has rightly been critiqued, because defining religion and separating it from culture is a notoriously difficult task. In addition, the integrity of Christian faith can equally be distorted when mixed with elements that do not originate in another religion, such as cultural values or political ideologies.[136] Because of this, many evangelicals define syncretism as

---

131. Van Rheenen, "Syncretism," 4; Carson, "Church and Mission," 219–20; Ott et al., *Encountering*, 276–81; Keller, *Gospel Contextualization*, 9; Hesselgrave, "Syncretism," 85.

132. Moreau, *Mapping*, 35.

133. Moreau, "Syncretism," 924.

134. Van Rheenen, "Syncretism," 7.

135. Droogers, "Syncretism," 10. See also Imbach, "Syncretism," 1062; Schmidt, "How Much," 27–28.

136. Richard, "Religious," 209–15; Droogers, "Syncretism," 13; Van Rheenen, "Syncretism," 3; Moreau, "Adapted Message," 331; Brown, "Contextualization," 127–33.

the mixing of Christianity with another "worldview".[137] Yet doing so raises a new set of challenges. As Moreau points out, "the very hiddenness of worldview makes it difficult—perhaps impossible—to grasp well enough to use as an analytic tool."[138] Indeed, the imprecision of the conceptual framework of worldview led to its being jettisoned by anthropologists.[139] For this reason, Moreau himself avoids classifying what is being mixed altogether, simply referring to the incorporation of "non-Christian elements."

Second, the fact that "syncretism" is used with an objective sense by some but with a subjective sense by others has led to confusion.[140] In the social sciences, the term is used objectively. As an example, Kamstra's definition ("the coexistence of elements foreign to each other within a specific religion")[141] is neutral, descriptive and non-evaluative. In theology and missiology, however, the term is usually used subjectively, as a negative evaluation, and so syncretism is a pejorative term.[142] In recent times, however, some non-evangelical theologians have used the term positively,[143] and some evangelicals have used it objectively, with the result that other terms are needed to distinguish the acceptable from the unacceptable. For example, Hollenweger speaks of "theologically responsible syncretism" where most evangelicals would simply use "contextualization".[144] In light of these multiple usages, some evangelicals advocate abandoning the term altogether. For example, Zehner uses "hybridity" instead, arguing that a neutral term helpfully forces evangelicals to actively evaluate the mixing in an ongoing way.[145] However, most evangelicals have retained the term "syncretism" to refer to unacceptable mixing, while using "contextualization" for acceptable mixing.[146]

137. For definitions of the term "worldview," see Hiebert, *Transforming Worldviews*, 25–26; Kraft, *Worldview*, 12.

138. Moreau, *Mapping*, 149.

139. Moreau, *Mapping*, 149.

140. Droogers, "Syncretism," 7.

141. Jaques Kamstra, *Synkretisme: Op de Grens tussen Theologie en Godsdienstenomenologie*. Leiden: Brill, 1970, 9–10, quoted in Droogers, "Syncretism," 10.

142. Droogers, "Syncretism," 12–13.

143. Harrison, *Mixed Religion*, x; Gort, "Syncretism"; Schineller, "Inculturation"; Schreiter, "Defining"; Pannenberg, *Basic*, 85–88.

144. Quoted in Davis, *Poles Apart?*, 23. Cf. Farah, "Complexity," 90; Sumithra, "Syncretism," 262.

145. Zehner, "Orthodox," 585–96. Cf. Burrows and Shaw, "Prologue," xix–xxiv; Burrows, "Theological Ideals," 20–37.

146. Sumithra, "Syncretism," 272; Tanchanpongs, "Developing," 110. What evangelicals describe as contextualization is described by social scientists as syncretism: M. Mullins, "Syncretistic Movements," 809.

A third difficulty relating to the use of the term "syncretism" is that it is used by different scholars to refer to two different types of mixing. Some use it to describe the holding of contradictory tenets.[147] For example, Baird uses the term to describe "cases where two conflicting ideas or practices are brought together and are retained without the benefit of consistency."[148] However, others use it to describe the outcome of a process where the two elements are "relativized"[149] or synthesized to create a third, new element.[150] For example, Kato speaks of a "synthesis" between the gospel and the elements from the receiving culture such that "a totally new 'gospel' appears."[151]

Fourth, further confusion regarding the meaning of syncretism arises from the fact that missiologists sometimes use the term to refer to a spiritually fatal condition ("the gospel is completely veiled and salvation is not possible"),[152] but on other occasions to refer to a spiritually non-fatal condition ("the gospel is augmented or diluted but not compromised so much that the message of salvation through Jesus alone is lost").[153] Hiebert acknowledges that the term is used in two senses:

> In one sense syncretism is a message that has lost the heart of the Gospel. In another sense, it is moving in the wrong direction, away from a fuller knowledge of the Gospel.[154]

Confusion arises where missiologists fail to explain which sense they intend, especially when an author switches between the two senses. For example, when Van Rheenan asserts that "we are always, to some degree, syncretistic," he is surely using the term in the spiritually non-fatal sense. But in the same article he defines syncretism as losing "the essence of the gospel."[155]

Finally, some have objected to any subjective use of the term, on the grounds that when used subjectively, it becomes a tool of oppression used by the powerful to "legitimate [their] own power in religious terms" and suppress diversity and challenges to their authority.[156] While this objection

---

147. Droogers, "Syncretism," 14. See also Nikides's definition: Nikides, "Response," 100.
148. Baird, *Category*, 147.
149. Sumithra, "Syncretism," 260.
150. Droogers, "Syncretism," 14.
151. Kato, "Gospel," 1227.
152. Wolfe, "Insider," 22.
153. Wolfe, "Insider," 22.
154. Hiebert, "Syncretism," 44. Cf. Kato, "Gospel," 1227.
155. Van Rheenen, "Syncretism," 8.
156. Droogers, "Syncretism," 16 (see generally 16–20).

is usually voiced by social scientists and non-evangelical theologians,[157] IM proponents have sometimes quoted it when responding to allegations that IM is syncretistic. For example, Richard writes,

> in Christian circles [syncretism] is most often used as a pejorative against developments in non-Western churches that do not neatly align with Western Christianity.[158]

Kraft is even more explicit:

> This problem is, of course, tied to the question of power. Those with the power to admit or to keep others out of organizations supposedly endorsed by God tend to set their standards according to their own cultural norms rather than according to the intent of God.[159]

In summary, confusion exists regarding the meaning of syncretism, and objections to its traditional evangelical usage (that is, in an evaluative, negative sense) have been forcefully made, and alternatives proposed.

Regarding how the terms syncretism and contextualization are used in this book, Tanchanpongs's comment is helpful here:

> At the end of the day, you can call it as you wish, but biblical authenticity of the Christian faith in a given context must still be evaluated somehow.[160]

The aim of this book is to perform such an evaluation, and beyond a simple definition of terms, to seek a method for distinguishing permissible and impermissible mixing of biblical faith with foreign forms. Notwithstanding the problems associated with the terms "contextualization" and "syncretism," they remain the generally accepted ones for referring to permissible and impermissible mixing, and so are used in this book with the meanings traditionally attached to them by evangelicals: "contextualization" refers to appropriate articulations and applications of Scripture, and "syncretism" refers to inappropriate ones. At the same time, care is taken to avoid the confusion and abuses described above. Of course, the decision to use the terms in this way does not resolve the important question of how to distinguish the appropriate and permissible from the inappropriate and impermissible, and it is to this question that we now turn.

---

157. Harrison, *Mixed Religion*, xv.
158. Richard, "Religious," 209.
159. Kraft, "Contextualizing Communication," 131.
160. Tanchanpongs, "Developing," 113.

iii. How are the two concepts to be distinguished?

Missiologists frequently point out that it is extremely difficult to distinguish contextualization from syncretism.[161] Indeed, the literature abounds with assertions that the two concepts are "in tension"[162] or "seemingly opposed,"[163] and that "there is a very fine line between the two."[164] Likewise, missionaries are depicted as needing to "walk a very narrow path"[165] or as standing "on a razor's edge."[166] The reason for this difficulty is that (as the above discussion of definitions makes clear) the two terms describe one and the same process: the process of relating Scripture to a given context.[167] In common evangelical usage, the only difference is a subjective and evaluative one, whereby contextualization is used for a positive evaluation and syncretism for a negative one. Consequently, as Corwin notes, discussion of this issue often resides "at the level of subjective feeling rather than objective standards," leading him to facetiously comment,

> What's the rule-of-thumb definition for the difference between contextualization and syncretism? Simple: it's contextualization when I do it, but syncretism when you do it![168]

Nevertheless, missiologists have attempted to propose objective methods for distinguishing the two concepts.

One approach (sometimes called the structuralist approach)[169] is to focus on the contextualizing process. In this approach, the focus is upon evaluating the elements of the culture. If the elements are deemed to be neutral or permissible, then using them is appropriate contextualization, but if they are impermissible, it is syncretism. So, for example, Poston applies this approach to argue that where Christians use local *cultural* forms, that is contextualization, but where they use local *religious* forms, that is syncretism.[170] This approach has been critiqued for failing to consider how a particular form is used and what meaning is given to it. Tanchanpongs, for example, says that this

---

161. Van Rheenen, "Syncretism," 9; Owens, "Syncretism," 74–80; Tanchanpongs, "Developing," 109–10; Moreau, "Identifying," 64.

162. Whiteman, "Function," 55.

163. Poston, "You Must Not," 243.

164. Connor, "Culture," 28.

165. Poston, "You Must Not," 243.

166. Hubbard, "Foreword," vii.

167. Van Rheenen, "Syncretism," 9.

168. Corwin, "Telling," 282.

169. Tanchanpongs, "Developing," 115–16.

170. Poston, "You Must Not," 248–50.

approach fails to recognize that "meaning is a function of *both* the cultural-linguistic system *and* its actual usages by people."[171]

Others have advocated focusing on the *outcome* of the contextualizing process when seeking to distinguish syncretism from contextualization. Tanchanpongs, for example, using a cooking metaphor, states, "Authenticity is measured not as much by the presence of certain ingredients, but by the actual outcome of the cooking . . . itself."[172] A variety of outcome-focused tests have been offered. Some claim that the key question is whether the gospel has been truncated[173] or distorted,[174] or has lost its integrity or message.[175] Others propose investigating whether or not scriptural truths have been nullified.[176] Still others suggest asking whether or not the contextualizing process has produced a genuinely biblical framework of beliefs and practices.[177] While these tests are unobjectionable (undoubtedly all evangelicals agree that the gospel should not be distorted), by themselves they have proven insufficient in distinguishing contextualization from syncretism. This is because they merely raise new questions, such as how one determines whether gospel distortion has occurred. More specific criteria are needed.

In light of this need, some have sought to identify a "gospel core," proposing that only distortion of this core should be labeled as syncretism. For McGavran, this core is a belief in the Trinity, the Bible and the basic commands. He proposes that "anything which damages this core is forbidden syncretism."[178] This approach, however, has encountered a range of difficulties. First, proponents of the approach have not been able to agree on what the gospel core actually is.[179] Second, critics, such as Harvie Conn, argued that the Bible itself makes no such distinction between a gospel core and the rest of its message, and warned that the approach creates a canon within a canon.[180] Thus whereas proponents of this approach

---

171. Tanchanpongs, "Developing," 118 (emphasis original).

172. Tanchanpongs, "Developing," 116.

173. Sumithra, "Syncretism," 262–63.

174. Jennings, "Suburban," 166.

175. Hiebert et al., *Folk Religion*, 378.

176. Jennings, "Suburban," 169; Wessels, "Biblical," 52; Rommen and Netland, *Christianity*, 19; Sumithra, "Syncretism," 273; Carson, "Church and Mission," 254.

177. Hiebert et al., *Folk Religion*, 378; Brown, "Contextualization," 127–33.

178. McGavran, "Biblical," 41. See further Haleblian, "Problem," 101; Archer, "Contextualization," 215.

179. Larkin, *Culture* (1988), 107–13; Haleblian, "Problem," 101; Blomberg, "Implications," 226.

180. Conn, "Normativity," 196–97.

attempted to identify "essential, basic and critical elements of Scripture," critics responded that "the entire biblical corpus and all that Scripture is intending to communicate" is "essential, basic and critical."[181] Ultimately, the "gospel core" approach has not proven helpful in distinguishing syncretism from contextualization.[182]

In 1984, Paul Hiebert proposed a model for distinguishing contextualization from syncretism called "critical contextualization."[183] According to this approach, if a pre-existing form is either uncritically rejected (and replaced with a foreign form) or accepted by believers, syncretism is likely to ensue. However, if a four-stage process of critical contextualization is followed by the relevant community of believers, the outcome is likely to be authentic contextualization. The four stages are as follows:

1. Exegesis of the cultural form in question to ascertain its meaning and function;
2. Identification and exegesis of relevant Scripture;
3. A critical evaluation of the form in light of biblical teaching; and
4. The development and implementation of a new contextualized practice (the old form may be retained, rejected, or modified).

Hiebert's critical contextualization helpfully identifies important steps to be taken in distinguishing syncretism from contextualization, and has been widely embraced by evangelicals.[184] However, for reasons discussed below (chapter 1, §3.b.iv.), something more is needed to bring clarity and consensus to the IM debate.

Finally, some missiologists have suggested that no single test or method can be devised which neatly distinguishes syncretism from contextualization. Instead, they propose a range of questions that need to be considered.[185] These include asking whether the contextualized practice

- emphasizes or minimizes the differences between biblical faith and the alternative system of beliefs and values;[186]

---

181. Tanchanpongs, "Developing," 115.

182. Tanchanpongs, "Developing," 115.

183. Hiebert, "Critical Contextualization" (1984); Hiebert, *Anthropological Insights*, 171–92; Hiebert, "Critical Contextualization" (1987); Hiebert, "Syncretism," 43–44.

184. Pocock et al., *Changing*, 332; Owens, "Syncretism," 74–80; Schlorff, "Translational Model," 323.

185. See, for example, Pocock et al., *Changing*, 324; Owens, "Syncretism," 74–80.

186. Van Rheenen, "Syncretism," 9; Hesselgrave, "Traditional Religions," 147–49; Connor, "Culture," 91–93.

- emphasizes or minimizes the sufficiency of Christ;[187]
- produces a church that is identical to society, or one which provides appropriate biblical critiques of society;[188]
- helps believers turn from or retain idolatrous allegiances;[189]
- permits the text's norms to take priority over those of the context.[190]

As with Hiebert's critical contextualization, these questions have proven valuable to missionaries and their worth is broadly acknowledged.[191] However, again, for reasons discussed immediately below, they have proven inadequate to resolve the IM debate. Something more is needed.

iv. Conclusion: the gap in the missiological literature

Missiological attempts to distinguish syncretism from contextualization have not brought consensus to the IM debate because the Bible's teaching regarding permissible and impermissible religious mixing has not been thoroughly studied and understood. The criteria offered by missiologists to distinguish syncretism from contextualization have generally not been formulated inductively from biblical texts, with the result that the Bible's potential to bring clarity to this crucial issue remains untapped. Missiologist A. Scott Moreau has acknowledged the fact that the current missiological discourse concerning contextualization and syncretism lacks biblical grounding. In an article on the topic, he lists a number of biblical texts that deal with syncretism, and then writes:

> For each of the biblical examples, careful exegetical work needs to be done by the Christian community. It is quite clear that there are biblical boundaries on the extent of allowable religious intermingling—but that those boundaries are not always as easy to draw as we might think.[192]

What is needed is a study that performs this "careful exegetical work," examining the biblical data relating to contextualization and

---

187. Rommen and Netland, *Christianity*, 106; Sumithra, "Syncretism," 266.
188. Tanchanpongs, "Developing," 120.
189. Hesselgrave, "Syncretism," 91–95; Moreau, *Mapping*, 129.
190. Conn, *Eternal Word*, 179.
191. Ott et al., *Encountering*, 275–76; Corwin, "Telling," 282–83.
192. Moreau, "Identifying," 51. See further Moreau, *Mapping*, 21.

syncretism—including both appropriation *and* resistance texts—and then developing appropriate evaluative criteria.

Evangelicals agree that any contextualized practice must conform to Scripture.[193] Yet, with regard to the use of the forms from other faiths, there is no agreement or clarity as to what the teaching of Scripture actually is. Hiebert's critical contextualization appropriately calls on communities of believers to identify and interpret relevant scriptural teaching and then apply it to the practice in question. In the case of the IM debate, what is needed, then, is an identification of texts concerning the use by believers of the forms of other faiths, and then a study of those texts that produces a broad and balanced description of the Bible's teaching on this matter. As it stands, this gap in the literature impedes progress in the IM debate.

c. A key issue: the relationship between form and meaning

Missiologists have long debated the relationship between form and meaning.[194] The term "form" is given a broad meaning in this debate, and includes terms, expressions, and practices such as religious rituals.[195] In recent times, two distinct positions on the relationship between form and meaning have emerged within evangelicalism, one pioneered by Kraft, and the other most clearly articulated by Hiebert. Kraft's theory has been heavily drawn on by proponents of IM. At stake in this debate is whether, and to what extent, it is appropriate for believers to use the forms of other faiths. This debate is crucial for the purposes of this book.

i. Kraft

In the 1960s, Nida pioneered the concept of dynamic equivalence in Bible translation, an approach that uses the forms of the receptor language (such as grammatical structures and idioms) to convey the meaning of the original text.[196] In the following decade, Kraft began applying the concept of dynamic equivalence to contextualization and church planting,[197] proposing that missionaries use local cultural and religious forms to express Christian

---

193. Ott et al., *Encountering*, 276; Tanchanpongs, "Developing," 109–10; Hiebert, "Syncretism," 44; Rommen and Netland, *Christianity*, 19.

194. For a history of this debate, see Hiebert, "Form," 102–5.

195. Kraft, *Christianity in Culture* (1979), 64; Schlorff, "Translational Model," 312.

196. Nida and Taber, *Theory*, 200.

197. Kraft, "Dynamic Equivalent," 114–23.

meanings. In support of his proposal, Kraft argues that meanings are not located in cultural forms but rather are constructed by, and located within, people.[198] Cultural and religious forms are "essentially neutral vehicles" that people use to convey meaning.[199] Kraft writes,

> The principle here seems to be that Christianness lies primarily in the functions served and the meanings conveyed by the cultural forms employed, rather than in the forms themselves.... The forms of culture are important not for their own sake but for the sake of that which they convey.[200]

According to Kraft, God's primary concern in not what form a worshiper uses, but what meaning the worshiper attaches to the form (that is, the worshiper's allegiance).[201] Syncretism occurs not because a borrowed religious form is used, but rather because an allegiance to someone or something other than the Christian God is attached to a form.[202] Since "the devotion to God, or lack of it, lies in the way in which the forms are used,"[203] Kraft concludes that almost any cultural and religious form can be used to express allegiance to God through Christ.[204] Thus he encourages missionaries not to introduce foreign, "Christian" forms, but rather to help believers in a given context to attach new meanings to pre-existing religious forms—that is, to change their faith allegiance.[205] For example, he encouraged a missionary in Japan to build Christian shrines which local believers could recognize as "places of power" and so convey the meaning that Christianity is powerful.[206]

Kraft's approach was initially drawn upon by Parshall as he pioneered C4 methodology.[207] And more recently it has been explicitly drawn upon by IM proponents as they have developed and justified IM methodology. For example, the following statement by Common Ground bears witness to Kraft's influence:

---

198. Kraft, "Communicating the Gospel," 34–35; Kraft, "Meaning Equivalence," 162.
199. Kraft, *Christianity in Culture* (1979), 95. See further Kraft, *Anthropology*, 35.
200. Kraft, *Christianity in Culture* (1979), 99.
201. Kraft, "Dynamic Equivalent," 115; Moreau, *Mapping*, 89; Wolfe, "Insider."
202. Kraft, *Christianity in Culture* (2005), 233; Moreau, *Mapping*, 89.
203. Kraft, *Christianity in Culture* (1979), 97.
204. Kraft, *Christianity in Culture* (1979), 93.
205. Kraft, "Christian Ethnotheology," 117; Moreau, *Mapping*, 152.
206. Kraft, "Meaning Equivalence," 161. See further Moreau, *Mapping*, 154.
207. Parshall, *New*, 55–61; Parshall, *Muslim*, 77–82.

> Muslim forms with transformed meaning can become ways of practically living out Jesus' command.. . . . There is no intrinsic spiritual power imbued in Islamic Forms (the Mosque, ritual prayers, fast, etc.). . . .The spiritual power which is present in Islamic forms is dependent upon the faith/belief/conscience of the practitioner.[208]

ii. Hiebert

Kraft's theory has been criticized on the grounds that his distinction between form and meaning is too simplistic and too radical.[209] Haleblian, for example, argues that form and meaning cannot "easily be separated like oil and water," with the result that forms are not always neutral, empty vessels.[210] A number of alternative explanations of the relationship between form and meaning have been offered. These range from Lingenfelter's extreme position that the forms of other faiths are *never* neutral (but rather inherently sinful),[211] to more nuanced arguments that there is no single relationship between form and meaning.[212] The most widely accepted of these is that of Hiebert.

Hiebert maintains that form cannot be completely divorced from meaning in the contextualizing process.[213] One reason for this is that the meaning attached to forms is created and controlled by dominant groups in society.[214] He says it is unrealistic to expect that a particular form "with a deep history within a context" can be stripped of this meaning and given a Christian one, especially where there is strong pressure from the dominant group to accept the meaning traditionally attached to the form.[215] In addition, he argues that not all forms are value-free, but rather that some are

---

208. Quoted in Smith, "Assessment," 36. See also Travis and Travis, "Contextualization," 14; Lewis, "Integrity," 46; Ridgway, "Insider," 79; Higgins in Corwin, "Humble Appeal," 16–17.

209. See, for example, Carson, "Limits," 207–8; Hesselgrave and Rommen, *Contextualization*, 67.

210. Haleblian, "Problem," 105.

211. Lingenfelter, *Transforming*, 19–22.

212. Moreau, *Mapping*, 89; Hesselgrave, "Great Commission," 140; Schlorff, "Translational Model," 318–19.

213. Hiebert, "Form," 107.

214. Hiebert, "Form," 106.

215. Hiebert, "Form," 106–10. See also Zehner, who argues that the original meaning attached to local forms cannot easily be discarded, since the use of the form triggers associations and engages an underlying "cognitive grid" for locals for whom the form has a history. Zehner, "Orthodox," 596.

intrinsically oppressive and evil and so cannot be used to communicate the gospel.[216] Hiebert contends that the relationship between form and meaning is complex and varied. He places forms on a spectrum, ranging from those which have a loose or arbitrary link to meaning, through to those which have a tight link to meaning.[217] Hiebert suggests that while the former can usually be contextualized (that is, given a new, Christian meaning), the latter cannot, because they are too closely tied to non-Christian meanings.[218] He warns that any attempts to do so are likely to produce misunderstanding and syncretism.[219] Given this, Hiebert stresses the need for a thorough examination of local forms—stage one of his critical contextualization—to determine the strength of the link between the form and its meaning in the culture.[220] Thus Hiebert is not opposed to all use of local forms, but warns that some are so saturated in non-Christian meaning that any use by Christians is likely to result in distortions of the gospel.

iii. How are Kraft's and Hiebert's positions justified?

These two opposing theories concerning form and meaning are at the heart of the IM debate.[221] Much is at stake. If Kraft is right, IM methodology can be embraced as appropriate contextualization, but if Hiebert is right, each IM practice needs to be carefully analyzed and relevant dangers guarded against. It is essential, then, to consider how the two positions are justified.

Both Kraft and Hiebert are anthropologists and draw primarily on the social sciences rather than the Bible to justify their positions.[222] For example, Kraft depends on theories from the disciplines of linguistics, translation, communication and anthropology.[223] In the same way, Hiebert draws on studies made by cultural anthropologists and communications theorists.[224] Kraft, however, also draws on the Bible to illustrate his position. Referring to the story of Elijah and the prophets of Baal (1 Kgs 18),

---

216. Hiebert, "Form," 106.
217. Hiebert, "Form," 111–14.
218. Hiebert, "Form," 117.
219. Hiebert, "Form," 117–18.
220. Hiebert, "Form," 117.
221. Moreau, *Mapping*, 160.
222. For discussions of this, see Wan, "Critique"; Hesselgrave and Rommen, *Contextualization*, 59–69; Hesselgrave, *Paradigms*, 261–74.
223. Kraft, *Christianity in Culture* (1979), 64; Kraft, *Communication Theory*, 82–85; Moreau, *Mapping*, 152.
224. Hiebert, "Form," 109–11.

he suggests that the worship forms used by Elijah and those used by the followers of Baal were "very similar."[225] The crucial difference was that of allegiance. Thus, concludes Kraft, the story illustrates that worship forms are "quite incidental to the allegiance that is being expressed through them"; only the latter is "a matter of eternal salvation."[226]

Although Kraft originally provided this biblical text for illustrative purposes only, subsequent missiologists have taken up and developed his suggestion that the Bible itself witnesses to the neutrality of religious forms, and have sought to build a comprehensive biblical case for Kraft's approach to form and meaning. Davis, for example, cites a series of terms and rituals that were first used by pagans, and only later by God's people. In the OT, these include the term El, the covenant-making ritual, circumcision, festivals and feasts, and the architecture and design of the temple;[227] and in the NT, baptism and the Greek philosophical term *logos*.[228] He notes that liberal theologians have long concluded that these appropriations are evidence that biblical faith evolved out of Canaanite and Greek religions.[229] He rejects this conclusion, and suggests instead that the appropriations are biblical evidence of the neutrality of forms, whereby the people of God borrowed pagan religious forms and invested them with new meaning:

> God took what was already in the pagan culture and "transformed" it by giving it both distinctive outward form and new inner meaning.[230]

Syncretism was guarded against, not by avoiding pagan forms, but by avoiding pagan meanings.[231] Davis concludes that "there is nothing inherently wrong in cultural borrowing."[232] He conceives of the biblical examples as "precedents"[233] for missionaries today, and so goes on to make a passionate plea for missionaries to use local forms:

> Whatever else one may deduce, one must accept the fact that Yahweh is in the business of validating all cultures by using what

---

225. Kraft, "Dynamic Equivalent," 118.

226. Kraft, "Dynamic Equivalent," 117–18. For a discussion of Kraft's hermeneutical approach, see Kraft, *Christianity in Culture* (2005), 153–66.

227. Davis, *Poles Apart*, 129–34.

228. Davis, *Poles Apart*, 138.

229. Davis, *Poles Apart*, 128. See further Block, "Other Religions," 46.

230. Davis, *Poles Apart*, 131, cf. 129.

231. Davis, *Poles Apart*, 133.

232. Davis, *Poles Apart*, 131.

233. Davis, *Poles Apart*, 128.

is there (even the architecture!), and transforming it for His usage. If Yahweh did it, why are His servants (missionaries) so reluctant to follow suit?. . . If Israel could borrow from OTHER SURROUNDING CULTURES which were familiar to them, why is it wrong for Asian Christians to borrow from THEIR OWN CULTURES?. . . Surely the heart cry of the African is to express his worship to God, not in unfamiliar foreign forms and meanings, but in local forms that are vital to him because they belong to his own culture.[234]

Davis's method has been taken up by other missiologists. For example, in justifying their statement that "the Bible itself gives us the basis for contextualization,"[235] Ott, Strauss, and Tennent cite Davis and imitate his method: they list a series of pagan forms that were apparently appropriated by Israel and the church, and argue that such appropriations demonstrate that God himself used these pagan religious forms to facilitate the life and worship of his people, all the while "reloading" them with "rich, new meaning to communicate divine truth."[236] The logic is that if God did so, contemporary missionaries can (and should) do so as well.

The same argument has been taken up by IM proponents to provide biblical justification for IM's use of Muslim forms. For example, IM proponent Petersen[237] finds a consistent pattern in the OT whereby Israel appropriates pagan forms but gives them a new meaning.[238] He lists a series of examples to prove his thesis (including the covenant ceremony, Hittite covenant forms, the ritual of circumcision, and the names used for God),[239] suggesting that they are evidence of a deliberate contextualizing policy on the part of God designed to "make the meaning of the divine truths all the more clear to the original audiences in question."[240] Petersen concludes that God was setting a precedent that we are to follow:

---

234. Davis, *Poles Apart*, 134 (emphasis original).

235. Ott et al., *Encountering*, 270.

236. Ott et al., *Encountering*, 271, 273 (see generally 270–74). For other presentations of the biblical precedent argument, see Glasser, "Old Testament," 32–51; Gilliland, "Contextualization," 52–73.

237. Petersen's interest is IM among Hindus, but the biblical argument is the same. Petersen, "Possibility."

238. Petersen, "Investigation," 124.

239. Petersen, "Investigation," 117–22.

240. Petersen, "Investigation," 118.

If it was previously modeled in the pages of the Old Testament, then it must also form an integral part of our contemporary approach to the evangelization of all peoples.[241]

Another IM proponent who uses this argument is Talman. He claims that many Israelite worship forms (including the term for God and the shape of the temple) were borrowed from the Canaanites,[242] suggesting that this happened because God wanted to "communicate his message with maximum impact by using ideas, terms, forms, and elements that were already familiar to the audience."[243] Syncretism was avoided, he says, because the borrowed forms were reinterpreted.[244] However, Talman's argument is more sophisticated than the arguments of Kraft, Davis, and Petersen, since, unlike those scholars, he also acknowledges the presence of a series of OT texts that point to "a strong exclusivist strand" (that is, texts which resist foreign forms).[245] Talman explains the coexistence of these two apparently opposing sets of texts (that is, appropriation and resistance texts) by suggesting that Israel engaged in a process of absorption and rejection, whereby good or neutral forms were appropriated (and, if necessary reinterpreted), but intrinsically evil ones were rejected.[246] Ultimately, he follows Kraft, Davis and Petersen in justifying IM's appropriation and reinterpretation of Muslim forms on the basis of biblical precedent, but in a more nuanced way, since he suggests that believers today must both borrow good forms but also reject bad ones:

> The OT's dual stance toward other religions provides a foundation for insider approaches today, with negative features of other religions being rejected, and positive aspects emulated. . . . As they evaluate their religious heritage, they retain the good and reject, reinterpret or relegate the bad.[247]

iv. Conclusion: the gap in the literature regarding form and meaning

The debate between Kraft and Hiebert regarding the relationship of form and meaning is crucial to the IM debate. Yet no substantial study has been

241. Petersen, "Investigation," 118.
242. Talman, "Old Testament," 49–57.
243. Talman, "Old Testament," 51.
244. Talman, "Old Testament," 51, 57.
245. Talman, "Old Testament," 51–52.
246. Talman, "Old Testament," 51, 57.
247. Talman, "Old Testament," 56.

done to investigate the compatibility of the theories with the biblical data. What is needed is a study that evaluates the competing theories in light of both appropriation and resistance texts.

While attempts have been made to provide a biblical justification for Kraft's theory, these suffer from two weaknesses. First, they deal mainly with appropriation passages and thus fail to give a biblically balanced picture.[248] Second, their analysis of the relevant biblical texts is usually brief: ordinarily they do not engage in an in-depth exegetical study of the texts, nor do they consider whether subsequent developments in salvation history might prevent the texts being treated as precedents.[249] What is needed is a biblical-theological study of a balanced selection of texts which relate to the relationship of form and meaning, and the appropriateness of using the forms of other faiths.

4. Assumptions, research methodology, delimitations, and definitions

a. Assumptions

Several key assumptions are outlined here.[250]

1. It is assumed that the Bible is God's inspired word, that it is a coherent unity, and that as God's revelation it is sufficient to equip believers to determine how to serve God in any culture at any time.[251]

2. It is assumed that, notwithstanding the Bible's unity, there is both continuity and discontinuity between the OT and NT.[252]

3. It is assumed that the Bible should be given a normative role in the contextualizing process.[253] This does not mean that an explicit biblical command or precedent is needed for a missiological method to

---

248. Talman is an exception in this regard. See Talman, "Old Testament," 51.

249. See Davis, *Poles Apart*, 128-34; Ott et al., *Encountering*, 270-74; Petersen, "Investigation," 117-22; Talman, "Old Testament," 49-55.

250. For a discussion of the way some of these assumptions shape responses to the contextualization debates, see Moreau, *Mapping*, 55-56.

251. See Moreau, *Mapping*, 57-60; Coleman, *Analysis*, 20; Van Rheenen, "Syncretism," 19.

252. See Satterthwaite, "Biblical History," 43-51.

253. See Moreau, *Mapping*, 57; Pocock et al., *Changing*, 324.

be valid, but rather that all methods need to be shaped by, consistent with, and evaluated against relevant biblical teaching.[254]

4. It is assumed that the meaning of a biblical text is constrained by authorial intent as expressed in the text (see further chapter 1, §4.b.iii. below).[255]

5. It is assumed that the hermeneutical task is to seek this meaning and to apply it to the contemporary context, and that this task should be performed using commonly accepted literary, grammatical, and historical exegetical tools.[256] Although some have proposed replacing the "grammatico-historical" interpretive method with a "culturo-linguistic" one, it is assumed in this book that the "grammatico-historical" method is a reliable way to discover the meaning of the biblical text.[257] As we engage in the task of seeking the meaning of a biblical text, we should avoid the naïve realist mistake of assuming that it is possible to perfectly understand both the biblical text and the contemporary cultural context into which it is applied, or to come to the task free from biases from our own cultural background.[258] However, this does not mean that the task of critically evaluating missiological methods in light of Scripture should be abandoned, but rather that it should be performed carefully, with humility and in dialogue with a range of viewpoints.[259]

6. It is assumed that the goal of those who advocate for IM methodology (that is, that unreached Muslim peoples might have the opportunity to hear and respond to the gospel) is an excellent one which is consistent with God's missional purposes in the world, and that those engaged in ministry to and with Muslims (both those who use IM methods and those who do not) are co-workers with God in his mission.

---

254. See Coleman, *Analysis*, 20; Ashford, "Great Commission," 177–207; Waterman, "Roots," 57.

255. See Vanhoozer, *Meaning*, 43–97, 201–80.

256. Moreau, *Mapping*, 95–96.

257. See Moreau, *Mapping*, 91; Kraft, *Christianity in Culture* (2005), 104; Carson, *Biblical Interpretation*; Espiritu, "Ethnohermeneutics"; Tappeiner, "Response"; Whelchel, "Ethnohermeneutics."

258. In his discussion of epistemology, Hiebert distinguishes between "naïve realists" (who believe that we can know reality in all its fullness) and "critical realists" (who recognize that our grasp of truth is imperfect, but believe that it can nevertheless be improved through diligent study of Scripture and the relevant cultural context). Hiebert, *Anthropological Reflections*, 19–51. See also Strauss, "Role," 99–128; Jennings, "Suburban," 169.

259. See further Coleman, "Coleman Responds," 49.

b. Research methodology

The methodology employed in this book is as follows. In chapters 2–5, selected appropriation and resistance texts from the OT and NT are studied. Drawing on a range of exegetical tools, especially those of biblical theology (BT), the message intended by the author in each passage is sought, and the text is placed in its biblical theological context. At the same time, interpretations given to these texts by participants in the IM debate, and claims made on the basis of these to justify or critique IM, are evaluated and the implications for the IM debate are outlined. In chapter 6, the results are synthesized to produce a summary of the Bible's teaching regarding how, with regard to the use of the forms of other faiths, syncretism may be distinguished from contextualization.

What follows is a further elaboration of three key features of this methodology.

i. Why a focus on biblical analysis rather than field research?

Attempts to evaluate IM practices purely through biblical analysis have, in the past, drawn sharp criticism from IM proponents, who question the value of studies done in isolation from field research and personal experience of IM.[260] In light of this, some justification for my decision to focus on biblical analysis rather than field research is necessary.

The evaluation of contextualized practices involves a number of stages, as Hiebert's critical contextualization model makes clear. These include exegesis of a particular local form to ensure its meaning and function is properly understood ("form-exegesis"), and exegesis of relevant biblical texts to identify the Bible's teaching on the matter ("text-exegesis"). While field research and experience are needed to perform form-exegesis well, this is not the case with text-exegesis,[261] and it is text-exegesis that I propose to do in this book. Although I do live and serve in a Muslim-majority context, and regularly engage in Muslim-form-exegesis as part of my ministry here, because of the significant gaps in the literature identified above regarding the relevant biblical teaching, in this research I have chosen to focus on text-exegesis. This means that I will not be drawing conclusions about whether particular Muslim forms should be used in particular contexts. Rather, my

---

260. See chapter 1, §1.3.a.viii.3. above and also Greer, "Review," 204.

261. This is not to say that the biblical exegesis stage cannot be enriched through engagement with the perspectives of scholars from a variety of social and cultural backgrounds. See further Coleman, "Coleman Responds," 52.

goal is to identify and articulate the biblical teaching that needs to be considered by those who are making such decisions in whatever context they find themselves. It is my hope that my research will be applied to a variety of specific contexts by BMBs and missionaries who understand the meaning and function of Muslim forms in their specific contexts.

ii. Why a preference for biblical theology?

The decision to use the hermeneutical tools of BT requires explanation.[262] A strength of BT is that it begins with the themes and categories raised by the text itself, before moving to seek contemporary applications.[263] By contrast, in missiological debates, this order is often reversed, that is, participants begin with categories and themes raised in the field, then take those to Scripture. For example, Rick Brown writes,

> I had been a rejectionist, and it was hard for me to accept that God was blessing insider movements. . . . But as I worked with godly Messianic Muslims from different countries, it became evident that God was leading them and blessing them. And as I searched the Scriptures, I found justification for diversity and contextualization.[264]

This approach (moving from field to Scripture) is necessary and desirable. Nevertheless, there is a danger that categories and themes foreign to biblical texts will be imposed on them, and that their original meaning will thus be missed or distorted. Therefore a study which seeks to be sensitive to the agenda set by the texts themselves should prove to be a helpful contribution to the IM debate.[265]

Another strength of BT is that it seeks to explain how the OT relates to the NT, and is sensitive to the progressive nature of revelation.[266] As dis-

---

262. The term BT has come to refer to a range of approaches, and so it is necessary to further clarify: I propose to employ the method that is described by Klink and Lockett in their taxonomy of types of BT as "Biblical Theology as History of Redemption" and which is applied in the *New Dictionary of Biblical Theology*. Klink and Lockett, *Understanding*, 59–89; Alexander and Rosner, *NDBT*, 3–114, 115–864.

263. Carson, "Current Issues," 29; Klink and Lockett, *Understanding*, 82; Rosner, "Biblical Theology," 3–10; Vanhoozer, "Exegesis," 52–63.

264. Corwin, "Humble Appeal," 9. Cf. Rebecca Lewis's comments in Corwin, "Humble Appeal," 8.

265. See further, Tennent, "Followers," 109; Smith, "Assessment," 31; Nikides, "Response," 110.

266. Klink and Lockett, *Understanding*, 61, 85.

cussed above, participants in the IM debate have not always considered the salvation-historical setting of texts, and have sometimes ignored the progressive nature of revelation, particularly through the practice of treating texts from earlier salvation-historical eras as precedents which justify contemporary practice. Therefore, a study which uses the hermeneutical tools of BT should be a useful contribution to the debate.

iii. Why a focus on identifying authorial intent?

According to the biblical precedent argument, biblical texts which depict God and his people using pagan forms function as precedents for believers today to use Muslim forms. Because this argument amounts to a claim that the biblical texts can be *applied* in a certain way, it is necessary to consider the hermeneutical principles associated with what Doriani calls the "theory and practice of application."[267]

Evangelical scholars writing in the field of hermeneutics generally agree that the interpretative process involves two stages: exegesis (identifying the original, intended meaning) and application (identifying the contemporary relevance).[268] Although they propose a variety of methods for identifying a text's application, on one foundational matter there is a strong consensus: the contemporary application of a text must be based on, and controlled by, the text's original meaning. Doriani writes,

> *Application* rests upon exegesis.... We cannot expect to discover the contemporary meaning of the Bible unless we know its original meaning.[269]

Likewise, Osborne insists that a text must be applied "in the same way it was used in the original setting.... The most important thing . . . is to base the application . . . on the intended meaning of the text."[270] Similarly, Fee and Stuart state,

---

267. Doriani, *Biblical Application*, 1–11.

268. They do not agree, however, on what amounts to the best terminology to describe the second stage. Doriani uses the term "application"; Fee and Stuart use "hermeneutics"; Osborne uses "contextualization"; Hirsch uses "significance"; Vanhoozer uses "application" and "appropriation." Doriani, *Biblical Application*, 3, 18–27; Fee and Stuart, *How to Read*, 23–31; Osborne, *Hermeneutical*, 410–33; Hirsch, "Meaning," 202–24; Vanhoozer, *Meaning*, 375.

269. Doriani, *Biblical Application*, 3–4, 19.

270. Osborne, *Hermeneutical*, 432–33, 441.

> The only proper control for [application] is to be found *in the original intent of the biblical text*....Otherwise biblical texts can be made to mean whatever they mean to any given reader. But such hermeneutics becomes total subjectivity....*A text cannot mean what it never meant.*[271]

Hirsch defends this foundational principle of application on ethical grounds:

> To treat an author's words merely as grist for one's own mill is ethically analogous to using another man merely for one's own purposes.[272]

Vanhoozer defends the principle by drawing upon speech-act theory. A biblical text, he points out, is a communicative act. Responsible readers will respect the aim of the communicative act,[273] and so the significance for a contemporary reader can only be identified once the reader has "first understood the communicative act for what it is."[274] The reader must attend to the same matter that the author intended.[275] Thus, he concludes, performance of the application stage of hermeneutics depends on the successful completion of the exegesis stage.[276] Vanhoozer goes on to warn that if readers "ignore the author's intended meaning as a goal and guide . . . , a text becomes a screen on which readers project their own images or a surface that reflects the interpreter's own face."[277]

Therefore, as we analyze appropriation and resistance texts in this study, the goal will be to identify the meaning intended by the author, as evident in the text. Given our special focus on the question of using the forms of other faiths, the *specific* goal will be to identify *whether or not the biblical author intended to communicate a message about using the forms of other faiths*, and if so, what that message was.

In regard to a focus on authorial intention, three qualifications need to be noted. First, the task of identifying the author's intended meaning does not involve a search for extra-biblical clues as to the actual subjective intentions of the author. Rather, it necessitates studying inferences in the text itself that enable the interpreter to identify "the theological concerns

---

271. Fee and Stuart, *How to Read*, 29–30 (emphasis original).
272. Hirsch, *Aims*, 91.
273. Vanhoozer, *Meaning*, 402.
274. Vanhoozer, *Meaning*, 260.
275. Vanhoozer, *Meaning*, 402.
276. Vanhoozer, *Meaning*, 260.
277. Vanhoozer, *Meaning*, 263. For similar articulations of this principle, see Klein et al., *Introduction*, 482; Köstenberger and Patterson, *Invitation*, 790.

and emphases that the . . . author has chosen to make known."[278] Second, some have helpfully questioned whether the interpretative process can really be neatly divided into a two-stage process of exegesis and interpretation, instead proposing that the two are fused and the boundary between them is fuzzy and permeable. These scholars do not reject the principle that application must be based on exegesis. They simply question whether it is possible to neatly separate them.[279] Third, beginning in the twentieth century, substantial challenges began to be made to this interpretative approach, and a number of evangelical defenses of the possibility and desirability of seeking the author's intended meaning subsequently appeared. Since both IM advocates and critics would appear to accept the evangelical consensus that it is possible and desirable to identify authorial intent, it is not necessary to engage this debate here.[280]

An additional, related matter warrants discussion at this point. A more specific body of literature exists which addresses the question of whether biblical *narratives* can function as precedents for Christians today.[281] This literature is of particular relevance for our purposes, since many of the texts claimed as precedents are narrative texts.

At issue here is whether descriptive history can or should be taken as normative for the church.[282] The fundamental principle that emerges from the literature is that, ultimately, the question needs to be resolved by reference to authorial intention. Fee, for example, writes,

> The major task of the interpreter of historical narrative is to discover the author's (and Holy Spirit's) *intent* in the recording of that history. . . . Historical precedent, to have normative value, must be related to intent. That is, if it can be shown that the purpose of a given narrative is to *establish* precedent, then such precedent should be regarded as normative.[283]

Similarly, Larkin asserts, "Historical material does not become authoritative historical precedent unless the author intends it so."[284]

Further, this crucially important authorial intent is revealed in the text, since, as Doriani notes, "Biblical narratives guide readers in their

---

278. Köstenberger and Patterson, *Invitation*, 386–87.
279. See Frame, *Doctrine*, 67, 97; Doriani, *Biblical Application*, 18–27.
280. See further Vanhoozer, *Meaning*, 373; Hirsch, *Validity*, 1–287.
281. See Fee, *Gospel and Spirit*, 83–104; Johnson, *Acts*, 4–13; Liefeld, *Interpreting*, 49–60; Köstenberger and Patterson, *Invitation*, 242–44; Walsh, *Old Testament*, 121–30.
282. Fee, *Gospel and Spirit*, 85.
283. Fee, *Gospel and Spirit*, 90, 92 (emphasis original).
284. Larkin, *Culture* (2003), 112. Cf. Doriani, *Biblical Application*, 199.

proper use. . . . Narratives suggest when the author intends a protagonist to set a precedent."[285] A text might do this explicitly or implicitly, but the important point is that the text itself contains "sufficient direction for readers."[286] Thus the role of the interpreter is to seek clues in the text itself regarding whether or not the author intended the narrative to function as a precedent.[287] Kostenberger justifies this approach by reference to the nature of biblical narrative:

> Biblical historical narrative is more than an accurate account of past events; it is a selective presentation of the facts designed to present a theological evaluation of that record—one that will bring about a proper spiritual and ethical response on the part of its readers.[288]

Thus the interpreter's task is to seek clues in the text that identify the author's authoritative interpretation of events and desired response. If there is evidence in the text that the response which the author intended to elicit from the reader was in fact the imitation of a particular protagonist's actions, then the text should indeed be applied as a precedent. If not, then to claim the text as a biblical precedent is to misuse it. After all, "only what is in keeping with the authorial intention expressed in the text carries with it biblical authority."[289]

Three cautions emerge from the literature concerning the use of biblical narratives as precedent. First, some of the events recorded in biblical narratives have a distinct and special salvation-historical function, and should be recognized as unique and unrepeatable.[290] It would be a mistake, therefore, to treat such texts as precedential.[291] Second, there are special risks and difficulties associated with treating God's actions as having precedential value, since not everything that God does is something which humans are called, or even permitted, to imitate.[292] Importantly, where

---

285. Doriani, *Biblical Application*, 207, 211.
286. Doriani, *Biblical Application*, 210.
287. Doriani, *Biblical Application*, 201.
288. Köstenberger and Patterson, *Invitation*, 244, see further 242, 372, 390, 741.
289. Köstenberger and Patterson, *Invitation*, 743. Regarding how to identify whether the biblical author intended that a text function as a precedent, see Doriani, *Biblical Application*, 195; Larkin, *Culture* (2003), 107–12; Fee, *Gospel and Spirit*, 94; Köstenberger and Patterson, *Invitation*, 385.
290. Liefeld, *Interpreting*, 58. See also, Doriani, *Biblical Application*, 86–87; Johnson, *Acts*, 5–13; Garner, "High Stakes," 270–72.
291. Carson, "Church and Mission," 232.
292. Cf. the distinction between God's communicable and incommunicable

God or Christ exercise "the prerogatives of deity . . . these acts we cannot directly imitate."[293] Third, interpreters need to be very careful when seeking to draw a universal norm from a particular historical event through the use of analogy. An example, suggests Fee, would be to argue for the necessity of water baptism for all believers on the basis of Jesus' baptism.[294] Fee argues that such analogizing involves a logical *non sequitur* and is usually bad exegesis.[295] He concludes that "the use of historical precedent as an analogy by which to establish a norm is never valid in itself."[296] Thus both general hermeneutical literature on the theory of application, and also specialized literature regarding the use of biblical narratives as precedents, affirm the fundamental importance of identifying authorial intent. For this reason, doing so is a key goal of the biblical analysis in this book.

iv. Schema for examining biblical texts

The schema used in the examination of biblical texts in chapters 2–5 is as follows. Each passage is analyzed in the following three stages:

a. **The relevance of the text to the research problem:** For a text to be relevant, it needs to deal with the use of the forms of other faiths by God's people *in their worship of the true God*. A text that depicts God's people using the forms of other faiths to worship other deities is not relevant.

b. **The meaning of the text for the original audience:** The goal of this stage is to discover the meaning intended by the author at the time of writing, and so the text is analyzed in its original historical, literary and cultural context.[297] The analysis begins with the following question: *Is there evidence in the text that the author is seeking to persuade the reader to appropriate or resist foreign forms?* If evidence of such an authorial intent is identified, it is presented and analyzed. If it is not, it follows that the purposes of the author must lie elsewhere, and so an additional question is asked: *What then is the author's purpose?* Finally, as we shall see in chapters 2–5, an inductive study of each

---

attributes in systematic theology: Horton, *Christian Faith*, 223–72.

293. Doriani, *Biblical Application*, 206.

294. Fee, *Gospel and Spirit*, 94.

295. Fee, *Gospel and Spirit*, 94.

296. Fee, *Gospel and Spirit*, 94.

297. Klink and Lockett, *Understanding*, 66; Vanhoozer, "Exegesis," 52–63; Beale, *We Become*, 23; Rosner, "Biblical Theology," 3–10; Goldsworthy, "Gospel," 50; Carson, "Worship," 15; Rosner, "Biblical Theology," 3–10.

of these texts highlights "worship" (defined below: chapter 1, §4.d.) as a major theme and concern in all the texts. Because of this, we conclude this stage with the summary question: *What does the text teach about worship and forms?*

c. **The meaning of the text today:** In the case of OT texts, this stage begins with considering *relevant redemptive-historical developments*, and then identifying how the OT text relates to the NT gospel.[298] As Goldsworthy notes, the gap which must be bridged by Christians seeking to apply OT texts relates not only to time and culture, but also to theology.[299] The hermeneutical tools of BT are required at this point to identify "the kind of bridge needed to overcome the gap between the text and the modern Christian."[300] This stage concludes with identifying *the implications of the text for the IM debate*.

Texts selected for analysis and how they were selected

The followings texts have been selected for analysis in this book:

	Appropriation texts	Resistance texts
Old Testament	Genesis 17	Exodus 32–34
	Exodus 12–13	Deuteronomy 12
	1 Chronicles 28	Hosea 8
New Testament	Acts 2–7	Acts 15
	Acts 15	1 Corinthians 8–10
	1 Corinthians 8–10	Colossians 2

The following criteria were used to select these texts.[301]

First, the texts needed to deal with (or have at least been put forward in the relevant debates as dealing with) the use of the forms of other faiths

---

298. Goldsworthy, "Gospel," 46, 123, 126; Satterthwaite, "Biblical History," 43–51; Vanhoozer, "Exegesis," 52–63. See Goldsworthy, "Relationship," 81–88; Doriani, *Biblical Application*, 240–42; Beale, *We Become*, 23.

299. Goldsworthy, "Gospel," 22, 50; Vanhoozer, "Exegesis," 52–63; Klink and Lockett, *Understanding*, 61.

300. Goldsworthy, "Gospel," 49. See also Rosner, "Biblical Theology," 3–10.

301. For non-exhaustive lists of appropriation and resistance texts from which the twelve selected texts were chosen, see chapter 1, §3.a.viii.1. and §4.b.iv.

by the people of God. Such texts speak most directly to the IM claim that BMBs can use Muslim forms.

Second, an equal number of appropriation and resistance texts have been selected. As noted in the literature review, the IM debate lacks biblical balance: most of the debate focuses around appropriation texts, while resistance texts are often ignored. Both appropriation and resistance texts need to be studied in order to understand why the forms of other faiths are sometimes used but sometimes rejected in Scripture.[302]

Third, texts frequently quoted in the IM and contextualization debates have been given preference where possible. However, because very few resistance texts have to date been cited in the debate (see chapter 1, §3.a.viii.1. above), three of the six resistance texts (Exodus 32–34, Hosea 8 and Colossians 2) are being introduced to the debate here for the first time. It is hoped that doing so will be a helpful contribution. At the same time, two texts (Acts 15 and 1 Corinthians 8–10) have been cited by both IM proponents and IM critics to support their respective arguments, and so these two texts were deemed particularly worthy of selection.

Fourth, so far as possible, texts were chosen from a range of salvation-historical eras, and from a variety of genres (narrative, law, prophecy, epistle), to ensure that the picture that emerges reflects as closely as possible the breadth and richness of biblical teaching on the matter. While it was possible to satisfy this criterion when selecting the resistance texts, it was not possible when selecting the appropriation texts, since most of the appropriation texts cited in the literature are historical narrative texts.

Finally, because a large number of appropriation texts have been cited in the IM and contextualization debates concerning forms, selecting only six for analysis has required omitting many others, and so some additional explanation is warranted here. Some texts were not selected because they do not satisfy the above criteria. For example, 1 Corinthians 7:14–24[303] does not deal explicitly with the use of the forms of other faiths. Likewise, texts that use terms like *El* and *logos*[304] deal with the appropriation of *terms* rather than *forms* ("forms "is defined below: chapter 1, §4.d.). Further, some appropriation texts deal with the appropriation of *cultural* forms (such as the covenant ceremony or Hittite covenant forms),[305] not the forms of other *faiths*. Nevertheless, other texts remain that do satisfy the above criteria and could have

---

302. See Carson, *Exegetical Fallacies*, 54–55, 93–94; Glaser, *Bible*, 26–31.

303. Cited in Massey, "Misunderstanding," 12–13; Ridgway, "Insider," 85; Lewis, "Integrity," 45–46; Lewis, "Promoting," 76.

304. Cited in Davis, *Poles Apart*, 138; Petersen, "Investigation," 117–22; Talman, "Old Testament," 49–57.

305. Cited in Davis, *Poles Apart*, 129–34; Petersen, "Investigation," 117–22.

been selected.³⁰⁶ Ultimately, the six selected were chosen because they provide the best and clearest examples of the biblical precedent argument.

My decision to omit 2 Kings 5 requires particular explanation here, given how frequently this text is cited in the debate. This text was indeed considered for inclusion as a possible OT appropriation text, but I ultimately gave preference to Gen 17, Exod 12–13 and 1 Chr 28 for the following two reasons. First, a number of exegetical uncertainties (concerning the meaning of Naaman's request and of Elisha's enigmatic response) make it difficult to draw firm conclusions based on this text. As Tennent writes, "there are sufficient ambiguities about the text to make it difficult to use in any proper exegetical way to contribute substantially to this discussion."³⁰⁷ Second, the three texts that were chosen contain a message concerning what forms the intended readers (the Israelites) themselves should use. This is not the case in 2 Kings 5: regardless of whether it contains a permission from Elisha for Naaman the Aramite to worship in the temple of Rimmon (a matter which is debated), this text is clearly not concerned with the matter of what forms the intended readers (the Israelites) should use. Therefore, this text is less directly relevant to the construction of a biblical precedent argument than the texts which I have chosen.³⁰⁸

c. Delimitations

The delimitations for this book are as follows. First, as discussed above, this book does not engage in field research. Instead, the focus is on identifying relevant biblical teaching, and considering its implications for the IM debate. This means that the goal is not to affirm or reject IM, but rather to articulate the biblical framework that can be used by form-selectors (both BMBs and foreign missionaries) when developing contextualized practices in their specific contexts.

---

306. See Gen 14:17–24 (Melchizedek's religion), Gen 15:7–18 (covenant curse ceremony), Gen 44:1–15 (Joseph's divination cup), Num 21:4–9 (Moses' bronze snake), Num 22–24 (Balaam's omens and divination), 2 Kgs 5 (Namaan's bowing down in the temple of Rimmon), Matt 2:1–12 (the Magi's star), Matt 28:19 (baptism), and John 4:1–42 (Samaritan worship forms).

307. Tennent, "Followers," 108.

308. See Baeq, "Contextualizing," 197–207; Higgins, "Biblical Basis," 213–16. On John 4:1–42 (another frequently cited appropriation text which I have not selected for study here), see Garner, "High Stakes," 259–60; Wolfe, "Insider," 150–54; Patterson, "Essential," 370.

INTRODUCTION

Second, no attempt is made to draw on the analytical tools of cultural anthropology or related social sciences. Rather, the focus is on using those of biblical scholarship.

Third, the focus is primarily upon IM methodology in Muslim contexts. There is little engagement with IM in Hindu or Buddhist contexts.

Fourth, the book does not seek to engage the broad range of biblical and theological issues raised by IM methodology (such as those relating to identity, ethics, ecclesiology, conversion, soteriology, revelation, theology of religions, the use by believers of the Qur'an, and the prophethood of Muhammad).[309] Rather, its more narrow focus is the use of Muslim forms by BMBs and missionaries.

Fifth, the book explores the possibility that using the forms of other faiths might produce syncretism, but it does not attempt to consider other possible causes of syncretism, nor to identify actual manifestations of syncretism in particular places. Some participants in the IM debate have suggested that the contemporary "Western church "is syncretistic (a syncretism of Christianity and consumerism or individualism).[310] This is a valuable discussion, but it is beyond the scope of this book.

Finally, I would like to acknowledge the limitations and biases that arise from my own personal experience and circumstances. I have written this book while engaging in ministry to Muslims in a Muslim-majority country in Southeast Asia. In my ministry, I use some contextualized Muslim forms, but choose not to use others. I have friends and colleagues (both local and foreign) who embrace IM methodology, seek to catalyze IM and are themselves part of an IM. I chose this topic out of a genuine desire to be better equipped by Scripture to make contextualized form-selections. Notwithstanding the fact that the bulk of this book is biblical analysis, I do acknowledge that my field experiences are likely to have influenced the way I have approached this research.

d. Definitions

In addition to the definitions given above for contextualization and syncretism (chapter 1, §3.b.), the following definitions of "form" and "worship" are important for our purposes.

---

309. On these issues, see Coleman, *Analysis*, 1–255; Azumah, "Islam," 7–24; Tennent, "Followers," 101–15; Strange, *Their Rock*, 53–236; Ibrahim and Greenham, *Critique*, 1–454.

310. See Brown, "Contextualization," 131; Owens, "Syncretism," 74–80; Farah, "Complexity," 88.

Form: The term "form" is used and defined in a range of academic disciplines, including semantics, linguistics, semiotics, anthropology and philosophy, and within these disciplines, it sometimes has a technical and specialized meaning.[311] However, notwithstanding the fact that missiologists draw upon the insights of experts from these fields when discussing the term "form," it has not been given a special or technical meaning within missiology.[312] Rather, in missiology, "form" (often "cultural forms" or "external forms") refers broadly to any "observable parts" of a culture which are used to serve functions and convey meaning.[313] Parshall writes,

> Cultural forms are the high-profile practices or customs that are visible to the onlooker. Meanings lie behind the forms and are often hidden and misunderstood by the outsider.[314]

In this book, "form" is given this broad meaning, and refers to religious practices and rituals, and objects used in worship.[315] Thus the Muslim *sholat* prayer ritual, a Muslim prayer mat, the Muslim practice of fasting during *Ramadan*, the Muslim pilgrimage to Mecca (the *hajj*), and the Muslim observance of *zakat* (alms-giving) are all "Muslim forms."[316]

Worship: As we shall see in chapters 2–5, when the texts selected for study in this book are analyzed inductively, worship emerges as an important theme in all of them. Therefore it is helpful to provide a definition here. In popular Christian usage, the term is often given a narrow meaning, referring to Sunday gatherings, or, more narrowly still, to certain parts of those gatherings (such as singing and prayer).[317] However, in the field of BT, worship has a much broader reference, describing the entire process by which people "engage with God."[318] It is concerned with "the fundamental question of how we can be in a right relationship with God and please him in all that we do."[319] Thus it is "a comprehensive category describing the Christian's total existence."[320]

---

311. See Hesselgrave, *Communicating*, 39–78; Hiebert, "Form," 101–21.

312. Hesselgrave and Rommen, *Contextualization*, 127–96.

313. Kraft, *Christianity in Culture* (1979), 64. See generally, Kraft, *Christianity in Culture* (1979), 64–69; Moreau, *Mapping*, 87–90; Tillich and Kimball, *Theology*, 54–55; Hiebert, "Form," 101–21.

314. Parshall, *Muslim*, 77.

315. See Hiebert, "Form," 101–21.

316. See further Parshall, *Muslim*, 79–82.

317. Peterson, *Engaging*, 16–17.

318. Peterson, *Engaging*, 20.

319. Peterson, *Engaging*, 18.

320. Peterson, *Engaging*, 18.

Many biblical theologians have set out to construct a biblical theology of worship.[321] In doing so, they have noted the inadequacy of merely focusing upon the derivation of the English word worship,[322] and have instead performed studies of the usage of key Hebrew and Greek terms that can be rendered by the English word worship. These terms include the Hebrew verbs הָוָה, *chawah* ("to bow down"), דָּבַע, *ʿavad* ("to serve"), תָּרֵשׁ, *sharat* ("to minister" or "to serve"), and אָרֵי, *yareʾ* ("to fear"); and the Greek verbs προσκυνέω, *proskuneō* ("to bow down, to pay homage"), λατρεύω, *latreuō* ("to serve"), δουλεύω, *douleuō* ("to serve"), and φοβέομαι, *phobeomai* ("to revere" or "to respect").[323] These scholars have also recognized the importance of going beyond mere word studies and including analyses of passages which do not use these terms, but which are thematically important to the topic of engaging with God.[324] Based on these studies, they propose the following definitions. Block defines worship as "reverential human acts of submission and homage before the divine Sovereign in response to his gracious revelation of himself and in accord with his will."[325] According to Carson,

> Worship is the proper response of all moral, sentient beings to God.... Human worship of God properly responds to the redemptive provisions that God has graciously made.... It manifests itself in all our living ..., both in adoration and in action, both in the individual believer and in corporate worship.[326]

Peterson proposes that worship is

> an engagement with [God] on the terms that he proposes and in the way that he alone makes possible.... [It involves] homage, service and reverence, demonstrated in the whole of life.[327]

---

321. See Peterson, *Engaging*; Peterson, "Worship," 855–63; Block, *For the Glory*; Ross, *Recalling*; Carson, "Worship," 11–62; Scobie, *Ways*, 567–612; Hattori, "Theology," 21–50.

322. Block, *For the Glory*, 8; Peterson, *Engaging*, 17; Carson, "Worship," 13–15.

323. See Firth, "Worship," 5–6; Peterson, *Engaging*, 55–74; Block, *For the Glory*, 1–27; Peterson, "Worship," 856–57.

324. Peterson, *Engaging*, 56; Carson, "Worship," 15, 18–19; Ross, *Recalling*, ch. 1.

325. Block, *For the Glory*, 23.

326. Carson, "Worship," 25–26.

327. Peterson, *Engaging*, 20, 73. For other definitions of worship, see Rayburn, *O Come*, 20–21; Schaper, *In His Presence*, 13.

Because worship is engaging with God on his terms, it follows that any worship which is not done on God's terms is false worship. In fact, false worship is an important concept in the Bible.[328] As Block notes:

> Those who direct their worship to other gods, or who worship the living God in ways contrary to his revealed will worship falsely.[329]

As we shall see, the principle that true worship is engaging with God on his terms emerges repeatedly throughout this book. Where this principle is articulated, it may appear to some that I am advocating for the "regulative principle," according to which all elements of corporate worship must be based on specific scriptural directions. However, this is not my focus. The regulative principle is specifically concerned with the public corporate worship of God, whereas I am addressing the much broader matter of the way God's people engage him in all of life. As well, whereas the regulative principle prohibits the use of modes of worship which are not expressly sanctioned in Scripture, as we shall see, I do not argue for the application of this restriction in the NT era.[330]

5. Projected contribution to the field

At stake in the debate over whether the use of Muslim forms in IM should be embraced as contextualization or rejected as syncretism is nothing less than the integrity of the gospel, the salvation of BMBs and the building of biblically authentic churches in Muslim-majority parts of the world.[331] The potential for cross-cultural missionaries to be the cause of syncretism has often been acknowledged by missiologists.[332] In light of this, it is crucial that missionaries, seeking to determine what methodology to use, be equipped with a detailed and balanced study of the Bible's teaching on this issue. As well, BMBs who are deciding whether or not to use Muslim forms need to know what, according to the Bible, they should consider as they make such decisions. There is thus a need for a study that draws on the resources of

---

328. See Ross, *Recalling*, §Introduction to Part 3; Glaser, *Bible*, 181; Garner, "High Stakes," 266–67.

329. Block, *For the Glory*, 24.

330. See Frame, *Worship*; Gore, *Covenantal Worship*; Ritchie, *Regulative Principle*.

331. Wolfe, "Insider," 8–9; Moreau, *Mapping*, 160; Higgins, "Key," 155–56; Lewis, "Integrity," 41–48; Nikides, "Response," 93; Garner, "High Stakes," 255–57.

332. Hesselgrave, "Syncretism," 71–95; Moreau, *Mapping*, 129; Waterman, "Insider," 297.

the discipline of biblical studies to articulate the Bible's teaching on the use by God's people of the forms of other faiths. I hope that this book will go some way in meeting this need, and in so doing, progress the IM debate, and also equip both BMBs and cross-cultural missionaries to engage in biblically authentic contextualized ministry in Muslim-majority contexts.

2

Old Testament Appropriation Texts

1. Introduction

IN THIS CHAPTER, THREE OT appropriation texts are studied: Genesis 17, Exodus 12–13 and 1 Chronicles 28. The goal is to identify the attitude of the biblical authors to the use by God's people of the forms of other faiths, and so draw implications for the IM debate. A secondary goal is to evaluate the claims that have already been made about these texts, since these texts have been put forward as "biblical precedents" which justify the use of the forms of other faiths by believers today.

2. Genesis 17 and circumcision

The first OT appropriation text is Genesis 17. This text describes an interaction between God and Abram/Abraham in which God confirms his covenant with Abram (17:1), clarifies his covenant promises (17:6), and declares that the covenant promises will be fulfilled through Sarah (17:16). God designates circumcision as the sign of this covenant, commanding Abraham and every male in his household to be circumcised (17:9–14). Abraham obeys this command (17:23–27). The context for these covenantal promises and commands is that God has already promised land, offspring, and blessing in 12:1–3, and established his covenant with Abram in 15:1–21.[1]

---

[1]. Woodbridge, "Circumcision," 411–12. The focus in the biblical analysis sections is to identify the authorial intent as expressed in the final form of the text, and so debates regarding the dating and redactional history of the text are beyond our scope. On these, see Williamson, *Abraham*, 188–267; Mathews, *Genesis*, 193–99; Williamson, "Circumcision," 122–23.

a. The relevance of the text to the research problem

Texts are deemed relevant if they deal with the use by God's people of the forms of other faiths, or have at least been cited by participants in the debate as such texts. Genesis 17 satisfies both criteria. As the following analysis demonstrates, it is indeed a text in which a form with pagan origins is appropriated by God's people for use in the worship of Yahweh. The fact that it has been cited by proponents of the biblical precedent argument (Ott, Strauss, and Tennent; McDermott; Davis; and Petersen)[2] makes it especially relevant for our purposes.

i. A form borrowed from other faiths

Circumcision was practiced by peoples of other faiths in the ANE long before it was designated as the sign of the covenant for the Israelites in Genesis 17. The oldest archeological discovery attesting to the practice was unearthed in Syria and dates from about the twenty-ninth century BC.[3] There is archeological evidence of circumcision being practiced in Egypt from the twenty-third century BC,[4] and in Canaan from the fourteenth century BC.[5] Jeremiah 9:24–25 refers to the Egyptians, Edomites, Ammonites and Moabites as practitioners of circumcision.[6] Thus circumcision was widely (but not uniformly)[7] practiced by Israel's neighbors, many of whom adopted the rite long before the time of Abraham.

Although it is clear that teenage and adult males from other faiths were circumcised, it is difficult to ascertain its meaning for them, as there is very little direct evidence on the matter.[8] Historians propose that it probably had a social function, marking either entrance into puberty, or marriage into a tribe.[9] Some have suggested that it may also have served a religious function. Hall, for example, suggests that it functioned both as a fertility rite, and as a

---

2. Ott et al., *Encountering*, 271; McDermott, *Can Evangelicals*, 82; Davis, *Poles Apart*, 130–31; Petersen, "Investigation," 120–21.

3. Sasson, "Circumcision," 473–76.

4. Pritchard, *ANE Texts*, 326; Hall, "Circumcision," 1025.

5. Pritchard, *ANE in Pictures*, 332.

6. Hamilton, *Genesis*, 469.

7. See Hamilton, *Genesis*, 469; Mathews, *Genesis*, 198; Wenham, *Genesis*, 23.

8. Wenham, *Genesis*, 23.

9. Walton, *Genesis*, 450–51; Hamilton, *Genesis*, 469, 472; Mathews, *Genesis*, 198; Sasson, "Circumcision," 473–76; Williamson, "Circumcision," 122.

magical apotropaic rite, aimed at warding off evil.[10] He cites a late (ca. 100 AD) Phoenician myth in which circumcision functions in this way, proposing that this myth probably preserves an ancient, pre-Abrahamic, belief.[11] Ultimately, it is not possible to be certain whether Israel's neighbors used circumcision in their worship, or merely for social reasons.

It does seem, however, that when the form was adopted by Israel, it was modified, and given a new meaning. It was modified in that it became for Israel an *infant* rite (Israelite boys were to be circumcised on the eighth day: 17:12), rather than one performed upon attaining puberty or adulthood.[12] It was given a new meaning in that it became a sign of the covenant between Yahweh and the Israelites (17:11), thus marking a "theological rite of passage into the covenantal community."[13]

ii. Used to worship Yahweh

When we recall the definition of worship in chapter 1, §4.d., according to which the term refers to the entire process by which people engage with God, it is clear that circumcision was indeed a form used by the Israelites in their worship of Yahweh. According to 17:11, circumcision is the sign of the covenant with Yahweh, and thus the mark of membership of the worshiping community.[14] According to 17:14, any male not circumcised must "be cut off" from this community and so excluded from the possibility of worshiping Yahweh.

In conclusion then, circumcision was a form used by the peoples of other faiths which was appropriated for use by Israelites in their worship of Yahweh in Genesis 17. This text is therefore relevant to the research problem.

---

10. Hall, "Circumcision," 1026.

11. Hall, "Circumcision," 1026.

12. Hartley, *Genesis*, 140; Sarna, *Genesis*, 385; Wenham, *Genesis*, 24; Arnold, *Genesis*, 172.

13. Walton, *Genesis*, 451. See also Mathews, *Genesis*, 198; Hamilton, *Genesis*, 472; Wenham, *Genesis*, 23; Woodbridge, "Circumcision," 411–13; Motyer, "Circumcision," 204; Williamson, "Circumcision," 123; Arnold, *Genesis*, 172.

14. Hamilton, *Genesis*, 470–72; Woodbridge, "Circumcision," 411–12; Schreiner, "Circumcision," 138.

b. The meaning of the text for the original audience

i. Is there evidence in the text that the author is seeking to persuade the reader to appropriate foreign forms?

Genesis 17 has been advanced as part of the biblical precedent argument. Proponents of this argument claim that texts like Genesis 17 depicting the appropriation of a foreign form do more than merely justify the use by the Israelites of that particular form (here, circumcision). Rather, they claim that these texts function as precedents, *justifying by analogy the appropriation of other forms*.[15] Therefore, at issue here is not whether there is evidence in Genesis 17 of an authorial intent to persuade the reader to use the specific form of circumcision, but rather, whether there is evidence of an intention to persuade the reader to appropriate foreign forms *generally*, with God's appropriation of circumcision functioning as an example which the Israelites are to imitate. As the following analysis demonstrates, there is no evidence of such an intention in the text of Genesis 17.

Importantly, in this text, circumcision is not depicted as a foreign form. Walton comments, "the text does not give the modern reader a hint that circumcision was practiced widely in the ancient Near East."[16] The form is simply commanded by God (17:10), with no reference to, or acknowledgement of, the fact that it is a form already in use by the surrounding nations. This is not to suggest that the biblical author is unaware that it is a pre-existing form, but it does suggest that *the fact that the form is a borrowed one is not important to the author's purposes in the text*. If the author's purpose in Genesis 17 was to encourage the Israelites to engage in a process of borrowing pagan forms by analogy, with the appropriation of circumcision functioning as a precedent for such borrowings, then one would expect that the fact that circumcision was a borrowed form would be emphasized, or at the very least, acknowledged. That it is not strongly suggests that its status as a borrowed form is not relevant to what the author is seeking to communicate. The reader is encouraged to practice circumcision, *not* because it is a borrowed form, but because it has been commanded by God (17:9–14, 23). Thus *historically*, circumcision was an appropriated form. But *hermeneutically* and *theologically*, it is not.

The proponents of the biblical precedent argument do not actually discuss the question of authorial intent in the biblical texts which depict appropriations of foreign forms. They do discuss, however, a related

---

15. See Ott et al., *Encountering*, 271; Davis, *Poles Apart*, 131–34, 141; Talman, "Old Testament," 51, 55–56; Petersen, "Investigation," 117–18, 127.

16. Walton, *Genesis*, 450–51.

matter: the matter of why God gave borrowed forms to Israel in the first place. They contend that God did so because he was engaging in contextualization. Davis, for example, argues that God gave foreign forms (including circumcision) to the Israelites to enable them to worship using forms that were culturally familiar to them.[17] Likewise, IM advocate Petersen suggests that God gave foreign forms (including circumcision) to Israel as part of a "strategic decision of the Holy Spirit" aimed at making Yahwism understandable in the ANE context:

> *Forms* have been recruited, as it were, in order to serve the divine *purpose* of truth communication. In other words, the use of such *forms* have [sic] helped make the *meaning* of the divine truths all the more clear to the original audiences.[18]

Petersen suggests that pagan forms were appropriated as part of a divine strategy of cultural adaption for the sake of effective communication which mirrored (and indeed pre-dated) Paul's strategy in 1 Corinthians 9:19–23 of becoming all things to all people: "[God] became, as it were, an 'ancient near easterner' in communicating effectively to those people."[19] Thus according to proponents of the biblical precedent argument, forms were appropriated for reasons relating to contextualization.

There is no evidence in the text of Genesis 17 to support this claim. In fact, there are no indications at all in the text as to why a form already in use by Israel's neighbors, rather than a newly created one, is selected as the sign of the covenant. The author simply does not address this question. It seems that this detail *is not important to the author's purposes in Genesis 17*. Thus something which is *historically* true (the fact that circumcision was an appropriation from pagans) seems to be *theologically* insignificant. Ultimately, Genesis 17 provides no information to explain why a pagan form is appropriated. Therefore, any attempts to explain the appropriation, including those put forward as part of the biblical precedent argument, should be recognized for what they are: speculations.[20] Given that there is no evidence in Genesis 17 of an authorial intention to persuade the reader to appropriate the forms of other faiths, we must conclude that the author's purpose lies elsewhere.

---

17. Davis, *Poles Apart*, 134.

18. Petersen, "Investigation," 118 (see generally 117–27).

19. Petersen, "Investigation," 124, see also 117–18. See further McDermott, *Can Evangelicals*, 81–82, 89.

20. For other possible explanations, see Block, "Other Religions," 46–47.

ii. What then is the author's purpose?

The author's purpose in Genesis 17 is to persuade the reader to respond in faith to God's gracious covenantal promises by practicing the rite of circumcision.[21] The author is not seeking to encourage the reader to engage in a wide-ranging process of borrowing pagan forms, with God's appropriation of circumcision functioning as a precedent. Rather, the author is encouraging the reader to use one specific form, circumcision, because doing so has been commanded by God. The following analysis bears this out.

The *context* for 17:1–27 helps to elucidate the purpose of the text. In Genesis 12:1–3, God promises to confer land, offspring and blessing on Abram. The central concern in 12:1—18:15, of which our text forms a part, is the fulfillment of these promises.[22] The narrative tension in 12:1—18:15 derives from whether Abraham and Sarah can learn to trust that God will in fact fulfill these promises. The focus in 13:1—15:21 is the promise of land, whereas the focus in chapters 16:1—18:15 is the promise of offspring.[23] In both sections, obstacles emerge which seem to threaten the promise and test the faith of Abraham and Sarah. In 13:1—15:21, the obstacle is Lot, because he competes for the land.[24] In 16:1—18:15, it is Sarai's barrenness, and then Ishmael's birth (since Ishmael threatens to supplant the promised line).[25] The central theological truth communicated in these two sections is that God is able to overcome the obstacles and bring about what he has promised.[26] Thus the section climaxes with the rhetorical question: "Is anything too hard for the LORD?" (18:14).

The task for Abraham and Sarah, and ultimately for the reader, is to learn to have faith that God will fulfill his promises, and to express this faith by obeying God's commands.[27] As such, the repeated pattern in 12:1—18:15 is as follows: God makes (or reaffirms) promises;[28] Abraham and Sarah doubt that God will fulfill them (particularly in response to obstacles that arise);[29] they eventually arrive at a place of trust expressed through obedi-

---

21. Greidanus, *Preaching Christ*, 163–64; von Rad, *Genesis*, 201; Deenick, *Righteous*, 15–52.
22. Greidanus, *Preaching Christ*, 159; Walton, *Genesis*, 445.
23. Walton, *Genesis*, 454.
24. Walton, *Genesis*, 445.
25. Walton, *Genesis*, 454.
26. Walton, *Genesis*, 425, 454; DeLapp, *Type-Scenes*, 17–28.
27. Brueggemann, *Genesis*, 151; Mathews, *Genesis*, 196–97.
28. 12:2–3, 7; 13:14–17; 15:1, 4–5, 7; 17:1–8, 15–16; 18:10.
29. 12:10–20; 13:5–7; 15:2–3, 8; 16:1–6, 15–16; 17:17–18; 18:11–15.

ence; and this leads to the advancement of God's plans.[30] As Walton argues, the fact that this pattern is repeated strongly suggests that understanding it is key to understanding the author's purpose:

> Our methodology requires us to pursue the purpose that the author has for the text. . . . These elements, obstacle and advance, appear chapter after chapter. Since they serve as a common denominator in otherwise disparate narratives, we infer that they represent the author's primary focus.[31]

Thus the context of 17:1–27 suggests that the author's central concern here is to depict the process by which God's people learn to have faith in his promises, and to express that faith through obedience to his commands.

An analysis of the *structure* of 17:1–27 confirms this conclusion. McEvenue identifies a chiastic structure in 17:1–27 which places the command to circumcise as the central (and thus most important) panel, reinforcing the conclusion that obedience to this command is the key concern of the text.[32] An analysis of the narrative arc also reveals the same concern. The passage begins with God making a series of promises (relating to offspring, an everlasting covenant, and land: 17:1–8), and then commands (Abraham and his descendants must keep the covenant, and practice the rite of circumcision: 17:9–14). An additional promise is made (it will be through Sarah that the offspring promise will be fulfilled: 17:15–16). Thus the narrative tension, established in 17:1–16, concerns whether Abraham will trust God's promises, and so obey the commands.[33] Abraham's initial response is to doubt (17:17–18). But after God reaffirms the promises (17:19–22), Abraham comes to a position of trusting obedience which he expresses by circumcising all the males in his household (17:23–27). The narrative tension is resolved when Abraham undergoes circumcision, and so demonstrates that he has learned faith.[34] Thus the text's structure strengthens the above conclusion regarding the author's purpose in this text.

An analysis of the *content and grammar* of 17:1–27 further supports this conclusion. As the narrative unfolds, the author directs the reader's attention to the fact that Abraham is required to make a specific response to God's promises.[35] This is brought into sharp focus by the emphatic pronoun

---

30. 13:18; 15:6, 9–21; 17:19–27. Cf. 22:1–19. Mathews, *Genesis*, 196–97, 205.
31. Walton, *Genesis*, 424–25.
32. McEvenue, *Narrative*, 158.
33. Greidanus, *Preaching Christ*, 162.
34. Greidanus, *Preaching Christ*, 163.
35. Walton, *Genesis*, 451; Wenham, *Genesis*, 20.

הָתָּא, *'attah* ("as for you"), in 17:9. As Hamilton notes, "After a series of 'I wills' by God, Abraham becomes the subject of a verb, instead of an object."[36] What follows in 17:9–14 is a detailed presentation of the command to circumcise, climaxing with the warning that those who do not obey will be cut off (17:14).[37] At issue in the narrative at this point then is *not* whether Abraham has understood the principles of contextualization, especially the importance of using local forms which are familiar to his neighbors. Rather, at issue is whether Abraham will express faith in God's promises through precise obedience to the *specific* command to circumcise.

The author carefully depicts Abraham's response to God, which unfolds in two stages. At first, Abraham lacks faith. He interrupts God's speech to laugh incredulously at God's announcement that Sarah would give birth (17:17),[38] and then proposes an alternative to God: that God fulfill his promise through Ishmael (17:18).[39] According to Wenham, 17:17–18 function rhetorically to allow "for the reader's own doubts to surface as well."[40] Yet as a result of God's patient and nurturing words of affirmation in 17:19–22, Abraham's faith is revitalized, and he obeys (17:23–27).[41] The fact that the author does not gloss over Abraham's struggle to learn faith, but instead focuses attention on it, strongly suggests that the author's purpose here is to display "the character of faith,"[42] and so equip the reader to engage in the same struggle, learning how to have this faith that expresses itself in obedience.[43]

Yet the call in this text is not merely a call to have faith that expresses itself as a general, unspecified obedience. Rather, it is a specific call to obey the command to circumcise. This is apparent from the fact that 17:9–14 has a clear view to future generations. The fact that the command applies not only to Abraham but also to his descendants is affirmed no less than three times (17:9, 10, 12). As well, grammatically, there is a shift from second person singular (17:9), to second person plural (17:10–12).[44] Hamilton notes: "God is speaking to those not yet born."[45] Further, the description

---

36. Hamilton, *Genesis*, 468.
37. Mathews, *Genesis*, 205.
38. Wenham, *Genesis*, 25.
39. Hamilton, *Genesis*, 477; Wenham, *Genesis*, 25.
40. Wenham, *Genesis*, 25.
41. Hartley, *Genesis*, 142.
42. Hartley, *Genesis*, 142.
43. Brueggemann, *Genesis*, 156.
44. Mathews, *Genesis*, 204; Hamilton, *Genesis*, 468.
45. Hamilton, *Genesis*, 468.

in 17:23–27 of Abraham's circumcising of *all* the males in his household (בְּכָל, *kol*, "all" or "every," appears three times in 17:23, 27) underscores the importance of *all* God's people practicing the rite.⁴⁶ Thus the specific response called for from the reader in 17:1–27 is circumcision.⁴⁷ The author's purpose in this text,aAs Greidanus concludes,

> [is] to *persuade* Israel (with the Lord's wonderful promises, the threat of being cut off from the covenant community, and their Patriarch's example) to keep God's covenant by circumcising all males.⁴⁸

An analysis of 17:1–27 has revealed that the purpose of the author is to persuade the reader to practice the rite of circumcision as an expression of faith in God's covenant promises. This strengthens the above conclusion that the author's purpose is *not* to persuade the reader to engage in a general process of borrowing the forms of other faiths. Indeed, these two purposes are not simply different: they are almost contradictory. The focus in 17:1–27 is squarely upon the need for obedience to God's specific command to circumcise. There is no permission (explicit or implicit) for the Israelites to take the initiative, imitate God and become the form-selectors themselves.

iii. What does the text teach about worship and forms?

In accordance with the schema for examining biblical texts described in chapter 1 (chapter 1, §4.b.iv.), we turn now to a discussion of what the text teaches about worship and forms (defined above: chapter 1, §4.d.). Four important points emerge.

1. True worship is God-given

First, this text makes it clear that true worship is God-given. In this text, God makes engagement with himself possible and prescribes its terms.⁴⁹ The role of Israel is not to design the worship practice, but simply to respond in faithful, submissive and precise obedience. God is not depicted in 17:1–27 as a model appropriator whom the Israelites are to imitate.

---

46. Mathews, *Genesis*, 204.
47. Mathews, *Genesis*, 201; Hamilton, *Genesis*, 468–69.
48. Greidanus, *Preaching Christ*, 163.
49. Peterson, *Engaging*, 20, 26–27, 33, 73; Durham, *Exodus*, 424; Block, *For the Glory*, 25; Garner, "High Stakes," 266–67; Scobie, *Ways*, 567; Ross, *Recalling*, ch. 2, and §"Introduction to Part 4."

Instead, God is presented as the one who unilaterally makes worship of himself possible, and then prescribes precisely how it is to be done.[50] The unequal nature of the relationship between God and Abraham becomes clear when the actions of the two in 17:1–27 are contrasted. For his part, God confirms and establishes the covenant (17:1, 7), makes promises (17:2–8, 15–16, 19–21), issues commands (17:1, 9–13), threatens excommunication (17:14), and assigns new names to the protagonists (17:4, 15, 19). In the OT, naming is an expression of the authority of the name-giver over the one named.[51] By contrast, Abraham falls down prostrate (17:3), listens (17:1–16, 19–21) and obeys exactly in accord with God's commands (17:23–27).[52] On the one occasion where Abraham does attempt to have a role in shaping the future of the covenant through his proposal that Ishmael be the heir (17:18), his suggestion is flatly rejected (17:19–21). In these matters, God refuses to negotiate.[53] God alone sets the terms for worship and for the advancement of his covenantal plans. Hamilton notes, "The covenant with Abraham is something God initiates, something he maintains, and something he brings to fulfilment."[54] The appropriate response for God's people is simply to submissively and obediently receive the terms of worship which God himself lays down.

The reference to Ishmael in 17:18 actually forms part of a sustained polemic in the broader Abrahamic narrative *against* human initiative in worship.[55] In 16:1–3, Abram and Sarai take the matter of producing offspring into their own hands, rather than waiting for God to fulfill his promise (see 12:2; 15:4–5).[56] Ishmael is born (16:4), and Abraham, out of a lack of faith in God's promise to give Sarah a child, suggests Ishmael as an alternative (17:18). Ishmael thus represents human initiative rather than submissive responsiveness in worship. He is a "human solution"[57] to a perceived inadequacy in God's plan, and he functions as "a temptation for Abraham to trust in the fruit of his own work rather than in the promise."[58] God rebukes Abraham and affirms his plan and promise (17:19–21). That God introduces this

---

50. Motyer, "Circumcision," 204; Deenick, *Righteous*, 17–18.
51. Walton, *Genesis*, 449–50.
52. Hartley, *Genesis*, 141–42; Mathews, *Genesis*, 207.
53. Hamilton, *Genesis*, 478–79.
54. Hamilton, *Genesis*, 465.
55. Mathews, *Genesis*, 192–93, 196–97.
56. Cf. 12:10–20 for another example of Abram taking matters into his own hands due to a lack of faith in God's promises. Brueggemann, *Genesis*, 151.
57. Wenham, *Genesis*, 25.
58. Brueggemann, *Genesis*, 152. See further, Hamilton, *Genesis*, 477.

speech with the emphatic particle לְבָא, *'aval* ("indeed" or "on the contrary"), makes his contradiction of Abraham's proposal all the more stark.[59] Human initiative in worship is flatly and emphatically rejected.

In light of this broader polemic against human initiative in worship, the notion that the author in 17:1–27 is seeking to encourage the Israelites to imitate God and borrow foreign forms must be dismissed. In 17:1–27, the reader is not granted permission to imitate God's act of form-appropriation. Rather, selection of worship forms is exclusively God's prerogative. In 17:1–27, God is not a model to be imitated, but an authority to be obeyed.

2. At This Stage in Salvation History, Acceptable Forms Are Those That Are God-Given

Second, in the old covenant era, the principle that God prescribes the terms of worship extends to the selection of forms. What makes a worship form valid at this stage in salvation history is simply that it is God-given. In Genesis 17, the history of previous usage of circumcision by Israel's neighbors is irrelevant. Israel does not need to know about this history in order to understand and obey the command in 17:9–14. As Sarna notes, what is determinative in making circumcision a valid form here is simply that God commands it: "The operation owes its sanction not to any natural reason but solely to its being divinely ordained."[60] We saw earlier that there is no evidence in the text of an intention on the part of the author to persuade or equip the reader to borrow foreign forms. The simplest explanation for this is that it is not Israel's role to select worship forms. Since it is not Israel's role, there is no need for the people to be persuaded or equipped to perform the task. Under the old covenant, God alone selects and gives forms to Israel. Therefore, what makes a form acceptable is quite simply the fact that it is given by God.

3. The Function of the Form of Circumcision Is to Enable People to Respond to God in Faith

Third, in 17:1–27, the form of circumcision functions as the means by which Abraham expresses his faith-response to God. Abraham's act of obedience in 17:23–27 is a sign of trust and thus commitment to God,[61] and the

---

59. Wenham, *Genesis*, 25.
60. Sarna, *Genesis*, 386.
61. Hartley, *Genesis*, 139.

"means by which Abraham and his seed ratify God's lordship over them."[62] The structure of 17:1–27 makes this clear. The promises of offspring, land and everlasting covenant precede the command to circumcise (17:9–14) and are expressed unilaterally:"I have made you . . . I will make you . . . I will establish . . . I will give" (17:3–8).[63] Circumcision is thus the *response* required of those to whom the promises are made.[64] The emphatic אַתָּה, *'attah* ("as for you"), in 17:9 stands in parallel to the emphatic אֲנִי, *'ani* ("as for me"), in 17:4. This parallel highlights the link between the promise and the command, and emphasizes the fact that Abraham's act is a *response* to God's. This is reinforced by the requirement in 17:14 that uncircumcised males "be cut off" (נִכְרְתָה, *nikhretah*) (that is, either excommunicated or executed).[65] Since failure to circumcise is evidence that the required faith-response is lacking, the uncircumcised can have no part in the covenant community.[66] As Walton notes, circumcision

> is not a condition for the covenant as a whole . . ., but it is a condition for an individual's entry into the community of the elect. It is a sign of participation, a symbol of subordination, and an initiation into relationship as defined by the covenant.[67]

In getting circumcised, Abraham does not *cause* the promises to be fulfilled. Rather, he confirms that he trusts them, and he takes hold of covenant membership in order that he might receive that which is promised.[68] Circumcision thus functions as "a confirmation sign, one bearing witness to Abraham's belief that God would fulfill his promises with respect to progeny."[69]

---

62. Hamilton, *Genesis*, 471–72.

63. On whether the Abrahamic covenant is unilateral or bilateral, see Youngblood, "Abrahamic," 31–46; Williamson, *Sealed*, 77–93; Gentry and Wellum, *Kingdom*, 259–338.

64. Walton, *Genesis*, 467.

65. Hamilton, *Genesis*, 473–74.

66. Woodbridge, "Circumcision," 411–12.

67. Walton, *Genesis*, 467.

68. Woodbridge, "Circumcision," 411–12.

69. Hamilton, *Genesis*, 472. See also Woodbridge, "Circumcision," 412.

4. THE LINK BETWEEN THE FORM AND ITS MEANING IS NOT ARBITRARY

Fourth, circumcision is given as a *sign* of the covenant (17:11). Commentators have explored whether it is a sign for God (to remind him of his promises: cf. 9:12–17), or a sign for Abraham and the Israelites (to remind them of God's promises), or both.[70] Whichever is correct, it is important to note the close link between the sign and that which is signified (that is, between the form and its meaning). The text is not explicit as to why *circumcision*, rather than some other form, has been selected as the sign of the covenant. Nevertheless, the text does invite the reader to draw a connection between the repeated promises made in the text relating to offspring (17:2, 4, 5, 6, 16, 19, 21), and the fact that the chosen sign is a mark on the male reproductive organ. Thus there is probably an inference that God chooses circumcision to be the sign because of its intrinsic symbolic link to procreation.[71] If this is correct, circumcision is chosen because of its symbolic potential. Williamson concludes, it is "to remind Abraham and his descendants of the covenant promises—especially the promise of 'seed.'"[72] Thus Genesis 17 contains important teachings concerning forms and worship.

iv. References to circumcision in the rest of the OT

A study of subsequent references to circumcision in the OT affirms the above conclusions regarding the meaning of Genesis 17. Most significantly, not one reference can be found in which the biblical author either acknowledges the foreign origins of the form, or seeks to persuade the Israelites to treat God's original appropriation as a model which they are to imitate. On the contrary, subsequent OT references reinforce the understanding that the giving of the form in Genesis 17 is not a model of appropriation to imitate, but rather simply a command to obey.

In Exodus 4:24–26, for example, Yahweh threatens to kill Moses, apparently because he is uncircumcised. This is an exegetically difficult passage because the Hebrew pronouns are used ambiguously. Nevertheless, it is

---

70. Williamson, *Abraham*, 176–81; Williamson, "Circumcision," 123; Wenham, *Genesis*, 23–24; Hamilton, *Genesis*, 470–72.

71. Deenick, *Righteous*, 48–51; Hartley, *Genesis*, 140–41; Hamilton, *Genesis*, 470–72; Mathews, *Genesis*, 204.

72. Williamson, "Circumcision," 123. Not all draw this inference: Walton, *Genesis*, 467; Williamson, *Abraham*, 176–81; Wenham, *Genesis*, 23–24.

clear that the problem is uncircumcision and the solution is circumcision.[73] The account highlights the importance of Moses being circumcised before he can participate in carrying out God's mission and thus the importance of obedience to the command in Genesis 17.[74] This emerges again in Exodus 12:44, 48, where circumcision is a condition for participation in the Passover.[75] Again, in Joshua 5:2–8, members of the wilderness generation must be circumcised before they can take possession of the land.[76] In all these texts, the emphasis is not upon God's original appropriation of circumcision as a precedent, but rather upon the importance of complete and precise obedience to the specific command to circumcise.

A study of OT references to circumcision also affirms the above conclusion regarding the function of the form. Many OT references to circumcision involve a figurative use of the term.[77] The person who disobeys God is described as having an "uncircumcised heart."[78] As well, the person who is unreceptive to God's word has an "uncircumcised ear."[79] This figurative usage affirms the above conclusion that circumcision functions as more than merely an external mark: it is also a means of expressing an *inner reality*, that is, faith.[80] So, for example, in Deuteronomy, a circumcised heart is one that possesses certain heart attitudes (fear of God and love for God: 10:16–20; 30:6) which express themselves in acts of obedience and service (10:16–20).[81] In fact, having the appropriate heart attitude (circumcision of the heart) is preliminary to, and even more important than, having the outward mark (Jeremiah 9:25–26).[82] In Ezekiel 44:9, only those who are circumcised in heart *and* flesh are permitted to enter the new temple.[83] Thus the figurative usage of circumcision in the OT emphasizes the strong link between the form of circumcision and inner heart attitudes (love and faith), which express themselves in obedience.[84] This affirms the above conclusion

---

73. Williamson, "Circumcision," 124; Woodbridge, "Circumcision," 412; Hall, "Circumcision," 1026–27.

74. Woodbridge, "Circumcision," 412; Williamson, "Circumcision," 124.

75. Woodbridge, "Circumcision," 412–13.

76. Woodbridge, "Circumcision," 412–13.

77. Sarna, *Genesis*, 387; Hamilton, *Genesis*, 481–82; Williamson, "Circumcision," 124–25.

78. Lev 26:41; Jer 9:25; Ezek 44:7, 9. See also Deut 10:16; 30:6; Jer 4:4.

79. Jer 6:10.

80. Wenham, *Genesis*, 31; Motyer, "Circumcision," 205.

81. Woodbridge, "Circumcision," 412–13.

82. Williamson, "Circumcision," 125.

83. Woodbridge, "Circumcision," 412–13.

84. Brueggemann, *Genesis*, 155.

that the function of the form of circumcision in Genesis 17 is to be a means by which an inner heart attitude (faith) is expressed.[85]

c. The meaning of the text for Christians today

We now consider the meaning of the text today. The ultimate goal is to identify the implications of the text for the IM debate. However, before we can do this, it is necessary to identify relevant redemptive-historical developments.

i. Relevant redemptive-historical developments

With the coming of Christ, physical circumcision as a sign of the covenant has become obsolete.[86] This is because in his death, Christ fulfills the covenant and undergoes the true and ultimate circumcision. Believers receive this true circumcision when they are united to Christ by faith.[87] Thus in the new covenant age, "circumcision of the heart" becomes a reality and physical circumcision is no longer required.[88]

Notwithstanding this significant covenantal development, NT references to circumcision nevertheless affirm the above conclusions concerning Genesis 17 and circumcision. Once again, not a single reference can be found in which God's giving of the form of circumcision is used by a NT author to encourage readers to engage in a process of contextualized appropriation of the forms of other faiths. Instead, God's giving of circumcision to Abraham is used in the NT to make a very different point: that circumcision was a means by which Abraham expressed his faith-response to God. Paul points out that Abraham's justification came prior to his circumcision (see Gen 15:6 and 17:23–27) and concludes that circumcision could not have been the means by which Abraham attained the status of covenant member (Rom 4:1–12; Gal 3:6–9). Rather, circumcision was a "seal" (σφραγῖδα, *sphragida*) of Abraham's righteousness by faith (Rom 4:9–12). As a seal, it ratified or confirmed Abraham's faith. God's command to circumcise thus functioned as an opportunity for Abraham to

---

85. See further Williamson, "Circumcision," 125.

86. Acts 15:1–21; 1 Cor 7:17–20; Gal 2:1–3; 5:1–11; 6:11–16; Phil 3:1–3; Col 2:8–14. Walton, *Genesis*, 450.

87. Col 2:11–14. Borgen, "Paul," 85–102.

88. Rom 2:28–29; Phil 3:3. Cf. Acts 7:51. Schreiner, "Circumcision,"138; Wenham, *Genesis*, 31; Motyer, "Circumcision," 205. For an in-depth analysis of circumcision in the NT, see Deenick, *Righteous*, 97–210. On whether baptism replaces circumcision as sign of covenant membership, see Hamilton, *Genesis*, 482–83.

express his faith-response to God.[89] Similarly, for the author of Hebrews, Genesis 17 is a depiction of Abraham's faith-response to God's promises (Heb 11:11–12).[90] Thus NT references to circumcision affirm the above analysis regarding the function of the form.

An additional relevant NT teaching concerns the dangers associated with misuse of the form. In a number of his letters, Paul responds to a false teaching that a person must be circumcised in order to be saved.[91] Paul insists that physical circumcision is obsolete, and concludes that whether or not a person is circumcised is a matter of indifference (Gal 5:6; 1 Cor 7:18–19).[92] However, this does not mean that a believer's decision regarding whether or not to be circumcised is unimportant. On the contrary, Paul warns that there will be spiritually disastrous consequences for anyone who undergoes circumcision *on the basis that it is necessary for salvation*:

> Mark my words! I, Paul, tell you that if you let yourselves be circumcised, Christ will be of no value to you at all.. . .You who are trying to be justified by the law have been alienated from Christ; you have fallen away from grace (Gal 5:2–4).

Practicing circumcision in itself is not problematic (cf. Acts 16:1–3).[93] But when circumcision is promoted as a requirement for salvation, it is clearly so.[94]

An important principle regarding forms emerges here. Though a person's status as circumcised or uncircumcised is a matter of indifference, the form of circumcision can nevertheless be a spiritually dangerous one. *If it is practiced for the wrong reasons, the result can be nothing less than a loss of the gospel.* This is why Paul adopts such an aggressive stance towards those advancing the false teaching.[95] Indeed, in Philippians 3:2, he refers to them

---

89. Schreiner, "Circumcision," 138; Woodbridge, "Circumcision," 413–14; Mathews, *Genesis*, 197.

90. Mathews, *Genesis*, 208.

91. See Acts 15:1, 5; Gal 2:12, 5:2–12, 6:12–15; Phil 3:1–11; Titus 1:10. See further, Woodbridge, "Circumcision," 413–14.

92. Hamilton, *Genesis*, 481; Mathews, *Genesis*, 199; Woodbridge, "Circumcision," 413–14.

93. Woodbridge, "Circumcision," 413–14.

94. Rom 2:28–29; 3:30; 4:9–12; 1 Cor 2:11; 3:11; Gal 6:15; Phil 3:2–3. Mathews, *Genesis*, 190. This analysis assumes a traditional understanding of Paul and not that promoted by advocates for the "New Perspective on Paul" (according to which Paul objects to Jewish promotion of circumcision as a boundary marker). Engaging in that debate is beyond our scope here. See Dunn, *New Perspective*; Wright, *Justification*; Carson et al., *Justification and Variegated Nomism*; Johnson and Waters, *Faith Alone*.

95. See Gal 1:8–9; 5:12.

as κατατομήν, *katatomēn* ("mutilators of the flesh"). The verb used here is the same as that used in the LXX to describe prohibited pagan mutilations.[96] The implication is that the false teachers are encouraging something equivalent to the gashing of the body practiced in the fertility religions.[97] In our analysis of Genesis 17, we saw that the correct use of the form of circumcision was as an expression of faith in response to God's promises. Here, in the NT, the corollary is made explicit: an incorrect use of the form of circumcision—as a *means* of gaining salvation—has spiritually fatal consequences.

Finally, we noted above (chapter 2, §2.b.iii.1.) that under the old covenant, worship is God-given—that is, God makes it possible and prescribes its terms. With the coming of Christ, there is both continuity and discontinuity in this regard. God still makes worship possible: in the new covenant he makes it possible through Christ (Heb 4:14-15; 8:1; 10:19-22).[98] And he still prescribes its terms: he prescribes faith in Christ, expressed in continued dependence on and obedience to him (Rom 1:5; 3:25; 12:1; Eph 2:8-10; 4:22-24).[99] However, God no longer makes the same detailed prescriptions of outward forms as he did in the old covenant era. Just as physical circumcision becomes obsolete in the new covenant, so too do many other outward prescribed forms.[100] Christ fulfills and replaces many of the old covenant prescribed forms, and so now true worship is defined by a focus on Christ, not the use of prescribed forms.[101] The result is that new covenant Christians have far greater freedom in selecting worship forms than did their old covenant counterparts.[102]

ii. The implications of Genesis 17 for the IM debate

Let us now consider the implications of our analysis of Genesis 17 for the IM debate.

---

96. Lev 21:5 (LXX).

97. Motyer, "Circumcision," 205.

98. See Peterson, *Engaging*, 228-37.

99. Peterson, *Engaging*, 102, 144, 174-76, 220, 238-46; Peterson, "Worship," 859-62; Clowney, "Worship," 111.

100. See, for example, Mark 7:18-20; John 2:19; Rom 7:1-6; 1 Cor 5:7; Heb 5:14.

101. There are nevertheless still some divinely-prescribed new covenant forms, such as the Lord's Supper and baptism. See Peterson, *Engaging*, 124-26.

102. See further Peterson, *Engaging*, 26, 30-31, 35, 124-26; Carson, "Worship," 38; Ross, *Recalling*, § "Conclusion for Part 1"; Scobie, *Ways*, 576.

1. Genesis 17 is not a Precedent for Appropriating Foreign Forms

Genesis 17 has been advanced by proponents of the biblical precedent argument as one of a series of texts which provides biblical precedent for believers today to use the forms of other faiths. However, for the following reasons, applying the text in this way is a misuse of the text.

As we saw in chapter 1 (chapter 1, §4.b.iii.), whether or not a biblical text can be treated as a precedent depends ultimately upon authorial intention.[103] Since biblical narratives "suggest when the author intends a protagonist to set a precedent,"[104] the interpreter's task is to seek evidence in the text regarding whether the author intended the text to function as a precedent. No such evidence was found, either in the text of Genesis 17, or in any of the subsequent biblical references to circumcision. What was discovered in the text of Genesis 17, however, was a clear authorial intent to persuade the reader to obey God's specific command to circumcise (regardless of the form's origins), as well as both a strong polemic against human initiation in worship and an affirmation that selecting and giving worship forms is God's prerogative alone. Therefore, Genesis 17 could not have functioned as a precedent for appropriating foreign forms for the original audience. As such, it cannot function that way for contemporary believers. After all, as Fee and Stuart explain,

> *A text cannot mean what it never meant.* . . . The true meaning of the biblical text for us is what God originally intended it to mean when it was first spoken.[105]

In characterizing Genesis 17 as a precedent for appropriating foreign forms, proponents of the biblical precedent argument have made a number of hermeneutical errors. First, they have failed to investigate authorial intent in the texts they cite. Ott, Strauss, and Tennent, McDermott, Davis, and Petersen all argue that God's giving of circumcision to the Israelites justifies contemporary form-appropriations,[106] yet none of them engages

---

103. Doriani, *Biblical Application*, 19, 3–4, 199, 207; Osborne, *Hermeneutical*, 432–33, 441; Fee and Stuart, *How to Read*, 29–30; Vanhoozer, *Meaning*, 402; Fee, *Gospel and Spirit*, 90, 92; Larkin, *Culture* (1988), 112; Köstenberger and Patterson, *Invitation*, 242, 244, 372, 390, 741.

104. Doriani, *Biblical Application*, 201.

105. Fee and Stuart, *How to Read*, 29–30 (italics original). See further, Köstenberger and Patterson, *Invitation*, 727–808.

106. Ott et al., *Encountering*, 271; McDermott, *Can Evangelicals*, 82; Davis, *Poles Apart*, 130–34; Petersen, "Investigation," 120–21.

in a detailed exegesis of Genesis 17 (or other circumcision texts) in order to identify if establishing a precedent was in fact the intention of God (the original appropriator), or of the biblical author who recorded God's giving of the form to Israel. As a result, they have imposed an agenda on the text (that of promoting contextualization), which the above analysis has shown to be foreign—even contradictory—to the author's actual agenda. Vanhoozer describes this as "reading against the textual grain."[107] Fee and Stuart warn that when this is done, meanings that were not intended are read into texts, and "biblical texts can be made to mean whatever they mean to any given reader." Ultimately, they conclude, "hermeneutics becomes total subjectivity."[108]

The second hermeneutical error concerns a failure to show sensitivity to divine-human distinctions. As discussed in chapter 1, works on hermeneutics have warned of the special dangers associated with treating God's actions as having precedential value, since not everything that God does is something that humans are permitted to do. Where God exercises "the prerogatives of deity . . . these acts we cannot directly imitate."[109] As discussed above, selection of worship forms was a divine prerogative in the OT. None of the proponents of the biblical precedent argument raises this divine-human distinction nor discusses whether the selection of forms is a divine prerogative in the OT. Rather, they proceed on the assumption that God's action is something that humans can (or even must) imitate. As a result, their conclusion drawn from Genesis 17 is unreliable.

Third, those who characterize Genesis 17 as precedent also make the hermeneutical error of treating an event that is unique in salvation history as repeatable. As discussed in chapter 1, works on hermeneutics have pointed out that the purpose of some narrative texts is not to establish a precedent but rather to record a distinct and unrepeatable event in salvation history.[110] As we saw above, the giving of the sign of the covenant in Genesis 17 is treated throughout Scripture as just such a unique event. The appropriate response from Israel was not to select other foreign forms by analogy which might also function as signs of the covenant, nor even as worship forms more generally. Rather, the appropriate response was to obey the command to circumcise.

107. Vanhoozer, *Meaning*, 373–75.

108. Fee and Stuart, *How to Read*, 29–30.

109. Doriani, *Biblical Application*, 206. See also Osborne, *Hermeneutical*, 207; Duvall and Hays, *Grasping*, 482.

110. Liefeld, *Interpreting*, 58; Doriani, *Biblical Application*, 86–87; Johnson, *Acts*, 5–13; Garner, "High Stakes," 270–72.

We have seen that Genesis 17 cannot be treated as a precedent for the appropriation of the forms of other faiths by new covenant believers. Of course, this does not settle the question of whether there is biblical justification for such appropriations. It simply means that they cannot be justified on the basis of Genesis 17.

2. Other implications for the IM debate

Notwithstanding the obsolescence of physical circumcision in the new covenant age, Genesis 17 nevertheless remains relevant because it teaches general principles concerning worship and forms (chapter 2, §2.b.iii. above) that continue to have force in the new covenant age. As Block notes,

> When we explore the forms of Israelite worship and their underlying theology, we discover a remarkable continuity of perspective between the Testaments. Jesus does not declare the old theology obsolete; rather, in him, the theology underlying Israelite worship finds its fulfillment.[111]

Thus even though the author's purpose in Genesis 17 is not to equip the Israelites to select worship forms, this text does contain general principles concerning worship and forms capable of informing new covenant form-selectors as they express their considerable freedom to select worship forms. What follows is a consideration of the implications of these principles for the IM debate.

First, the above analysis of Genesis 17 demonstrates that the author's primary concern is to equip the reader to engage with God in the way God has prescribed; that is, the author's primary concern is true worship. An important point emerges here: in a text concerning the use of forms by God's people, the author's focus is not contextualization (that is, how God's message is to be related to and applied in a particular context), but rather worship (that is, how God's people relate to and engage with God). In light of this, I propose that a fundamental concern of form-selectors should be *the impact of a given form on true worship*.

Second, Genesis 17 establishes that true worship is God-given, whereas human-initiated worship is false. The privilege of engaging God in worship is a gracious gift of God. The appropriate human response is to receive this gift. Form-selectors should seek forms which will uphold this dynamic. Given that the way of worship that God gives in the new

---

111. Block, *For the Glory*, 7. See also Carson, "Worship," 38; Ross, *Recalling*, §"Introduction to Part 1" and ch. 2; Peterson, *Engaging*, 172, 176, 253.

covenant era is faith in Christ, expressed in dependence and obedience, forms should be selected based on their capacity to facilitate this. Whether or not a form is the best one in the circumstances should depend first and foremost on the (likely) impact of using the form on the capacity of believers to express and grow in Christ-dependence.

As we saw in chapter 1, two tests that have been advanced for use in the selection of contextualized forms are Kraft's allegiance test and IM proponents' "biblical compatibility" test. According to the allegiance test, any religious or cultural form that can be used to express allegiance to God is deemed potentially suitable (see chapter 1, §3.c.i. above). According to the biblical compatibility test, provided that local forms are not immoral or prohibited in the Bible, and that they are given a Christian meaning, they are deemed potentially suitable (see chapter 1, §3.a.vi. above). A shortcoming of both tests is that they do not direct the attention of form-selectors to the importance of preserving the dynamic described above, whereby the privilege of engaging God in worship is graciously given by him, not initiated or merited by his people. A given Muslim form might pass both the allegiance test and the biblical compatibility test, and yet not be a helpful form because it introduces concepts of human initiation or merit-accumulation into the worship of BMBs. This text points to the need for a test which goes further than simply asking about allegiance and moral neutrality, and instead specifically calls form-selectors to consider whether a given form facilitates or hinders an understanding of worship as something which God gives and his people receive.

Third, the form of circumcision functions in Genesis 17 as a means by which Abraham can express his faith-response to God. If this reflects a general biblical teaching regarding the function of forms (on this, see chapter 2, §3.b.iii.3. below), then this reinforces the importance of the test being advanced here: specifically, that form-selectors ask whether a given form facilitates or hinders worshipers to express dependence on Christ.

In their writings, proponents of the biblical precedent argument focus attention on the importance of selecting forms that are culturally familiar to the worshiper.[112] However, in Genesis 17, the crucial issue is not cultural familiarity, but rather whether the form helps the worshiper to make the appropriate faith-response to God's gracious provision of a way to worship him. It would be unfortunate if, in an attempt to ensure that the forms used are culturally familiar, BMBs and missionaries failed to give sufficient weight to this textually more significant matter.

---

112. Davis, *Poles Apart*, 134, 141; Petersen, "Investigation," 117–18, 127; Talman, "Old Testament," 56–57.

Fourth, regarding the debate between Kraft and Hiebert concerning the strength of the connection between form and meaning (see chapter 1, §3.c.), Genesis 17 lends support to Hiebert's position. In our analysis, we identified a probable close symbolic link between the form of circumcision (a mark on the male reproductive organ), and that which the form signified (Abraham's trust in God's promises to make him fruitful). Thus, there is an intrinsic link here between form and meaning. This lends support to Hiebert's claim that form and meaning cannot always easily be separated.[113] An implication for the IM debate is that form-selectors who are considering using Muslim forms will need to consider how strong the connection between a given form and its meaning in Muslim worship is, and whether it is possible for BMBs to discard or modify the Muslim meaning.

Finally, in the above analysis of Paul's discussion of the form of circumcision, we saw that if a form is used for the wrong reasons (specifically, as a means of gaining salvation), the result can be spiritually fatal. Just as Christ would be of no value to the Galatians if they practiced circumcision in order to be justified (Gal 5:2), so too the misuse of forms today could render Christ of no value to worshipers. This highlights the importance of acknowledging the potential power and impact of using forms incorrectly, and also the importance of carefully reflecting upon worshipers' motivations and beliefs in using forms. Of course, any forms can potentially be misused, not just the forms of other faiths. However, close attention to the matter of motivations and beliefs is critical in this context, since what is being proposed is that BMBs use forms which they previously used in Muslim worship *with Muslim motivations and beliefs*. Thus, BMBs need to consider why they used particular Muslim forms in their pre-conversion Muslim worship, and whether there is a danger that any motivations and beliefs that contradict or undermine the principles of Christian worship will continue to surface if they use the form in their worship as believers.

3. Exodus 12–13 and the Passover

Our second OT appropriation text is Exodus 12:1—13:16. This text functions as the climax to an extended narrative (7:8—13:16) in which God demonstrates his superiority over Pharaoh and the Egyptian gods through a series of signs and plagues, and so persuades Pharaoh to allow the Israelites to leave Egypt (see 5:2; 8:18–19; 12:12, 31–36).[114] The text contains three sections. First, instructions are given regarding what the Israelites

---

113. Hiebert, "Form," 106–10.
114. Alexander, *From Paradise*, 170; Longman, *Immanuel*, 186–87.

must do to survive the firstborn plague and leave Egypt (12:1–27). Second, the historical Passover and exodus event itself is narrated (12:28–42). Third, instructions are given regarding the perpetual commemoration of the event (12:43—13:16).[115]

a. The relevance of the text to the research problem

This text is relevant because it has been advanced as part of the biblical precedent argument. Davis, a pioneer of the biblical precedent argument which has since been embraced both by IM advocates and by those writing in the field of contextualization more broadly, depicts the Passover as a feast which probably had pagan origins and concludes that, although the feast is given a new meaning in Exodus 12, "the pagan roots remain."[116] As the following analysis bears out, Davis's claim may be true, but it is speculative.

i. A form borrowed from other faiths

Beginning with Wellhausen in the nineteenth century, many historical critics have contended that the Passover and Unleavened Bread feasts did not originate with the exodus events, but were instead adaptations of pre-existing ANE pagan cultic feasts.[117] Wellhausen argued that originally the Feast of Unleavened Bread was a Canaanite agricultural feast and the Passover was a pastoral nomadic feast which involved the offering of sheep and cattle. He claimed that the two feasts were originally both unrelated to each other and also unconnected to the exodus, and were only amalgamated and associated with the exodus during Josiah's reign.[118]

A number of subsequent historical critics built upon Wellhausen's theory. Gray, for example, posited that the Passover was originally a sacrificial meal with an apotropaic purpose.[119] Pedersen argued that it was originally a pagan spring-time rite aimed at ensuring the successful

---

115. Alexander, *From Paradise*, 170–71. 12:1—13:16 forms a single, unified compositional unit. See Bruckner, *Exodus*, 91. On the debates concerning the redactional history of this text, see chapter 2, §3.a.i. below and Durham, *Exodus*, 161; Childs, *Exodus*, 184; Armerding, "Festivals," 300–301.

116. Davis, *Poles Apart*, 131–32.

117. On the history of this view, see Kraus, *Worship*, 1–25; Alexander, "Passover," 1–6; Childs, *Exodus*, 184–95.

118. Wellhausen, *Prolegomena*, 83–120.

119. Gray, *Sacrifice*, 337–82.

movement of the flock to summer pasture.[120] De Vaux agreed that it was originally a spring-time sacrifice, but proposed instead that the goal was to guarantee the fecundity and prosperity of the flock.[121] Numerous other theories have been put forward, including that the Passover originally had links with "circumcision, demonism, fertility cult or the first-born oblation."[122] Thus the theories vary widely in detail, but have in common the notion that the two feasts were originally pagan in origin, separate from each other and unrelated to the exodus.[123]

When it comes to evaluating these theories, it is important to begin by recognizing that cultic sacrifice was commonplace in the ANE, and so it is plausible that the Passover rite, with its sacrificing of a lamb or kid, was originally a borrowed rite.[124] Further, the Passover and Feast of Unleavened Bread were celebrated in spring (13:4),[125] and along with Israel's other feasts, were at least partially rooted in the agricultural cycles: in Deut 16:1–9, the dates for the three main feasts—Passover, Weeks and Tabernacles—are calculated by reference to agricultural milestones.[126] According to ANE paganism, the success of the agricultural cycles was thought to be closely tied to the correct performance of the religious cult, and so the timing of pagan feasts was also set by the agricultural cycles.[127] In light of this, the proposition that Israel's feasts, including the Passover and Feast of Unleavened Bread, may have had pagan ANE prototypes is reasonable.[128]

However, for the following five reasons, no firm conclusions can be drawn regarding the veracity of the proposals.

First, the proposition is based on supposed similarities between pagan ANE feasts and the biblical feasts, and yet there is very little evidence concerning the relevant ANE feasts. Rost, for example, points to similarities between the biblical Passover and a supposed semi-nomadic migratory festival aimed at protecting the flock. He writes that the setting for both feasts is a people on the move, and the rite for both involves an apotropaic use of

---

120. Johannes Pedersen, "Passahfest und Passahlegende," *ZAW* 62 (1934) 161–175, quoted in Bokser, "Feasts,"756.

121. De Vaux, *Ancient Israel*, 484–92.

122. Stewart, "Passover," 871. See further, Soggin, *Israel*, 91–93, 97–98; Segal, *Hebrew*, 147–48, 239–40.

123. Bokser, "Feasts," 759.

124. Enns, *Exodus*, §Exodus 11:1–13:16. See generally Walton, *Ancient*, 87–161.

125. Bruckner, *Exodus*, 103.

126. Soggin, *Israel*, 93; Ross, *Recalling*, ch. 13; Wright, *Old Testament*, 98; Longman, *Immanuel*, 185; Armerding, "Festivals," 301.

127. Armerding, "Festivals," 301; Talmon, "Gezer," 177–87.

128. Armerding, "Festivals," 301.

blood.¹²⁹ The problem is that no evidence exists for such an ancient migratory festival. Rost's reconstruction of the festival is, as Haran points out, entirely speculative.¹³⁰ Likewise, de Vaux points to the similarities between elements of the biblical feasts and those of feasts celebrated by Bedouin in the twentieth century.¹³¹ However, whether or not these modern Bedouin feasts preserve ancient elements is also a matter of speculation.

Second, plausible arguments against the theory that the feasts were Canaanite borrowings have also been advanced. For example, Halbe rejects the claim that the Feast of Unleavened Bread originated as a Canaanite agricultural festival on the grounds that the month of Abib is too early for a festival to mark the conclusion of the harvest. He suggests that it is unlikely that a seven-day festival would have been celebrated at the beginning of the harvest.¹³² Halbe's reasoning is as speculative as that of Rost and de Vaux above. Yet his arguments do highlight the difficulty of arriving at any firm conclusions in this matter.

Third, arguments based on the etymology of פֶּסַח, *pesach* ("Passover"),¹³³ are also inconclusive. In Akkadian, the same root is used in the sense of appeasing, and so the term might preserve vestiges of a pagan apotropaic rite.¹³⁴ In Hebrew, פֶּסַח, *pesach* can mean "to limp" or "to skip," and so some see here the vestige of a dance performed at a pagan festival. However, others see only a reference to the angel of death skipping over the Israelite households.¹³⁵ Etymological arguments for the pagan origin of the feasts are thus inconclusive.

Fourth, because the theories regarding the pagan origins of the feasts are based on the historical-critical method, their speculative nature needs to be acknowledged.¹³⁶ The historical-critical method proceeds on the basis that there are four sources for the Pentateuch (J, E, D, and P) and that each of these sources can be dated.¹³⁷ Different Pentateuchal texts are

---

129. L. Rost, "Weidewechsel und Altisraelitischen Festkalendar," *ZDPV* 66 (1943) 205-216, quoted in Childs, *Exodus*, 189.

130. Haran, *Temples*, 320-21.

131. De Vaux, *Ancient Israel*, 484-93. See also Propp, *Exodus*, 434-36.

132. Jörn Halbe, "Erwägungen zu Ursprung und Wesen des Massotfestes," *ZAW* 87 (1975) 325-334, quoted in Alexander, "Passover," 4 (see also 11, 19).

133. 12:11, 21, 27, 43, 48. Cf. 12:13, 23.

134. Plastaras, *God*, 150-51.

135. Bosman, "פֶּסַח," 642-644; Longman, *Immanuel*, 187, 224; Stewart, "Passover," 381; Hamilton, *Exodus*, 184-85; Stuart, *Exodus*, 278.

136. Alexander, "Passover," 3-6.

137. For recent approaches to dating the sources, see Baden, *Redaction*; Stackert, *Prophet*.

attributed to different sources, and then the history of the feasts is reconstructed on the basis of different emphases and concerns in the different texts.[138] For example, Wellhausen based his conclusions on the following line of reasoning. First, he attributed certain Pentateuchal references to the feasts to J,[139] and others to P.[140] Then he noted that the J references mention the Feast of Unleavened Bread in isolation from the Passover, whereas P references mention both feasts together. Then, based on his theory that J is tenth/ninth century and P is sixth/fifth century, he concluded that the Passover must not have existed when J was composed, and so the two feasts must have originally been unconnected.[141] Thus Wellhausen's conclusions are arrived at on the basis of a series of speculations regarding the existence of the different sources, their dating, the attribution of particular biblical texts to particular sources, and the reasons for the omission of a reference to the Passover in some texts concerning the Feast of Unleavened Bread. In recent times, the speculative nature of the historical-critical method has been highlighted.[142] Studies have questioned the validity of the criteria used to date the different sources,[143] as well as those used to distinguish them in the first place.[144] Scholars have also pointed out the unreliability of concluding, on the basis of a text's silence with regard to a practice, that it did not exist at the time a source was composed.[145] Ultimately, the historical-critical theories cannot be substantiated.

Fifth, the text itself does not portray the feasts as adaptations of existing feasts. As far as the text is concerned, new feasts are inaugurated in 12:1—13:16.[146] Further, as Stuart notes, it is possible to infer from the fact that elaborate care is taken in 12:1—13:16 to describe every detail of the ceremony, that this is not merely an adaptation of an existing rite well-known to the Israelites, but rather, a new practice.[147] Regarding the historical-critical claims that the two feasts were originally unrelated to each other and to the exodus, in 12:1—13:16 itself, they are inextricably linked, and the elements of the feasts are closely tied in meaning to the exodus event that is being

---

138. Wellhausen, *Prolegomena*, 1–16, 83–111.
139. Exod 23:15–16 and 34:18–22.
140. Exod 12:1–20, 28, 43–49; 13:1–2; Lev 23:5–8; Num 9:1–14; 28:16–25.
141. Wellhausen, *Prolegomena*, 83–107. See also Alexander, "Passover," 1–2.
142. Armerding, "Festivals," 301; Alexander, "Passover," 3–6.
143. Rendtorff, *Problem*; Hurvitz, *Linguistic*.
144. Van Seters, *Abraham*; Van Seters, "Place," 169–70; Whybray, *Making*.
145. See Alexander, "Passover," 5.
146. Longman, *Immanuel*, 185–86.
147. Stuart, *Exodus*, 289.

commemorated. For example, the reason given in the text for the eating of unleavened bread is as a commemoration of the fact that the Israelites left Egypt in haste (12:34; 13:3); there is no hint in the text that a different meaning was previously attached to it.[148] Thus the text itself offers no explicit support for the proposition that the feasts are pagan appropriations.

In conclusion, that ANE pagan spring-time feasts pre-existed the events of Exodus 12–13 is not in doubt, and thus the proposition that the feasts were borrowed forms is plausible. Nevertheless, for the above reasons, there can be no certainty as to the extent to which there was actual dependence on such pagan prototypes.[149]

ii. Used to worship Yahweh

There is no doubt that the Passover and Feast of Unleavened Bread were used in the worship of Yahweh. According to 12:1—13:16, the feasts were to be celebrated as a "sacrifice to Yahweh" (12:27) and a commemoration of Yahweh's act of salvation in the exodus (12:14, 17, 26–27, 42; 13:3, 8–9, 14–16).

In conclusion then, it is possible, but not certain, that the feasts which became the Passover and Feast of Unleavened Bread were originally pagan feasts borrowed and adapted in Exodus 12–13 for use in the worship of Yahweh. Either way, this text is relevant for our purposes because it has been used to support the biblical precedent argument.[150]

b. The meaning of the text for the original audience

i. Is there evidence in the text that the author is seeking to persuade the reader to appropriate foreign forms?

According to the biblical precedent argument, OT form appropriations (such as the appropriation of the feasts in Exodus 12–13)[151] function as precedents for believers today to appropriate other forms by analogy.[152] If 12:1—13:16 is in fact intended to function in this way, it should be possible to find evidence

---

148. Armerding, "Festivals," 301.

149. On the significance of OT/ANE parallels generally, see Currid, *Against*; Poythress, *Interpreting Eden*; Weeks, *Admonition*; Weeks, "Problems," 287–306; Machinist, "Distinctiveness," 420–42.

150. Davis, *Poles Apart*, 131–32.

151. Davis, *Poles Apart*, 131–32.

152. See Ott et al., *Encountering*, 271; Davis, *Poles Apart*, 131–34, 141; Talman, "Old Testament," 51, 55–56; Petersen, "Investigation," 117–18, 127.

in the text that the author is seeking to persuade the reader to appropriate other pagan forms, with the appropriation of the feasts functioning as model appropriations. However, there is no such evidence in the text.

Most importantly, as with Genesis 17, the forms in this text are not actually portrayed as borrowed forms. Rather, so far as the text is concerned, the feasts originate with Yahweh's commands (see 12:1–20; 12:43–49; 13:1–16.).[153] There is no hint that what is actually taking place is a borrowing or adaptation of existing rites. This does not rule out the possibility that, historically, an appropriation was taking place. But it does highlight the very important hermeneutical and theological point that, even if such an appropriation took place, it was nevertheless irrelevant to the message which the author sought to communicate. Since there is no recognition in the text that the feasts are appropriated forms, it is not possible to conclude that the author is seeking to persuade the reader to make other form-appropriations by analogy.

When Davis quotes Exodus 12–13 as evidence for the biblical precedent argument, he does not actually investigate or discuss the author's intention in this text. However, he does discuss a related matter: why God gave pagan forms to the Israelites. He proposes that God did so for reasons related to contextualization, suggesting that God appropriated pagan forms so that Israel could use forms that were culturally familiar to them.[154] In fact, this notion is common to all proponents of the biblical precedent argument. For example, Talman suggests,

> [OT appropriations are] God's intentional contextualization through Abraham and other patriarchs to present a culturally meaningful witness to the surrounding nations.... This seems to reflect Yahweh's desire to communicate his message with maximum impact by using ideas, terms, forms, and elements that were already familiar to the audience.[155]

Thus according to proponents of the biblical precedent argument, pagan forms were appropriated for reasons relating to contextualization. However, there is nothing in 12:1—13:16 to support this claim. The author makes no attempt to explain why pagan feast forms are appropriated. Indeed, the feasts are not even portrayed as appropriated forms at all. Therefore the suggestion that God was motivated by reasons relating to contextualization is speculative and has no grounding in the text.

---

153. Longman, *Immanuel*, 185; Scobie, *Ways*, 576.
154. Davis, *Poles Apart*, 134.
155. Talman, "Old Testament," 50–51. Cf. Petersen, "Investigation," 118.

In conclusion, there is no evidence in the text of an authorial intention to persuade the reader to appropriate foreign forms. The author's purpose must lie elsewhere.

ii. What then is the author's purpose?

The author's purpose in 12:1—13:16 is to persuade the reader to commemorate God's gracious act of salvation in the exodus by observing the feasts with an understanding of their meaning. The author is not seeking to encourage the reader to imitate God's appropriation of pagan feast forms by appropriating *other* pagan forms. Rather, the author is seeking to encourage and equip the reader to use the *specific* forms commanded in the text. The following analysis bears this out.

A striking structural feature of 12:1—13:16 is the interweaving of narrative material and liturgical instructions.[156] In the account of the first nine plagues (7:8—10:29), a narrative pattern is established which involves the announcement of the plague, its execution, its impact, and Pharaoh's reaction.[157] But this pattern is broken in our text: the plague is announced in 11:1-10, but the narration of its execution and impact, and of Pharoah's reaction, does not come until 12:29-42. The pattern-breaking material in 12:1-28 consists of detailed instructions regarding the initial and future observances of the feasts (12:1-27). Not only that, but the narration of the escape from Egypt (12:33-42; 13:17—14:30) is also interrupted by additional instructions regarding the future observance of the feasts (13:1-16). This repeated insertion of liturgical instructions seems "to interfere with the flow of the narrative."[158] That the author is willing to do so strongly suggests that the author's specific purposes in this text are to highlight the importance of future generations observing the feasts, and to equip them to do so. In seeking to explain the "awkwardness" of the liturgical interruptions, Stuart writes, "The answer, we suggest, is that the writer, Moses, was thinking of the best interests of his audience. . . [who] would need to follow these instructions carefully."[159]

An analysis of other structural features of the text reinforces this understanding of the author's purpose. The text is structured in such a way that the detailed instructions concerning the sacrifice of the Passover lamb are given

---

156. Enns, *Exodus*, §Exodus 11:1–13:16.
157. Enns, *Exodus*, §Exodus 11:1–13:16.
158. Stuart, *Exodus*, 269. See also Enns, *Exodus*, §Exodus 11:1–13:16.
159. Stuart, *Exodus*, 270.

no less than three times: 12:1–20, 12:21–27, and 12:43–51.[160] This repetition emphasizes the importance both of the rite and of precise obedience to the divine stipulations. In addition, both sets of instructions concerning the first Passover sacrifice conclude with a climactic command that future generations commemorate the event (12:17–20; 12:24–27).[161]

An analysis of the content of the text further reinforces the proposition that the author's purpose is to persuade and equip the reader to observe the feasts. In a variety of ways, the author emphasizes the *importance* of observing the feasts. The event being commemorated by the feasts is so important, in fact, that Israel's calendar is to be shaped by it (12:2): the first month of the Canaanite year occurred in autumn, whereas the exodus occurred in spring (13:4), and thus God gives the Israelites a different calendar to their neighbors.[162] As well, certain key commands and threats are emphasized through repetition. The positive command to observe the feasts repeatedly surfaces (12:14, 17, 25, 42; 13:5, 10). As well, the negative warning that anyone who fails to participate "must be cut off" (הִכָּרְתָה, *nikhrtah*) is stated twice (12:15, 19). Thus an individual's ongoing membership of the covenant community depends upon obedient observance of the feasts. Further, the fact that the meaning of the feasts must be passed on to subsequent generations is also stated twice (12:25–27; 13:8). Bruckner comments, "The striking repetition of phrases in this passage is not accidental. The Passover and Feast of Unleavened Bread event and observance as a feast has constitutional force for God's people."[163]

Another way in which the author highlights the importance of observing the feasts is by explaining their function for Israel. The feasts are commemorations of the exodus event (12:14, 24–27; 13:3, 9, 16), and so must be observed in order to ensure that Israel remembers God's constitutive act of deliverance. Observing the feasts will also have a broader, more far-reaching impact on worshipers. In 13:9, Yahweh explains that observing the Feast of Unleavened Bread will function as a "sign" (אוֹת, *'ot*) and a "reminder" (זִכָּרוֹן, *zikhron*) "that this law of the LORD is to be on your lips." Thus, observance of the feast was crucial because as Stuart explains,

> it triggered remembrance of the covenant law by which the Israelites were kept in proper relationship with God and for which he had brought them out of Egypt in the first place.[164]

---

160. Bruckner, *Exodus*, 91.
161. Alexander, *From Paradise*, 171.
162. Stuart, *Exodus*, 272–73.
163. Bruckner, *Exodus*, 94.
164. Stuart, *Exodus*, 315.

Thus the text repeatedly emphasizes the importance of observing the feasts.

The text also functions to *equip* readers to observe the feasts. In 12:40—13:10, detailed instructions are given regarding *when* (12:40–42, 51; 13:3–6, 10) and *where* (12:46) the feasts are to be observed, *who* may participate (12:43–45, 47–49), and *what* must be done (12:46; 13:6–8).[165]

As well as emphasizing the *importance* of observing the feasts, and *equipping* the reader to do so, the text also helps readers to understand the *meaning* of the feasts. First, in 12:12, Yahweh announces that the tenth plague is a "judgment on all the gods of Egypt." Thus when the Israelites commemorate the exodus, they acknowledge Yahweh's superiority over other gods and his sovereignty over all peoples.[166] Second, in 12:13, Yahweh declares that he will spare the Israelites from the plague: "I will pass over you" (פָּסַחְתִּי עֲלֵכֶם, *pasachti 'alekhem*).[167] Thus a commemoration of the exodus also involves an acknowledgement of Yahweh as *rescuer* of his people.[168] This is affirmed again in 12:17: the Feast of Unleavened Bread must be observed "because it was on this very day that I brought your divisions out of Egypt." Third, according to 12:13 (and 12:22–23), this rescue only comes to those who put their faith in Yahweh's promise to rescue them by obediently putting blood on their doorframes. Thus a commemoration of the exodus also involves a recognition of the importance of submitting to Yahweh's lordship in faith and obedience.[169] Fourth, in 12:42, the author asserts that just as Yahweh kept "vigil" (שִׁמֻּרִים, *shimmurim*) on the night of rescue, so too subsequent generations must honor Yahweh by keeping "vigil" (שִׁמֻּרִים, *shimmurim*) for him.[170] Thus the observation of the feasts is an act of responsive gratitude.[171] This notion is reaffirmed in 13:8, where the Israelites are commanded to tell their children that they observe the Feast of Unleavened Bread "because of what the LORD did for me when I came out of Egypt." Thus the text helps the reader understand the meaning of the feasts.

Therefore, an analysis of 12:1—13:16 shows that authorial purpose was to persuade and equip the reader to observe the feasts with a full understanding

---

165. Stuart, *Exodus*, 307.

166. Stuart, *Exodus*, 278–79.

167. פֶּסַח, *pesach* could mean "to limp," "to stand watch over," "to dance or skip," or "to pass over." Regardless of which is correct, it clearly refers to a process by which the Israelites escape the plague. See further Bosman, "פֶּסַח," 642–644; Longman, *Immanuel*, 187; Stewart, "Passover," 381; Hamilton, *Exodus*, 184–85; Stuart, *Exodus*, 278.

168. Longman, *Immanuel*, 186–87.

169. Bruckner, *Exodus*, 93–94.

170. Stuart, *Exodus*, 306; Bruckner, *Exodus*, 99–100.

171. Stuart, *Exodus*, 306.

of their meaning. The author is not concerned with the potential for God's appropriation of pagan feast forms to function as a precedent for additional appropriations of pagan forms by the reader. On the contrary, the focus is upon the need for the reader to precisely obey God's specific and detailed commands concerning the observation of the feasts themselves.

iii. What does the text teach about worship and forms?

Four important principles concerning worship and forms emerge in this text.

1. True Worship is God-given

First, the text affirms that true worship is God-given.[172] In this text, God not only provides a great rescue for his people (12:17, 29–36), but he also provides the means by which they might take hold of it (the ritual involving the putting of blood on the doorframes: 12:7, 13, 22–23), and also the means by which they might commemorate it (the two feasts: 12:14–16, 24–27; 13:3, 9, 16).[173] God is not portrayed in 12:1—13:16 as a model appropriator which the Israelites must imitate, but rather as the one who authoritatively and unilaterally prescribes the terms of worship. A comparison of the actions of God and those of the people in this text highlights their very different roles. God issues commands regarding the initial and perpetual observance of the feasts, both directly to Moses and Aaron (12:1–20; 12:43—13:2) and indirectly, through Moses, to the people (12:21–27; 13:3–16). The people, by contrast, listen to the commands (12:21–26, cf. 13:3–16), bow down and worship (12:27), and obey God's commands completely and precisely (12:28). The affirmation in 12:28 that the people completely obey is repeated in 12:50 (cf. 12:35), emphasizing the fact that the human role in worship is to receive that which is graciously given by God. Block writes, "What makes Israelite worship distinct is that it is set by Yahweh and the elements are chosen by him"[174] In 12:1—13:16, selection of worship forms is exclusively God's prerogative. The appropriate human response is submissive and meticulous obedience.

---

172. Peterson, *Engaging*, 20, 26–27, 33, 73; Durham, *Exodus*, 424; Block, *For the Glory*, 25; Garner, "High Stakes," 266–67; Scobie, *Ways*, 567; Ross, *Recalling*, ch. 2.
173. Bruckner, *Exodus*, 92–93.
174. Block, *Deuteronomy*, 440.

2. At this stage in salvation history, acceptable forms are those that are God-given

Second, we see again that, at this stage in salvation history, what makes a worship form valid is that it is God-given. The author of Exodus 12–13 is at pains to emphasize that the precise instructions for the feasts originate with Yahweh. The repetition of the giving of the instructions (from Yahweh to Moses and Aaron, then from Moses to the people: 12:1–13 and 12:21–27; 12:14–20 and 13:3–10) makes clear that, notwithstanding the fact that the people hear the instructions from Moses, they are ultimately from Yahweh. This is further emphasized in 12:28 and 12:50. The fact that the author makes no attempt to equip the reader to select different forms themselves also reinforces this basic observation that, at this stage in salvation history, worship forms are given by God and received by his people. The Israelites are not given the freedom to make form-selections themselves. For the Israelites, if a form is given by God, it is acceptable; if it is not, it is not acceptable.

3. The function of the forms is to enable people to respond to God in faith

Third, in 12:1—13:16, the God-given forms function as a means by which the Israelites express their faith-response to God. This is clear with the putting of blood on the doorframes (12:7, 22). According to 12:13, the blood is a "sign" (אוֹת, 'ot). As a sign, the blood signifies the fact that the occupants have responded in faith to the promise of protection.[175] It is a sign "showing faith on the part of those who reside inside."[176] Not only is it a sign for *God*, in the sense that it prompts him to pass over the marked house, but it is also a sign "for you" (לָכֶם, lakhem) (12:13), that is, for *the Israelites*. The sign was for the people's benefit in the sense that it required them "to undertake an action that involved more than mere ideation, but one demonstrating their confidence in God's power to kill and rescue."[177] In putting the blood on the doorframes, the people do not *cause* their deliverance, but rather they *take hold* of that which God, on his own initiative, graciously offers and eventually brings about. Alexander comments:

> The narrative consistently implies that the LORD was not coerced into helping by the people's actions, but acted freely. . . .

---

175. Hamilton, *Exodus*, 184.
176. Stuart, *Exodus*, 276.
177. Stuart, *Exodus*, 276.

Nowhere does the text suggest that the people persuaded God to act on their behalf by the offering of sacrifices or the performance of meritorious deeds; their deliverance from Egypt is portrayed as an act of sovereign grace.[178]

Thus the form of putting of blood on the doorframes functions as a *means* by which the people express their faith and submit to his lordship and rescue plan.

Similarly, the form of eating unleavened bread also functions as the *means* by which the Israelites express their faith-response to God. For participants in the original exodus event, the act of taking unleavened bread on the journey was an expression of faith that God would rescue (12:32–34). Because they believed Yahweh's promise to rescue them, the Israelites left in haste, rather than taking the time to mix leaven into their dough and wait for it to rise.[179] The act of making unleavened bread demonstrated willingness to participate in a hasty departure, and so expressed faith in Yahweh's promise to deliver them that very night.[180] These acts did not cause the deliverance to take place. Rather, they were expressions of confidence that it would indeed take place and of a readiness to receive it.

Likewise, for subsequent generations of Israelites, the eating of unleavened bread was not an act by which they obtained salvation or covenant blessings. Rather, it functioned as a "memorial" (זִכָּרוֹן, *zikhron*), commemorating the salvation and blessings already theirs (12:14; cf. 13:3).[181] Because Yahweh had commanded the Israelites to commemorate the exodus by eating unleavened bread, doing so was a faith-response.[182] The corollary was also true: failure to do so exhibited a lack of faith, and so anyone who ate leavened bread during the feast had to be "cut off" (12:15).[183] Thus the forms given in Exodus 12–13 function as the legitimate means by which the Israelites express their faith-response to God.

---

178. Alexander, "Passover," 17. *Contra* some historical critics who find here the vestiges of a pagan apotropaic rite (whereby the blood functions magically to ward off evil). See Bokser, "Feasts," 757; Alexander, "Passover," 7–8.

179. Stuart, *Exodus*, 294–95.

180. Stuart, *Exodus*, 276.

181. Stuart, *Exodus*, 282.

182. Stuart, *Exodus*, 283.

183. Stuart, *Exodus*, 283–84; Hamilton, *Exodus*, 187–88.

4. The Link between the Forms and Their Meanings is not Arbitrary

In Exodus 12–13, there is a close link between the prescribed forms and their meanings. In 12:3–11, precise instructions are given regarding how the Passover meal is to be eaten. Many contain symbols of haste, pointing to the readiness of the Israelites for the imminent, hurried departure from Egypt.[184] The meal must be eaten the "same night" as the animal is sacrificed (12:8). It must be "roasted over the fire" (12:8–9), a method associated in ANE thought with travelling, due to the lack of pots for boiling.[185] No time is to be taken to eviscerate the animal: it must be cooked whole (12:9).[186] Since they will be travelling the next morning, the leftovers must be burned that night (12:10). The Israelites must be fully dressed and ready for travel while eating the meal, even to the point of carrying a staff (12:11).[187] The concluding command of the section functions as a summary: "Eat it in haste; it is the LORD's Passover" (12:11).

Interestingly, not all of these actions were necessary from a practical perspective to facilitate a quick departure. Evisceration, for example, does not actually take very much time.[188] Putting on sandals and picking up a staff takes even less! However, they were *symbols* of haste, and so pointed to the dramatic and sudden rescue which Yahweh was about to bring about.[189] What is evident here is a strong link between form and meaning. The Passover meal is to be eaten in such a way that culturally accepted symbols of haste, as well as forms intrinsically associated with haste, are used to picture the dramatic exodus deliverance.

The eating of unleavened bread is another form that has a very close link to the meaning given to it. Eating unleavened bread reminds subsequent generations of the exodus precisely because the exodus generation took unleavened bread with them, on account of there being no time to prepare leavened bread (12:34, 39).[190] The eating of different food simply would not carry the same symbolic meaning or power.

Other elements of the feasts also point to the original deliverance. For example, the requirement that the Passover meal be eaten indoors (12:46)

---

184. Bruckner, *Exodus*, 92–93; Stuart, *Exodus*, 277–78.
185. Bruckner, *Exodus*.
186. Bruckner, *Exodus*, 93.
187. Waltke and Yu, *Old Testament*, 382; Bruckner, *Exodus*, 93.
188. Bruckner, *Exodus*, 93.
189. Bruckner, *Exodus*, 92–93.
190. Waltke and Yu, *Old Testament*, 382; Stuart, *Exodus*, 283.

functions to remind the Israelites of the need for the exodus generation to stay inside their blood-marked houses during the tenth plague.[191] Likewise, the requirement that "the whole community of Israel" celebrate the feast (12:47) reminds worshipers that the whole community of Israel was rescued on that night (see 12:3, 6, 19). In all this, we see that the prescribed form is *very closely linked* to its meaning. Sometimes the link is a historical one (the Israelites are commanded to re-enact an event from the original Passover), and sometimes it is an existing culturally-recognized one (such as the link between roasting and travelling). Either way, it is clear that the rituals prescribed are, as Enns concludes, "inextricably bound . . . to the departure itself."[192] In Exodus 12–13, form and meaning are not easily separated.

5. Forms have the potential to shape beliefs and worldview

Exodus 12–13 highlights the worldview-forming power of worship forms. Enns notes the detailed nature of the instructions given in Exodus 12–13, the fact each is imbued with symbolic meaning, and the fact that this meaning must be passed on to subsequent generations (12:26; 13:8–9; 13:14). He concludes:

> One thing we can learn from this is the importance the Bible places on ritual. . . . Ritual breeds familiarity. It seeps into one's subconscious and, however subtly, begins to exert a formative influence. . . . Ritual has always been and will always be a means of securing for future generations the power and reality of the gospel.[193]

Thus Exodus 12–13 highlights the potential for rituals or forms to shape worldview.

iv. References to the feasts in the rest of the OT

An analysis of subsequent OT references to the feasts affirms the above. Not one OT reference can be found where the biblical author seeks to persuade the readers to treat Yahweh's (possible) appropriation of the pagan feast forms as permission to appropriate and adapt other pagan forms. In fact, not

---

191. Stuart, *Exodus*, 309.
192. Enns, *Exodus*, §Exodus 11:1–13:16.
193. Enns, *Exodus*, §Exodus 11:1–13:16. Cf. Zahniser, *Symbol*, 64–66; Shaw, "Dynamics," 1–19.

one reference can be found in which the biblical authors even acknowledge that the feasts are borrowed forms. Instead, subsequent references to the feasts reinforce the understanding that Exodus 12–13 contains commands which are to be obeyed.[194] For example, in Numbers 9:1–14, the emphasis is on the importance of precise obedience to Yahweh's commands concerning the Passover (Num 9:1–3, 5, 8). When a question arises concerning the celebration of the feast by those who are ritually unclean, the Israelites do not develop a procedure themselves based on what they have learned from Yahweh's previous form-giving. Rather, they enquire directly of Yahweh, and then follow the precise commands he gives (Num 9:6–13). Likewise, in 2 Chronicles 30:1—31:1, the obedience of the people to the prescriptions of the Law of Moses as they celebrate the Passover is emphasized (30:9, 15–16). Similarly, in 2 Kings 23:21–23, the emphasis is on the keeping of the feast as an expression of obedience to Yahweh's commands. The account of the same event in 2 Chronicles 35:1–19 also highlights that the Passover is observed in accordance with the prescriptions in the Book of Moses (35:12).[195]

Throughout the OT, Yahweh's giving of the feasts is not presented as a model form-borrowing which the Israelites must imitate, but rather as a set of commands which they must receive and obey. Historically speaking, the feasts may be borrowed forms, yet this is never given any theological significance by any of the OT authors.

c. The meaning of the text for Christians today

We now consider the meaning of the text for Christians.

i. Relevant redemptive-historical developments

Exodus 12–13 called the Israelites to observe the feasts as a commemoration of God's deliverance of Israel from bondage in Egypt. Yet with the coming of Christ, the observance of these feasts becomes obsolete, because Christ, in his death, becomes the true Passover sacrifice (1 Cor 5:7; 1 Pet 1:18–19),[196] securing an even greater deliverance: the deliverance from bondage to sin and death (Rom 3:24; 6:1–3; Gal 4:3–5).[197] It is this greater deliverance which Christians are to commemorate by observing the Lord's Supper, which

---

194. On these texts, see Alexander, "Passover," 8–16.
195. Armerding, "Festivals," 309.
196. Stuart, *Exodus*, 271.
197. Waltke and Yu, *Old Testament*, 392; Scobie, *Ways*, 596.

replaces the Passover.[198] When Jesus institutes this new commemoration, he follows the Passover custom by explaining the elements of the meal, but shifts the focus from the events of the exodus to those of his own death.[199]

The ongoing significance of the feasts lies in the fact that NT authors draw upon various elements of them to communicate new covenant truths. Importantly for our purposes, these truths do not relate to contextualization. In fact, not one NT author refers to the feasts in order to build an argument for the contextualized borrowing of the forms of other faiths. Instead, when the NT authors refer to the feasts, their purpose is to explain the meaning of Christ's death and its implications for believers. All four Gospels depict the death of Christ as the fulfillment of the meaning of the Passover feast.[200] On the Mount of Transfiguration, Jesus speaks with Moses and Elijah "about his ἔξοδον, *exodon* ("exodus" or "departure"), which he was about to bring to fulfillment at Jerusalem (Luke 9:31)."[201] The fact that Jesus' death coincides with the Jewish commemoration of the Passover is highlighted in all four gospels.[202] In the Synoptic Gospels, the last supper is a Passover meal, and Jesus identifies himself with the Passover sacrifice.[203] In John, Jesus' death is also portrayed as a Passover sacrifice.[204] John even quotes from Exodus 12:46 to explain why Jesus' bones are not broken (John 19:36).[205] The purpose of the gospel writers is to communicate that Jesus' death is redemptive, and that it secures deliverance for God's people.[206]

Likewise for Paul, the value of the feasts for Christians lies in the fact that they prefigured Christ, and so help to elucidate the meaning of his death. Paul characterizes the feasts as only "a shadow of the things that were to come," with Christ being the "reality" (Col 2:17). As shadows which prefigure Christ, the feasts point to and illuminate the meaning of Christ's death. And

---

198. Matt 26:17-30; Mark 14:12-26; Luke 22:7-23; 1 Cor 11:23-33. Cf. Gal 4:10; Rom 14:5-6; Col 2:17. Scobie, *Ways*, 596; Alexander, *From Paradise*, 174-75; Stewart, "Passover," 873; Enns, *Exodus*, §Exodus 11:1-13:16.

199. Waltke and Yu, *Old Testament*, 392.

200. Scobie, *Ways*, 596; Longman, *Immanuel*, 113-15.

201. Stuart, *Exodus*, 282.

202. Matt 26:17-30; Mark 14:12-26; Luke 22:7-23; John 19:14, 31.

203. Matt 26:17-30; Mark 14:12-26; Luke 22:7-23. Waltke and Yu, *Old Testament*, 392; Alexander, *From Paradise*, 174.

204. John 19:14; 31-33, 42. Alexander, *From Paradise*, 174. On the theme of Jesus as the fulfillment of OT feasts generally in John's gospel, see Davies, *Gospel*, 296.

205. A historical difficulty exists regarding the timing of the meal when John's account is compared to the Synoptic Gospels. See Alexander, *From Paradise*, 174-75; Blomberg, *Historical Reliability*, 237-53.

206. Longman, *Immanuel*, 113-15; Alexander, *From Paradise*, 175.

so Paul describes Christ as "our Passover lamb" who "has been sacrificed" (1 Cor 5:7). Peter also seems to depict the death of Christ as the ultimate Passover sacrifice (1 Peter 1:18–19; cf. Exod 12:5).[207] In his death, Jesus secures a far greater deliverance than the one commemorated by the Passover. The ongoing value of the Passover is that it is a paradigm or type of this ultimate deliverance and so illuminates its meaning. Stuart concludes, "The ultimate purpose of the Old Testament Passover instruction is to point forward to Christ, to the purpose of his death."[208] Thus the meaning of Exodus 12–13 for Christians lies not in its function as an example of contextualized appropriation of foreign forms which believers are to imitate, but rather in the fact that the feasts elucidate the meaning of Christ's death.

ii. The implications of Exodus 12–13 for the IM debate

Let us now examine the implications of our analysis of Exodus 12–13 for the IM debate.

1. EXODUS 12–13 IS NOT A PRECEDENT FOR APPROPRIATING FOREIGN FORMS

Exodus 12–13 has been put forward as part of the biblical precedent argument as one of a number of texts which provides biblical precedent for believers today to borrow and adapt the forms of other faiths.[209] However, to apply Exodus 12–13 in this way is to misuse the text. We saw in chapter 1,§4.b.iii. that a contemporary application of a text must be based on, and controlled by, the text's original meaning, and yet there is no evidence whatsoever in Exodus 12–13 that the author intended to communicate a message about borrowing and adapting forms. Further, the notion that this text is a precedent for borrowing pagan forms is actually in tension with authorial intention as disclosed by the text: to persuade and equip the reader to observe the feasts precisely according to Yahweh's commands, since the selection of forms is exclusively Yahweh's prerogative.

A study of subsequent references to the feasts in both the OT and the NT revealed that God's (possible) appropriation and adaptation of pagan feasts is never drawn on as an example of contextualized borrowing which

---

207. Other interpretations of this text are possible. See Alexander, *From Paradise*, 174; Hamilton, *Exodus*, 181.

208. Stuart, *Exodus*, 274. See also Armerding, "Festivals," 310.

209. Davis, *Poles Apart*, 131–32.

believers are to imitate. Therefore, Exodus 12–13 cannot be applied as a precedent for appropriating the forms of other faiths. The conclusion to the contrary is based on a number of hermeneutical errors. These are discussed above in relation to Genesis 17 (chapter 2, §2.c.ii.1.), and are not repeated here.

2. Other implications for the IM debate

Like Genesis 17, Exodus 12–13 contains a number of principles regarding worship and forms that continue to have relevance in the new covenant age. These principles need to be taken into account as new covenant believers exercise their greater freedom regarding form-selection.

First, the above analysis of Exodus 12–13 affirms the importance of evaluating a form's helpfulness through the lens of a biblical theology of worship. The author's primary concern in this text is not contextualization. Rather, it is to ensure that God's people are engaging God in the way he makes possible and prescribes; that is, the author's concern is worship. If this is the concern of the biblical author, then it also needs to be the concern of form-selectors today. Specifically, form-selectors need to carefully consider the impact of any given form on the capacity of the user to engage in true worship.

Second, Exodus 12–13 highlights the fact that true worship is God-given: the role of God's people is to receive and use the way to engage God that he himself provides. As we have seen, for new covenant believers this does not involve the use of the same outward forms as it did for old covenant believers, but rather it involves faith in Christ, expressed in dependence and obedience. Therefore, when the impact of a given form on true worship is being evaluated, at issue is *whether the form facilitates or hinders this faith-response to Christ.*

A shortcoming of the "biblical compatibility" test advocated by some IM proponents (see chapter 1, §3.a.vi. above) is that it does not direct the attention of form-selectors to this matter. The priority in the biblical compatibility test seems to be cultural familiarity: provided a Muslim form is not inherently "negative," "dark," or "immoral," it can be retained.[210] A better test is one that prioritizes worship over cultural familiarity, prompting form-selectors to seek those forms which *best* facilitate true worship (Christ-dependence) in the circumstances.

---

210. See Lewis in Brogden, "Inside Out," 35; Talman, "Old Testament," 49–57; Higgins, "Key," 156; Brown, "Biblical Muslims," 70–73.

Third, the function of God-given forms in Exodus 12–13 is to enable God's people to respond in faith to the rescue and covenant blessings that God graciously bestows upon them. Forms are not a means by which blessings can be obtained. An implication is that form-selectors need to consider whether a given form will function in this way, that is, as a means by which believers make a faith-response to God *who has already graciously offered salvation and blessing*. If a given Muslim form has previously been used in a different way (for example, as a means of accumulating merit in order to earn blessing), then it may not be the best choice in the circumstances.[211]

Fourth, Exodus 12–13 provides further support for Hiebert's proposition that the connection between forms and their meanings can sometimes be very close, even intrinsic, with the result that the two cannot easily be separated.[212] In Exodus 12–13, some of the forms have intrinsic links to their meaning. An important implication is that not all forms are equally good candidates for use by believers. Some are more appropriate and effective than others for facilitating a meaningful faith-response. This insight casts doubt upon the veracity of Kraft's proposal that almost all forms are "neutral vehicles" which can be invested with new Christian meanings.[213] Indeed, the link between form and meaning can be very strong, such that it may not be easy, or even possible, to detach the meaning previously associated with a form.

Finally, Exodus 12–13 highlights the worldview-forming power of worship forms. This further underscores the importance of carefully ensuring that the forms used in worship today reflect gospel truths and facilitate the appropriate faith-response. It also reinforces the importance of avoiding forms which distort or confuse the message of the gospel, or which replace the appropriate faith-response with notions contrary to the gospel (such as notions of merit-accumulation or deity-manipulation).

Thus notwithstanding the fact that Exodus 12–13 cannot be applied as a precedent for appropriating foreign forms, the text does contain a number of important implications for the IM debate.

4. First Chronicles 28 and the temple

The third and final OT appropriation text is 1 Chronicles 28. This text is part of an extended narrative (21:1—29:25) in which David makes

---

211. Green, "Guidelines," 233–34, 245–49.

212. Hiebert, "Form," 106–10.

213. Kraft, *Christianity in Culture* (1979), 95, 99; Kraft, *Christianity in Culture* (2005), 233; Kraft, *Anthropology*, 35; Kraft, "Dynamic Equivalent," 115.

preparations for the construction of the temple. In our text, David publicly commissions Solomon to build the temple (28:1–10), gives him detailed plans for its construction (28:11–19) and exhorts him to perform the task courageously (28:20–21).[214]

a. The relevance of the text to the research problem

This text is relevant to the research problem because it has been cited in connection with the biblical precedent argument. A number of proponents of this argument (Davis; Ott, Strauss, and Tennent; and Talman)[215] have noted that the design of Solomon's temple was similar to that of some existing pagan temples, and so have argued that the temple is another example of a pagan form which was appropriated by God's people. First Chronicles 28 is the only text put forward in connection with this argument.[216] As the following analysis bears out, broadly speaking, the claim is accurate: Solomon's temple was probably similar in design to some existing pagan temples, but there were some differences.

i. A form borrowed from other faiths

Considerable archeological evidence has been uncovered from all over the ANE regarding the design, layout, size, construction, and furnishings of pagan temples of the period.[217] Unfortunately, however, almost no archeological evidence of Solomon's temple has been recovered.[218] The only information we have about Solomon's temple is the material in 1 Kgs 6–7, 1 Chr 22–29, and 2 Chr 2–3, and this material does not enable a complete reconstruction—partly because the temple accounts are selective in their focus, and partly because they contain technical Hebrew construction terms whose precise meanings elude modern scholars.[219] Because of this, it is not

---

214. Thompson, *Chronicles*, 189. On the tension between the accounts of Solomon's commissioning in 1 Chr 28 and 1 Kgs 1–2, see Japhet, *Chronicles*, 483; Hooker, *Chronicles*, 109.

215. Davis, *Poles Apart*, 132; Ott et al., *Encountering*, 271; Talman, "Old Testament," 50.

216. Davis, *Poles Apart*, 132. There is no equivalent of 1 Chr 28 in either Samuel or Kings.

217. Meyers, "Temple," 354; Kitchen, *Reliability*, 122.

218. Kitchen, *Reliability*, 122; Meyers, "Temple," 354; Monson, "Solomon's Temple," 929, 931.

219. Monson, "Solomon's Temple," 929–30; Meyers, "Temple," 353.

possible to draw firm and detailed conclusions about the extent to which Solomon's temple was similar to contemporary ANE temples.[220] Nevertheless, when the biblical projections are compared to the archeological evidence, it is clear that, at least in general terms, Solomon's temple did indeed resemble existing pagan temples in a number of ways.

In terms of design and layout, Solomon's temple shares a number of features with temples from northern Syria and northern Mesopotamia:

> a rectangular plan, a pillared entrance on the short southern wall, a tripartite division (internal walls), a raised platform or niche opposite the door, and an elevated holy of holies or inner sanctum at the far end.[221]

Regarding size, Solomon's temple also "stands within a long-established range of size for temples of its type during the third to first millennia."[222] With respect to construction materials, historians have identified many similarities, including the use of three-layered stone masonry topped with cedar beams, and the use of wood-paneling with gold overlay.[223] Regarding furnishings, similarities have also been identified, including the use of standing columns, movable stands with ablution bowls, and a range of other cultic items.[224] With respect to decorative motifs, many similarities have also been noted, such as cherubim, palm trees, and open flowers.[225]

On the basis of these comparisons, historians generally agree that Solomon's temple was probably very similar in both design and features to existing pagan temples of the period.[226] One temple in particular, the King 'Ain Dara temple in northern Syria, has been hailed as a "striking parallel" to Solomon's temple in terms of size, date and iconography, such that it can be said to provide a "physical corollary to the OT's word picture of Solomon's temple."[227]

220. Keel, *Symbolism*, 161.

221. Monson, "Solomon's Temple," 932. See also Kitchen, *Reliability*, 126; Keel, *Symbolism*, 151.

222. Kitchen, *Reliability*, 126 (see generally 123–24).

223. Kitchen, *Reliability*, 126.

224. Kitchen, *Reliability*, 125–27.

225. Block, "Other Religions," 47–48; Keel, *Symbolism*, 141–44. On the similarities between the symbolism and ideology associated with Solomon's temple, and that of its pagan counterparts, see Monson, "Solomon's Temple," 932–34; Block, "Other Religions," 47–48; Walton, *Ancient*, 118, 127.

226. Kitchen, *Reliability*, 126–27; Wessels, "Biblical," 55; Block, "Other Religions," 47–48; Meyers, "Temple," 355.

227. Monson, "Solomon's Temple," 932; Kitchen, *Reliability*, 123–24. For detailed comparisons of Solomon's temple with this and other ANE temples, see further

Nevertheless, Solomon's temple had no exact parallels in the ANE, and important differences can be identified.[228] For example, unlike pagan temples, the holy of holies was square, not rectangular, and it contained no icon representing Yahweh.[229] In fact, unlike pagan temples, Solomon's entire temple complex contained no images of the deity or of humans.[230] Thus Solomon's temple resembled contemporary pagan temples in many ways, and yet was different in certain important respects.

ii. Used to worship Yahweh

The temple was undoubtedly used in the worship of Yahweh. It is described in the text as "a place of rest for the ark" (28:2), "the footstool of our God" (28:2), a house for Yahweh's name (28:3), and a "sanctuary" (28:10). Indeed, the broader narrative of which our text is a part makes it clear that the temple is right at the centre of Yahweh's plans for his people to worship him (1 Chr 17, 21–29, 2 Chr 2–7).[231]

In conclusion then, while Solomon's temple was not an exact copy of existing pagan temples, it did resemble them in many ways. Thus it may be characterized as a pagan form that was appropriated and adapted for use in the worship of Yahweh.

b. The meaning of the text for the original audience

i. Is there evidence in the text that the author is seeking to persuade the reader to appropriate foreign forms?

Proponents of the biblical precedent argument claim that this form-appropriation functions as a biblical precedent for believers today to borrow and adapt the forms of other faiths.[232] The veracity of this claim depends upon whether evidence can be found in the text that the author *intended* to persuade the reader to treat the appropriation as a precedent (see chapter 1, §4.b.iii. above). There is no evidence in the text of any such authorial

---

Monson, "New 'Ain Dara Temple," 20–35; Keel, *Symbolism*, 111–76; Monson, "Solomon's Temple," 931–34; Kitchen, *Reliability*, 122–27.

228. Meyers, "Temple," 355.

229. Keel, *Symbolism*, 154, 157; Walton et al., *Bible Background*, 419.

230. Monson, "Solomon's Temple," 934; Glaser, *Bible*, 74; Scobie, *Ways*, 572.

231. Pratt, *Chronicles*, 28–29; Waltke and Yu, *Old Testament*, 761–62.

232. Davis, *Poles Apart*, 132–34; Ott et al., *Encountering*, 271; Talman, "Old Testament," 50.

intention. Indeed, there is not even any acknowledgement in the text that the design and features of the temple are in fact borrowed forms. Rather, the plans for the temple are presented as originating with Yahweh, who gives them to David, who in turn gives them to Solomon (28:12, 19).

These plans may well have strongly resembled pagan temples of the time, and thus, *historically speaking*, an appropriation may have been taking place. Yet the fact that the pagan origins of the form are ignored suggests that the form's status as a borrowed one was of no importance whatsoever to the message which the author sought to communicate. Thus a likely *historical* reality (form appropriation) has no *literary* or *theological* significance here. In these circumstances, it is simply not possible to conclude that the author is seeking to persuade and equip the reader to borrow foreign forms.

In putting forward his case for the biblical precedent argument, Davis cites 28:11 and 19, and correctly acknowledges that, according to the text, the temple's design originates with Yahweh.[233] But he then goes further and suggests that Yahweh's reasons for giving a borrowed form related to contextualization.[234] Indeed, all proponents of the biblical precedent argument maintain that God appropriated pagan forms out of a desire to contextualize his communication to Israel or to the surrounding nations.[235] The problem with this argument is that it is completely unsubstantiated by the text. There is no explanation in the text as to why God gave the Israelites a borrowed form. The notion that he did so for the sake of contextualization is purely speculative.

The speculative nature of this argument is underlined by a brief survey of other attempts to explain the similarities between Solomon's temple and ANE pagan temples. Historical critics such as Gunkel and Delitzsch exclude the possibility that the design of Solomon's temple originated with Yahweh, and propose that the Israelites simply borrowed ideas from their neighbors.[236] Some evangelicals, by contrast, suggest that the similarities can be attributed to the fact that pagans have some understanding of divine truth, albeit a limited and distorted one.[237] Ross writes,

---

233. Davis, *Poles Apart*, 132.

234. Davis, *Poles Apart*, 134.

235. Talman, "Old Testament," 50–51; Petersen, "Investigation," 117–27; Ott et al., *Encountering*, 271.

236. Niehaus, *Ancient*, 23–30.

237. Niehaus, *Ancient*, 16, 29–30, 178.

> One must conclude that a certain amount of truth, or at least a proper instinct for religious matters, existed in the pagan systems.[238]

An alternative evangelical explanation is provided by Niehaus, who proposes that similarities can be attributed to "demonic inspiration of false religion."[239] He classifies pagan forms that resemble God-given worship forms as "theological counterfeits" that were "imposed upon the ancients by the misleading inspiration of fallen angels."[240]

It is beyond the scope of this book to evaluate the relative merits of these competing explanations. The point here is simply that the explanation for the similarities offered by the proponents of the biblical precedent argument (that God was motivated by a desire to contextualize) is just one of many which have been put forward, none of which has any support in 28:1–21. Ultimately, all these explanations are speculative, and so to draw conclusions from such speculations relating to theology or ministry methodology is unjustified and dangerous. The following observation from Scobie is apposite here:

> Biblical theology is concerned not with hypothetical theories of origins, but with the OT material in its final canonical form, and with its theological significance.[241]

In conclusion, no evidence can be found in the text that the author sought to persuade the reader to appropriate foreign forms for use in Yahweh-worship.

ii. What then is the author's purpose?

The author's purpose in 28:1–21 is to persuade the reader to express trust in God through devotion to the Davidic kingship and to temple worship, on the basis that these institutions are God-given. The author is not seeking to persuade the reader to borrow pagan forms generally, but rather to use the specific forms (the kingship and the temple) that are the focus of the text. The following discussion bears this out.

An analysis of the message of the book as a whole helps to elucidate the author's purpose in 28:1–21. The book of Chronicles is written to a post-exilic

---

238. Ross, *Recalling*, ch. 6. See also Beale, *Temple*, 88.
239. Niehaus, *Ancient*, 179.
240. Niehaus, *Ancient*, 181.
241. Scobie, *Ways*, 577.

audience.²⁴² Not only were these returnees facing economic difficulties, foreign threats, and domestic conflicts, they were also experiencing theological disappointment, since the restoration had not brought the abundant blessings that had been predicted by the prophets.²⁴³ Chronicles is written to provide this struggling community with guidance "for attaining a greater realization of the blessings of the Kingdom of God in their time."²⁴⁴

The Chronicler stresses the importance of commitment to the Davidic kingship and to temple worship. Waltke writes,

> In the Chronicler's theology the restored community is organized around two central institutions: the Davidic throne and the Jerusalem temple. . . . [Commitment to these institutions] is the stuff that furthers the kingdom of God in spite of trouble.²⁴⁵

Indeed, as Pratt notes, seventeen of the twenty-one chapters devoted to David concentrate on his preparations for the temple (1 Chr 13–29).²⁴⁶ Likewise, Solomon's chief achievement is the construction of the temple (2 Chr 2:8).²⁴⁷ Further, the later kings who are portrayed as exemplars are those who renovate the temple or otherwise show devotion to it.²⁴⁸ Thus the book as a whole is concerned to impress upon the reader the crucial roles of the Davidic kingship and the temple. Hahn concludes,

> For the Chronicler, the key to history is the kingdom of David, established by divine covenant and embodied in the temple at Zion and its liturgy. As the rise of this liturgical empire in the past triggered blessings for God's chosen people and for the world, so its future restoration will bring to fulfillment God's plan for history.²⁴⁹

An analysis of the content of 28:1–21 reveals that this general concern of the book is also very much the focus of this text. In 28:1–21, these two

---

242. On the dating of Chronicles, see Pratt, *Chronicles*, 9–12.

243. Ezek 34:26; Joel 3:18–21; Amos 9:11–15. Pratt, *Chronicles*, 14–15; Hahn, *Chronicles*, 1.

244. Pratt, *Chronicles*, 15.

245. Waltke and Yu, *Old Testament*, 761–62. See further, Pratt, *Chronicles*, 25; Hahn, *Chronicles*, 4–5.

246. Pratt, *Chronicles*, 25.

247. Waltke and Yu, *Old Testament*, 761.

248. See 2 Chr 14:1–2; 15:8–15; 17:2–9; 23:17; 24:4–14; 29:3—31:21; 33:1–19; 34:3—35:18. Waltke and Yu, *Old Testament*, 761–62. See further, Pratt, *Chronicles*, 28–29.

249. Hahn, *Chronicles*, 13.

institutions are legitimized by the fact that they have their origins not in the will of humans, but in the will of God himself.

First, regarding the kingship, David's dynasty is portrayed as legitimate because it is chosen by God (28:4–7).[250] The fact of divine election is emphasized through intensification: God chose "Judah," and from the house of Judah "my house," and from that house, "me," and from all "my sons," "Solomon" (28:4–5). The scope of the election is broad: God gives David a jurisdiction which is comprehensive ("over all Israel," 28:4), and for an unlimited duration ("forever," 28:4). And the fact that Solomon is David's divinely-appointed successor is asserted no less than four times (28:5, 6, 10; 29:1).[251]

Second, regarding the temple, the author makes it clear that this too comes into being as a result of God's will.[252] Although David had attempted to initiate the building project, God rejected David's proposal (28:2–3) and instead commissioned Solomon for the task (28:6, 10). Not only that, but God provides detailed plans for the temple (28:11–19). There is some question over whether or not 28:12 affirms that the plans were divinely inspired: רוּחַ, *ruach*, in 28:12 can mean either "mind" or "spirit," and so the plans that David gives to Solomon could simply be "all that he had in mind," or could be "all that was with him by the Spirit."[253] However, there is no doubt that divine inspiration is what is claimed in 28:19:

> "All this," David said, "I have in writing as a result of the LORD's hand on me, and he enabled me to understand all the details of the plan."

The phrase used here מִיַּד יְהוָה, *miyyad yhwh* (lit. "from the hand of the LORD"), is a formula denoting divine revelation in prophetic contexts (Ezek 1:3; 3:14).[254] Indeed, the Chronicler is at pains to emphasize that *every* detail of these most elaborate plans came from God: "all" (כֹּל, *kol*) appears no less than 8 times in 28:12–19. By depicting the temple worship established by David and Solomon as divinely initiated and commissioned, the Chronicler urges his post-exilic readers to participate in it in their day.[255] Of course, the Chronicler's readers could not worship at Solomon's temple because it had been destroyed by the Babylonians. But they could participate in the temple

250. Pratt, *Chronicles*, 191.
251. Japhet, *Chronicles*, 488; Thompson, *Chronicles*, 190.
252. Pratt, *Chronicles*, 191.
253. Van Pelt et al., "רוּחַ," 1073–78; Thompson, *Chronicles*, 192; Hill, *Chronicles*, 326; Klein, *Chronicles*, 525; Jonker, *Chronicles*, 165.
254. Hill, *Chronicles*, 326; McKenzie, *Chronicles*, 215; Japhet, *Chronicles*, 498.
255. Pratt, *Chronicles*, 194.

worship established by the Davidic dynasty by worshiping at the Second Temple, which was built on the same site, under the guidance of the same Levitical priesthood, and using the same cultic items listed in 28:13–18. As Pratt notes, the Chronicler is concerned to "authorize David's plans for worship" as being of ongoing validity for the returnees, notwithstanding the destruction of Solomon's temple.[256]

The divine origin of temple worship is further emphasized through an allusion to the tabernacle. Just as Moses was once shown a "plan" (תַּבְנִית, *tavnit*) for the tabernacle (Exod 25:9, 40), so too David is given a "plan" (תַּבְנִית, *tavnit*) for the temple (28:11 12, 19).[257] Just as the "plan" (תַּבְנִית, *tavnit*) given to Moses began with instructions for the shrine (Exod 25:8–9), followed by instructions concerning its furnishings (25:10–39), so too the "plan" (תַּבְנִית, *tavnit*) given to David follows a similar sequence (28:11–12, then 28:13–18).[258] By establishing a continuity with the worship established in Moses' day, the Chronicler further legitimizes the temple worship established by the Davidic dynasty.[259]

Thus the reader is encouraged to be devoted to the Davidic kingship and the temple worship because they both have their origins in the will of God. But why did God establish these institutions? According to the broader theology of the book, God did so in order "to establish *his* reign on earth."[260] There are hints of this broad goal in our text: in 28:2 the temple which God commissions is to be *his* house, and in 28:5, David's throne is actually *God's* throne (28:5).[261] Ultimately, then, the reader must be devoted to these institutions because God expresses his own kingship through them.[262]

The authorial intent to urge commitment to these two institutions is again evident in 28:20–21, where David urges Solomon to be diligent in performing "all the work for the service of the temple" (28:20), and reassures him that God is with him in this venture (28:20). In the same way, "the post-exilic audience can and must be devoted to the temple in their

---

256. Pratt, *Chronicles*, 194. See also Thompson, *Chronicles*, 193; Knoppers, *Chronicles*, 940–41; Braun, *Chronicles*, 275; Japhet, *Chronicles*, 485; Hill, *Chronicles*, 326; Hooker, *Chronicles*, 110.

257. McKenzie, *Chronicles*, 215; Japhet, *Chronicles*, 485.

258. Knoppers, *Chronicles*, 940.

259. Knoppers, *Chronicles*, 940–41; Thompson, *Chronicles*, 193; Hill, *Chronicles*, 325; Klein, *Chronicles*, 524–25; Braun, *Chronicles*, 271–72; De Vries, *Chronicles*, 220.

260. Hahn, *Chronicles*, 76.

261. See also 1 Chr 29:23 and 2 Chr 9:8, Hahn, *Chronicles*, 76–77; Hill, *Chronicles*, 324; Pratt, *Chronicles*, 193.

262. Hahn, *Chronicles*, 75–77.

own day," knowing that God is with them also in this matter.²⁶³ Thus the author's purpose in 28:1–21, as evident in the text itself, is not to persuade the reader to borrow foreign forms, but rather to persuade the reader to use the specific God-given forms described in the text.

iii. What does the text teach about worship and forms?

We turn now to a discussion of what the text teaches about worship and forms. Three points emerge.

1. TRUE WORSHIP IS GOD-GIVEN

First, the text affirms the foundational principle that true worship is God-given. In 28:1–21, it is God who commissions the temple (28:6, 10), decides who will build it (28:6, 10), provides the detailed plans for its construction (28:12–19), and provides the workforce needed for its construction (28:21). Temple worship is a gracious gift of God.

The role of God's people is not to imitate God in his role as form-selector (or form-appropriator). Rather, it is to obediently receive and use the worship forms that he provides. Indeed, the importance of humble obedience to God is emphasized in this text.²⁶⁴ The success of Solomon's reign will depend upon his obedience (28:7). David urges Israel's leaders to obey (28:8) and warns Solomon of the consequences of failure to do so (28:9).²⁶⁵ Solomon must "do the work" that God has given him to do (28:10, 20). At no point is initiative or freedom in the selection of worship forms encouraged. On the contrary, Solomon and Israel must submissively and precisely receive and use that which God provides.²⁶⁶

Indeed, the reader is reminded of the inappropriateness of human initiation in worship in 28:2–3, where David explains that he had previously proposed to initiate temple construction himself, but God had refused on the grounds that David was a warrior who had shed blood. This is an allusion to the incident in 17:1–15 which contains a sharp polemic against human initiation in worship.²⁶⁷ When Yahweh rejects David's proposal in

---

263. Pratt, *Chronicles*, 195. See also Pratt, *Chronicles*, 31; Braun, *Chronicles*, 273.
264. Japhet, *Chronicles*, 486–87, 491; Pratt, *Chronicles*, 192.
265. Thompson, *Chronicles*, 191.
266. The same emphasis can be found in Solomon's private commissioning in 22:2–19.
267. 2 Sam 7:1–17 (the parallel text) is similar in both content and rhetorical force.

17:1–15, he points out that his relationship with David has actually been characterized by *him* acting on *his* initiative for David, not the reverse (17:7–10).[268] Then, in an ironic reversal of David's intention to build a "house" (בַּיִת, *bayit*) for Yahweh (17:4), Yahweh declares that he will build a "house" (בַּיִת, *bayit*) for David (17:10).[269] Thus 17:1–15 rejects "the sufficiency of any human initiative in the matter of temple building,"[270] and indeed any human presumption in worship generally.[271]

It is clear, then, that in 28:1–21 and its context, the selection of worship forms is exclusively God's prerogative. Therefore the notion that 28:1–21 seeks to encourage the Israelites to imitate God and appropriate foreign forms must be rejected. Humans are not to imitate God as form-selector, but rather receive from God the means of worship that he graciously provides.

2. At This Stage in Salvation History, Acceptable Forms are Those that are God-given

The second point follows on from the first: because selection of worship forms is God's prerogative, it follows that, at this stage in salvation history, the thing which makes a worship form valid is its God-givenness. As we saw above, what makes the temple a legitimate place for worship is the fact that God commissions it and gives it to his people. At no point in the text does the author take any steps to persuade or equip readers to select worship forms themselves. The simple reason is that it was not Israel's role to select worship forms. The reader is not told why God chose the particular design that he did, because the reader does not need to know God's reasons. Instead, the reader simply needs to recognize the God-givenness of temple worship, and be devoted to it. Therefore, the question of whether the design of the temple was borrowed from pagan temples is irrelevant and of no concern to the author.

---

268. Jonker, *Chronicles*, 124–25.

269. There is a wordplay on בַּיִת, *bayit* here, which can refer to a "temple" or a "dynasty." Wilson, "בַּיִת," 655–657; Jonker, *Chronicles*, 125.

270. Dumbrell, *Covenant*, 49.

271. Jonker, *Chronicles*, 123–28. Cf. 13:1–14, where Uzzah is destroyed by Yahweh because he touches the ark. Jonker writes: "It was not the bringing of the ark to Jerusalem that was denounced when Uzzah was killed by Yahweh, but the improper, exclusively human effort exerted in doing so." Jonker, *Chronicles*, 124.

3. God is intimately concerned with the details of worship forms

Third, the text affirms the importance of worship forms and God's concern that they conform to his plan and will. The plans which Yahweh gives to David (28:12, 19) are remarkable in their detail and comprehensiveness. Everything, from the floor plans to the weight of gold and silver for the various cultic items, is given to David by God (28:11–19). Nothing is left to chance. The picture that emerges here is of a God who is intimately concerned with every detail relating to the forms that his people will use to worship him. There is no hint that other forms can be substituted for the ones that God graciously gives here.[272] Thus 1 Chronicles 28 contains important teachings concerning forms and worship.

iv. References to the design of the temple in the rest of the OT

An analysis of other OT references to the design and features of the temple affirms the above conclusion that Yahweh's (possible) appropriation of the design of pagan temples is not an exemplary appropriation which the Israelites are supposed to imitate. Not a single OT reference can be found in which the author seeks to persuade the reader to treat Yahweh's appropriation of the temple form as a precedent for Israelite form-appropriation generally. Indeed, not a single OT reference can be found in which there is even an acknowledgement that a form-appropriation has taken place. Instead, other OT references to the temple's design and features reinforce the teaching of 28:1–28 that the temple is something given by God, which his people should use obediently.

In Exodus 25–31, God gives Moses the design of the tabernacle and its furnishings, and then in Exodus 35–40, the construction is narrated. Because the tabernacle is the temple's salvation-historical predecessor, and because the design and features of the former significantly influence the latter,[273] these texts are relevant here. There is no indication in Exodus 25–31 and 35–40 that the design and features that are given by God to Moses are in fact borrowed from pagan sanctuaries.[274] Further, there is no evidence in the

---

272. In this regard, it is worth recalling that there were theologically significant differences between Solomon's temple and ANE pagan temples. For example, Solomon's temple had no icons or images. Cf. Exod 20:4–5; 32:1—34:35; Deut 5:8–9; Ps 106:19–20.

273. Cf. 1 Kgs 8:4. See Scobie, *Ways*, 569; Longman, *Exodus*, 169. Many critical scholars reverse the order of dependence, contending that the tabernacle was a later reconstruction modeled on Solomon's temple. Friedman, "Tabernacle," 292–300.

274. Notwithstanding the fact that there is some historical evidence that the

text of an authorial intent to equip readers to engage in the process of form-selection themselves. On the contrary, the emphasis falls upon the fact that the tabernacle is a gift from God which is designed by God and which will enable the people to enjoy God's presence amongst them—provided they receive it obediently. The tabernacle must be constructed precisely according to the pattern God shows Moses (25:8, 40; 26:30; 27:8).[275] Leaving no detail to chance, God even fills those responsible for the artistic design with his Spirit (31:3). Thus the Israelites are not responsible for the design. Instead, their role is to construct the tabernacle precisely according to God's instructions, something which they do in Exodus 35-40.

Exodus 25-31 affirms the above observations that God is intimately concerned with the details of worship forms (see chapter 2, §4.b.iii.3.). In this text, matters such as dimensions, materials, construction-methods, and even the placement of individual furnishing items are described in scrupulous detail. As many have noted, there is a rich symbolic significance to the details given here.[276] The tabernacle's design proclaims "the presence of a holy God in the midst of a sinful camp," with each of the details conveying important theological truths.[277] No room is given for human modifications to this divine plan, because that which is given by God is meaningful and is just as he intends.

Another relevant text is 1 Kings 6-7, which narrates the construction of the temple. The details of the design and furnishings are given, but there is no attempt to provide a rationale for these features. Importantly, there is no hint that what is taking place is a borrowing. Any resemblance that the temple might bear to pagan temples is once again of no concern to the author, and thus of no importance to the intended message. Instead, the text is concerned to emphasize the importance of obedience (6:11-13; cf. 9:1-9). Provan aptly summarizes the text's rhetorical force: "God is not half so impressed with structures as with obedience."[278]

Ezekiel 40-43, concerning the construction of a new temple, is also relevant here. The proportions of this new temple are given in considerable detail, but as with the Exodus, Kings and Chronicles texts, there is no acknowledgement of any pagan influence on the design, nor is there any

---

tabernacle resembled pagan tent-sanctuaries. See Averbeck, "Tabernacle," 818-19; Davis, *Poles Apart*, 132.

275. Longman, *Exodus*, 132.

276. See Longman, *Exodus*, 134-42; Hamilton, *Exodus*, 447-526; Janzen, *Exodus*, 191-225; Childs, *Exodus*, 512-52.

277. Longman, *Exodus*, 135-36.

278. Provan, *Kings*, 74. 2 Chr 3-4 is the parallel text to 1 Kgs 6-7, and is similar in both content and rhetorical force.

indication that the readers are given these details in order to equip them to make analogous contextualized form-selections. Instead, Ezekiel's intention seems to be to give his exilic audience hope that a splendid restoration will indeed take place and that God will dwell with them once again. This is evident not only in the climax to the section in 43:1–12 where the glory of the Lord fills the new temple (counteracting Yahweh's departure from the old temple in Ezekiel 8–11), but also in the closing words of the book itself: "The LORD is there" (48:35).[279]

Thus when the OT authors discuss the design and features of the temple (or its predecessor or successor), their concern is not contextualization. Any possible resemblance to pagan temples is not explained, or even acknowledged. Yahweh's giving of sanctuaries to Israel is *never* presented as a model appropriation of foreign forms which the Israelites are to imitate. Instead, they are gracious gifts which enable Israel to enjoy God's presence, and which they must construct and use precisely according to God's instructions.

c. The meaning of the text for Christians today

i. Relevant redemptive-historical developments

The NT authors present Jesus as the fulfillment and replacement of the tabernacle (John 1:14) and the temple (Matt 12:6; John 2:12–22), and thus as the true mediator of God's presence.[280] In the new covenant age, God's presence is no longer in the Jerusalem temple (Matt 27:51),[281] but instead he dwells amongst his people by his Spirit, with the result that the Christian community can also be characterized as the new covenant temple.[282] Like the old covenant temple, the new covenant temple is God-given, God-designed, and inextricably linked to the Davidic king.[283]

Because the new covenant temple is not a physical building, the NT does not contain any texts like Exodus 25–31 or 1 Chronicles 28 which provide details concerning the design and features of a physical building. Nevertheless, there is one NT text concerning the design of OT sanctuaries

---

279. McConville, *Exploring*, 104; House, *Theology*, 343.

280. See Eph 2:20–22; Col 2:9–10; 1 Pet 2:4–8. Peterson, "Worship," 860–63; Peterson, *Engaging*, 202; Longman, *Exodus*, 170–73.

281. Scobie, *Ways*, 592.

282. 1 Cor 3:16–17; 2 Cor 6:16; Eph 2:20–22. Scobie, *Ways*, 592–93; Waltke and Yu, *Old Testament*, 761.

283. Eph 2:20; 1 Pet 2:4–8; cf. Matt 16:18. On the links between the new covenant temple and the Davidic king, see Beale, *Temple*, 216–44.

which is relevant here. In Hebrews 8–9, the writer reveals that the OT tabernacle was modeled on the heavenly dwelling place of God.[284] The writer describes this heavenly dwelling place as the "true tabernacle" which was constructed "by the Lord, not by a mere human being" (8:2; cf. 9:11). The earthly tabernacle, by contrast, was merely "a copy and shadow of what is in heaven" (8:5; cf. 9:24). The term "copy" (ὑποδείγματι, *hupodeigmati*) suggests that the earthly tabernacle is a replica of the heavenly archetype.[285] The term "shadow" (σκιᾷ, *skia*) implies a foreshadowing (of that which believers will experience in heaven), and so "suggests the earthly sanctuary mimics enough of the original to point God's people to greater, heavenly realities."[286] Thus the OT tabernacle is both an imitation of the heavenly sanctuary and also an anticipation of the ultimate redemption that will be accomplished there. Hence the pattern which God showed Moses in Exodus 25:9 and 20 (and therefore presumably also the pattern which God showed David in 1 Chronicles 28)[287] was based on God's heavenly dwelling place.[288] This means that, according to the Bible, regardless of any resemblances that might have existed between OT sanctuaries and ANE pagan temples, *it was the design and features of heaven itself, not that of ANE pagan temples*, that influenced the design and features of the OT sanctuaries. In giving the plans, then, God was not motivated by a desire to contextualize. Rather, he was commissioning a sanctuary that would reflect and point towards his own dwelling place, the place where Christ's perfect redemptive work would one day be accomplished, and indeed the place where God's people will one day fully experience his presence and blessing.[289]

ii. The implications of 1 Chronicles 28 for the IM debate

We now consider the implications of our analysis for the IM debate.

---

284. See Block, *For the Glory*, 257–58.

285. Bruce, *Hebrews*, 183–84.

286. See 10:1 for another usage of "shadow" connoting anticipation. Guthrie, *Hebrews*, 280.

287. After all, the temple's basic design is very similar to the tabernacle's. Longman, *Exodus*, 169.

288. Scobie, *Ways*, 588; Block, *For the Glory*, 257.

289. Scobie, *Ways*, 594, 604–5.

1. First Chronicles 28 is not a precedent for appropriating foreign forms

Yahweh's giving to Israel of a design for the temple which resembled that of pagan temples has been claimed as a biblical precedent which gives permission to believers today to borrow and adapt the forms of other faiths.[290] However, this claim is flawed and must be rejected. There is no evidence in 1 Chronicles 28 of an intention on the part of the author to persuade or equip readers to engage in contextualized form-appropriation. On the contrary, the authorial intention which is evident concerns the importance of readers obediently receiving the forms which are selected and graciously given by God. Since the text does not authorize Israel to borrow and adapt forms, and since contemporary application of a text must be based on, and controlled by, the text's original meaning (see chapter 1, §4.b.iii. above), 1 Chronicles 28 cannot be treated as a precedent for contextualized form-appropriations today. A study of other OT references to the design and features of sanctuaries confirms this conclusion, since those texts affirm the exclusive divine prerogative to design and select forms, as well as Israel's role as submissive form-receiver.

Further evidence of the shortcomings of the biblical precedent argument is found in the assertion in Hebrews 8–9 that the OT tabernacle was an imitation of the heavenly original. Regardless of actual *historical* resemblances which might have existed between Israelite sanctuaries and their pagan counterparts, the theological significance of the design and features of OT sanctuaries ultimately lies in the fact that they reflect and point to a heavenly reality. Thus the revealed intention of the design and features of biblical sanctuaries has nothing whatsoever to do with contextualization.

In conclusion, 1 Chronicles 28 and related texts cannot be applied as precedents for appropriating foreign forms. The notion that they can is based on a series of hermeneutical errors, which are discussed above in relation to Genesis 17 (chapter 2, §2.c.ii.1.) and are not repeated here.

2. Other implications for the IM debate

First Chronicles 28 teaches principles concerning worship and forms that have ongoing relevance in the new covenant era and which therefore need to be taken into account by form-selectors today. Four implications are identified here.

---

290. Davis, *Poles Apart*, 132; Ott et al., *Encountering*, 271; Talman, "Old Testament," 50.

First, the above analysis once again highlights the importance of selecting forms with reference to the likely impact of the form on a worshiper's ability to engage in true worship. Whereas IM proponents emphasize the importance of BMBs using contextualized forms, the author's concern in 1 Chronicles 28 is not actually contextualization. Rather, it is *true worship*: worship which honors God by using the means he has given his people to approach and relate to him. This is not to say that contextualization is unimportant. Rather, it is to say that a concern to ensure that forms are contextualized must not be given priority over that which has consistently emerged in this chapter as the chief preoccupation of the biblical authors in texts dealing with worship forms: whether or not God's people are engaging in true worship.

Second, since 1 Chronicles 28 affirms the principle that true worship is God-given, this text further strengthens the foundational contention in this book that a form should be evaluated according to whether or not it helps the worshiper to receive and use God-given worship. While God-given worship for the original readers of 1 Chronicles 28 involved devotion to temple worship, for new covenant believers it involves devotion to Jesus, the true "temple" (chapter 2, §4.c.i. above). Therefore a key question for believers engaged in contextualized form-selection needs to be: *Does this form facilitate or hinder an all-of-life devotion to, and dependence on, Christ?* I propose that this test, with its focus on worship, is a better one than the "biblical compatibility" test proposed by some IM proponents (see chapter 1, §3.a.vi.), which instead focuses attention on the inherent morality of a form and prioritizes contextualization (cultural familiarity) over worship.

Third, in our analysis of all three OT texts in this chapter, we have seen that the old covenant era is one in which worship forms are prescribed by God, such that what makes a form acceptable is simply that God has commanded that it be used. When we recognize this, we see that the biblical compatibility test (see chapter 1, §3.a.vi.) is based on a misreading of the relevant OT texts. In justifying the biblical compatibility test, IM proponent Talman suggests that there is a pattern in the OT whereby "good" forms are borrowed by the Israelites and "bad" ones (that is, those with a "dark, deceptive, destructive" character)[291] are rejected.[292] He concludes that this forms a precedent for today, whereby believers should borrow "positive" forms which are compatible with the Bible, and reject "negative," biblically incompatible forms.[293] Yet as we have seen throughout this

---

291. Talman, "Old Testament," 51.
292. Talman, "Old Testament," 49–57.
293. Talman, "Old Testament," 56–57. See also Lewis's comments in Brogden,

chapter, at issue in the OT texts is not whether certain worship forms are good or bad, positive or negative. Rather, at issue is *whether or not their use is commanded by God*. The OT authors do not seek to equip the Israelites to make an assessment of the intrinsic morality of forms and then select appropriate ones. Rather, they seek to persuade them to use the forms God prescribes and avoid those he does not prescribe.

Fourth, we saw above that in 1 Chronicles 28 (and Exodus 25–31), God is intimately concerned with the details of worship forms, ensuring that even the smallest details of the design and furnishings of the sanctuaries conform to his will. This casts further doubt upon Kraft's claim that forms are "essentially neutral vehicles" which can be used and given new meanings.[294] It reinforces Hiebert's understanding that the link between form and meaning is sometimes very close.[295] Certainly, new covenant believers enjoy a greater freedom with regard to the selection of worship forms than did the Israelites (chapter 2, §2.c.i. above), but as this freedom is exercised, form-selectors need to be aware of the potential for a form's meaning to be closely, perhaps inseparably, linked to the form itself.

Thus notwithstanding the fact that 1 Chronicles 28 cannot be applied as a precedent for appropriating foreign forms, the text does contain a number of important implications for the IM debate.

5. Conclusion

In this chapter, we have studied three OT appropriation texts. A consistent picture has emerged. None of the texts can be characterized as biblical precedents for believers to use the forms of other faiths. At the same time, all of the texts contain principles concerning worship and forms with remarkably similar emphases, highlighting God's initiative and authority in determining how his people respond to him. As we have seen, the implications of these principles for contextualization and the IM debate are significant.

We now turn to an analysis of OT resistance texts.

"Inside Out," 35.

294. Kraft, *Christianity in Culture* (1979), 95. See further Kraft, *Anthropology*, 35; Kraft, *Christianity in Culture* (1979), 93.

295. Hiebert, "Form," 106–10.

3

Old Testament Resistance Texts

1. Introduction

IN THIS CHAPTER, THREE OT resistance texts are studied: Exodus 32–34, Deuteronomy 12 and Hosea 8. Our aim, as with chapter 2, is to identify what message the biblical authors intend to communicate concerning the forms of other faiths, and then to draw implications for the IM debate.

2. Exodus 32–34

The first resistance text is Exodus 32–34. Exodus 32:1-6 records the sin of Israel and Aaron while Moses is on Mount Sinai. The people ask Aaron to make a god (or gods), and Aaron responds by collecting gold from the people and making an idol in the shape of a young bull. He then builds an altar and revelrous worship ensues. Exodus 32:7—34:35 first shows how the sin results in a serious rupture in the covenant relationship and then depicts the process by which this rupture is repaired so that the covenant can be remade.[1]

a. The relevance of the text to the research problem

For a text to be relevant, it needs to be one in which the forms of another faith are used by God's people to worship God (and not merely other gods). As the following analysis shows, Exodus 32–34 is indeed such a text.

---

1. Childs, *Exodus*, 557. There is general agreement that Exod 32–34 is a single, unified compositional unit. On the debates regarding the redactional history of the text, see Moberly, *Story*, 157–86; Durham, *Exodus*, 426; Childs, *Exodus*, 557–58, 562.

i. Forms borrowed from other faiths

The forms used in 32:1–6 are undoubtedly forms used by Israel's neighbors to worship their gods. First, the use of idols in worship was universally practiced by Israel's neighbors.[2] Indeed, the second commandment (Exod 20:4–6), which prohibited idols, was unique in the ANE. No parallel has been found.[3] Thus idol-worship is certainly the form of another faith.

Second, when Aaron chooses the shape of "a young bull" (עֵגֶל, *'egel*)[4] for the idol (32:4), he engages in a borrowing at that level too. In the ANE, the young bull was a symbol of fertility and power, and was the single most common animal used to represent gods.[5] Egypt, the Levant, Anatolia, and Mesopotamia all had bull-cults,[6] and thus the idol's shape was undoubtedly a borrowing. Scholars have proposed a range of possibilities regarding *which* bull-cult Aaron borrowed from.[7] However, this cannot be determined with certainty.[8] What is important for our purposes is that bull-cults were very common in the ANE and so Aaron and the Israelites would have had ample exposure to them. Thus the bull-shaped idol is a borrowed form.

Third, Aaron's altar is also a borrowed form. In 32:5, Aaron builds an altar "in front of [the idol]" (לְפָנָיו, *lepanav*). It was standard practice in ANE religion to position altars in front of idols, so as to ensure that the gods would see the offerings made and accept them.[9] By contrast, Yahweh prescribed that the altar be positioned in the courtyard of the tabernacle, with no direct line of sight to the ark in the holy of holies.[10] Thus the altar is a borrowed form.

Finally, the Israelites' revelrous feast is also a borrowed form. In 32:6, the Israelites engage in "having fun" or "revelry" (צחק, *tzchq*).[11] צחק, *tzchq*

---

2. von Rad, *Old Testament*, 214–15; Lods, "Images," 138–42. See generally Hoerth et al., *Peoples*; Finegan, *Myth*.

3. Stuart, *Exodus*, 451.

4. See Lu, "עֵגֶל," 320–21.

5. Van Dam, "Golden Calf," 368; Kitchen, "Golden Calf," 158–59.

6. Van Dam, "Golden Calf," 368.

7. See Kitchen, "Golden Calf," 158–59; Oswalt, "Golden," 13–20; Bailey, "Golden Calf," 97–115; Stuart, *Exodus*, 569, 669–70; Longman, *Exodus*, 133; Tsumura, "Canaan," 126–27; Van Dam, "Golden Calf," 368–69; Spencer, "Golden Calf," 1068–69; Key, "Traces," 20–26.

8. Childs, *Exodus*, 565.

9. Stuart, *Exodus*, 666.

10. Stuart, *Exodus*, 666.

11. Stuart, *Exodus*, 666.

can have sexual connotations.[12] Evidence exists that Israel's neighbors engaged in ritualized orgies at their places of worship, possibly in the hope of securing fertility for the land through sympathetic magic. For example, prostitutes can be found amongst lists of temple personnel in Canaanite and Akkadian texts.[13] As well, the prohibition in Deuteronomy 23:17-18 seems to be directed against such "sacred prostitution,"[14] although not all agree.[15] Because of this, some have concluded that 32:6 describes a pagan-style religious orgy.[16] The evidence is not sufficient to permit a firm conclusion here. Of the six other occurrences of צחק, *tzchq* in the *piel* form in the OT, a sexual nuance is present in three (Gen 26:8; 48:14, 17) and absent in the other three (Gen 19:14; 21:9; Judg 16:25). Further, 32:18 (where Moses tells Joshua that he hears עַנּוֹת, *'annot*) does not resolve the matter, since עַנּוֹת, *'annot* could be translated as "an orgy," as "Anat" (a Canaanite goddess), as "cultic singers" or "music," or as "a hubbub or din." Thus, like 32:6, 32:18 may or may not suggest sexual behavior.[17]

However, even if no sexual reference is intended, the revelrous feast is nevertheless influenced by pagan worship practices. Whereas the law required that the Israelites eat fellowship offerings in the courtyard of the tabernacle, in the ANE, worshipers at idol-worship feasts usually ate their portion of the offerings at or around the shrine.[18] Exodus 32:6 seems to depict just such an idol-feast. As well, the description in 32:17-19 of the feast matches what is known of pagan worship practices. In 32:17, Moses and Joshua hear "the noise of the people" (אֶת־קוֹל הָעָם בְּרֵעֹה, *et-qol ha'am bere'oh*). This phrase implies wild celebration and unrestrained boisterousness.[19] So loud is the noise, in fact, that Joshua, a military general, mistakes it for the sound of battle (32:17).[20] Thus Stuart proposes that what is depicted here is "the sort of shrieking that pagans thought appropriate to rousing the gods."[21] Further, in 32:19, Moses sees the Israelites "dancing" around

---

12. See Allen, "צחק," 796-97; Hamilton, *Exodus*, 532-33.

13. Walton et al., *Bible Background*, 197.

14. Sprinkle, "Sexuality," 749-50.

15. Tigay, *Deuteronomy*, 480-81; van der Toorn, "Prostitution," 510-12; Lipiński, "Prostitution," 48-56.

16. Waltke and Yu, *Old Testament*, 469; Childs, *Exodus*, 556.

17. Stuart, *Exodus*, 666-67, 676; Hamilton, *Exodus*, 532-33; Deem, "Anath" 29; Rendsburg, "Hebrew," 192; Edelman, "*Annôt*," 355; Whybray, "*Annôt*," 122; Andersen, "Lexicographical Note," 111.

18. Stuart, *Exodus*, 666.

19. Durham, *Exodus*, 430; Stuart, *Exodus*, 675.

20. Stuart, *Exodus*, 675.

21. Stuart, *Exodus*, 675.

the idol, another practice commonly associated with pagan worship in the ANE.²² As well, the revelrous feast does not appear to resemble any of the Yahweh-given feasts in 23:14–17.²³ For these reasons, even those who reject the notion that chapter 32 depicts *sexual* activity nevertheless conclude that the Israelites are "copying the worship styles of idolatry"²⁴ and engaging in a "ritual that followed practices well known to the Ancient Near East."²⁵ Thus this revelrous feast would also be a borrowed form.

ii. Used to worship Yahweh

There is debate regarding whether it is Yahweh or other gods that the Israelites are attempting to worship in 32:1–6.²⁶ As the following analysis makes clear, while there is ambiguity surrounding the Israelites' request in 32:1, what eventually takes place in 32:4–6 is most likely an attempt to worship Yahweh.

The Israelites' request in 32:1 is for אֱלֹהִים, *'elohim* who will go before them. It is difficult to determine whether they are asking for an idol to represent Yahweh or to represent other gods.²⁷ The question cannot be resolved on purely grammatical grounds, since אֱלֹהִים, *'elohim* can be singular, "god/God," or plural, "gods," depending on the context. Ordinarily in the OT, where אֱלֹהִים, *'elohim* is used with plural verbs (as it is here), the plural, "gods," is intended. But sometimes it refers to Yahweh (Gen 20:13, 35:7; 1 Sam 4:8; 2 Sam 7:23).²⁸ Some argue that the fact that the context is one of dissatisfaction with Moses (the Israelites refer to him disparagingly as "this

---

22. Stuart, *Exodus*, 676–77.
23. Bruckner, *Exodus*, 222.
24. Stuart, *Exodus*, 666.
25. Sasson, "Worship," 152.
26. See Oswalt, "Golden," 18–20; Moberly, *Story*, 46–47; Hamilton, *Exodus*, 531–34; Spencer, "Golden Calf," 1069; Durham, *Exodus*, 419–22; Waltke and Yu, *Old Testament*, 469; Stuart, *Exodus*, 664–65.
27. For arguments that they are requesting an idol of Yahweh, see Bailey, "Golden Calf," 97–115; Hyatt, *Exodus*, 304; Moberly, *Story*, 46–48. For arguments that they are requesting an idol for other gods, see Stuart, *Exodus*, 663; Durham, *Exodus*, 419; Oswalt, "Golden," 13–20; Sasson, "Bovine," 380–87; Brichto, "Worship," 1–44; Childs, *Exodus*, 564.
28. See Fretheim, "אֱלֹהִים," 405–6; Moberly, *Story*, 47–48; Van Dam, "Golden Calf," 368–69; Hamilton, *Exodus*, 531–32; Stuart, *Exodus*, 662.

fellow": 32:1)²⁹ leads to the conclusion that the people are turning away from Yahweh to polytheism.³⁰ However, this is speculative.

More persuasive, in fact, are the contextual arguments that the Israelites seek an idol *to represent Yahweh*. First, the people's request is simply that an idol be made, not that a new deity or deities be sought.³¹ Second, when Aaron makes just one idol (32:4a) and calls a feast to Yahweh (32:5), there is no surprise, opposition or disappointment expressed by the people. Rather, they receive the idol enthusiastically and use the same combination of אֱלֹהִים, *'elohim* with plural verbs to refer to it (32:4b) as they had used in their request in 32:1, suggesting that what Aaron makes is in line with their request.³² Therefore it seems that the people's request in 32:1 is for an idol to represent Yahweh and not other gods.

Yet even if it is not, what ensues in 32:4–8 is almost certainly worship of Yahweh. In 32:4, Aaron makes the idol and then the people declare, "This is your אֱלֹהִים (*'elohim*), O Israel, who brought you up out of Egypt." Throughout Israel's history, the deliverance from Egypt is associated with Yahweh and with no other god.³³ Indeed, the phrase the people use in 32:4 is almost identical to Yahweh's self-description in 20:2. Thus the people conceive of a continuity between Yahweh and the idol.³⁴ For this reason, most agree that by 32:4, the Israelites are associating the idol with Yahweh and viewing it as a means of worshiping him.³⁵

Additional details in 32:5–8 confirm this. In 32:5, Aaron explicitly identifies Yahweh as the object of the worship, announcing a "sacred feast

---

29. Bruckner, *Exodus*, 221.
30. Stuart, *Exodus*, 662–63.
31. Hamilton, *Exodus*, 532.
32. The fact that the Israelites use אֱלֹהִים, *'elohim* with plural verbs in 32:4 to refer to just one idol strongly suggests that both 32:1 and 32:4 are references to God (singular), not gods. Canonical support for this is found in Neh 9:18, which quotes Exodus 32:4, but uses אֱלֹהִים, *'elohim* with a *singular* demonstrative, making explicit that just one God was being worshpped. Hamilton, *Exodus*, 532; Van Dam, "Golden Calf," 368–69; Sailhamer, *Pentateuch*, 311; Spencer, "Golden Calf," 1066; Oswalt, "Golden," 16; Bailey, "Golden Calf," 99–100.
33. Stuart, *Exodus*, 665.
34. Moberly, *Story*, 46–47.
35. *Contra* Bruckner, *Exodus*, 221; Bailey, "Golden Calf," 99–100. A range of possibilities has been put forward regarding exactly how the Israelites might have conceptualized the relationship between the idol and Yahweh. For some, the idol functionally replaced Moses or the ark and tabernacle, for others it functioned as a pedestal or an emblem for Yahweh, and for still others, it was simply an image of Yahweh. See Spencer, "Golden Calf," 1068; Moberly, *Story*, 46–47; Sasson, "Bovine," 386–87; Bailey, "Golden Calf," 97–98; Eissfeldt, "Lade," 190–215; Toews, *Monarchy*, 52–53; Stuart, *Exodus*, 665; Van Dam, "Golden Calf," 369; Oswalt, "Golden," 14–20.

for Yahweh" (חַג לַיהוָה, *chag layhwh*).[36] Not only that, but he uses precisely the same phrase as is used earlier in Exodus (and indeed throughout the OT) for festivals to Yahweh.[37] Aaron could hardly have made the associations between the idol and Yahweh any stronger. (Those who interpret 32:1 as a request for other gods agree; they suggest, however, that Aaron is attempting to "salvage" the situation and help the people "revert" to Yahweh worship.)[38] Then in 32:6, the people sacrifice burnt offerings and present fellowship offerings. These are the "the very offerings that Yahweh had specified for himself."[39] Finally, the fact that in 32:8 Yahweh characterizes the people's sin as a violation of the second commandment (making and using idols), rather than of the first commandment (having other gods), confirms that the problem here is the use of an idol to worship Yahweh, and not a change of allegiance.[40] Thus Exodus 32 depicts an attempt to worship Yahweh using the idol as the "new point of focus."[41]

In conclusion, this is indeed a text dealing with an attempt by God's people to use the forms of other faiths to worship Yahweh.

b. The meaning of the text for the original audience

i. Is there evidence in the text that the author is seeking to persuade the reader to resist the forms of other faiths?

There is abundant evidence in Exodus 32–34 of an authorial intent to persuade the reader not to repeat the sin of false worship committed by Aaron and the Israelites described in this narrative. However, as we shall see, what makes the worship false is not simply that the forms of other faiths are involved, but that in using these forms, the Israelites have violated God's commands and rejected the God-given way to worship.

---

36. See Alexander, *From Paradise*, 187.

37. See Exod 10:9; 12:14; 13:6; Lev 23:6, 31, 34, 39 and Hos 9:5. Durham, *Exodus*, 421.

38. Stuart, *Exodus*, 664–65.

39. Durham, *Exodus*, 422. See Exod 10:25; 18:12; 20:24–25; 24:5; 29:18, 25, 28 42; 30:9, 28; 31:9. Stuart, *Exodus*, 666; Alexander, *From Paradise*, 187.

40. Durham, *Exodus*, 422; Stuart, *Exodus*, 668; Alexander, *From Paradise*, 187.

41. Durham, *Exodus*, 421–22.

1. The Author Resists the False Worship by Depicting its Consequences

The author strongly resists the false worship by portraying the disastrous impact of it on the covenant relationship and by showing that the process of repairing this rift is far from straightforward. While the sin itself takes just 6 verses to describe (32:1–6), the description of its terrible consequences is 88 verses long (32:7—34:35), suggesting that resisting the false worship is at the very heart of the author's purposes here.

The Israelites' very status as the people of God is profoundly threatened.[42] Whereas up until this point in Exodus, the Israelites have always been "my people" (עַמִּי, *'ammi*),[43] now in 32:7, Yahweh disowns them, referring to them in his speech to Moses as "your people" (עַמְּךָ, *'ammecha*), whom "you brought up" (תִיעֲלֶה, *heʿeleyta*). In 32:10, Yahweh's anger burns and he announces his intention to destroy the people and make a new start with Moses. Thus the entire redemptive plan of Exodus 1–31 is "thrown into terrifying jeopardy. . . . The special treasure-people . . . are suddenly in danger of becoming a people with no identity at all, a non-people."[44] In 32:11–14, this disaster is averted when Yahweh relents as a result of Moses' intercession. As intercessor, Moses does not attempt to minimize the guilt of the people. Rather, he bases his appeal entirely on Yahweh's character, honor, and purposes.[45] Thus even though destruction is averted, the seriousness of the people's sin and the reality of the wrath incurred is in no way diminished.[46]

In 32:15–24, Moses descends the mountain. In 32:11 he had asked Yahweh, "Why should your anger burn against your people . . . ?"; now that he witnesses the false worship himself, it is his own anger that burns (32:19).[47] By presenting Yahweh and Moses' anger in two separate stages, the author emphasizes the seriousness of Israel's sin "doubly and very effectively."[48] So serious is this sin, in fact, that it prompts Moses to break into pieces the precious tablets of the Testimony (32:19), which, we have just been told, were the writing of God himself (32:15–16).[49] This is a highly

---

42. Childs, *Exodus*, 567.

43. Exod 3:7, 10; 5:1; 7:4, 16; 8:1, 8, 20–23; 9:1, 13, 17, 27; 10:3; 12:31; 22:25. Moberly, *Story*, 49–50.

44. Durham, *Exodus*, 417.

45. Moberly, *Story*, 50; Alexander, *From Paradise*, 187.

46. Moberly, *Story*, 50; Childs, *Exodus*, 567.

47. Hamilton, *Exodus*, 543.

48. Durham, *Exodus*, 430.

49. Stuart, *Exodus*, 674.

significant ceremonial and symbolic act.[50] For some, it announces the complete annulment of the covenant.[51] For others, it communicates that the covenant has been breached and so punishment will follow.[52] Either way, the seriousness of the sin is graphically portrayed.

Next, Moses grinds the idol into dust and forces the Israelites to drink the dust mixed with water (32:20). Although the significance of this action is debated, the total destruction is clearly an uncompromising repudiation of the false worship,[53] and the forced drinking is possibly a sign of the judgment that the Israelites will shortly experience.[54]

In 32:25—33:11, the author continues to portray the devastating consequences of the sin. About three thousand Israelites are slain (32:25–29). Fretheim comments: "Radical sin is believed to call for radical measures."[55] Next, Moses attempts to make atonement for the "great sin" of the people through further intercession (32:30–32).[56] He fails: Yahweh affirms in 32:34 that further judgment awaits ("I will punish them for their sin"), and in 32:35, Yahweh strikes the people with a plague.

Yet a problem remains. The false worship has demonstrated the sinfulness of the people and this requires that Yahweh withdraw his presence from them, lest he destroy them (33:3).[57] The special presence of Yahweh with his people is one of the fundamental signs of their covenant status (33:15–16; 34:9),[58] and the withdrawal of his presence is the ultimate penalty.[59] Indeed, intimacy with God was the whole goal of the exodus.[60] The description of the people's distress and mourning in 33:4–6 reflects the gravity of this punishment.[61] The withdrawal of divine presence is symbolized by the pitching of the tent of meeting not merely "outside the camp," but "some distance away" (33:7).[62] This stands in tragic contrast to Yahweh's original plan to

50. Stuart, *Exodus*, 677.

51. Bruckner, *Exodus*, 225; Longman, *Exodus*, 133; Alexander, *From Paradise*, 187.

52. Moberly, *Story*, 53; Stuart, *Exodus*, 677.

53. Cf. Exodus 23:24. See Stuart, *Exodus*, 678; Spencer, "Golden Calf," 1067-68; Van Dam, "Golden Calf," 370.

54. Waltke and Yu, *Old Testament*, 470.

55. Fretheim, *Exodus*, 289.

56. The phrase "great sin" appears three times in this chapter: 32:21, 30, 31. Hamilton, *Exodus*, 547.

57. Stuart, *Exodus*, 689–90; Moberly, *Story*, 60.

58. Moberly, *Story*, 63; Stuart, *Exodus*, 704.

59. For example, see Lev 20:3; 22:3. Stuart, *Exodus*, 692.

60. Waltke and Yu, *Old Testament*, 471.

61. Stuart, *Exodus*, 691–92.

62. Moberly, *Story*, 63–64.

dwell in the midst of the camp (Exod 25–31; Num 2).[63] The people originally made the idol because they craved access to the divine presence. Ironically, by their sin, this is the very thing that they forfeit.[64]

In 33:12—34:35, the gradual restoration of the broken covenant relationship takes place. Moses continues his intercession (33:12–16, 18; 34:8–9), Yahweh agrees to be present with his people once again (33:14, 17), the shattered tablets are replaced (34:1–4), Moses is given a special experience of Yahweh's presence (34:5–9), and the broken covenant is remade (34:10–30). Significantly, Yahweh's statement in 34:10 contains the language of *making* (not merely *renewing*) a covenant. Indeed, in keeping with the making of a covenant, all the standard features of the covenant structure are present in 34:10–30 (that is, preamble, prologue, stipulations, sanctions, and witness and document clauses).[65] That a new covenant is actually *made* and not merely *renewed* highlights just how close Israel has come to losing everything. Further, this restoration is only possible because of Yahweh's gracious and merciful character (33:19; 34:6–9), and not because the people merit forgiveness.[66] Indeed, they continue to be characterized by "wickedness, rebellion and sin" (34:7).[67] Thus, once again, the gravity of the sin is in no way diminished. On the contrary, the sin has had devastating consequences, and healing and restoration have been hard-won.

Although the focus in 32:7—34:35 is upon the penalties imposed by Yahweh in response to the people's sin, the author also demonstrates that the sin has direct consequences in the lives of the people. Yahweh declares in 32:7 that by their sin, the people "have corrupted themselves" (שִׁחֵת, *shichet*).[68] According to Beale, the author highlights these corrupting effects through the literary device of mockingly identifying the Israelites with the idol that they worship.[69] He shows that throughout 32:7—34:35, the Israelites are portrayed as wild and untrained bulls. They are "stiff-necked" (32:9; 33:3,5; 34:9), they "have been quick to turn away" (32:8), they are "running wild" (lit. "let loose") (32:25).[70] Thus in an artful "narrative taunt," the author depicts the bull-worshipers as rebellious and stubborn bulls that are

63. Moberly, *Story*, 63–64; Stuart, *Exodus*, 694.
64. Moberly, *Story*, 63; Stuart, *Exodus*, 691.
65. Stuart, *Exodus*, 712–13, 719–21.
66. Moberly, *Story*, 67–68; Alexander, *From Paradise*, 187; Mackay, *Exodus*, 564; Waltke and Yu, *Old Testament*, 472.
67. Moberly, *Story*, 90.
68. This is the reflexive *piel* of שחת, *shcht*. Van Dam, "שחת," 92–93; Bruckner, *Exodus*, 222.*Contra* Stuart, *Exodus*, 668.
69. Beale, *We Become*, 76–78, 82.
70. Beale, *We Become*, 77–78.

running wild.[71] The point is that false worship has a corrupting effect on the "inner spiritual being" of the worshipers.[72]

Thus in 32:7—34:35 the author resists the false worship in the strongest possible terms by showing that the sin corrupts the people, brings them to the brink of annihilation, and puts the entire redemptive plan in peril. Indeed, as Janzen notes, Exodus 32–34 is "Israel's version of the universal human turn in Genesis 2–3."[73]

2. The Ultimate Problem with the Worship Is That It Is Disobedient and Human-Initiated

The author resists the use of these borrowed forms to worship Yahweh. However, ultimately what makes the worship problematic is that it amounts to a violation of God's commands regarding how he is to be worshiped and a rejection of the way to worship that he is providing.[74]

The making and using of idols is prohibited by the second commandment (20:4–6; cf. 24:3 and 24:7). Thus the worship in 32:1–6 is disobedient worship. Yahweh makes this explicit in 32:8, and then uses a metaphor for disobedience ("stiff-necked") to characterize the people in 32:9 (cf. 33:3, 5).[75] Further, the prominence in the narrative of the tablets that contain the laws inscribed by God himself (32:15–19; 34:1–4) also serves to highlight that the basic problem here is disobedience. Later, when Moses describes the people's sin, he also characterizes it as a violation of the command prohibiting idols.[76] Thus, first and foremost, Israel's worship is problematic because it violates Yahweh's revealed will.[77] The borrowed forms function as the agent of the sin, but what makes the act a sin is that it is in violation of God's commands.

When Exodus 32–34 is read in its broader context within the book of Exodus, however, a deeper problem emerges: in making the idol, Israel is not merely disobeying Yahweh, but is also rejecting Yahweh's own provision of a true and effective way to access his presence and worship him. The sin of 32:1–6 takes place while Moses is on top of the mountain receiving

71. Beale, *We Become*, 78.
72. Beale, *We Become*, 82.
73. Janzen, *Exodus*, 226.
74. Durham, *Exodus*, 422.
75. Stuart, *Exodus*, 668, 684.
76. There are substantial similarities between the wording in 32:31 and in 20:23. Moberly, *Story*, 57.
77. Ryken and Hughes, *Exodus*, 1500.

instructions from Yahweh for the building of the tabernacle.[78] Thus the tragic irony is that at the very moment that the Israelites seek to create a vehicle for Yahweh's presence and so enable worship, Yahweh is providing a true way for this need to be met.[79] Indeed, the account of the idol worship in chapters 32–34 functions as a dislocating interruption to the full account of the tabernacle's origins, coming in between Yahweh's instructions for its building (chapters 25–31) and the account of its construction (chapters 35–40).[80] It is thus strategically placed to highlight the contrast between true (God-given) and false (human-initiated) worship.[81]

That the people's sin is a rejection of God-given worship and a replacing of it with a false alternative is emphasized through a series of parallels between these two approaches to worship. For example, in 25:1–9, Yahweh prescribes that the people should offer their gold and other precious materials for the construction of the tabernacle so that he can "dwell among them" (25:8). What happens in 32:1–6, however, is that the people offer their gold for the construction of an idol which they hope will convey Yahweh's presence (32:4b, 5b).[82] Thus the idol replaces the God-given divine dwelling place.[83] As well, there are striking parallels between the false worship in 32:1–6 and the covenant confirmation ceremony in 24:1–11. In both passages, Aaron plays a role (24:1, 9; 32:1–3, 5), an altar is built (24:4; 32:5), offerings are made (24:5; 32:6), and offerings are eaten in the presence of Yahweh (24:11; 32:6).[84] Thus the people's false worship of 32:1–6 is depicted as a substitute for, and replacement of, the whole covenantal system of God-given worship.

In conclusion, though the use of certain borrowed forms is roundly condemned in Exodus 32–34, the text is not a blanket condemnation of the use of borrowed forms *per se*. The borrowed forms are the *means* by which the Israelites commit the sin, but ultimately, what makes their worship sinful here is that it is done in violation of God's commands concerning how he is to be worshiped, and in rejection of the way to worship that he is providing.

---

78. See Exod 24:15–18 and chapters 25–31. Van Dam, "Golden Calf," 370–71; Sailhamer, *Pentateuch*, 310.

79. Van Dam, "Golden Calf," 370–71; Stuart, *Exodus*, 669.

80. Stuart, *Exodus*, 659.

81. Van Dam, "Golden Calf," 370–71; Longman, *Exodus*, 131–32.

82. Moberly, *Story*, 46–47.

83. Moberly, *Story*, 47.

84. Van Dam, "Golden Calf," 370–71; Durham, *Exodus*, 422.

ii. What does the text teach about worship and forms?

Let us now consider what the text teaches about worship and forms. Three points emerge.

1. True worship is God-given

First, a fundamental worship principle that emerges here is that true worship is God-given. Throughout the book of Exodus, Yahweh alone makes worship of himself possible, and Yahweh alone determines how it is to be done.[85] It is Yahweh who rescues the Israelites from slavery in Egypt so that they might worship him.[86] It is Yahweh who prescribes the terms of the covenant relationship when he gives the laws (20:1—23:19).[87] It is Yahweh who initiates construction of the tabernacle (25:8), who provides detailed plans for its construction which must be followed "exactly" (25:9; cf. 25:40; 26:30, 27:8), who provides the materials needed (12:35-36), and who gives the craftsmen the ability they need to build it (31:3).[88] And it is Yahweh who gives regulations regarding priests and offerings, and so determines the terms on which the people can engage him (29:1-46).[89] Thus Yahweh makes worship possible and determines what is acceptable worship.[90] What makes the worship in 32:1-6 problematic is that it is done in violation of God's commands and in rejection of the way he is providing.

2. Human-initiated worship is false worship

Second, the corollary is that human-initiated worship is false worship. The worship of 32:1-6 is unacceptable not just because it is in violation of Yahweh's commands but also because it is done at the people's initiative and on their terms.[91] This can be seen in Yahweh's statement in 32:8 that the people have turned aside from "the way" (דֶּרֶךְ, *derekh*) that he commanded them. דֶּרֶךְ, *derekh* typically refers to a "path" or a "way of life."[92] The Israelites are

---

85. Peterson, *Engaging*, 20, 26–27, 73.
86. Exod 3–19. See especially 3:12; 4:23; 7:16; 8:1, 20; 9:1, 13; 10:3.
87. Peterson, *Engaging*, 26–29.
88. Longman, *Exodus*, 131–32.
89. Peterson, *Engaging*, 33.
90. Durham, *Exodus*, 424; Block, *For the Glory*, 25; Garner, "High Stakes," 266–67; Scobie, *Ways*, 567; Ross, *Recalling*, ch. 2; Peterson, *Engaging*, 35.
91. Durham, *Exodus*, 424.
92. Merrill, "דֶּרֶךְ," 989–93; Moberly, *Story*, 49; Durham, *Exodus*, 425.

therefore rejecting the God-given path or way, and substituting it with their own.[93] Significantly, when in 33:13 Moses successfully intercedes to restore the covenant relationship, he asks Yahweh, "teach me your ways (דְּרָכֶךָ, *derakhecha*)."[94] Thus true worship is shown to be a seeking and following of the way given by God. For this reason, human initiative in worship of the sort depicted in 32:1–6 is inherently problematic,[95] since it necessarily entails a rejection of the God-given way.[96] The people's error is thus to replace "God's initiative on their behalf with their own."[97]

In this text, then, the borrowed forms are the means by which the people commit this sin of rejecting God-given worship and substituting it with human-initiated worship. This is highlighted in 34:10–28 where, in remaking the covenant, Yahweh focuses on the dangers posed to the purity of Israel's worship by the false worship of the nations.[98] The nations will be a "snare" to Israel by encouraging an imitation of their worship practices (34:11–12).[99] Therefore, Israel must destroy the worship forms used by the nations (34:13) so that these forms cannot function to entice Israel away from God-given worship.[100] Israel must also avoid making a covenant with the nations and intermarrying with them, lest Israel be drawn into their false worship (34:15–16).[101] Further, Israel must avoid a series of cultic practices associated with Canaanite worship, such as making idols (34:17), consuming blood (34:25),[102] and cooking a goat in its mother's milk (34:26).[103] Thus the focus in 32:10–28 is on the problem of Israel expressing its faith "in the symbols of the surrounding religious culture rather than in the way prescribed by Yahweh."[104] Worship that is not God-given, but is instead designed and initiated by humans, is false worship.

---

93. Ryken and Hughes, *Exodus*, 1509.

94. Moberly, *Story*, 73.

95. Peterson, *Engaging*, 26.

96. Spencer, "Golden Calf," 1065.

97. Bruckner, *Exodus*, 221.

98. Moberly, *Story*, 97; Stuart, *Exodus*, 722; Mackay, *Exodus*, 566–67.

99. Mackay, *Exodus*, 567; Stuart, *Exodus*, 723.

100. Mackay, *Exodus*, 567.

101. Stuart, *Exodus*, 723.

102. See Stuart, *Exodus*, 732.

103. There is evidence that the practice in 34:26 was a Canaanite cultic fertility practice, although this evidence is not conclusive. See Stuart, *Exodus*, 539–40; Haran, "Seething," 23–35; Labuschagne, "You Shall Not," 6–17; Moorhead, "Cooking," 261–71.

104. Moberly, *Story*, 98.

3. A RISK INHERENT IN USING BORROWED FORMS IS THAT UNWANTED MEANINGS WILL BE IMPORTED

Third, a risk inherent in using borrowed forms is that unwanted meanings will be imported. The forms of ANE religion were imbued with meanings concerning the nature and character of the gods, and how and why they were to be worshiped. It is evident in 32:1–6 that some of these meanings are imported into Israel's worship along with the borrowed forms. Because these imported meanings are contrary to the principles of God-given worship revealed in Exodus, the result is a distortion of true worship.

A foundational conviction in ANE idolatry was that the divine presence could be secured through the making and keeping of an idol.[105] In 32:1–6, the Israelites believe that they can secure Yahweh's presence in this way. Their demand in 32:1 for an idol that will "lead us" or "go before us" (יֵלְכוּ לְפָנֵינוּ, *yelkhu lepaneynu*), is a demand for divine presence.[106] Then, when they see the newly-constructed idol, they show that they believe that they have secured Yahweh's presence by declaring "here is your god" (32:4b), and then by bowing down to the idol and sacrificing to it (32:8).[107] This pagan notion of providing one's own means of securing the deity's presence is "offensive"[108] from the perspective of Exodus. In Exodus, Yahweh's presence cannot be accessed by human initiative, but instead is graciously given on his terms.[109] Access to Yahweh's presence is carefully guarded: anyone who enters Yahweh's presence without observing the appropriate regulations will die (28:35, 43; 30:20, 21).[110] By responding to the false worship of 32:1–6 with a removal of his presence (33:3), Yahweh demonstrates to the people that they cannot demand and control his presence in this way.[111]

Another belief in ANE idolatry was that through worship, the gods came under human control.[112] Not only were the idols made by humans, but the gods which they represented were also thought to be fed by humans—in much of ANE pagan understanding, it appears the gods could not feed themselves and so were dependent on such offerings.[113] Further,

---

105. Peterson, *Engaging*, 35; Ross, *Recalling*, ch. 9; Van Dam, "Golden Calf," 368.
106. Stuart, *Exodus*, 663.
107. Stuart, *Exodus*, 669.
108. Peterson, *Engaging*, 35.
109. See chapters 25–31, especially 25:8; 29:45–46.
110. See also Lev 16:2–34; Heb 9:1–28. Longman, *Exodus*, 135–36.
111. Waltke and Yu, *Old Testament*, 469.
112. Van Dam, "Golden Calf," 368.
113. Stuart, *Exodus*, 451; Walton, *Ancient*, 144, 177–78.

there was a belief that correctly performed rituals created an obligation on the part of the deity and so directly brought about the desired result in a cause-and-effect fashion. The phrase *ex opere operato*, "by the ritual it is effected," has been used to describe this magical way of thinking.[114] Exodus 32:1-6 depicts the Israelites in control of their idol. They demand it (32:1), craft it (32:4), and "feed" it (32:5-6). Yet this pagan understanding is repugnant from the perspective of Exodus. In Exodus, Yahweh is an invisible, intangible, incomparable, living and speaking God who must not be reduced to an inanimate, static image created and maintained by humans.[115] Thus the result of using this foreign form to worship Yahweh is that the Israelites have developed a distorted understanding of who Yahweh is and how he is to be worshiped. Indeed, they have arrived at a *pagan understanding of Yahweh* and are depicted as worshiping a "grotesque parody" of Yahweh.[116] If there is to be restoration, these distorted understandings of Yahweh will need to be corrected. This explains the need for the theophany in 34:5-7 in which Yahweh proclaims his name and reveals his character to Moses.[117] Thus the text shows that using a borrowed form can cause confusion regarding the nature and identity of God.

ANE religion also minimized the importance of ethical behavior.[118] Typically the gods made few ethical demands of their worshipers, since their focus was upon being fed through offerings.[119] This pattern of thinking is evident in 32:1-6. The Israelites construct an idol and make sacrifices to it, but they do not construct an equivalent of the tablets, since their bull-idol makes no ethical demands.[120] Related to this, as discussed above (chapter 3, §2.a.i.), ANE idol-worship was sometimes associated with ritual sexual practices, possibly aimed at securing fertility through sympathetic magic. If 32:6 and 32:17-19 imply that an orgy takes place, then this is further evidence of the importation into Israel's worship of motives and ethical permissiveness associated with ANE idol-worship.[121] Moses' characterization of the people as "out of control" (32:25) only confirms this picture in which Israel worships Yahweh without regard to his ethical

---

114. Waltke and Yu, *Old Testament*, 469.

115. 20:4-6, 23; 34:17. Waltke and Yu, *Old Testament*, 416; Durham, *Exodus*, 421-22. See further Oswalt, "Golden," 13-20.

116. Moberly, *Story*, 47-48.

117. Stuart, *Exodus*, 715-16.

118. Stuart, *Exodus*, 451.

119. Walton, *Ancient*, 149; Stuart, *Exodus*, 451; Ross, *Recalling*, ch. 20.

120. Durham, *Exodus*, 421-22; Stuart, *Exodus*, 669.

121. Williams, *Making*, 55.

demands. Again this pagan theology of worship is in stark contrast to the picture of true worship in Exodus, where Yahweh makes detailed and exacting ethical demands (20:1—23:33). In fact, in Exodus, worship can only take place within the context of a covenant relationship in which Israel is required to "obey me fully" (19:5).[122]

We have seen that in 32:1–6, the forms of ANE idolatry are not borrowed in isolation from the meanings associated with them. Rather, the meanings are imported together with the forms. And because these meanings contradict the principles of true worship, the result is that a series of distorted understandings enter into Israel's worship.[123] Along with the pagan forms come pagan beliefs, attitudes, and ethics. Thus the text warns that a risk inherent in using the forms of other faiths is the importation of false meanings.

iii. References to Exodus 32 in the rest of the OT

Later OT references to our text affirm the above conclusions regarding the text's meaning. For example, Deuteronomy 4:15–18 reinforces the conception of true worship as God-given and revealed, and false worship as an unauthorized replacement of it. There, Moses explains that the reason why Israel must not make an idol to represent Yahweh is because God at Sinai did not reveal himself in any form.[124] Likewise in Psalm 106:19–20, the sin of Exodus 32:1–6 is described as one of *exchanging* true God-given worship for a false, human-made substitute.

The most significant OT passage, however, is 1 Kings 12–14. First Kings 12:25–33 is strikingly reminiscent of Exodus 32:1–6: Jeroboam makes two golden bull-idols and declares, "Here are your gods, Israel, who brought you up out of Egypt." He then proceeds to hold an unauthorized festival and make offerings to the idols.[125] As the following analysis demonstrates, the rhetorical intent of the two texts are also remarkably similar, and thus 1 Kings 12–14 functions to reinforce the importance of the theological principles concerning worship outlined above from Exodus 32–34.

---

122. Peterson, *Engaging*, 27–30.
123. Stuart, *Exodus*, 691; Kitchen, "Golden Calf," 158–59.
124. Harman, *Deuteronomy*, 62–63.

125. Aberbach and Smoler identify no less than thirteen parallels between the two texts. Aberbach and Smoler, "Golden Calves," 129–34. Based on these similarities, some speculate that the Exodus 32 narrative was created as a polemic against Jeroboam's cult. See Durham, *Exodus*, 420; Moberly, *Story*, 162; Van Dam, "Golden Calf," 371; Childs, *Exodus*, 559–60.

First Kings 12 (like Exodus 32) describes a situation in which the Israelites use a borrowed form (a bull-idol) to worship Yahweh. The identification of the idols with the אֱלֹהִים, *'elohim* who brought Israel out of Egypt (1 Kgs 12:28) suggests that this is indeed an attempt to worship Yahweh (notwithstanding the fact that, so far as Yahweh is concerned, they are effectively worshiping other gods: 14:9).[126] In 1 Kings 12:25-33 (as in Exodus 32-34) the false worship is resisted in the strongest possible terms. Jeroboam's new places of worship are condemned (13:1-5, 32); he and his family will die dishonorable and degrading deaths (14:10-12); his dynasty will come to an end (14:10, 14); and the Northern Kingdom will be scattered and rejected by God (14:15-16).[127] In addition, the author gives his own evaluation: Jeroboam's worship is "sin" and an "evil" that will lead to the downfall and destruction of his dynasty (12:30; 13:33-34).[128] In the remainder of 1 and 2 Kings, Jeroboam's role in facilitating false worship is repeatedly referred to as Israel's characteristic sin[129] which ultimately leads to the judgment of exile (2 Kgs 17:20-23).[130]

The worship in 1 Kings 12-14 is problematic for the same reasons as the worship in Exodus 32-34. It amounts to a violation of Yahweh's commands, both regarding idols (Exod 20:4-6) and places of worship (Deut 12:5-7, 13-14).[131] Indeed, Jeroboam is explicitly contrasted with "my servant David, who kept my commands" (14:8). As well, Jeroboam's worship amounts to a rejection of the God-given way to worship, in favor of a human-made alternative. Just as the author of Exodus contrasted God-given tabernacle worship with human-initiated bull-idol worship, so too the author of Kings contrasts God-given temple worship with Jeroboam's bull-idol worship, especially through a wordplay on "house" (בַּיִת, *bayit*).[132] The problem Jeroboam faces is that his political rival has a house, the "house of Yahweh" or "temple" (בֵּית־יְהוָה, *beyt-yhwh*) (12:27). His solution is to replace it with his own house, the "house of high places" or "shrine" (בֵּית בָּמוֹת, *beyt bamot*) (12:31). Just as the worship at the בֵּית־יְהוָה, *beyt-yhwh* is accompanied by priests, an altar, and

---

126. Provan, *Kings*, 109-12; Moberly, *Story*, 165-67; Wyatt, "Calves," 68-91.
127. Provan, *Kings*, 113.
128. Spencer, "Golden Calf," 1066.
129. 1 Kgs 15:26, 34; 16:31; 21:22; 22:52; 2 Kgs 3:3; 9:9; 10:29, 31; 13:2, 6, 11; 14:24; 15:9, 18, 24, 28.
130. Provan, *Kings*, 109.
131. Provan, *Kings*, 109-12.
132. Wilson, "בַּיִת," 655-657; Provan, *Kings*, 109-10.

festivals,¹³³ so too is the worship at Jeroboam's בֵּית בָּמוֹת, *beyt bamot*.¹³⁴ That Jeroboam's worship is the product of human initiative rather than divine provision is repeatedly emphasized: it is Jeroboam who makes the idols (12:28), who sets them up (12:29), who appoints the non-Levitical priests (12:31), and who institutes a festival (12:32) at a time "of his own choosing" (12:33).¹³⁵ Jeroboam's false worship is thus an unauthorized and human-initiated replacement of God-given temple worship.

First Kings 12–14 (like Exodus 32–34) also highlights the fact that a risk inherent in using borrowed forms is that unwanted meanings will be imported. Jeroboam seems to have absorbed the belief in ANE idolatry that deities could be manipulated and obligated to act by the owners of the idols.¹³⁶ Yet the narrative repeatedly shows that Yahweh is different to ANE gods. For example, Jeroboam tries to arrest the prophet that God sends to condemn his idolatry (13:4), but instead Jeroboam's own hand is shriveled and the altar at his new shrine in Bethel is split (13:4–5).¹³⁷ Next, Jeroboam attempts to purchase the prophet's favor by offering him food and a gift (13:7), but the prophet, in obedience to Yahweh's command, refuses such attempts at manipulation (13:9).¹³⁸ In 14:1–20, Jeroboam still thinks he can manipulate a prophet of Yahweh into making a positive prophecy, using disguises and gifts to achieve his goals, yet once again he fails: the prophet simply announces Jeroboam's judgment.¹³⁹ Thus 1 Kings 12–14 (like Exodus 32) warns of the danger of unwanted meanings being imported with the forms of other faiths, resulting in a distortion of true worship.

c. The meaning of the text for Christians today

Having considered the meaning of the text for the original audience, we now turn to its meaning for Christians today.

---

133. Priests (8:1–11), altar (6:20–22; 8:22, 31, 54, 64; 9:25), and festivals (8:2, 65).

134. Priests (12:31), altar (12:32) and festivals (12:32). Provan, *Kings*, 109–11.

135. For a discussion of the parallels with Exodus 32:1–6, see Provan, *Kings*, 110–11.

136. Van Dam, "Golden Calf," 368; Waltke and Yu, *Old Testament*, 416, 469; Stuart, *Exodus*, 451.

137. Provan, *Kings*, 113–14.

138. Provan, *Kings*, 114–15.

139. Provan, *Kings*, 117–19.

i. Relevant redemptive-historical developments

Exodus 32–34 warns against replacing God-given worship with a false, human-initiated substitute, and so calls readers to enter God's presence to worship him only in the way he makes possible and prescribes.[140] For the original readers, this meant worshiping in the tabernacle,[141] making the prescribed sacrifices and offerings,[142] and depending on the mediation of properly ordained priests.[143]

According to the NT, these elements of the OT cult were temporary foreshadowings of Christ (Heb 10:1) who fulfills and replaces the cult and opens a new and more perfect access to God's presence for worship.[144] Christ is the fulfillment and replacement of the tabernacle[145] and the temple,[146] and is the true mediator of God's presence.[147] True worship is no longer tied to any physical place;[148] instead, Christ is now the "place" where God is met.[149] Christ is also the perfect once-for-all sacrifice for sin, rendering the ongoing making of offerings and sacrifices inappropriate.[150] He is also the Great High Priest that brings to an end the ministry of the Levitical priests.[151] In the new covenant era, Christians enter into God's presence to worship, not by using the institutions of the OT cult, but instead through faith in Christ, expressed as continuing dependence on and obedience to Christ.[152] As temples of the

---

140. Peterson, *Engaging*, 20.

141. Exod 25–31 and 35–40.

142. Lev 1–7 and 16.

143. Exod 28–29; Lev 8–10.

144. Block, *For the Glory*, 73; Carson, "Worship," 23–24; Waltke and Yu, *Old Testament*, 476–78; Peterson, *Engaging*, 80, 108.

145. John 1:14—he "pitched a tabernacle" (ἐσκήνωσεν, *eskēnōsen*) among us—recalls the instruction in Exod 25:8–9 to make a "tabernacle" (LXX σκηνῆς, *skēnēs*). Peterson, *Engaging*, 93.

146. Matt 12:6; John 2:12–22.

147. See also Col 2:9–10; Eph 2:20–22; 1 Pet 2:4–8. Peterson, *Engaging*, 202; Peterson, "Worship," 860–63; Longman, *Exodus*, 170–73.

148. John 4:20–24. Peterson, "Worship," 860; Carson, "Worship," 23–24.

149. Matt 1:22–23; 27:51; 28:18–20; John 1:51. Peterson, *Engaging*, 83, 93, 100–101; Peterson, "Worship," 559–60; Longman, *Exodus*, 170–73.

150. Heb 7:27; 9:24–28; 10:1–18. Peterson, "Worship," 861–63; Peterson, *Engaging*, 129.

151. Heb 2:17; 4:14–16; 7:25–27; 8:6–13. Peterson, *Engaging*, 229–31.

152. Rom 3:25; 6:1–23; 12:1; Col 3:9–10; Eph 4:22–24; Heb 4:14–16; 10:19–23. Peterson, "Worship," 859–63; Peterson, *Engaging*, 102, 144, 174–76, 220, 238–43; Clowney, "Worship," 111.

Holy Spirit, new covenant believers live their entire lives in God's presence, and so are always engaging in worship.[153]

Because access to God's presence is secured once and for all through Christ, the NT does not contain detailed prescriptions of "outward forms, locations and ceremonials" for accessing God's presence for worship.[154] There is therefore no need for a new covenant equivalent of Exodus 25–31 (or indeed an equivalent of the book of Leviticus).[155] With the fulfillment of the cult comes a greater freedom with regard to worship forms.[156] The NT does prescribe some forms to be used in public gatherings of believers,[157] but these do not function as means of accessing God's presence for worship as the OT forms did. Certainly, there is no NT equivalent of the detailed legal cultic material present in the OT.[158] In fact, the question at the heart of this book regarding whether or not the forms of other faiths should be borrowed was not one that the Israelites ever needed to confront, since they lived during a stage in salvation history when worship forms were largely prescribed. The fact that new covenant believers have considerable freedom with regard to the selection of forms used to express dependence on Christ constitutes a significant discontinuity between the old and new covenant eras.

Despite this discontinuity, there is also continuity, in that the principles concerning worship and forms in Exodus 32–34 continue to apply.[159] God still sets the terms of acceptable worship, declaring that only worshipers who depend on Christ's finished work are able to enter his presence for worship.[160] Two NT references to Exodus 32:1–6 highlight this continuity. First, in Acts 7:38–42, Stephen cites the incident as an example of the kind of disobedience that is now causing Stephen's opponents to reject Christ.[161] Whereas Israel's rejection of God was expressed in Moses' era by a rejection of the tabernacle worship, now it is expressed in a rejection of Christ. Second, in 1 Corinthians 10:1–13, Paul refers to a series of Moses-era events (including that of Exodus 32:1–6), then

---

153. Rom 12:1–2; 1 Cor 6:19–20; Heb 10:19. Peterson, "Worship," 860–63; Clowney, "Worship," 117.

154. Peterson, *Engaging*, 100.

155. Clowney, "Worship," 116.

156. Carson, "Worship," 37–38; Ross, *Recalling*, §"Conclusion for Part 1."

157. Clowney provides a list which includes corporate prayer (1 Tim 2:1); the public reading of Scripture (1 Tim 4:13); the expounding of Scripture in preaching (1 Tim 4:13); singing (Col 3:15). Clowney, "Worship," 117.

158. Clowney, "Worship," 116.

159. See Peterson, *Engaging*, 172, 176, 253.

160. Gal 2:21; 5:4; Heb 4:14–16; 10:19–23.

161. Spencer, "Golden Calf," 1066; Childs, *Exodus*, 573.

explains that these events were "written down as warnings for us" (10:11), and so warns the Corinthians not to fall into false worship as the Israelites did.[162] Thus notwithstanding the redemptive-historical changes regarding worship inaugurated by Christ, the principles regarding worship and forms in Exodus 32–34 continue to apply.[163]

ii. The implications of Exodus 32–34 for the IM debate

We now consider the implications of Exodus 32–34 for the IM debate. There are important differences between the forms used in 32:1–6, and those proposed by IM proponents. For example, in 32:1–6, an idol is used, whereas IM proponents are not advocating the use of idols. However, the text is still relevant because it is a text which deals with the use by God's people of borrowed forms to worship the true God, and because it contains theological principles concerning worship and forms. The fact that the NT affirms the ongoing relevance of these principles underlines the importance of considering the implications of this text for the IM debate.

1. Exodus 32–34 is not a blanket prohibition on using the forms of other faiths, but it does warn of the dangers

Exodus 32–34 is not a blanket prohibition on the use of the forms of other faiths by God's people. While the author undoubtedly mounts a vehement polemic against the use of specific borrowed forms in 32:1–6, this cannot be broadened to a general prohibition on all usage of borrowed forms. The ultimate problem with the worship in 32:1–6 is not simply that the forms are borrowed, but rather that the worship is a violation of God's commands and a rejection of God-given worship. Thus if there is a blanket prohibition in this text, it is a prohibition on attempting to worship God in a way that is not the God-given way.

The part played by the borrowed forms in the sin of 32:1–6 is that they are the means by which the sin is committed. In this respect, the forms play a key role in rendering the worship false. Thus while the text is not a blanket prohibition on using the forms of other faiths (such as Muslim forms), it does highlight the dangers associated with doing so. This is explored further below.

---

162. Childs, *Exodus*, 573.
163. Van Dam, "Golden Calf," 371.

2. Other Implications for the IM debate

Five other implications are identified here. First, the author's primary focus in Exodus 32–34 is to protect against *the corruption of true worship*. Thus once again we see that in a text concerning the use of the forms of other faiths, the issue of primary concern to the biblical author is *not* contextualization, but rather true worship. This affirms the need for a biblical theology of worship to be a crucial frame of reference in the form-selection process. Where BMBs or missionaries are considering using Muslim forms, they need to evaluate the impact of such use on true worship.

Second, in Exodus 32–34, true worship is God-given. Those who want to engage God in worship must engage with him in the way he makes possible, and on the terms he proposes. As we saw above, for new-covenant believers, this no longer involves using the prescribed outward forms of the OT cult, but instead requires a continuing dependence on Christ and his finished work. Therefore, a key question for BMBs and missionaries who are considering the use of Muslim forms is whether doing so is likely to *facilitate* or *hinder* this dependence on Christ.

Third, in Exodus 32–34, the false worship is human-initiated, and so the text highlights the dangers of using forms associated with human initiation in worship. An implication for the IM debate is that if there are Muslim forms associated with human effort or initiative in entering God's presence to worship, rather than depending on Christ's finished work, then there is a danger that using such forms will draw worshipers away from the "way" given by God. Form-selectors need to choose forms that facilitate worship of God through total dependence on Christ, and avoid forms that have the potential to promote patterns of thinking associated with human initiation in worship.

Fourth, the text also highlights the problem of unwanted meanings being imported along with borrowed forms. If BMBs are considering using Muslim forms, it will be important to identify the meanings attached to those forms for the BMBs in previous Islamic usage, and to consider whether such meanings are likely to remain attached to the forms and so hinder the BMBs in their Christian worship. For example, if a particular form was previously associated with merit-accumulation and garnering divine favor, then it needs to be considered whether using the form is likely to facilitate patterns of thought which undermine complete dependence on Christ's work.[164]

---

164. Cf. Green, "Guidelines," 233–34, 245–49.

Finally, regarding the debate concerning the relationship between form and meaning, Exodus 32–34 lends biblical support to Hiebert's claim that form and meaning cannot always be easily separated.[165] At the same time, it casts doubt upon Kraft's claim that forms borrowed from other faiths are "neutral vehicles" that can be used to express allegiance to the true God.[166] The forms of other faiths in Exodus 32–34 are neither neutral nor harmless. Rather, they produce false worship.[167] The meanings associated with them are not separated from the forms; rather, they remain attached and result in confused allegiance and distortion concerning how to engage God in worship.

Thus Exodus 32–34 contains important implications for the IM debate.

3. Deuteronomy 12

Our second OT resistance text is Deuteronomy 12. It contains laws regulating Israel's worship. The Israelites are commanded to destroy all vestiges of Canaanite worship in the land and to ensure that they do not imitate Canaanite practices (12:2–4; 12:29–32). Instead, they are to worship Yahweh in the place he chooses, using the offerings he prescribes (12:5–14). They are permitted to slaughter animals in other places, but only non-sacrificially (12:15–28).[168]

a. The relevance of the text to the research problem

As the following analysis demonstrates, this text is concerned with the use by the Israelites of the forms of other faiths to worship Yahweh, and so is relevant to the research problem.

---

165. Hiebert, "Form," 106–10.

166. Kraft, "Communicating the Gospel," 162; Kraft, *Christianity in Culture* (2005), 233; Kraft, *Anthropology*, 35; Kraft, "Dynamic Equivalent," 115; Kraft, *Christianity in Culture* (1979), 93–99.

167. Ross, *Recalling*, ch. 9.

168. Deut 7:1–26 is a closely related text (see also Exod 20:22–26; 23:24–26; 34:13 and Lev 18:3; Num 33:50–52). There is general agreement that 12:1–32 forms a single, unified compositional unit. See Christensen, *Deuteronomy*, 263. *Contra* Block, *Deuteronomy*, 324–25. On the substantial historical critical debate concerning this text, see McConville, *Law*, 21–40; McConville and Millar, *Time*, 89–139; McConville, *Deuteronomy*, 214–16; Craigie, *Deuteronomy*, 216; Biddle, *Deuteronomy*, 206.

i. Forms borrowed from other faiths

The text itself asserts that the forms discussed in 12:2-4, 29-31 are the worship forms of other faiths. In 12:2, the Israelites are commanded to destroy the "sanctuaries" (מְקֹמוֹת, *meqomot*)[169] where "the nations you are dispossessing worship their gods." Likewise, in 12:3, the worship articles which must be destroyed are explicitly identified as Canaanite[170] forms: "*their* altars, . . . *their* sacred stones, . . . *their* Asherah poles, . . . the idols of *their* gods."[171] Again, in 12:4 (repeated in 12:31), the worship that is forbidden is worship that imitates the Canaanites: "You must not worship the LORD your God in their way." In 12:30, the Israelites must not say: "How do these nations serve their gods? We will do the same."

The text's explicit assertion that the worship forms discussed in 12:2-4 and 29-31 were Canaanite worship forms is supported by historical enquiry into Canaanite religious practices. That Canaanites worshiped at open-air sanctuaries of the kind referred to in 12:2 is widely accepted,[172] as is the fact that they used the various worship articles described in 12:3. They used the stone "altars" (מִזְבְּחֹת, *mizbechot*) to present food and drink offerings; they erected stone "pillars" (מַצֵּבֹת, *matztzevot*), for cultic purposes; and in their worship they also used "Asherah poles" (אֲשֵׁרֵי, *'asherey*), which were standing wooden objects (or perhaps trees) representing the Canaanite mother goddess Asherah.[173] Finally, the cult of child sacrifice referred to in 12:31 is associated with various Canaanite deities, the chief amongst them being the god Molek.[174] The forms described in 12:2-4, 29-31 are thus undoubtedly forms from other faiths.

---

169. Merrill, *Deuteronomy*, 220; McConville, *Deuteronomy*, 218.

170. The term "Canaanite" is used in this book (notwithstanding the objections of some that it is ethnically and linguistically imprecise) since the focus here is the contrast between the religion of the Israelites, and all the other religious practices of the nations around them. See Biddle, *Deuteronomy*, 210; Brueggemann, *Deuteronomy*, 143.

171. In the Hebrew, each of these nouns appears with a third person plural suffix.

172. Christensen, *Deuteronomy*, 241.

173. Christensen, *Deuteronomy*, 241-42; Block, *How I Love Your Torah*, 108; Biddle, *Deuteronomy*, 207; Olyan, *Asherah*, 1-3; Margalit, "Asherah," 264-97. On the claim that Asherah poles were not borrowed forms but were in fact native to Israel, see Olyan, *Asherah*, 33-37; Biddle, *Deuteronomy*, 207-9.

174. Craigie, *Deuteronomy*, 220; Heider, *Cult*, 93-400; Oden, "Persistence," 36; Wyatt, "Calves," 68-91.

ii. Used to worship Yahweh

The problem addressed in 12:2-4, 29-31 is the use of these Canaanite forms *to worship Yahweh*. This is not to say that the author of Deuteronomy is indifferent to the possibility that the Israelites might also worship Canaanite gods. That possibility is frequently addressed.[175] However, the focus in 12:2-4, 29-31 is the use of Canaanite forms to worship Yahweh. This is evident in 12:4 (which is repeated in 12:31a): לֹא־תַעֲשׂוּן כֵּן לַיהוָה אֱלֹהֵיכֶם, *lo taʿasun khen layhwh ʾeloheykhem*—lit. "you shall not act thus to Yahweh your God." The meaning here is that "the Israelites must not worship the Lord in the ways that Canaanites worshiped their gods."[176] Thus what is in view here is using Canaanite shrines (12:2), worship articles (12:3), and cultic rituals (12:30-31) to worship Yahweh.[177] Therefore, this text is relevant to the research problem.

b. The meaning of the text for the original audience

i. Is there evidence in the text that the author is seeking to persuade the reader to resist the forms of other faiths?

There is extensive evidence in Deuteronomy 12 of an authorial intent to persuade the reader to resist Canaanite forms. Moses mounts his case both through a series of direct commands, and also by providing a series of theological reasons as to why using Canaanite forms is problematic. However, the ultimate problem with using Canaanite forms is that to do so is to reject God-given worship for a human-initiated substitute.

1. The author resists the use of foreign forms through direct commands

The most direct strategy employed by Moses to prevent the borrowing of Canaanite forms is through a categorical prohibition (12:4, 31a). Israel is

---

175. See 4:28; 6:12-16; 7:4, 16; 8:19; 11:16, 28; 13:1-11; 17:2-7; 28:14; 29:25-28; 30:17-18; 31:16-29; 32:15-18, 21.

176. Tigay, *Deuteronomy*, 120. See also Biddle, *Deuteronomy*, 207; Block, *Deuteronomy*, 326; Christensen, *Deuteronomy*, 265; McConville, *Deuteronomy*, 219; Craigie, *Deuteronomy*, 218. *Contra* Lundbom, *Deuteronomy*, 426, 439.

177. Tigay, *Deuteronomy*, 120; Craigie, *Deuteronomy*, 218; Block, *Deuteronomy*, 304-5; Biddle, *Deuteronomy*, 219.

not to borrow Canaanite rites or imitate their worship in any way.[178] The fact that this command appears both at the beginning and at the end of the unit strongly suggests that a key purpose of 12:1–31 is to resist foreign religious influences.[179]

There is also a series of supporting commands in 12:2–3 and 29–30 which function to ensure that the prohibition is obeyed. According to 12:2–3, the Israelites must expunge the land of all traces of non-Yahwistic worship. They must "destroy completely" (אַבֵּד תְּאַבְּדוּן, 'abbed te'abbedun) the Canaanite shrines (12:2) and "break down" (נִתַּצְתֶּם, nittatztem), "smash" (שִׁבַּרְתֶּם, shibbartem), "burn up" (תִּשְׂרְפוּן, tisrefun), and "cut down" (תְּגַדֵּעוּן, tegadde'un) their various worship articles (12:3). The verbs here convey violence, urgency and completeness.[180] There must be "no residue of paganism remaining."[181] The goal seems to be, at least partly, to remove the temptation to borrow Canaanite worship forms.[182] But it is also to "wipe out their names from those places" (12:3b). In ANE thought, worship sites were strongly associated with the deity worshiped there. As McConville states, "the religious associations of a place went deep."[183] The destruction of the shrines and associated worship articles was designed to break this strong connection and remove all memories of the false worship, that it might not influence the Israelites in their worship of Yahweh.[184]

The command in 12:29–30, where the Israelites are forbidden to inquire about Canaanite worship practices, also functions as a supporting command to the foundational prohibition of 12:4, 31a. Here there is a recognition that the eradication of Canaanite worship places and articles will not in itself guarantee obedience to the foundational prohibition, since the Israelites might still imitate Canaanite worship practices if knowledge of such practices survives.[185] Therefore the Israelites are not even permitted to learn about pagan worship forms. Christensen summarizes the strategy: "It is best to remain ignorant of that which might infect them."[186] Thus Moses persuades the reader not to use Canaanite forms through both a foundational prohibition, and also a series of supporting commands.

178. McConville, *Deuteronomy*, 228; Christensen, *Deuteronomy*, 265.
179. Wright, *Deuteronomy* (1996), 159; McConville, *Law*, 56–59.
180. Block, *Torah*, 108.
181. Merrill, *Deuteronomy*, 220.
182. Craigie, *Deuteronomy*, 216; Block, *Deuteronomy*, 305.
183. McConville, *Deuteronomy*, 218–19.
184. McConville, *Deuteronomy*, 218–19; Christensen, *Deuteronomy*, 241–42.
185. Biddle, *Deuteronomy*, 218.
186. Christensen, *Deuteronomy*, 265–66.

2. The author also resists the use of foreign forms through depicting Canaanite worship as dangerous, detestable and ineffective

Another way Moses persuades the reader to avoid Canaanite forms is through a biting polemic against Canaanite worship. He depicts Canaanite worship as dangerous to those who practice it. In 12:30, Moses likens Canaanite worship to a snare set to trap the Israelites and divert them from true worship.[187] Israelites who inquire about Canaanite rituals are like people stumbling into a trap.[188] Curiosity in this area can have fatal consequences.[189] Such is the seductive power of Canaanite worship forms that they will remain a threat even after those who originally used them, the Canaanites, have been destroyed (12:30).[190] Moses thus warns the Israelites to "be careful" or "take care for yourself" (הִשָּׁמֶר לְךָ, *hishshamer lekha*) (12:30) and avoid Canaanite forms as an act of self-preservation.[191]

The commands in Deuteronomy 12 form part of a broader strategy in the book whereby any threat to the purity of the Israelites' worship (both from within Israel and without) is removed. The status of *herem* (חרם), which means "devoted to destruction," is applied to the Canaanite inhabitants of the land (7:1–2, 25–26; 20:15–18) because they pose a threat to Israel's fidelity to Yahweh (7:3–5; 20:18). The strategy of removing threats is also applied to apostates (13:12–18), false prophets who incite apostasy (13:5), and people who show contempt for a judge or priest (17:12). The rationale is: "you must purge the evil from among you" (13:5; cf. 17:12; 19:11–13, 19; 21:18–21; 22:22, 23–24; 24:7). Thus the goal is not to give offenders their due, but to protect and preserve the spiritual health of the nation. Thus Canaanite forms are just one of a number of dangerous threats to Israel's spiritual health which must be eradicated.[192]

Canaanite worship is also detestable to Yahweh. The things the Canaanites do in their worship are "detestable things the LORD hates" (12:31). The term תּוֹעֲבַת, *toʿavat* ("detestable" or "an abomination"), is a very strong one which occurs frequently in Deuteronomy to refer to, amongst other

---

187. McConville, *Grace*, 141. For other texts in which foreign religion is portrayed as a snare, see 7:16, 25 and Exod 23:24; 34:12; Josh 23:13; Judg 2:3. Lundbom, *Deuteronomy*, 439.

188. Tigay, *Deuteronomy*, 127.

189. Biddle, *Deuteronomy*, 219.

190. Brueggemann, *Deuteronomy*, 146; McConville, *Deuteronomy*, 228.

191. Lundbom, *Deuteronomy*, 434.

192. Block, *Deuteronomy*, 331, 407; Wright, *Deuteronomy* (2012), 179, 185. On *herem*, see Naudé, "חרם," 276–277; Lilley, "Herem," 169–77; Nelson, "Herem," 40–54.

things, people who lead others into idolatry (13:12–15; 17:2–4; 18:9–12), idols (7:25–26; 27:15), and practices associated with idolatrous worship (20:18).[193] As McConville notes, it is "the deuteronomic term for what is cultically reprehensible."[194]

Moses also depicts Canaanite worship as ineffective. The description of the locations of the Canaanite shrines in 12:2 ("on the high mountains, on the hills and under every spreading tree") contrasts sharply with the single place where Yahweh definitively reveals himself (12:5, 7), and depicts the Canaanite worshipers as groping in vain for contact with the divine. McConville remarks that Moses is "scathing . . . of the indiscriminateness of the Canaanites' worship."[195] Likewise Block suggests that it is as if they "feel obligated to claim for liturgical purposes every potential place where a god might be contacted."[196] Thus Canaanite worship is dangerous, detestable and ineffective, and so to use Canaanite forms is foolish.

3. The ultimate problem with using Canaanite forms is that to do so is to reject God-given worship for a human-initiated substitute

We have seen that Moses forcefully resists the use of Canaanite worship forms. However, the ultimate reason that using such forms is problematic is not that using the forms of other faiths is always wrong, but rather that Yahweh is prohibiting the use of these foreign forms here, and also that to use them here would amount to a rejection of Yahweh's provision of a true and effective way to worship him.

The foundational positive assertion in this text is that Yahweh is providing for true worship: he will choose a place (12:5, 11) where Israel can make prescribed offerings (12:6, 14) and rejoice in his presence (12:7, 12). This Yahweh-given way (12:5–28) is sharply contrasted with the way of the Canaanites (12:2–4, 29–31).[197] The contrast is effected first through use of the term "place" (מָקוֹם, *maqom*). The "places" (מְקֹמוֹת, *meqomot*) where the Canaanites worship are to be destroyed (12:2) and the names of their gods wiped out from that "place" (מָקוֹם, *maqom*) (12:3). Instead, the Israelites

---

193. Grisanti, "תעב‏," 314–318; Lundbom, *Deuteronomy*, 342; Merrill, *Deuteronomy*, 184.
194. McConville, *Deuteronomy*, 351.
195. McConville, *Deuteronomy*, 218–19.
196. Block, *Torah*, 105.
197. McConville, *Deuteronomy*, 219.

must seek the "place" (מָקוֹם, *maqom*) that Yahweh chooses (12:5).[198] A second way the contrast is effected is through the term "name" (שֵׁם, *shem*). Regarding the Canaanite gods, the Israelites must wipe out "their names" (שְׁמָם, *shemam*) from the worship places (12:3), and instead, they must seek the place where Yahweh will put "his name" (שְׁמוֹ, *shemo*) (12:5).[199] Through this contrast, Moses establishes that there are two alternative ways of worshiping Yahweh: using Canaanite forms and using Yahweh-given forms. The Israelites must choose correctly. To choose Canaanite forms is to reject true, Yahweh-given worship.

That Israel has a choice to make is emphasized through another verbal parallel: in 12:5, Israel must "seek" or "choose" (תִדְרְשׁוּ, *tidreshu*) the place chosen by Yahweh; by contrast, in 12:30, Israel must not "seek" or "choose" (תִדְרֹשׁ, *tidrosh*) the Canaanite gods in order to learn about Canaanite worship forms.[200] The contrast is stark; a choice must be made.[201]

Thus while this text does strongly resist the use of foreign forms, the ultimate problem with using the forms is not that it is always wrong to use all forms of other faiths, but rather because to use them here would be to violate God's direct commands and to reject the way of worship that he is providing. Ultimately, what is being resisted here is rejecting God-given worship and replacing it with a false, human-initiated substitute.

ii. What does the text teach about worship and forms?

We now turn to a discussion of what the text teaches about worship and forms. Three points emerge.

---

198. Craigie, *Deuteronomy*, 216–17; Merrill, *Deuteronomy*, 220. McConville and Wright suggest that the singular "place" (מָקוֹם, *maqom*) is deliberately used in 12:3 (even though it refers to a plurality of shrines) in order to establish this strong, antithetical contrast with the singular place of 12:5. The singular form of the noun in 12:3 can be taken distributively, and so the contrast can be effected without compromising grammatical precision. McConville, *Deuteronomy*, 218; Wright, *Deuteronomy* (1996), 170.

199. Merrill, *Deuteronomy*, 107; McConville, *Deuteronomy*, 220–21; Wright, *Deuteronomy* (1996), 159–60.

200. McConville, *Deuteronomy*, 228; Christensen, *Deuteronomy*, 265.

201. That a choice must be made is also highlighted by the structure of the unit. See Lundbom, *Deuteronomy*, 419.

1. True Worship is God-given

First, a defining feature of true worship is that it is God-given. In this text, it is Yahweh who makes worship possible and sets its terms.[202] The prerogative of choosing the worship place is entirely Yahweh's: Israel must worship at "the place the LORD your God will choose" (12:5). The repetition of this phrase no less than five times (12:11, 14, 18, 21, 26) highlights the importance of the place being chosen by Yahweh. In the history of Deuteronomy 12's interpretation, a great deal of effort has been poured into identifying the location of the place referred to here in geographical terms.[203] Yet, as Wright points out, this focus inverts "the priority of the text."[204] The text is concerned not with the location of the place, but instead with the fact that it is chosen by Yahweh.[205] Indeed, the failure to name the place might well be an intentional rhetorical device to focus attention on that which truly legitimizes the place for worship: its Yahweh-chosenness. Wright notes: "What matters is not 'where?' but 'who?'"[206]

The theme of Yahweh's choice is an important one in Deuteronomy.[207] Just as Yahweh chooses the place of worship here, so too he chooses Israel (4:37; 7:6–7; 10:15; 14:2), the priests (18:5; 21:5), and he will choose the king (17:15).[208] Throughout Deuteronomy, *it is Yahweh who sets the terms* for Israel's life and worship. According to McConville, "it is this that underlies his whole relationship with them."[209]

The importance of divine choice of worship place becomes further apparent when Deuteronomy is read in light of its many parallels with ANE suzerain-vassal treaties.[210] Because the place Yahweh chooses will be a dwelling place for his name (12:5), there is probably an allusion here to the ANE practice whereby suzerain kings dwelled in palaces, the location of which was entirely at their discretion. Client princes would be required to visit

---

202. Peterson, *Engaging*, 33; Durham, *Exodus*, 424; Block, *For the Glory*, 25; Garner, "High Stakes," 266–67; Scobie, *Ways*, 567.

203. Many, assuming a late dating for Deuteronomy, identify Jerusalem as "the place," and suggest that the purpose of the unit is to provide an apologia for Jerusalem as the legitimate place of worship. See Wright, *Deuteronomy* (1996), 163; McConville and Millar, *Time*, 121–22.

204. Wright, *Deuteronomy* (1996), 163.

205. Block, *Torah*, 105; McConville and Millar, *Time*, 121.

206. Wright, *Deuteronomy* (1996), 163.

207. McConville and Millar, *Time*, 121–22; McConville, *Law*, 30.

208. McConville, *Deuteronomy*, 219–20; Block, *Torah*, 105; Lundbom, *Deuteronomy*, 428.

209. McConville, *Law*, 30.

210. See Mendenhall, "Covenant," 50–76; Barré, "Treaties," 653–56.

periodically to assert their loyalty and offer their tributes, but they would never choose the suzerain's dwelling place for him.²¹¹ Thus Yahweh sets the terms of true worship, and this includes selecting the place of worship.

Because Yahweh sets the terms of worship, the part of humans is simply to receive and obey the divine prescriptions.²¹² When they go to the chosen place of worship, the Israelites must "observe everything I command" (12:14) and "be careful to obey" (12:28). They must do "what is right in the eyes of the LORD" (12:25), as opposed to what is "right in their own eyes" (וְהַיָּשָׁר בְּעֵינָיו, *hayyashar be'eynav*) (12:8).²¹³ The unit is framed by strong reminders of the importance of precise and unrelenting obedience (12:1, 32). Thus Moses' theology of worship is profoundly Yahweh-centric. According to Deuteronomy 12, true worship "transpires in God's place by God's invitation on God's terms. . . . Ultimately acceptable forms and styles of worship are not determined by worshipers."²¹⁴

2. Human-initiated Worship is False Worship

Second, human-initiated worship is false worship. Whereas true worship is made possible by God and has its terms set by God (12:5-28), the worship which is rejected as false (12:2-4, 29-31) is made possible by the worshipers, and it is the worshipers who set the terms.²¹⁵ Moses emphasizes that the Israelites must not worship anywhere they please (12:13) but only at the place that Yahweh chooses (12:14). As well, the worship activity must also not be human-designed (12:8). The problem with Canaanite worship is that it is human-designed and human-initiated. Moses never depicts Canaanite worship as something given by or commanded by Canaanite deities. Rather, it is simply things that the Canaanites do for their gods (12:30, 31).

As well, the concluding warning in 12:32 that the Israelites must not "add to . . . or subtract from" Yahweh's commands concerning worship is significant. Given the proximity of this warning to the command not to imitate Canaanite practices (12:31), it is best understood as an injunction to the Israelites not to supplement or adapt Yahweh-given worship "with

---

211. Merrill, *Deuteronomy*, 221; Mendenhall, "Covenant," 50–76; Block, *Torah*, 107.

212. Block, *Torah*, 110–11.

213. Lundbom, *Deuteronomy*, 438; Christensen, *Deuteronomy*, 248, 258. In the Deuteronomic History, the phrase "right in their own eyes" is used to describe the cultically and morally chaotic state of affairs of the period of the Judges: Judg 17:6; 21:5, cf. Prov 12:15; 21:1. Biddle, *Deuteronomy*, 213.

214. Block, *Deuteronomy*, 314.

215. Wright, *Deuteronomy* (1996), 162; McConville, *Law*, 30; McConville, *Deuteronomy*, 224–25; Craigie, *Deuteronomy*, 218.

their own cultic improvisations" based on practices borrowed from their neighbors.²¹⁶ To make any modifications to Yahweh-given worship is to render the worship false; to use Canaanite worship forms is "to exchange the only true source of salvation for lifeless and powerless substitutes."²¹⁷ The great danger posed by foreign forms, then, is that they stand as an alternative to Yahweh-given worship, an alternative which the Israelites might be tempted to use.

What makes false worship false is that it is human-designed and human-initiated. Once this is grasped, it becomes evident that the foundational reason why Canaanite forms are "detestable" (12:31) is, quite simply, because they are not given by Yahweh. In light of the close proximity of the term "detestable" to the child sacrifice reference in 12:31, some have assumed that what makes the Canaanite forms detestable is their intrinsic moral repugnancy.²¹⁸ Yet this overlooks the crucial theological principle in the passage: what distinguishes acceptable from unacceptable worship forms is whether or not they are prescribed by Yahweh. Indeed, not all of the "detestable" forms which must be eradicated are intrinsically morally repugnant. For example, although the Canaanite "altars" (מִזְבֵּחַ, *mizbeach*) must be broken down (12:3), the form of an altar cannot be intrinsically morally repugnant, since there is "an altar" (מִזְבַּח, *mizbach*) at the place Yahweh chooses (12:27). What makes Canaanite altars detestable is that, unlike the "altar of Yahweh" (מִזְבַּח יְהוָה, *mizbach yhwh*) in 12:27, they were not commissioned by Yahweh. Thus divinely-initiated worship is true, and human-initiated worship is false.²¹⁹

3. A risk inherent in using Canaanite forms is that Canaanite meanings will be imported

Third, our text warns that a risk inherent in using the forms of other faiths is that unwanted meanings will be imported. In 12:5-28, Moses presents a profound theology of true worship which explains three things: *why Israel should worship, what makes worship effective*, and what are the *appropriate social ethics in worship*. When this theology of true worship is contrasted

---

216. Block, *Deuteronomy*, 326. Cf. 4:2, where the context (4:3-31) is also a warning not to imitate pagan practices. Christensen, *Deuteronomy*, 265.

217. Wright, *Deuteronomy* (2012), 10.

218. Tigay, *Deuteronomy*, 127; Cairns, *Word*, 132-33. See also Mann, *Deuteronomy*, 66.

219. For other texts in Deuteronomy where this theme emerges, see 4:15-19; 9:7-29; 13:1-18; 17:2-4; 18:9-22; 26:14.

i. Why Israel should worship

In 12:5–28, Moses gives three reasons why Israel should worship.

First, worship is an opportunity to respond to Yahweh in thankfulness and reverent homage for blessings already conferred.[220] In 12:5–28, Moses catalogues the blessings which Yahweh is going to shower upon the Israelites: he will give them material prosperity (12:7), rest and security (12:9–10),[221] the land (12:9–10), and even permission to eat meat abundantly in non-sacrificial contexts (12:15, 20, 21). These blessings are the *grounds* for worship: Israel is to gather in worship *in response* to these blessings.[222] In 12:7, the Israelites will worship "because" (אֲשֶׁר, *'asher*) Yahweh has blessed them.[223] In 12:11, the Israelites will gather in worship once Yahweh has given them the land and rest (12:10).[224] McConville identifies a number of "careful correspondences" in Deuteronomy between Yahweh's giving of the land, and Israel's worship. For example, just as Israel אוב, *bo'* ("came") to the land (1:20, 31; 4:1), so they must now אוב, *bo'* ("come") to the place Yahweh chooses to worship (12:5). Just as Yahweh brings Israel to the מָקוֹם, *maqom* ("land") (1:31), so too Israel must come to the מָקוֹם, *maqom* ("place, sanctuary") to worship (12:5).[225] McConville concludes, "the worship of Israel responds to the salvation of Yahweh in the exodus and the gift of the land."[226] True Yahwistic worship is responsive.[227] It is done to acknowledge and commemorate God's provision.[228] Its mood, then, is celebratory and joyful: indeed the directive "to rejoice" or "to be glad" (שָׂמַח, *samach*) appears three times (12:7, 12, 18).[229]

---

220. Block, *Torah*, 109–10.

221. בָּטַח, *betach* ("live in security") in 12:10 carries the sense of the ability to trust without fear. Moberly, "בטח," 644–649; McConville, *Deuteronomy*, 224.

222. Block, *Torah*, 109–10; Willis, "Eat," 284.

223. Lundbom, *Deuteronomy*, 430–31.

224. McConville, *Deuteronomy*, 224–25.

225. McConville, *Law*, 32, 36, 58.

226. McConville, *Deuteronomy*, 222.

227. Willis, "Eat," 284–85; McConville, *Deuteronomy*, 231.

228. Craigie, *Deuteronomy*, 319–20.

229. See also 14:26; 16:11, 14; 26:11. Block, *Torah*, 115; Brueggemann, *Deuteronomy*, 143; Lundbom, *Deuteronomy*, 430–31.

Second, worship is an opportunity to participate in and enjoy the blessings given by Yahweh.[230] In 12:5–28, Moses anticipates a time when the Israelites will enjoy abundance and prosperity (12:7, 15, 17, 18, 21). Importantly, when they gather to worship, they will feast on this abundance together (12:7, 18). Thus the promises of blessing in the land (for example, 7:13–14) are actually fulfilled at the moment the people gather in worship which is characterized by feasting.[231]

Third, worship is an opportunity to enjoy fellowship with Yahweh.[232] The joyful feasting is "in the presence of the LORD your God" (12:7, 18; cf. 12:12).[233] Block suggests that the commands to worship in 12:5–14 are presented in the form of an invitation from a benevolent suzerain to his vassals to dine at his banquet table and enjoy communion and fellowship.[234] Thus true worship is responsive and relational.

This contrasts sharply with the reasons for worship associated with the forms prohibited in 12:2–4, 29–31. Pagan worship was done in order to *secure* the relevant deity's favor so that the deity would bless the worshiper.[235] ANE pagan worship was undergirded by cause-and-effect thinking: it was believed that if the worshiper did something for the god (for example, feed the god through presenting an offering), then the god would bless the worshiper on a *quid pro quo* basis.[236] This is evident in an inscription of the Assyrian King Arik-din-ili which indicates that he built the temple of Shamash "in order that the harvest of my land might prosper."[237] Similarly, the conception of worship as a means to secure blessing is evident in the following prayer directed to Baal:

> O Baal! If you will drive the strong one from our gates, the warrior from our walls, a bull, O Baal, we shall dedicate, a vow, Baal, we shall fulfill.[238]

Thus pagan and Yahwistic motivations in worship are diametrically opposed. Pagans worshiped not in order to give thanks for blessing, but rather

---

230. McConville, *Deuteronomy*, 223; Brueggemann, *Deuteronomy*, 143.
231. McConville, *Deuteronomy*, 231.
232. McConville, *Deuteronomy*, 223; Biddle, *Deuteronomy*, 217.
233. Willis, "Eat," 282–83.
234. See Block, *Torah*, 112–14.
235. Walton, *Ancient*, 177–78, 180; Willis, "Eat," 285.
236. Stuart, *Exodus*, 451.
237. Cited in Hurowitz, *Exalted House*, 323.
238. This prayer was found on a tablet discovered in Ugarit. Wyatt, *Religious*, 421–22.

to secure it. Their purpose was not to thank God for a freely given gift, but to compel and manipulate the relevant deity.

These pagan motives in worship are reflected in some of the forms prohibited in 12:3. For example, "pillars" (מַצֵּבֹת, *matztzevot*) were stone columns which had phallic symbolism and were used in fertility rituals aimed at *securing* agricultural success.[239] Likewise, "Asherah poles" (אֲשֵׁרָה, *'ashera*) represented the goddess Asherah, the female consort of Baal (himself a symbol of fecundity), and were also used in fertility rituals aimed at *securing* material prosperity.[240] Thus Canaanite forms were strongly associated with motivations that contradicted and undermined the principles of true, God-given worship. In prohibiting the forms, it appears Moses is seeking to prevent the unwanted importation of these meanings.

ii. What makes worship effective

In 12:5–28, Moses also explains that what makes worship effective and acceptable is simply that it is done precisely in accordance with Yahweh's commands regarding worship (12:1, 11, 14, 28, 32).[241] It is not because there is any kind of magical power in the worship place or rituals. Rather, using them constitutes effective and acceptable worship simply because Yahweh has chosen and prescribed them (12:5, 11, 13, 14, 18). This is in stark contrast to ANE pagan beliefs. Evidence suggests that ANE pagans believed that the forms themselves contained an intrinsic power and "causal force."[242] It seems they believed that by going to an appropriate place, using an appropriate worship article, and performing a correct ritual, their worship would be effective through a process of cause and effect.

Regarding place, ANE pagans believed that deities had limited spheres of jurisdiction and dwelling, and so worshipers needed to go to the deities' dwelling-places in order to access their presence and power.[243] Height and fertility were strongly associated with deity, and so the pagan worship places were typically "on the high mountains, on the hills" (12:2) or "under

---

239. Wright, *Deuteronomy* (1996), 111; Biddle, *Deuteronomy*, 207; Lundbom, *Deuteronomy*, 424.

240. Binger, *Asherah*, 146–47; Margalit, "Asherah," 284; Olyan, *Asherah*, 1–3; Biddle, *Deuteronomy*, 207–8, 220; Lundbom, *Deuteronomy*, 425.

241. McConville, *Deuteronomy*, 227–28.

242. Best, *Unceasing Worship*, 165–66. See also Stuart, *Exodus*, 450–54; Hunt, "Idols," 437–41; Curtis, "Idol," 376–81.

243. Craigie, *Deuteronomy*, 216. See further Farbridge, *Studies*, 27–49.

every spreading tree" (12:2).²⁴⁴ Moses rejects this theology associated with Canaanite worship places when he describes Israel's worship place as a place Yahweh will choose "to put his name there for its dwelling" (לָשׂוּם אֶת־שְׁמוֹ שָׁם לְשִׁכְנוֹ, *lasum et-shemo sham leshikhno*) (12:5). This carefully worded phrase affirms that although Yahweh will be present at the place of worship, his presence and influence are not limited to it; rather, it is one of a succession of places he will choose.²⁴⁵ As well, it dissuades Israel from adopting the Canaanite notion that the place of worship is one of intrinsic power. Indeed, "No place which becomes the object of Yahweh's choice takes on intrinsic significance."²⁴⁶ Rather, what makes it significant is the fact that Yahweh has chosen to put his name there. Therefore "God's people are not to become preoccupied with places, but with Yahweh."²⁴⁷

Regarding worship articles, ANE pagans also believed that an intrinsic power attached to them. They held that when used correctly, divine power was accessed and a change in reality was effected.²⁴⁸ Specific beliefs attached to each of the articles shaped the way they were used in worship. For example, it was believed that the life of the deity was in some way present in the idol, and thus the role of a worshiper was to provide the deity with the daily care and sustenance needed by any living individual.²⁴⁹ Altars were thought to be the tables of the gods, and thus the role of a worshiper was to present food and drink offerings on these altars.²⁵⁰ Asherah poles symbolized the female goddess Asherah, who acted as sexual partner to Baal and so brought fertility.²⁵¹ In 16:21–22, Israel is forbidden from setting up an Asherah pole beside the altar of Yahweh, presumably because to do so would imply that she was

---

244. Biddle, *Deuteronomy*, 208; Merrill, *Deuteronomy*, 220; Lundbom, *Deuteronomy*, 423–24.

245. The theology embedded in this phrase is often referred to as "name theology," which is seen as affirming that Yahweh is not bound to any place and that his people have no control over his presence. See further Wilson, *Out*, 1–257; Merrill, *Deuteronomy*, 221; Tigay, *Deuteronomy*, 120; von Rad, *Deuteronomy*, 38–40; Hundley, "Reexamination," 533–55; McConville and Millar, *Time*, 111–13, 121, 139; Christensen, *Deuteronomy*, 242–43; Brueggemann, *Deuteronomy*, 144.

246. McConville and Millar, *Time*, 139.

247. Millar, "Land," 626.

248. Walton et al., *Bible Background*, 182.

249. Stuart, *Exodus*, 450–51; Curtis, "Idol," 337–38.

250. See Ezek 39:17–20; 41:22; 44:16; Mal 1:7, 12. Block, *Torah*, 108; Curtis, "Idol," 378; Oppenheim, *Ancient*, 186–94; Rudman, "When Gods," 37–39.

251. McConville, *Deuteronomy*, 154; Lundbom, *Deuteronomy*, 425; Biddle, *Deuteronomy*, 211, 220.Binger, *Asherah*, 146–47; Margalit, "Asherah," 184; Olyan, *Asherah*, 1–3.

Yahweh's sexual partner, and that Yahweh could be induced to confer agricultural fertility to Israel in response to being given a consort.[252]

Regarding rituals, ANE pagans also believed in their intrinsic power. According to ANE pagan thinking, rituals were mechanisms by which deities could be controlled or manipulated.[253] What mattered was the use of proper techniques.[254] The rituals themselves were shaped by, and grounded in, pagan beliefs. Because ANE pagans believed in the power of ritual symbolic imitation, many rituals involved such imitation.[255] For example, it is thought that worshipers participated in ritual orgies with temple prostitutes in the hope that, through this symbolic act associated with human reproduction and fertility, they would induce Baal to send rain on the earth and so bring about agricultural fertility.[256]

In conclusion, ANE beliefs regarding what makes worship effective were sharply at odds with Moses' teaching in 12:5–28. These beliefs were strongly associated with the prohibited forms, and so any use of the forms would risk the importation of these unwanted meanings into the Israelites' worship.

iii. Appropriate social ethics in worship

In 12:5–28, Moses also prescribes appropriate social ethics in worship. Worshipers must show charity towards the marginalized and economically vulnerable.[257] As the people feast (12:7), those who have no capacity to produce their own income (servants and Levites)[258] must be provided for by those who do (12:12, 18). The values of social inclusivity and compassionate generosity in worship surface again in 14:27–29 and 16:11, 14, where Moses specifies that other vulnerable people must also be provided for, specifically

---

252. Lundbom, *Deuteronomy*, 526–27. The very thing prohibited in 16:21–22 appears later to have occurred in Israel's history. An inscription found in Quntillet 'Arjud, in the southern Negeb, from the period of the monarchy (ca. 800), refers to "Yahweh of Samaria and his Asherah." See Lundbom, *Deuteronomy*, 526–27.

253. Scurlock, "Magic," 464.

254. Biddle, *Deuteronomy*, 294; Walton, *Ancient*, 154.

255. Scurlock, "Magic," 464.

256. Gordon and Rendsburg, *Bible*, 160–61. Owing to limited historical and archeological data, it is not possible to build a complete picture of the practices and the theology undergirding them. See further, Sprinkle, "Sexuality," 749–50; Day, "Religion of Canaan," 831–37.

257. Block, *Torah*, 115; McConville, *Deuteronomy*, 223; Biddle, *Deuteronomy*, 217.

258. Levites had no tribal territory allotted to them: 12:12. Christensen, *Deuteronomy*, 248.

widows, orphans and aliens.[259] All members of society are to have access to Yahweh's presence and blessing.[260]

Moses' teaching on appropriate social ethics in worship in 12:5–28 contrasts starkly with the ethics associated with the pagan forms prohibited in 12:2–4, 29–31. To take just one example, in 12:31 Moses refers to the Canaanite practice of child sacrifice. This was probably a ritual reserved for circumstances where the worshiper sought an unusually substantial blessing, such as rescue from plague or imminent defeat in war.[261] According to Tigay, "Underlying child sacrifice was the belief that for the most earnestly desired benefactions from the gods, the most precious gifts had to be offered."[262] Thus whereas the vulnerable were to be included and provided for in Yahwistic worship, in Canaanite worship, they could be sacrificed by those with power.

The beliefs attached to the forms prohibited in 12:2–4, 29–31 are thus sharply at odds with Moses' theology of worship in 12:5–28. A risk inherent in using Canaanite forms would be that these unwanted meanings might be imported into the Israelites' worship, resulting in a distortion and corruption of true worship. As Tigay writes, the prohibited forms had "ineradicable pagan associations,"[263] and so they posed a serious threat to the purity of Israel's worship.[264] Moses' pre-emptive solution was to call for their eradication.

iii. References to Deuteronomy 12 in the rest of the OT

According to the authors of the Deuteronomic History, Israel failed to obey the commands in 12:1–32, and this failure led to false worship, syncretism, and apostasy. Canaanite worship sites were not all destroyed.[265] Sometimes the sites (often mountaintop sanctuaries) were reused for

---

259. Wright, *Deuteronomy* (1996), 166.
260. Block, *Torah*, 104.
261. Tigay, *Deuteronomy*, 464.
262. Tigay, *Deuteronomy*, 464. On child sacrifice, see Lev 18:21; 20:2–5; 2 Kgs 3:27. For a discussion of the relevant historical and archeological material, see Tigay, *Deuteronomy*, 464–66; Biddle, *Deuteronomy*, 220–21.
263. Tigay, *Deuteronomy*, 463. See also Biddle, *Deuteronomy*, 208.
264. McConville, *Deuteronomy*, 228; Biddle, *Deuteronomy*, 219.
265. Judg 2:2; 6:25–33.

worship of Yahweh.[266] As well, "pillars" (מַצֵּבֹת, *matztzevot*) were built,[267] and "Asherah poles" (אֲשֵׁרָה, *'ashera*) were set up.[268] All this resulted in prophetic censure,[269] national spiritual decline, and eventually exile.[270] Indeed, Deuteronomy 12 is often alluded to when the authors of the Deuteronomic History seek to explain the reasons for Israel's decline and exile. For example, it is said of King Ahaz that he engaged in the abominable practices of the nations, including child sacrifice (2 Kgs 16:3; cf. Deut 12:4, 31), and that he worshiped "on the hill tops and under every spreading tree" (2 Kgs 16:4; cf. Deut 12:2). Significantly, the climactic explanation for the exile in 2 Kings 17:9-11 also alludes to Deuteronomy 12:2-4:

> They set up sacred stones and Asherah poles on every high hill and under every spreading tree. At every high place they burned incense, as the nations whom the LORD had driven out before them had done.

Thus the subsequent allusions to Deuteronomy 12 underscore the importance of the command to eradicate Canaanite forms: Israel's failure to obey it led to judgment and exile.

c. The meaning of the text for Christians today

i. Relevant redemptive-historical developments

Deuteronomy 12 contains positive and negative commands, and these are now considered in turn.

Positively, Deuteronomy 12 calls readers to worship God only in the way he makes possible and prescribes.[271] For the original readers, this meant worshiping by going to the Yahweh-chosen place (12:5),[272] and making the prescribed offerings and sacrifices (12:6). For NT readers, Jesus is now the true "place" provided by God where worshipers "go" to

---

266. 1 Sam 9:13-14, 19, 10:5; 2 Sam 15:32; 1 Kgs 18:19. Lundbom, *Deuteronomy*, 423.

267. 1 Kgs 14:23; 2 Kgs 17:10. Lundbom, *Deuteronomy*, 424.

268. 1 Kgs 14:15, 23; 16:33; 2 Kgs 17:10; 21:3, 7.

269. Isa 10:10; 27:9; Jer 2:27; 3:9, 23; 17:2-3; Ezek 6:3-4; Mic 5:13[14]; Hos 4:13. Lundbom, *Deuteronomy*, 423-26.

270. 2 Kgs 17:7-23.

271. Peterson, *Engaging*, 20.

272. While this chosen place may have been Shiloh at first (1 Sam 1-4; Jer 7:12), by the time of Solomon, it was Jerusalem: 1 Kgs 8:44, 48; 2 Chr 7:12. Christensen, *Deuteronomy*, 260; Wright, *Deuteronomy* (1996), 163.

enter God's presence for worship (John 4:19-26).[273] Indeed, the invitation in Deuteronomy to "come" to the chosen place (12:5) in order to enjoy God's presence and "rest" (12:10) finds its fulfillment in Jesus' invitation in Matthew 11:28 to "come to me ... and I will give you rest."[274] Jesus is also the ultimate sacrifice, rendering the offerings and sacrifices prescribed in Deuteronomy 12 obsolete.[275] Christians depend on Jesus as the sacrifice already offered on their behalf, and in grateful response they offer "spiritual sacrifices" (1 Peter 2:5), and present their bodies as "living sacrifices" (Rom 12:1-2).[276] Thus, whereas the Israelites were called by Deuteronomy 12 to attend a specific place and make prescribed offerings, believers today are called to make a total life-response to Christ's saving work, expressed as faith in and obedience to Christ.

Although the forms prescribed in Deuteronomy 12 have now been superseded, the *principles* in Deuteronomy 12 regarding the nature of true worship have ongoing application: true worship is still God-given, not human-designed; and true worship is still a response to God's provision and not a means to manipulate God's blessings. As Firth notes,

> Obviously, we will not reproduce the *form* of worship that we find in the Old Testament. . . . But the theology that lies behind Israel's worship is of vital importance.[277]

Negatively, Deuteronomy 12 prohibits the Israelites from imitating Canaanite worship practices and calls them to eradicate Canaanite worship forms. These laws cannot be directly applied by new covenant believers as they engage with peoples of other faiths. Such a literal application is not possible: the Canaanite worship forms listed in 12:2-3 no longer exist (except in museums), and most believers today do not live "in the land" which is where these laws apply (12:1). But more importantly, a direct application is not theologically warranted, given that the application of the Mosaic law (of which Deuteronomy 12 is a part) is radically transformed with the coming of Christ. The question of how the Mosaic law applies in the life of Christians is a highly debated one. Although space does not permit an extended

---

273. Christensen, *Deuteronomy*, 244.

274. Block, *Torah*, 113. On the development of the theme of "rest" through the Canon, see Lundbom, *Deuteronomy*, 432.

275. 1 Cor 5:7; Eph 5:2; Hebrews 7:27; 9:24-28; 10:1-18. Peterson, "Worship," 860-62; Peterson, *Engaging*, 129; Lundbom, *Deuteronomy*, 429.

276. Lundbom, *Deuteronomy*, 429; Christensen, *Deuteronomy*, 259.

277. Firth, "Worship," 6-7.

discussion here, the following provides a framework for identifying the contemporary meaning of these laws.[278]

A starting point is that Jesus did not abrogate the Mosaic law, but instead fulfilled it (Mat 5:17–20). Although scholars differ regarding the precise implications, there is a general agreement that it entails both continuity (the law is not abolished) and discontinuity (it is fulfilled and thus its application is changed).[279] A study of specific laws whose fulfillment is explicit in the NT reveals a general pattern: even where a particular law no longer applies literally (discontinuity), its purpose or objective has ongoing importance (continuity).[280] Kruse summarizes the salvation-historical change in this way:

> The law continued to have an educative role for [Christians], but it was no longer the regulatory norm under which they lived. Christians were not bound to the actual demands of the law but had much to learn from the principles and values underlying them.[281]

Wright proposes a two-stage hermeneutical strategy for identifying the contemporary meaning of Mosaic laws: first, the interpreter must identify the function and objective of the law within the original Israelite context; and second, the interpreter must seek the contemporary significance, making every effort to "preserve the objective while changing the context."[282]

Applying Wright's approach here, we have seen that the function and objective of the negative laws in Deuteronomy 12 are to protect the purity of Israel's worship. The eradication of Canaanite forms had the purpose of removing Canaanite worship practices as a viable alternative to worshiping Yahweh in the way he had prescribed, and preventing the importation of false-worship theology associated with these forms. Application of this function and objective to contemporary contexts might caution believers today against using the forms of other faiths, if using them risks impairing true worship. Wright himself proposes that Deuteronomy 12 does not call contemporary Christians to engage in "violently literal iconoclasm," but that

---

278. On the law and gospel debate generally, see Kruse, "Law," 633–36; Strickland, *Five Views*.

279. Kruse, "Law," 633–36; VanGemeren, "Law," 13–58; Moo, "Law," 319–76; Satterthwaite, "Biblical History," 43–51; Goldsworthy, "Relationship," 81–88.

280. For example, see Lev 11:1–47 and Mark 7:1–23.

281. Kruse, "Law," 636.

282. Wright, *Deuteronomy* (1996), 13–14. See further Wright, "Authority," 31–48; Wright, *God's People*, 260–65.

it does call for an uncompromising confrontation of threats to the purity of the worship of God's people.[283]

ii. *The implications of Deuteronomy 12 for the IM debate*

The Canaanite forms prohibited in Deuteronomy 12 are different from Muslim forms. Yet notwithstanding these differences, the text is relevant to the IM debate because it deals with the use of the forms of other faiths by God's people (something that is advocated by IM proponents), and because of the abiding principles regarding worship and forms that it teaches.

Wright has commented on the importance of this text for missiological reflection. He writes,

> The seriousness with which Deuteronomy treats idolatry and the insidious nature of idolatry's enticement for God's people call for a more reflective and realistic treatment for the modern missiological context than is usually offered in many discussions of the question of world religions. There is a strength of language here (detestable . . .utterly abhor), matched by a strength of action . . . , that displays a divine attitude toward idolatry that cannot be easily relativised.[284]

The fact that Deuteronomy 12 portrays the Canaanite forms as dangerous snares to the people of God, that the Israelites are called to eradicate them in such uncompromising terms, and that Israel's failure to obey these commands results in false worship, judgment and exile, all underline the importance of considering the text's implications today. Indeed, given all this, it is surprising that Deuteronomy 12 has been so briefly and rarely discussed by participants in the IM debate.[285]

1. Deuteronomy 12 is not a blanket prohibition on using the forms of other faiths, but it does warn of the dangers

Deuteronomy 12 cannot be applied in the new covenant era as a law prohibiting all use of borrowed forms. IM critic Poston seeks to apply it in this way, concluding that "the importation of non-Christian religious practices

---

283. Wright, *Deuteronomy* (1996), 119.

284. Wright, *Deuteronomy* (1996), 119. See also Christensen, *Deuteronomy*, 244.

285. Brogden and Poston discuss it briefly. See Brogden, "Inside Out," 35; Poston, "You Must Not," 245.

into a Christian context is never to be tolerated."[286] However, Poston's application must be rejected for two reasons. First, he fails to consider relevant redemptive-historical developments concerning the application of the Mosaic law (chapter 3, §3.c.i. above). Second, what makes Canaanite forms problematic according to Deuteronomy 12 is not that all foreign forms are always problematic, but rather that using these Canaanite forms is prohibited by Yahweh, and that to use them would be to reject the way to worship that he is providing (chapter 3, §3.b.i. above).

For new covenant believers, Deuteronomy 12 does not simply prohibit all use of the forms of other faiths. What it prohibits is engaging with God in any way other than the way he has provided. But in this regard, Deuteronomy 12 does contain a warning for new covenant believers: there are risks associated with using the forms of other faiths, since they have the potential to draw believers away from using the God-given way to worship. Thus Deuteronomy 12 is not a blanket prohibition on using the forms of other faiths today, but it is a warning that such forms have the potential to undermine, corrupt and distort true worship. This is explored further below.

2. Other implications for the IM debate

Five other implications of the text for the IM debate are identified here.

First, in Deuteronomy 12 we have a text which resists foreign forms on the grounds that they pose a threat to the purity of Israel's worship. Thus, once again we see the importance of making a biblical theology of worship a key frame of reference in the process of form-selection. The primary concern of form-selectors should be to ensure that believers are engaging with God in the way he makes possible and on the terms he sets. BMBs and missionaries who are considering using Muslim forms must consider whether such use is likely to facilitate or hinder the worship of God in the way he himself has directed.

Second, Deuteronomy 12 warns that the forms of other faiths have the potential to corrupt and distort true worship. The text calls participants in the IM debate to a sober recognition of the potential influence of forms. Whereas Kraft downplays the influence of forms by characterizing them as "neutral vehicles" which can ordinarily be invested with new meanings, Deuteronomy 12 portrays the Canaanite forms as having such a potential to corrupt true worship that total eradication is required. The fact that Israel must eradicate the Canaanite forms (rather than simply invest them with new meaning) suggests that Kraft has underestimated the potential

---

286. Poston, "You Must Not," 245.

influence of forms, and that his proposal that almost any can be reused needs, at the very least, to be nuanced or qualified.

Third, Deuteronomy 12 highlights the fact that true worship is God-given, whereas false worship is human-designed and human-initiated. Since the God-given way to worship in the new covenant age is continuing dependence on Christ, it is crucial that where the use of Muslim forms is contemplated, the potential of these forms to draw believers away from Christ-dependence be carefully considered. It will be especially important to ask whether the particular forms in question have associations in the mind of worshipers with human initiation or human merit-accumulation in worship, since such associations could hinder the development of Christ-dependence.

Fourth, Deuteronomy 12 also highlights the fact that where foreign forms are used by God's people, there is a danger that false worship theology or meanings will be imported into their worship. Form-selectors today must carefully consider the potential of Muslim forms to bring with them unwanted meanings that might distort true worship. BMBs who are considering using Muslim forms will need to identify the meanings previously attached to those forms, and consider whether using them will introduce unhelpful concepts into their worship (for example, the notion that worship is a means of winning God's favor). A theological principle which Christensen identifies in Deuteronomy 12 is that "true religion is found in conscious rejection of every false dependence."[287] It may be that particular BMBs have historical associations with Muslim forms that could be described as false worship dependencies (such as a dependence on the performance of religious ritual to win God's favor). If this is the case, then a crucial question will be whether the use of those forms is likely to hinder this process of rejecting and eradicating these false dependencies.

Finally, in this book, I propose a test for form-selection that asks whether a particular form is likely to be *helpful* in achieving the goal of true worship. This test better reflects the concerns of Deuteronomy 12 than both Kraft's allegiance test (chapter 1, §3.c.i.) and IM proponents' "biblical compatibility" test (chapter 1, §3.a.vi.).

The focus of Kraft's test is upon the question of allegiance. Provided a form can be used to express allegiance to the true God, it is deemed potentially suitable. While Kraft's concern that allegiance be to the true God is a vital one, correct allegiance alone is insufficient. Deuteronomy 12 warns that worship can be directed towards the true God (and so with the correct allegiance), and yet still be false worship (because the worship is not done

287. Christensen, *Deuteronomy*, 249.

in the way God makes possible). Thus form-selectors need to go beyond simply satisfying themselves that the form is used to express allegiance to the true God, and also ask whether the form facilitates or hinders engaging with God in the way he makes possible.

According to the "biblical compatibility" test, forms are rejected as biblically incompatible if they are intrinsically immoral or otherwise explicitly prohibited in the Bible (see chapter 1, §3.a.vi.). Thus the focus of this test is the morality of the form. The problem here is that it is not intrinsically immoral forms and directly prohibited forms alone that can cause problems for worship. In Deuteronomy 12, a morally neutral form (an altar) is prohibited on the grounds that it still has the capacity to distort true worship because of the unwanted meanings attached to it (see chapter 3, §3.b.ii. above). Therefore, it is not only forms which are immoral or explicitly prohibited by Scripture which need to be rejected. What is needed is a test that calls form-selectors to evaluate the *helpfulness* of forms in assisting believers to engage with God in the way he makes possible and on the terms he sets. When this test is applied, certain Muslim forms which are not intrinsically immoral or explicitly prohibited in the Bible might nevertheless be rejected as not helpful (or simply not the best available option) in achieving the goal of facilitating true worship, on the grounds of their past associations for the worshiper. Thus both the "allegiance" test and the "biblical compatibility" test do not adequately warn of the potential dangers of borrowed forms.

4. Hosea 8

Our third and final OT resistance text is Hosea 8. This text is a judgment oracle, spoken by Yahweh against Israel. Scholars generally agree that the oracle was originally delivered during the Assyrian crisis of the northern kingdom's final two decades.[288] The oracle begins with a declaration that destruction looms because Israel has broken the covenant (8:1–3). Then details of Israel's covenant violation are provided. Israel has appointed illegitimate kings and used idols to worship Yahweh (8:4–7a). Israel has also sought security through entering into foreign alliances (8:7b–10). Finally, Israel has built illegitimate shrines and offered unacceptable sacrifices (8:11–14).[289]

---

288. See Wolff, *Hosea*, 137; Stuart, *Hosea*, 130.

289. Most agree that 8:1–14 forms a single, unified compositional unit. See Nogalski, *Hosea*, 115; Hwang, *Hosea*, 289–309; Stuart, *Hosea*, 129. On historical critical issues related to this text, see Nicholson, *God*, 202; Lim and Castelo, *Hosea*, 146.

a. The relevance of the text to the research problem

For a text to be relevant, it needs to deal with the use by the Israelites of the forms of other faiths to worship Yahweh. As the following analysis shows, this is indeed such a text.

i. Forms borrowed from other faiths

The forms referred to in 8:4–6 are undoubtedly the worship forms of other faiths. In 8:4–6, Yahweh critiques the Israelites for making idols, especially "the calf of Samaria" (cf. 4:17; 13:2; 14:8). Use of idols or images was prohibited for the Israelites (Exod 20:4–6, 23) but was the dominant form of religious expression amongst Israel's neighbors during Hosea's time. Idols in the shape of calves or young bulls were especially popular.[290] Thus in making and using idols, including the calf of Samaria, the Israelites borrowed worship forms.

The form referred to in 8:11 is also a borrowed one. According to 8:11, Israel has "multiplied altars" (הִרְבָּה מִזְבְּחֹת, *hirbah mizbechot*), that is, Israel has constructed multiple worship sites (cf. 4:13). The construction and use of multiple worship sites was not permitted in official Yahwism (Deut 12). It was, however, standard practice in ANE religion.[291] Thus in constructing and using a plurality of worship sites, the Israelites borrowed the forms of other faiths.[292]

ii. Used to worship Yahweh

According to Hosea 8, Israel has been using these borrowed forms to worship Yahweh. This is not to say that the Israelites of Hosea's day did not also engage in worship of other deities: it is clear from other parts of Hosea[293] and other OT books[294] that they did. However, the worship that is critiqued in Hosea 8 is worship directed to Yahweh. This is evident in 8:2, where, in response to the announcement of impending destruction in 8:1, Israel cries out, not to other deities, but to Yahweh (לִי, *li*: "to me"). Not only is Israel's cry directed to Yahweh, but it uses covenantal language:

---

290. See chapter 3, §2.a.i. above and Dearman, *Hosea*, 222.
291. See chapter 3, §3.a.i. above, and Hwang, *Hosea*, 27–28.
292. Stuart, *Hosea*, 135; McComiskey, "Hosea," 132.
293. 1:2; 2:2–15; 3:1; 4:13–14; 7:14; 9:1; 11:2. Munayer, *Hosea*, 129.
294. 2 Kgs 15:4; 15:35; 2 Chr 27:2; 28:2–4. McComiskey, "Hosea," 1–2.

"My God, we know you" (אֱלֹהַי יְדַעֲנוּךָ, *'elohay yeda'anukha*). The claim to "know" God in the OT is a claim to enjoy a special covenantal relationship with him, based on a knowledge of his saving work in history.²⁹⁵ Thus Hosea 8 deals with a people who direct their cries to Yahweh, and believe that they have a relationship with him.²⁹⁶

Confirmation of this comes in 8:5–6 with mentions of the "calf of Samaria." Most scholars conclude that this is a reference to the calf-idol erected in Bethel by Jeroboam in 1 Kings 12:28–29. There are two reasons for this. First, there is no historical evidence that a calf-idol ever existed in the capital city of Samaria.²⁹⁷ It seems more likely, therefore, that "Samaria" is used here metonymously, representing the whole northern kingdom of Israel.²⁹⁸ Although Jeroboam had built two calf-idols in the northern kingdom, one in Bethel and one in Dan, by the time Hosea 8 was composed the idol in Dan had probably been destroyed by the Assyrian king Tiglath-Pileser III, and hence the reference in 8:5–6 to a single calf-idol only.²⁹⁹ Second, the declaration in 8:6 that the calf of Samaria is "not God" (לֹא אֱלֹהִים, *lo 'elohim*) seems to be an allusion to, and a polemical reversal of, Jeroboam's claim in 1 Kings 12:28 that the calves are Israel's אֱלֹהִים, *'elohim* who brought them out of Egypt.³⁰⁰ Thus what is critiqued in 8:5–6 is worship at Jeroboam's Bethel cult. Importantly, this was a cult for the worship of *Yahweh*, not other deities (see chapter 3, §2.a.ii. above). This is clear from Jeroboam's description of the Bethel and Dan idols in 1 Kings 12:28.³⁰¹ Further evidence that these idols continued to be used for worship of Yahweh (and not other deities) is found in the fact that they escaped destruction during the reign of Jehu, who sought to purge the northern kingdom of Baal worship (2 Kgs 9–10).³⁰² If Jeroboam's famous idols had been associated with Baal worship, they would likely have been destroyed along with the temple of Baal in Samaria (1 Kgs 10:18–29).³⁰³

---

295. See 2:20; 4:1; 6:6; Prov 2:5; Jer 22:16. Dearman, *Hosea*, 219; Andersen and Freedman, *Hosea*, 489–90.

296. McComiskey, "Hosea," 120.

297. Dearman, *Hosea*, 225; McComiskey, "Hosea," 124; Nogalski, *Hosea*, 117.

298. Dearman, *Hosea*, 225; Stuart, *Hosea*, 132; McComiskey, "Hosea," 124.

299. Cf. 10:5, which speaks of the residents of Samaria fearing the destruction of "the calf of Beth-Aven" (עֶגְלוֹת בֵּית אָוֶן, *'egelot beyt aven*). Beth Aven, lit: "house of nothingness," is Hosea's polemical nickname for Bethel, "house of God." Garrett, *Hosea*, 183–84; Wolff, *Hosea*, 137.

300. Dearman, *Hosea*, 223, 226.

301. Cf. Exod 32:4 and discussion on chapter 3, §2.a.ii. above.

302. Dearman, *Hosea*, 225.

303. Dearman, *Hosea*, 225.

Further confirmation that the worship in Hosea 8 is directed to Yahweh comes in 8:11-13. Though the worship in 8:11-13 is performed at unauthorized *sites* (8:11),[304] the sacrifices are nonetheless offered to Yahweh, since Yahweh refers to them as "my sacrificial gifts" (זִבְחֵי הַבְהָבַי, *zivchey havhavay*) (8:13).[305] As well, the sacrifices are broadly in line with levitical guidelines: 8:11 refers to "sin offerings" (חָטָא, *chato'*) (cf. Lev 4:1-5:13) and 8:13 refers to eating the meat of sacrifices (cf. Lev 7:19-21; 19:5-8).[306] This strengthens the conclusion that what is depicted here is attempted worship of Yahweh, or in Dearman's words, "syncretistic, baalized forms of Yahwism."[307]

In conclusion, Hosea 8 deals with the use by the Israelites of the forms of other faiths to worship Yahweh.

b. The meaning of the text for the original audience

i. Is there evidence in the text that the author is seeking to persuade the reader to resist the forms of other faiths?

There is considerable evidence in the text that Hosea's purpose is to persuade the reader to refrain from using certain forms of other faiths. Hosea does this by announcing the dire consequences for the Israelites of using these forms. Ultimately, however, what renders the worship problematic is not simply the use of borrowed forms, but rather that such use amounts to a violation of God's commands and a rejection of the God-given way to worship. The following analysis bears this out.

1. THE AUTHOR RESISTS THE FALSE WORSHIP BY DEPICTING ITS CONSEQUENCES

In Hosea 8, the devastating consequences of the false worship are depicted. It is leading to nothing less than God's rejection and judgment, and a removal and reversal of covenant blessing. The oracle begins in 8:1a with an urgent call for the ram's horn to be sounded to warn Israel that an enemy is approaching.[308] Just as an eagle hovers over its prey before attacking (8:1b), so too

---

304. Israel has "multiplied altars" (8:11), in contravention of Deut 12.
305. McComiskey, "Hosea," 133.
306. McComiskey, "Hosea," 132-33.
307. Dearman, *Hosea*, 230.
308. Dearman, *Hosea*, 216. The phrase אֶל־חִכְּךָ שֹׁפָר, *'el-chikhkhekha shofar* (lit. "the

an enemy is preparing to attack Israel (8:3).[309] Alarmingly, as the judgment oracle unfolds, it becomes increasingly clear that this enemy is none other than Yahweh himself (8:4, 5b, 6b, 10b, 13b, 14b), even though he acts through the agency of foreign nations (8:7b-8, 10b, 13b; cf. 5:8-14).[310]

The initial announcement of impending judgment in 8:1–3 is followed in 8:4–14 by a breathtaking series of images which depict this judgment. The enemy's attack will be like a whirlwind (8:7). Famine will strike and foreigners will eat what Israel has planted (8:8).[311] The entire nation will be swallowed up by foreign nations (8:9). The Israelites will be oppressed by a foreign king (8:10) and driven into captivity once more (8:13).[312] Finally, utter destruction is announced, as Yahweh will "send fire upon their cities" (8:14). These images of judgment are delivered succinctly and in quick succession, such that their cumulative effect is to "jar the imagination with unthinkable punishments too horrible to contemplate."[313]

What makes the oracle especially confronting to Israelite sensibilities, however, is that the coming judgment is artfully depicted as a tragic reversal of all the blessings previously conferred by Yahweh under the covenant. Thus the image of Yahweh as an eagle, hitherto used positively to depict Yahweh as rescuer, protector, guide, and one who confers blessing (Exod 19:4; Deut 32:11–12), is "turned upside down": now Yahweh is an enemy eagle that attacks and pursues Israel (8:1, 3; cf. Deut 28:49).[314] Likewise, in 8:3, Hosea upends the cherished depiction of life under Yahweh's protection in Psalm 23:6, whereby "goodness" (טוֹב, tov) and love are said to "pursue" (רדף, rdf) the psalmist. In 8:3, because Israel has rejected "goodness" (טוֹב, tov), Yahweh will "pursue" (רדף, rdf) Israel as an enemy.[315] Further, the depiction of Israel in 8:8 as an article which was once precious, but has now been discarded as worthless, is a poignant allusion to Exodus 19:5, where Yahweh had announced that an obedient Israel would become his treasured possession.[316] The reversal theme resurfaces in 8:10. There, the verb "to gather" (קבץ, qvtz), typically used "to describe Israel's deliverance *from* exile" (Deut

---

horn to your mouth") has no verb, communicating urgency: "the horn to your mouth!" McComiskey, "Hosea," 119.

309. McComiskey, "Hosea," 119.
310. Hwang, *Hosea*, 293; Stuart, *Hosea*, 130; Munayer, *Hosea*, 491.
311. Stuart, *Hosea*, 134.
312. McComiskey, "Hosea," 133; Stuart, *Hosea*, 137.
313. Smith, *Hosea*, 133.
314. Dearman, *Hosea*, 216; Munayer, *Hosea*, 486.
315. Hwang, *Hosea*, 295.
316. McComiskey, "Hosea," 129.

30:3–4; Hos 1:11), is now used to describe "a gathering *for* exile."³¹⁷ In 8:13 there is also a harrowing allusion to Yahweh's famous self-description in Exodus 34:7 as one who maintains love "to a thousand generations, forgiving 'iniquity' (עָוֹן, *ʿawon*), transgression, and 'sin' (חַטָּאָה, *chattaʾah*)." Hosea announces that Yahweh "will remember their 'iniquity' (עָוֹן, *ʿawon*) and punish their 'sin' (חַטָּאָה, *chattaʾah*)" (8:13).³¹⁸ This is followed by a reversal of the exodus tradition: whereas Israel was once delivered from Egypt, now an "anti-exodus" will occur as Israel returns to Egypt (8:13).³¹⁹ In relation to this series of reversals, Lim and Castelo write,

> Essentially, Hosea reinterprets the national myth of Israel. Whereas previously Israel's story involved a deliverance from the nations and a conquest of them in the promised land, now it will include a defeat and dispersion among the nations.³²⁰

Thus Hosea 8 announces that all the blessing previously conferred under the covenant will be replaced with divine wrath, rejection, and destruction.³²¹

Hosea shows the link between the false worship and these dire consequences through a "cause and unintended effect" motif. Ironically, although the Israelites engage in false worship out of a desire to secure blessing and prosperity, in reality, their worship produces the opposite effect. In 8:4b, Yahweh states that the Israelites have made idols "in order that" (לְמַעַן, *lemaʿan*) "they might be destroyed" (יִכָּרֵת, *yikhkharet*).³²² The use here of the conjunction "in order that" (לְמַעַן, *lemaʿan*) is ironic.³²³ In making the idols, the Israelites certainly did not *intend* to bring about their own destruction, yet that is exactly what they have done.³²⁴ As Dearman notes,

---

317. Lim and Castelo, *Hosea*, 151.

318. Cf. Lev 26:16; Deut 28: 22, 33, 36, 45, 51, 68. Stuart, *Hosea*, 131, 134, 135, 137; Lim and Castelo, *Hosea*, 148; Dearman, *Hosea*, 232.

319. Hwang, *Hosea*, 307.

320. Lim and Castelo, *Hosea*, 151.

321. On this motif, see Hwang, *Hosea*, 307; Munayer, *Hosea*, 486; Wolff, *Hosea*, 147.

322. The suffix in יִכָּרֵת, *yikhkharet*, lit: "its destruction," could refer to the idol or to Israel's wealth, but in the context it is more likely to refer to the Israelites themselves, and thus the verse speaks of the people's destruction. Stuart, *Hosea*, 130; Hwang, *Hosea*, 296; Dearman, *Hosea*, 222. *Contra* Garrett, *Hosea*, 183; McComiskey, "Hosea," 123; Smith, *Hosea*, 135.

323. McComiskey, "Hosea," 123. Garrett describes it as sarcastic. Garrett, *Hosea*, 183.

324. Stuart, *Hosea*, 130.

The intended outcome is reversed.... The idol makers have brought on failure and destruction for Israel..., even if it was blessing and security that they intended to secure by them.[325]

Irony is also present in 8:5, where the calf-idol is said to arouse Yahweh's burning anger and compromise the people's "innocence" or "purity" (נִקָּיֹן, *niqqayon*). Far from functioning as intended (that is, as a medium of worship), the idol actually arouses divine wrath.[326] And, far from bringing about ritual purity, worship using the idol actually pollutes worshipers.[327]

This ironic cause-and-effect motif reappears in 8:7 with the phrase "they sow the wind and reap the whirlwind." By using idols, Israel has sown "wind" (רוּחַ, *ruach*), that is, something vain and useless.[328] Yet the outcome is far worse than the nothingness one might expect, since the wind is actually going to grow into a whirlwind that will destroy them.[329] The agricultural verb-pair "to sow" (זרע, *zrʿ*) and "to reap" (קצר, *qtzr*) sharply portrays the link between the sin and its unintended consequences.[330]

The motif reaches a climax in 8:11 with the assertion that although Israel has built a plurality of altars "for sin offerings" (לְחַטָּא, *lachatoʾ*), they have in fact become altars "for sinning" (לַחֲטֹא, *lachatoʾ*). The irony is profound. The altars were intended to facilitate *expiation* of sin, yet they actually function as a means of *committing* sin.[331] Through a clever pun on חטא, *chtʾ*, which can mean both "sin offering" and an act of "sin,"[332] Hosea declares "the surprising fate that multiplying cultic worship leads to the opposite of its intended effect."[333] As Beeby notes: "Religious zeal led to death, not life."[334] Furthermore in 8:13, Hosea shows that the act of making sacrificial gifts to Yahweh at unauthorized altars, no doubt intended to bring about forgiveness of sin, actually has the opposite—and tragic—effect of causing Yahweh to *remember* Israel's sin, and send the nation into exile![335]

---

325. Dearman, *Hosea*, 222.

326. Achtemeier, *Minor Prophets*, ch. 17.

327. Hwang, *Hosea*, 298.

328. Cf. Isa 41:29; Job 7:7; 15:2; Eccl 1:14 where רוּחַ, *ruach* ("wind") carries the sense of vanity, illusion, and nothingness. Achtemeier, *Minor Prophets*, ch. 17.

329. McComiskey, "Hosea," 128.

330. Hwang, *Hosea*, 299–300; Stuart, *Hosea*, 134.

331. Stuart, *Hosea*, 135–36; Dearman, *Hosea*, 230; Garrett, *Hosea*, 186.

332. Cf. Exod 29:14 and 32:31. Luc, "חטא," 87–93; Hwang, *Hosea*, 305.

333. Hwang, *Hosea*, 305.

334. Beeby, *Hosea*, 108.

335. Garrett, *Hosea*, 187.

Finally, the "cause and unintended effect" motif appears once more in 8:13–14 with a wordplay on אכל, *'khl* ("eat, consume"). Because the Israelites אכל, *'khl* ("eat") the meat of sacrifices offered at unauthorized sites, Yahweh will send fire that will אכל, *'khl* ("consume") Israel's fortresses (8:14).[336] Thus "the victims of the catastrophe are pictured as agents."[337]

In Hosea 8, Hosea shows that the Israelites' use of the forms of other faiths has brought about a crisis whereby "the end of saving history is imminent."[338] Hosea highlights the tragic irony at the heart of the Israelites' worship: that which is done to secure blessing, actually brings about the very opposite: curse and judgment.[339] Thus Hosea resists the false worship by depicting the dire consequences for the Israelites of engaging in it.

2. The Author Also Resists the False Worship by Depicting It as Ineffective and Dangerous

Hosea also resists the false worship by depicting it as ineffective and dangerous. In 8:5, Hosea announces that Yahweh has spurned the calf-idol. As a human-made article which is not God (8:6), the idol cannot facilitate true worship.[340] Indeed, such is its ineffectiveness and powerlessness that it will not even be able to prevent its own destruction (8:6b).[341] Likewise in 8:13, in a parody of the traditional priestly pronouncement that an offering has been accepted by Yahweh,[342] Hosea declares of the Israelites' offerings, "Yahweh does not accept them" (יְהוָה לֹא רָצָם, *yhwh lo ratzam*).

At the same time as stressing that the human-made idol is ineffective, Hosea also shows that it is dangerous, precisely because worshipers do not realize that it is ineffective, and so have a false sense of security. This is apparent in 8:2 when the Israelites respond with astonishment to the announcement of judgment in 8:1, protesting, "My God, we know You!" (אֱלֹהַי יְדַעֲנוּךָ, *'elohay yeda'anukha*). The claim "to know" (ידע, *yd'*) God suggests that the Israelites genuinely believe that they still enjoy an intimate

---

336. Hwang, *Hosea*, 291.
337. Eidevall, *Grapes*, 131.
338. Wolff, *Hosea*, 147.
339. Garrett, *Hosea*, 180, 193; Birch, *Hosea*, 103.
340. Achtemeier, *Minor Prophets*, ch. 17.
341. There are allusions to Exodus 32 here: Yahweh declares "my anger burns" (חָרָה אַפִּי, *charah 'appi*) in 8:5 (cf. Exod 32:10, 11, 19, 22), and the idol's complete destruction is announced in 8:6 (cf. Exod 32:19–20). The effect of these allusions is to confirm the seriousness of Israel's sin. Lim and Castelo, *Hosea*, 149; D. Simundson, *Hosea*, 69.
342. See Lev 1:17, 2:14, 3:5. Achtemeier, *Minor Prophets*, ch. 19; Garrett, *Hosea*, 188.

relationship with Yahweh as covenant partners and continue to be recipients of his favor.[343] The fact that they are still participating in Yahweh-worship no doubt reinforces this belief (8:4b-6, 11-13). Yet they are misguided. They do not realize that their worship has actually aroused Yahweh's anger (8:5), such that he will pursue them as an enemy (8:3).[344] False worship is particularly dangerous because it lulls worshipers into a false sense of security, blinding them to their need to engage Yahweh in true worship. Thus the false worship is both ineffective and dangerous.

3. The ultimate problem with the worship is that it is disobedient and human-initiated

Hosea resists the use of the forms of other faiths in the strongest possible terms. However, this text does not amount to a blanket prohibition. Rather, what makes the use of the forms problematic here is that such use amounts to a violation of Yahweh's own commands regarding how he is to be worshiped. In 8:1b, in a clause beginning with the particle יַעַן, *ya'an* ("because"), Yahweh explains why the judgment just announced in 8:1a will take place: Israel has broken "my covenant" (בְּרִיתִי, *beriti*) and rebelled against "my law" (תּוֹרָתִי, *torati*). "Covenant" (בְּרִית, *berit*) and "law" (תּוֹרָה, *torah*) function as poetic complements here, together referring to the entire tradition of Yahweh's dealings with Israel, but particularly the Mosaic legal stipulations.[345] The assertion in 8:1 then is that Israel has violated these stipulations. This idea is repeated in 8:3 with the allegation that Israel has spurned "the good" (טוֹב, *tov*). טוֹב, *tov* is an important term in Deuteronomy, used to describe the good that comes from Yahweh when Israel obeys.[346] To assert that Israel has rejected this good, then, is to assert that Israel has disobeyed Yahweh's revealed will and so forfeited the promised good.[347] Indeed, the causal connection between Israel's disobedience and Yahweh's judgment is emphasized through a wordplay on "spurn" (זנח, *znch*). Just as Israel "has spurned" (זָנַח, *zanach*) the good (8:3a), so too Yahweh "has spurned" (זָנַח, *zanach*) the

---

343. Cf. 2:20; 5:4. McComiskey, "Hosea," 120; Stuart, *Hosea*, 131; Garrett, *Hosea*, 181; Munayer, *Hosea*, 490.

344. McComiskey, "Hosea," 120.

345. Smith, *Hosea*, 134; Dearman, *Hosea*, 218; Garrett, *Hosea*, 181. Contra Wolff, *Hosea*, 137-38. On the historical-critical debate concerning the authenticity of the reference to covenant in 8:1, see Nicholson, *God*, 178-88.

346. See Deut 5:33; 6:24; 10:13; 12:28; 26:11; 30:9, 15. Gordon, "טוֹב," 353-357; Dearman, *Hosea*, 219; Garrett, *Hosea*, 181-82; McComiskey, "Hosea," 121. Contra Stuart, *Hosea*, 131.

347. Smith, *Hosea*, 134; Achtemeier, *Minor Prophets*, ch. 17.

calf-idol (8:5a).³⁴⁸ Thus Israel's conduct is problematic because it violates Yahweh's law. The subsequent discussion of Israel's idol making (8:4b-6) and multiplication of altars (8:11) must, therefore, be read in light of the relevant Mosaic prohibitions of such conduct (Exod 20:4-6, 23; Deut 12).³⁴⁹

That the basic problem is disobedience is reinforced in 8:11-12. In 8:11, Yahweh asserts that the altars which the Israelites have built have become "altars for sinning," but does not explicitly state why. However, in 8:12, he reflects on the Israelites' longstanding pattern of disregarding his laws: "Were I to write for him a multitude of my laws, they would be regarded as a strange thing."³⁵⁰ This strongly implies that the reason the altars are occasions for sinning is *because* they were constructed without due attention to Yahweh's laws (specifically, those in Deuteronomy 12 prohibiting a plurality of altars).³⁵¹ Indeed, there is a wordplay on "multiply" (רבה, *rvh*) in 8:11 and 8:12, which explicitly links the problem with its cause: Israel "multiplied" (הִרְבָּה, *hirbah*) altars (8:11) *because* Israel did not heed the "multitude" (רֻבֵּי, *rubbey*) of Yahweh's laws (8:12).³⁵² Therefore, the use of these forms of other faiths is condemned first and foremost because such use is disobedient—a violation of Yahweh's commands regarding how he is to be worshiped.

Another reason why such usage is condemned is because in disobeying Yahweh's commands regarding how he is to be worshiped, Israel is rejecting God-given worship and replacing it with a human-made alternative. In 8:6b, Yahweh scornfully says of the idol, "a metalworker has made it; it is not God." Thus a fundamental problem with the calf-idol is that it has its origin in Israel, not Yahweh.³⁵³ It is a human-made and human-designed way to worship. Yahweh's exclamation of disgust in 8:6a, "from Israel!" (מִיִּשְׂרָאֵל, *miyyisra'el*), could be taken as a reference to the idol ("it is from Israel!"), or to the people who made the idol ("they are from Israel!"). If it refers to the idol,³⁵⁴ then this clause strengthens the polemic against the idol based on its human origins. Indeed, the clause "it is not God" is structurally parallel to "it is from Israel," further highlighting the fact that

---

348. Hwang, *Hosea*, 294.

349. Wolff, *Hosea*, 144; Nogalski, *Hosea*, 122; Stuart, *Hosea*, 135-36.

350. My translation. Since the Torah already existed in written form in Hosea's day (4:6; 8:1), the sense here is that even if Yahweh were to write his laws again, many times, the Israelites, given their history of disobedience, would continue to ignore them. McComiskey, "Hosea," 132.

351. Stuart, *Hosea*, 135-36; McComiskey, "Hosea," 132.

352. Wolff, *Hosea*, 144; Hwang, *Hosea*, 305; Stuart, *Hosea*, 135-36.

353. McComiskey, "Hosea," 125.

354. McComiskey argues that it does: McComiskey, "Hosea," 125-26. *Contra* Achtemeier, *Minor Prophets*, ch. 17.

the human origin of the calf is what makes it so problematic.[355] Thus notwithstanding the fact that Hosea 8 is a text that resists the use of the forms of other faiths, the ultimate problem here is not the use of such forms *per se*. Rather, it is the rejection of God-given worship, and its replacement with a human-designed and initiated substitute. The foreign forms play a critical role in this: they are the means by which the sin is committed. But the ultimate problem is the rejection of God-given worship.

ii. What does the text teach about worship and forms?

We now turn to a discussion of what the text teaches about worship and forms.

1. True worship is God-given

In Hosea 8, it emerges once again that true worship is God-given: Yahweh alone makes true worship possible and Yahweh alone sets its terms.[356] Any worship that is outside the divinely prescribed parameters for worship is no longer true worship. In making the idol, the Israelites have rejected God-given worship and substituted their own, human-made form. This form is problematic because it functions as an alternative to, and substitute for, God-given worship.

2. Human-initiated worship is false worship

Since true worship is God-given, it follows that human-initiated worship is false worship. As we have seen, what makes the worship in Hosea 8 ultimately unacceptable is not simply that the forms of other faiths are used, but rather that these forms have been used at the *people's* initiative, and on their terms. Thus the defining feature of the false worship here is that it has its origins in people, not God.

---

355. McComiskey, "Hosea," 126.
356. Peterson, *Engaging*, 20, 26–27, 73.

3. A Risk Inherent in Using Borrowed Forms is that Unwanted Meanings will be Imported

Hosea 8 highlights the fact that when forms are borrowed from other faiths, there is a danger that the pagan meanings previously associated with them will also be imported. Because these pagan meanings contradict and undermine the principles of God-given worship, the result is a distortion of true worship. There are numerous indications in Hosea 8 that pagan meanings have been imported as well as the forms.

First, in ANE religion, obedience to divine prescriptions was not stressed as something important.[357] In fact, the gods generally did not issue commands. Walton explains,

> The ancients believed that . . . the gods simply were not very forthcoming about what constituted offence [and] . . . did not take it upon themselves to communicate their expectations.[358]

What was considered important in maintaining a deity's favor was not obeying divine laws, but rather the correct performance of rituals: "The performance of the cult was central and foundational to their religion."[359] It appears in 8:1–3 that the Israelites (who have been using the forms of ANE religion for centuries by this stage)[360] have been strongly influenced by this belief system. Although they violate Yahweh's law (8:1) and reject the good he offers to those who obey him (8:3), they nevertheless believe they "know" (ידע, *yd‘*) God and are entitled to his protection (8:2).[361] According to the beliefs of ANE religion, the Israelites can indeed expect to enjoy Yahweh's favor, since they have not stopped making offerings to him (8:11–13). Yet a fundamental tenet of Yahwism is that "knowledge of God" (דעת אלהים, *da‘at ’elohim*) is something enjoyed only by covenant partners who obey his laws (4:1; 6:6; cf. Exod 19:4–6; Deut 28).[362] Israel has broken Yahweh's covenant and rebelled against his laws (8:1). Therefore, Yahweh flatly rejects their claim to know him (8:3b) and, along with it, the erroneous beliefs of ANE religion that lie behind it.

---

357. Stuart, *Exodus*, 451.

358. Walton, *Ancient*, 149.

359. Walton, *Ancient*, 184. See also Stuart, *Exodus*, 451.

360. The Bethel calf-idol was built during Jeroboam I's reign (some time between 922–901 BC). Most scholars date the oracle in Hosea 8 to around 733 BC. Wolff, *Hosea*, 137; Stuart, *Hosea*, 130.

361. Stuart, *Hosea*, 131; Birch, *Hosea*, 79.

362. Hwang, *Hosea*, 294; Birch, *Hosea*, 79.

Second, according to ANE religion, an idol manifested and mediated the deity's presence, thus permitting the worshiper access to divine presence. After an idol's construction was complete, a ritual was performed to "actualize the presence of the god" in the idol.[363] The idol or image was not considered to *be* the deity, but rather "the deity was the reality that was embodied in the image."[364] This *belief* regarding access to the divine presence seems to have been imported into Israel's worship of Yahweh along with the *form* of the calf-idol. In light of Yahweh's insistence in 8:6 that the calf-idol "is not God," we can infer that the Israelites have indeed come to believe that it is God, or at least that it mediates his presence in some way.[365] Thus the form of the idol has not been borrowed in isolation from the meaning associated with it. Because this meaning is contrary to the principles of true worship—the concept that Yahweh's presence could be mediated by an idol was abhorrent in Yahwism[366] —the result is a distortion of true worship.

Third, ANE religion did not emphasize the need for worshipers to manifest love for, or loyalty to, the gods.[367] Rather, what counted was the correct and precise performance of rituals believed to bring about the desired effect in an impersonal, cause-and-effect fashion.[368] External ritual observance was prioritized over internal motivations and attitudes of the heart.[369] In the book of Hosea, it is clear that this pagan belief system has infiltrated Israelite worship of Yahweh. This is hinted at in 8:13, where the word for the sacrifices that the Israelites offer Yahweh is "my love-things" (הַבְהָבַי, *havhavay*).[370] According to McComiskey, this choice of word reminds the reader that the offering was intended to represent "the heart attitude of the people."[371] Yahweh's refusal to accept the offering in 8:13 reveals that the people have failed to cultivate the right heart attitude.[372]

This motif of prioritizing external observation of ritual over appropriate inner attitudes is a significant theme in the book of Hosea. For

---

363. Walton, *Ancient*, 120–21, 158. See also Walker and Dick, *Induction*, 4; Hornung, *Conceptions*, 229.

364. Walton, *Ancient*, 158; Walker and Dick, *Induction*, 6.

365. Birch, *Hosea*, 79; Stuart, *Hosea*, 132. See generally Dick, "Prophetic," 1–53; Zevit, *Religions*, 524–26.

366. Exod 20:4–6; 32:1–34:35; Deut 9:7–21; Ps 106:19; Isa 40:19–20; 44:9–20

367. Birch, *Hosea*, 69; Walton, *Ancient*, 134–37.

368. Achtemeier, *Minor Prophets*, ch. 11; Nicholson, *God*, 194.

369. Birch, *Hosea*, 69.

370. The meaning of this word is contested. McComiskey proposes it is best understood as a noun from the verb "to love" (אהב, *'hv*). McComiskey, "Hosea," 133.

371. See McComiskey, "Hosea," 133.

372. McComiskey, "Hosea," 133; Stuart, *Hosea*, 136–37; Hwang, *Hosea*, 305–6.

example, in 6:4, Yahweh bemoans the fact that Israel's "love" or "loyalty" (חֶסֶד, *chesed*) is fleeting, and so in 6:5 he says that he has, by his prophets, announced judgment on the people.[373] Then in 6:6 he further explains the reason for the judgment:

> For I desire "love/loyalty" (חֶסֶד, *chesed*) and not sacrifice, the knowledge of God (דַּעַת אֱלֹהִים, *daʿat ʾelohim*) rather than burnt offerings.

חֶסֶד, *chesed* and דַּעַת אֱלֹהִים, *daʿat ʾelohim* are poetic complements that together describe Yahweh's expectation of his people being bound to him in love, trust, faithfulness and obedience.[374] What is required here is a sincere engagement of one's heart in love and loyalty which permeates all of life.[375] Yet the Israelites do not understand this. Instead, they have absorbed the beliefs associated with the pagan forms they have borrowed, leading them to believe that Yahweh can be "placated by the observation of religious externals" alone.[376] The people have "come to view Yahweh as they viewed the pagan gods"[377] and "confused Yahweh with Baal."[378] Stuart observes, "the people have understood worship as their Canaanite neighbors understood it, as limited to ritual acts of sacrifice."[379]

This motif appears again in 7:14. Here, Yahweh declares of the Israelites, "They do not cry out to me from their hearts" (7:14a). The Israelites do cry to Yahweh for help, but their cry is not בְּלִבָּם, *belibbam* (lit: "in/with the heart"), meaning it is not engaging their reason and emotion, and so is not relational and sincere.[380] Instead, they "wail on their beds" (7:14b). The reason they wail is explained in the following clause: "They slash themselves, appealing to their gods for (עַל, *ʿal*) grain and new wine" (7:14c). The sense of עַל, *ʿal* here is "in order to get."[381] This appears to be a reference to a ritual that the Israelites have borrowed from Baalism, whereby the petitioner self-lacerates in order to persuade or coerce the deity to provide blessing (cf. 1

---

373. McComiskey, "Hosea," 91; Hwang, *Hosea*, 256; Smith, *Hosea*, 112.
374. Nogalski, *Hosea*, 99; McComiskey, "Hosea," 91; Wolff, *Hosea*, 120.
375. McConville, *Exploring*, 146; Achtemeier, *Minor Prophets*, ch. 11.
376. McComiskey, "Hosea," 89.
377. McComiskey, "Hosea," 89.
378. Achtemeier, *Minor Prophets*, ch. 11.
379. Stuart, *Hosea*, 109–10.
380. Dearman, *Hosea*, 350; Achtemeier, *Minor Prophets*, ch. 16. In Hebrew thinking, לֵב, *lev* ("heart") refers to emotion, mind and will, and so to cry from the heart is to express "a total commitment of one's being." Simundson, *Hosea*, 65.
381. McComiskey, "Hosea," 115.

Kgs 18:28).³⁸² Therefore, tragically, a relational cry from the heart has been replaced by a non-relational wail of physical anguish from the bed.³⁸³ Rather than simply asking Yahweh for help, the Israelites are seeking to coerce him to bless them through a self-harming ritual. As Achtemeier observes: "Yahweh is worshipped as if he were Baal, with wailing and with self-torture."³⁸⁴

Yahweh's plaintive statement in 8:12, in which he bemoans the fact that his laws are regarded by the Israelites as a "strange" or "foreign" (זָר, *zar*) thing, functions as an apt summary of what has occurred. So thoroughly have pagan beliefs come to dominate Israelite thinking, that it is *Yahweh's* laws, not those of pagan gods, that seem strange and foreign. Smith writes,

> Since the people have adopted their theological understanding of sacrifice, dietary laws, the character of the divine, and appropriate social behavior from their Canaanite culture, God's instructions in the Torah seem strange and inapplicable in their setting.³⁸⁵

We have seen that the book of Hosea demonstrates the difficulty of separating a worship form from the meaning historically associated with it. Hosea does not explain whether the borrowing of pagan forms led immediately to the importation of pagan meanings, or whether the process occurred over time. What is clear is that by Hosea's day both the pagan forms *and* their associated meanings are present in Israel's worship, leading to a disastrous distortion of true worship. In this way, Hosea warns of a significant danger associated with using borrowed forms: the danger of foreign meanings also entering into the worship of God's people.

iii. Hosea 8 and the rest of the OT

Second Kings 17 affirms that the judgments prophesied in Hosea 8 did in fact take place: Israel is defeated by Assyria and the people are exiled. Not only that, but the author of Kings affirms, with Hosea, that this judgment takes place because "the Israelites persisted in all the sins of Jeroboam" (2 Kgs 17:22), that is, the Israelites persisted in worshiping Yahweh using the Bethel calf-idol.³⁸⁶

---

382. Hwang, *Hosea*, 277.
383. McComiskey, "Hosea," 115; Simundson, *Hosea*, 65.
384. Achtemeier, *Minor Prophets*, ch. 16.
385. Smith, *Hosea*, 136. See also Garrett, *Hosea*, 187.
386. 2 Kgs 17:22 brings to a climax a central theme in the book whereby Israel's following in the sins of Jeroboam inexorably leads it to judgment and exile: see 1 Kgs 14:16; 15:30; 16:31; 2 Kgs 10:29, 31; 13:2, 11; 14:24; 15:9, 18, 24, 28. Nogalski, *Hosea*,

That the terrible judgments announced in Hosea 8 did in fact come to pass only underscores the importance of the accusations against Israel in Hosea 8. This is confirmed by recognizing that a number of key elements of Hosea's critique also emerge in the writings of other OT prophets. For example, a number of other prophets present critiques of idol-worship which are similar to that in Hosea 8:6, with the essential idea being that the idol "is not God."[387] Also Hosea is not alone in his critique of the pagan "magical" approach to worship, by which properly performed rituals were thought to produce the desired outcome in a cause-and-effect manner regardless of the heart attitudes of the worshiper (6:4-6, 7:14, 8:13). Indeed, the same critique surfaces in the works of a number of other OT prophets.[388] Thus Hosea's theological message concerning the use of the forms of other faiths is affirmed and reinforced by other OT writers.

c. The meaning of the text for Christians today

Having identified the meaning of the text for the original audience, we now consider its meaning today.

i. Relevant redemptive-historical developments

In Hosea 8, a judgment is announced on the Israelites because, in their attempt to worship Yahweh, they have rejected the way he prescribed and incorporated human-designed ways modeled on the worship of the surrounding nations. Therefore for Israel, this oracle is a call to worship Yahweh exclusively in the way he makes possible and prescribes in the Torah, avoiding idols and unauthorized worship sites, and instead worshiping at the Jerusalem temple, using all the divinely prescribed apparatus of the OT cult. For new covenant readers who live in the age of the fulfilled cult (see chapter 3, §2.c.ii. above), it is a call to depend exclusively upon Christ, who is the God-given and God-prescribed way to obtain and maintain God's favor and blessing in this era. At the same time, it is a call to resist all human-designed worship that springs from a theology which depends on something other than Christ for blessing and favor.

119, 125.

387. See Jer 10:1-5; Isa 37:19; 43:12-17; 44:6-20. Dearman, *Hosea*, 223; Nogalski, *Hosea*, 119.

388. See Isa 1:10-17, 29:13-14; Amos 4:4-13, 5:21-25; Jer 7:21-26; Ezek 16:15-21; 20:25-31; Mic 6:6-8; Mal 1:6-14; 3:3-4, 10-12. Peterson, *Engaging*, 45; McConville, *Exploring*, 146; Nogalski, *Hosea*, 123; Nicholson, *God*, 201-17.

Notwithstanding the discontinuity brought about by the coming of Christ, the theological principles in Hosea 8 have ongoing application. These principles need to be considered and applied by new-covenant believers as they engage with God through dependence on Christ, including as they seek worship forms which best facilitate this Christ-dependence.[389]

Indeed, a number of key principles from the text are affirmed in the NT. For example, the principle that emerges in Hosea 8:1–3, where Yahweh rejects the Israelites' claim to "know" him on the basis that they have disobeyed him, is also reaffirmed in the NT (John 8:39–44, 55).[390] Indeed, 1 John 2:4 is almost a summary of Hosea 8:1–3:

> Whoever says, "I know him," but does not do what he commands is a liar.

As another example, Hosea's polemic against a pagan-style external ritualism that ignores heart attitudes is picked up by Jesus himself when he quotes Hosea 6:6 in his critique of the Pharisees (Matthew 9:13, 12:7).[391] Thus the principles in Hosea 8 have ongoing relevance today and need therefore to be considered by new covenant believers when selecting worship forms.

ii. The implications of Hosea 8 for the IM debate

We now consider this text in relation to the IM debate.

The forms used by the Israelites in Hosea 8 are different from those being proposed for use in contextualized worship by IM proponents. Nevertheless, this text is relevant to the IM debate because it deals with an attempt by God's people to use the forms of other faiths to worship the true God. The fact that Hosea 8 contains such a scathing polemic against the Israelites' use of foreign forms, accompanied by such a devastating judgment, underlines the importance of carefully reflecting upon the oracle's implications for today.

1. Hosea 8 is not a blanket prohibition on using the forms of other faiths, but it does warn of the dangers

Hosea 8 is not a blanket prohibition on the use of the forms of other faiths by God's people. Certainly, Hosea sharply critiques the Israelites' use of

---

389. Smith, *Hosea*, 140–41.
390. Garrett, *Hosea*, 181.
391. Smith, *Hosea*, 113.

certain borrowed forms in this text. But this cannot be generalized as a prohibition on all usage of borrowed forms. The ultimate problem with the Israelites' worship is not simply that the forms of other faiths are used, but that the worship is disobedient and a rejection of God-given worship. What is prohibited, then, is attempting to worship God in any way other than the God-given way.

The role of the forms of other faiths is that they are the means by which the sin is committed. As such, even though Hosea 8 is not a blanket prohibition on using borrowed forms, it is a warning concerning the dangers associated with using them. This is explored further below.

2. Other Implications for the IM Debate

Five other implications of Hosea 8 for the IM debate are identified here.

First, the borrowed forms are resisted in Hosea 8 because they have a corrupting impact on true worship. Using the borrowed forms amounts to a violation of God's laws regarding worship, a rejection of his way to worship, and allows for the importation of meanings contrary to the principles of true worship. Although worship requirements have changed in the new covenant era, Hosea 8—like Exodus 32–34 and Deuteronomy 12—highlights the importance of making a *biblical theology of worship* a key frame of reference when seeking to evaluate the helpfulness of a particular borrowed form. Therefore, it is proposed that rather than simply asking whether using a particular Muslim form takes the contextualization process too far,[392] or crosses the line into syncretism[393] (as is often done in the IM debate), a more fruitful and biblically-grounded approach is to ask what is the likely (or proven) impact of using the form on true worship.

Second, a key principle to emerge in Hosea 8 (and indeed, in all the texts studied so far) is that true worship is God-given: it occurs only when God's people engage with him in the way he makes possible, according to the terms he sets. I propose, therefore, that a key question when considering the usefulness of a worship form is whether it is likely to facilitate or hinder the worship of God *in the way he himself has directed*. Since for new covenant believers, this involves faith in Christ, expressed in continuing dependence and obedience (see chapter 3, §3.c.ii. above), a vital question is whether Muslim forms are likely to facilitate or hinder this.

Third, Hosea 8 highlights the real possibility that borrowed forms can have a "Trojan horse"-type function, in that they can facilitate the

---

392. Racey, "How Far," 304.
393. Parshall, "My Thirty Year Odyssey," 86.

importation of dangerous meanings which distort true worship—even where they are *intended* as vehicles for the worship of the one true God. An implication is that form-selectors need to ask whether there are any meanings known to be attached to the forms which would undermine or contradict the principles of true worship. For example, has a particular form been associated with a belief that worship is something people do in order to earn divine favor and blessing? If so, the warning of Hosea 8 is that the form could distort and undermine true worship.

Fourth, by highlighting the dangers of unwanted meanings being imported along with borrowed forms, Hosea 8 affirms Hiebert's claim that forms cannot always be divorced from meaning in the contextualizing process, and that it can be unrealistic to expect that a particular form can be stripped of the meaning previously given to it by the worshiper—especially if that meaning is still given to it by the dominant group in society.[394] Hosea 8 also demonstrates the shortcomings of Kraft's claim that most forms, including forms from other faiths, are "neutral vehicles" which can be invested with new meanings and so can facilitate meaningful, culturally appropriate worship.[395] Hosea 8 actually paints a very different picture. In Hosea 8, the meanings historically associated with the borrowed pagan forms are present in Israel's worship, despite the people's intention to use them in worship of Yahweh. In fact, since Hosea's oracle was delivered after almost 200 years of unbroken worship by the Israelites at the Bethel calf-idol (see chapter 3, §4.b.ii.3. above), Hosea 8 gives an especially valuable insight into the long-term impact of the forms of other faiths. The impact has been devastating. By Hosea's day, the worldview of the Israelites is so drenched in pagan meanings and theology that Yahweh is treated *as if he were merely a Canaanite fertility or nature god*, and his own laws have become a strange and foreign thing (8:12). Hosea 8's warning needs to be heard in the IM debate. Form-selectors must consider whether the sustained use of Muslim forms by believers in a Muslim-majority context might lead to a similar outcome.

Fifth, Hosea 8 further highlights the shortcomings of Kraft's emphasis on allegiance. Kraft focuses attention in the contextualization process upon the matter of allegiance by suggesting that almost any forms can be used in Christian worship, provided the allegiance is correct (chapter 1, §3.c.i. above). Without denying that allegiance to the true God is essential, it is proposed here that this is an unhelpful focus. It is unhelpful because,

---

394. Hiebert, "Form," 106–10.

395. Kraft, *Christianity in Culture* (1979), 95, 99; Kraft, *Christianity in Culture* (2005), 233; Kraft, *Anthropology*, 35; Kraft, "Dynamic Equivalent," 115.

as we have seen in Hosea 8, worship directed to the true God (and so with the correct allegiance) can still be false worship that is unacceptable, even detestable, to God.

A compounding problem is that a focus on allegiance may give rise to a false sense of security. As we saw above, the Israelites' use of borrowed forms amounted to sin which elicited divine wrath rather than divine favor. The problem was that because the Israelites continued to express allegiance to Yahweh by offering worship to him, they believed themselves to be safe from judgment. Thus the Israelites labored under a false sense of security, thinking there was no need to pursue change, when in fact change was desperately needed. Hosea 8 depicts a people who believe they know God and enjoy his favor because their allegiance is to him, but in reality, use of the borrowed forms has rendered their worship false, and so they face destruction and divine rejection.

A focus on allegiance has the potential to create a similar sense of false security today, in that worshipers might satisfy themselves that their worship is directed to the true God (because it is in the name of Jesus), but fail to give adequate attention to the question of whether they are engaging God in the way he makes possible (that is, through faith in Christ, expressed in continuing dependence and obedience). A better focus than that of allegiance is worship. If the focus is on worship, form-selectors are not simply concerned to ensure that they are worshiping the true God, but also that they are worshiping him in the way he directs. The critical question becomes whether a given form *facilitates* or *hinders* such worship. This test better reflects the concerns in the biblical text. Thus a series of important implications for the IM debate arises out of Hosea 8.

5. Conclusion

In this chapter, we have studied three OT resistance texts. A consistent picture has emerged. While none of the texts can be characterized as a blanket prohibition on the use by new-covenant believers of the forms of other faiths, each one does contain strong warnings of inherent dangers.

In chapters 2 and 3, we have studied two sets of OT texts that are apparently in tension with one another: those which appear to permit the appropriation of the forms of other faiths (chapter 2), and those which appear to resist it (chapter 3). According to IM proponent Talman, this tension can be resolved by looking at the *nature of the form*. He proposes that in the OT, the positive elements of other religions are appropriated, while the negative ones are rejected.[396] However, in our analysis, we have read the texts in light of their salvation-historical setting, and seen that during the OT era (unlike during the NT era), forms are largely divinely prescribed. Once we recognize this, it becomes clear that the key to resolving the tension is not by evaluating the *nature of the form*, but rather by considering *who is making the form-selection*. In the OT appropriation texts, *God* selects the forms, whereas in the OT resistance texts it is *God's people* who select the forms. When God chooses a foreign form for use in worship, that form is acceptable because God has chosen it. When Israel does the same thing, the form is not acceptable, because Israel has chosen it. Thus what distinguishes the two sets of texts is not the nature of the form (whether it is deemed positive or negative), but rather whether the form is chosen by God or by people.

Far from being in tension, all six OT texts actually affirm the same principles: that under the old covenant, it is God's prerogative to select worship forms, and, more broadly, that true worship is God-given. This latter principle has ongoing relevance in the new covenant age, and is crucial to the development of a biblically grounded approach to contextualization. In selecting forms, new covenant believers must seek those that help them to engage with God in the way he directs and makes possible.

As we shall now see, this same principle emerges in the NT appropriation and resistance texts.

---

396. Talman, "Old Testament," 49–52.

4

New Testament Appropriation Texts

1. Introduction

WE NOW TURN TO NT appropriation texts. The analysis of the first two NT appropriation texts, Acts 2–7 and Acts 15, is presented in this chapter, while the analysis of the third NT appropriation text, 1 Corinthians 8–10, appears in the next. Acts 15 and 1 Corinthians 8–10 have been claimed by both IM proponents and IM critics as texts which give support to their respective positions, and so these two texts are studied in this book as both appropriation and resistance texts. To avoid unnecessary duplication, the analysis of these texts is not broken into two separate sections. Rather, the full analysis of Acts 15 is presented in this chapter, while the full analysis of 1 Corinthians 8–10 is presented in the next. In this way, the Acts texts are grouped together in chapter 4, and the Pauline texts in chapter 5. The goal of this chapter, as with previous chapters, is to identify the message of the biblical author as it relates to the use of the forms of other faiths, and then identify the implications for the IM debate.

2. Acts 2–7 and temple worship

The first NT appropriation text is Acts 2:42—7:60 as it relates to temple worship. This text describes a series of incidents in the life of the early church in which the temple is consistently in the foreground. Although 2:42—7:60 undoubtedly contains a series of smaller units, because the extended section describes a building conflict between the believing community and the temple authorities, climaxing in Stephen's martyrdom, many have stressed the importance of reading it as a single, larger unit in order to grasp Luke's literary and theological purposes.[1] For this reason, 2:42—7:60 as an ex-

---

1. Tannehill, *Acts*,64–79; Witherington, *Acts*, 228; Peterson, *Acts*, 244; Thompson,

tended unit is analyzed here, notwithstanding the fact that the texts which have been advanced in the context of the IM debate are just a handful of individual texts from within this unit.

a. The relevance of the text to the research problem

Acts 2:42—7:60 is relevant for our purposes because texts from this extended narrative (2:42, 46; 3:1; 5:12, 42) have been put forward by IM proponents as depicting believers from a Jewish background participating in temple worship, and so using the forms of another faith (Judaism). IM proponents propose that these texts are biblical precedents which give permission to BMBs to use Muslim worship forms today.[2] We begin our analysis of this claim by investigating, first, whether the Jewish forms can rightly be characterized as "forms of another faith," and second, whether the Jewish followers of Jesus as Christ (hereafter, Jewish believers) do in fact use the forms.

i. Can the Jewish forms be characterized as "forms of another faith"?

Unlike the pagan forms discussed in chapters 2 and 3, the forms in question here (the Jerusalem temple and its associated sacrifices and other rituals) are forms which God gave to his people in Scripture.[3] In this respect, they are not forms of another faith but rather are forms from the same Yahwistic faith. However, in the new covenant era, God's people are no longer required to use these forms: with the coming of Christ, they are fulfilled and rendered obsolete.[4] At the same time, in Acts, Jews who do not follow Jesus as Christ (hereafter, non-believing Jews) continue to use the forms as prescribed forms of their faith (Judaism). Therefore, while technically these are forms from an earlier era of the same faith, functionally, they are forms of another faith (in that they are used by non-believing Jews), and may be treated as such for the purposes of this research.

Acts, 145–73.

2. Higgins, "Identity," 118, 122; Higgins, "Key," 158–59; Higgins, "Inside What?," 77–80; Higgins, "Acts 15," 37–38; Ridgway, "Insider," 81; Roberts and Jameson, "Conversion," 202–3; Caldwell, "Jesus in Samaria," 30; Lewis, "Honoring," 18; Lewis, "Integrity," 42; Travis, "Messianic," 54–55; Talman, "Islam," 12 (see n18).

3. See Lev 1–7, 12–16, 22–24; Num 6–8, 15, 18, 28–30; Deut 12–18, 21–26; 1 Kgs 5–8; 1 Chr 22–29; 2 Chr 2–7.

4. See chapter 4, §2.b.ii. and iii. below and Thompson, *Acts*, 145–73. Of course, it may have taken believers a period of time to appreciate the implications of Christ's work in this regard.

ii. Do the Jewish believers use the Jewish forms?

However, there are considerable doubts concerning whether the Jewish believers do in fact *use* the Jewish forms in these texts. The IM precedent argument is based on the understanding that 2:42, 46; 3:1; 5:12 and 5:42 depict Jewish believers participating in temple worship.[5] Higgins, for example, writes that the church in Acts "remained within the religious expressions of the people of Israel, continuing to attend the Temple."[6] He proposes that these Jewish believers are members of an "insider movement" who fully participate in Jewish worship, notwithstanding the fact that such worship "was not led by believers and was not supportive of the new community's faith in Jesus as the Messiah and Lord."[7] IM proponents are not alone in concluding that Acts depicts early Jewish Christians participating in temple worship. Many writing outside the field of missiology draw the same conclusion. For example, Chilton concludes that the early Jewish believers "participated in the cult in the manner of devoted, nonpriestly Israelites."[8] However, Thompson's caution in this regard is apposite: he stresses the need to observe "what Luke does and does not say about the believers and the temple."[9] In fact, as we shall now see, a close examination of these texts reveals that Luke *never actually states that the believers participate in temple worship.*

Luke provides two broad summaries of the believers' activities in the temple precincts (2:42–47 and 5:12–16). Significantly, he makes no mention of participation in the sacrificial cult in either summary.[10] Indeed, all mentions of the believers' activities at the temple in this section are references to their activities at "the temple precincts" (ἱερόν, *hieron*), not at the "temple sanctuary" (ναός, *naos*).[11]

What then does Luke say concerning the believers' activities in the temple precincts? According to 2:42, the believers are devoted to "the

---

5. Higgins, "Identity," 118, 122; Higgins, "Key," 158–59; Higgins, "Inside What?," 77–80; Higgins, "Acts 15," 37–38; Ridgway, "Insider," 81; Roberts and Jameson, "Conversion," 202–3; Caldwell, "Jesus in Samaria," 30; Lewis, "Honoring," 18; Lewis, "Integrity," 42; Travis, "Messianic," 54–55; Talman, "Islam," 12 (see n18).

6. Higgins, "Inside What?," 77–78.

7. Higgins, "Key," 159.

8. Chilton, "Temple," 1162. For other similar conclusions, see Chance, *Jerusalem*, 36, 82–85; Barrett, "Attitudes," 347–50.

9. Thompson, *Acts*, 152. See also Blomberg, "Christian," 402. Lucan authorship of Luke-Acts is assumed in this book. For a discussion of the authorship of Acts, see Bock, *Acts*, 15–19; Peterson, *Acts*, 1–4; Keener, *Acts*, 1:402–16.

10. Thompson, *Acts*, 152; Scobie, *Ways*, 592; Hahn, *Worship*, 43.

11. Thompson, *Acts*, 145, 152. See further, Head, "Temple," 106–9.

prayers" (ταῖς προσευχαῖς, *tais proseuchais*).[12] Higgins takes this as a reference to the "prescribed prayers in the temple."[13] While Higgins's interpretation is possible,[14] "the prayers" could equally refer to the believers' "own appointed seasons for united prayer."[15] It is far from certain that this is a reference to participation in set temple prayers.

According to 2:46, the believers "continued together" (προσκαρτεροῦντες ὁμοθυμαδὸν, *proskarterountes homothumadon*) in the temple precincts. There is no hint here of participation with non-believing Jews in temple worship. Rather, 2:46 simply describes a gathering of believers in the temple precincts. Indeed, Luke's comment that the believers enjoy "the favor of all the people" (2:47) implies that they are identifiable as a separate group. It seems that their distinctive activities (2:42-45) have earned them a distinctive reputation.

According to 3:1, Peter and John go to the temple "at the time of prayer." This is a reference to the prayer service that accompanied the time for afternoon sacrifice (the *Tamid*) at the temple.[16] Importantly, Luke does not say that they go there for the purpose of participating in those temple prayers or sacrifices. It is *possible* that they have such a motive, but any such conclusion is based on speculation.

According to 5:12, the believers (or the apostles)[17] "gathered together" (ὁμοθυμαδὸν πάντες, *homothumadon pantes*) in the temple. Again, this text does not depict believers joining with non-believing Jews for worship. On the contrary, 5:13 makes it clear that the apostles are held in such awe that non-believing Jews do not dare draw near to them. Once again, they have a reputation as a distinct group.

Finally, 5:42 affirms that the apostles preach daily in the temple courts. Again, there is no hint here that they join with non-believing Jews in temple worship, nor that they use other Jewish worship forms. As Thompson notes,

> The *only* activity Luke records the believers doing in the temple in this context is proclaiming Jesus (4:2; 5:20, 25, 42). Thus it must be acknowledged that to see anything more in Luke's

---

12. The plural form with the article suggests that the reference is to specific, regular prayer times, rather than to prayer generally. Peterson, *Acts*, 162; Keener, *Acts*, 1:1011.

13. Higgins, "Key," 158.

14. Peterson, *Acts*, 162; Keener, *Acts*, 1:1011.

15. Bruce, *Acts*, 73. See also Bock, *Acts*, 151.

16. See Exod 29:38-41; Num 24:8. Witherington, *Acts*, 173; Keener, *Acts*, 2:1044-47; Peterson, *Acts*, 167.

17. See Bock, *Acts*, 230; Peterson, *Acts*, 214.

references to the believers' activity in the temple courts in Acts 2–5 is to read more into Acts than Luke himself has said.[18]

Thus throughout Acts 2–7, Luke never explicitly states that the believers participate in any elements of temple worship. Any conclusion that they do so is based on *conjecture*, and goes against the clear statements in the text that the believers formed a distinctive group, quite separate from non-believing Jews, and used the temple precincts to carry out their own activities.

The speculative nature of the conclusion that the believers participate in temple worship is evident in the tone used by those who make this claim. Barrett writes that it is "implied, though not actually stated" that Peter and John participate in temple worship.[19] Witherington suggests that the believers "probably" participated in temple worship.[20] Walton claims, "while *Luke does not explicitly say* that they go to pray, *it does look as though* he presents the apostles acting as devout Jews."[21] The text does not permit firm conclusions here.

Further, it is unnecessary to conclude from the fact of the believers' daily presence at the temple (2:46; 5:12, 42) that they are there to participate in temple worship, since their presence can be explained in other ways. Bock proposes that the believers meet there simply because it is a "known locale," and so "people know where to come."[22] Peterson suggests that they meet at the temple precincts because they provide an open space to gather.[23] Keener agrees, pointing out that the temple precincts provided the largest available open space in Jerusalem, and that there was a well established practice of special interest groups holding meetings there.[24] Others highlight the temple as the most strategic place for witness (indeed, in 5:20, they are commanded to go there *to preach*).[25] Of course, these suggestions are also speculations. The point is that the believers might have had other reasons for gathering in the temple precincts, and so we cannot deduce from their presence there that they necessarily participate in temple worship.

In conclusion then, contrary to the assertions of many, Acts 2–7 does not depict the people of God using Jewish worship forms. This is not to say that, historically speaking, such participation did not occur. Whether there

---

18. Thompson, *Acts*, 152–53.
19. Barrett, "Attitudes," 347.
20. Witherington, *Acts*, 163, 173.
21. Walton, "Tale," 136 (emphasis added).
22. Bock, *Acts*, 230.
23. Peterson, *Acts*, 163.
24. Keener, *Acts*,1:1031–32.
25. Witherington, *Acts*, 163; Peterson, *Acts*, 167; Blomberg, "Christian," 402.

is extra-biblical evidence that early Christians worshiped at the temple is another matter altogether, and is beyond the scope of this study. The goal here is to identify Luke's literary and theological purposes, and so articulate scriptural teaching on the issue. It is not to make historical enquiries as to the nature of early Christian worship practices, which, after all, may or may not have been in accord with God's plan for the church.

b. The meaning of the text for the original audience

i. Is there evidence in the text that the author is seeking to persuade readers to use the forms of their pre-conversion faith?

IM proponents claim that the texts which they cite from Acts 2–7 are precedents justifying the use by believers today of the forms of their pre-conversion faiths. For example, on the basis of these texts, IM proponent Higgins claims,

> a biblical precedent exists for new believers from Islam to remain in the mosque and continue to practice other religious expressions of Islamic life.[26]

The claim is thus based on an analogy: just as (so it is asserted) the early Jewish believers used Jewish worship forms, so too BMBs today can use Muslim forms.

As we saw in chapter 1 (chapter 1, §4.b.iii.), whether a text can be treated as a precedent ultimately depends upon whether evidence can be found in the text that the author intends it to function that way. Therefore, at issue here is whether there is evidence in Acts 2–7 that Luke's depiction of Jewish believers at the temple is aimed at persuading, first, Jewish believers to use Jewish forms, and second, readers from other faith backgrounds to use the forms of their previous faiths by analogy. As the following analysis bears out, no such evidence can be found.

Regarding Jewish believers, we begin by noting that temple participation might not even have been a possibility for Luke's original readers, given that Acts might well have been written after the temple's destruction in 70 AD.[27] But even if it was written before 70 AD, as demonstrated above, at no point in Acts 2–7 does Luke explicitly state that the early Jewish believers participate in temple worship. Any conclusion that they do participate

---

26. Higgins, "Key," 158.

27. Well-supported proposals for the date of Acts range from 64 to 90 AD, that is, from before and after the temple's destruction. Keener, *Acts*, 1:383–401.

is based on conjecture. It is therefore not possible to mount the case that Luke's purpose was to persuade Jewish believers to use Jewish forms. Surely if that had been his purpose, he would not have left the question of whether the believers actually use the forms to mere speculation. The fact that the text is not clear as to whether the forms were actually used, combined with the evident literary and persuasive skill of Luke as an author, makes it clear that he did not have this purpose in mind.

In making the biblical precedent argument from Acts 2–7, some IM proponents refer to the conclusions of certain historians that some Jewish believers did in fact participate in temple and synagogue worship for 50 years or more after the resurrection.[28] However, in light of the methodological assumptions in this book (chapter 1, §4.a. above) that the Bible as God's inspired Word is to be given a normative role in shaping theological understanding and ministry methodology (and not the actual historical practice of some Christians), this historical evidence is not relevant here. Our purpose is to identify what message Luke sought to convey regarding the temple. While some early Jewish believers may have continued to participate in the temple cult, this *historical* fact sheds no light on the *theological* question of whether such participation was in accord with God's will and plan for them.[29]

Regarding readers from other faith backgrounds, given that there is no evidence of an authorial intention to persuade Jewish believers to use Jewish forms, it follows that there is no evidence of an intention to persuade readers from other faiths to use the forms from their pre-conversion faiths by analogy. If the argument with respect to Jewish believers fails, then clearly the analogy fails too.

ii. What then is the author's purpose?

If Luke's purpose in Acts 2:42–7:60 is not to encourage the use of the forms of other faiths, what is it? Having noted that the view that Jewish believers participate in temple worship is based on reading "more into Acts than Luke himself has said," Thompson goes on to write,

---

28. Higgins, "Inside What?," 79; Higgins, "Identity," 118, 122; Massey, "Planting," 140. Higgins cites Whitacre's conclusion that Christians only separated from the temple and synagogue some 50 years after the events of Acts 2–7. See Whitacre, *John*, 244.

29. On the historical evidence, including a discussion of the parting of the ways between Christians and Jews, see Bauckham, "Parting," 135–51. For a discussion of the implications of the historical evidence for the IM debate, see Coleman, *Analysis*, 198–211.

It would be more fruitful to examine the narrative itself to see what Luke is emphasizing in this context.[30]

When we do this, it emerges that Luke's literary and theological purposes with respect to the temple are actually *strongly at odds* with the IM precedent argument. In Acts 2–7, far from encouraging Jewish believers to *participate* in temple worship, Luke is actually announcing the *end* of the temple system. His purpose is to show that Jesus fulfills and replaces the temple, and that the apostles replace the existing temple leadership. As Thompson explains,

> Simply put, the book of Acts highlights the end of the old temple system and law and the inauguration of a new 'authority structure' in the inaugurated kingdom of God by virtue of Jesus' lordship and the authority of his 'authorized delegates', the apostles.[31]

Scholarship regarding Luke's attitude to the temple is divided and a range of views exists. This stems from the fact that Acts 2–7 seems to contain two conflicting sets of texts: so-called "pro-temple" and "anti-temple" texts.[32] For example, the early believers gather daily at the temple (Acts 2–5), yet Stephen appears to be critical of it (Acts 7).[33] This has led some to conclude that Acts contains no coherent or consistent view of the temple.[34] Others downplay or reinterpret the "anti-temple" texts, and so conclude that Luke intends to convey an essentially positive view of the temple and to uphold its ongoing significance.[35] Still others suggest that the apparently conflicting attitudes reflect the historical process that early Christians went through as they came to understand the implications of Christ's death for the temple.[36] However, the view outlined above—that Luke is actually announcing that Jesus fulfills and replaces the temple—best accounts for the data. What we have in these texts is not "thoughtless" inconsistency on Luke's behalf[37] or conflicting views amongst early believers, but rather a seismic salvation-historical transition: Luke both upholds the temple as a God-given institution that pointed to Jesus, but at the same time, he

---

30. Thompson, *Acts*, 153.
31. Thompson, *Acts*, 145. Cf. Peterson, *Engaging*, 137.
32. Thompson, *Acts*, 145–46.
33. See Walton, "Tale," 136–44.
34. Barrett, "Attitudes," 355–65.
35. See Sylva, "Meaning," 261–75; Hurtado, *Lord*, 195–96; Chance, *Jerusalem*, 35–45.
36. Witherington, *Acts*, 163, 173; Peterson, *Acts*, 167.
37. Barrett, "Attitudes," 361.

announces that, with the coming of the one that the temple anticipated, the temple's time has come.[38] We will now consider the major sections in Acts 2–7 consecutively to substantiate this view.

Luke signals that important temple-related changes are afoot as early as 2:1–13. In the tongues of fire descending on the believers (2:3), there appears to be an allusion to previous key moments in salvation history where God's glory descends for the purpose of dwelling with his people: at Sinai (Exod 19:16–25), upon the tabernacle (Exod 40:34) and upon the temple (1 Kgs 8:10).[39] Indeed, just as Yahweh's glory once "filled" the tabernacle (Exod 40:34), and "filled the house" of Yahweh (1 Kgs 8:10), so too now a "sound like the blowing of a violent wind . . . filled the whole house" where the believers gather (Acts 2:2).[40] Perrin explains the significance:

> For Luke, then, Pentecost signaled the onset of a new epoch in salvation-history, and the end of the order under the current temple.[41]

That Luke has something important to say about the temple in the following section is suggested by its structure. Acts 2:46 and 5:42 are almost identical (both refer to the believers' activities at the *temple* and in their *homes*) and so act as a frame for the section. The "framed" material consists of events at the temple (3:1—4:22), at believers' homes (4:23—5:11), then at the temple again (5:12–41).[42] As Spencer notes, this "*spatial* antithesis between public temple and private house" is accompanied by a "*social* conflict between temple authorities and church leaders."[43] Through this structure, Luke contrasts the old order (the temple and its leadership) with the new (Jesus and the apostles), and demonstrates that the former is now replaced by the latter.

Acts 3:1–10 concerns a man who is lame and who is therefore excluded from the temple.[44] Whereas others in the story are going "into" (εἰς, *eis*) the temple (3:1–3), he is outside "at" (πρὸς, *pros*) the gate (3:2, 10), unable to participate in and benefit from the social and cultic activity that takes place inside.[45] Yet when he is healed in Jesus' name, he goes "into the temple"

---

38. Thompson, *Acts*, 147, 171–72. For other articulations of this view, see Bruce, *Acts*, 157; McKelvey, "Temple," 806–11; Schreiner, *Magnifying*, 633–34.
39. Perrin, *Jesus*, 63; Beale, *Temple*, 204–6; Fitzmyer, *Acts*, 234.
40. Perrin, *Jesus*, 63.
41. Perrin, *Jesus*, 63.
42. Thompson, *Acts*, 151–52.
43. Spencer, *Acts*, 42.
44. See Lev 21:17–20; 2 Sam 5:8. Witherington, *Acts*, 173–74; Bock, *Acts*, 162.
45. Thompson, *Acts*, 153–54.

(εἰς τὸ ἱερὸν, *eis to hieron*) with the others for the very first time (3:8).⁴⁶ His dramatic entry amounts to a "leaping over temple boundaries,"⁴⁷ intimating that Jesus is now providing that which the temple could not.⁴⁸ In this way, the healing highlights "the inadequacy of the temple system together with the overcoming of that old-system inadequacy through Jesus."⁴⁹

Peter's subsequent explanation of the miracle in 3:11–26 reinforces this understanding. Peter declares that *all* the promised blessings from God—promises made to Abraham (3:25), Moses (3:22), David (3:18, 20, 24) and through "all the prophets" (3:18, 21, 24)—are now fulfilled in, and available exclusively through, Jesus (3:19, 21, 25–26).⁵⁰ In the past, the temple was the place where forgiveness of sins was found; now it is Jesus (3:19–20).⁵¹ Importantly, Peter repeatedly uses the phrase "the name of Jesus" (3:6, 16; cf. 4:7, 10, 12, 17, 18, 30; 5:28, 40, 41).⁵² In the OT, God's people appealed to "the name of Yahweh," and it was to the temple that these appeals were directed, since the temple was "a house for the name of Yahweh."⁵³ Yet now such appeals are to be made to "the name of Jesus," who provides all the blessings hoped for during the OT era.⁵⁴ Thus the inadequacy of the temple (3:1–10) is contrasted with the all-sufficiency of Jesus, who is depicted as the one who brings to fulfillment all that the temple and the other OT institutions anticipated and pointed to (3:11–26).⁵⁵ Franklin writes,

> The miracle in the Temple points to the fulfillment of its life in Jesus so that now the 'name' of Jesus brings that salvation to

---

46. The term used for his "complete healing" (ὁλοκληρίαν, *holoklērian*) (3:16) appeared in the LXX to refer to unblemished animals offered in sacrifice. Thus the man has gone from a blemished and excluded outcast, to one who is recognized inside the temple as whole and unblemished. Witherington, *Acts*, 182.

47. Spencer, *Journeying*, 55.

48. Witherington, *Acts*, 176; Bock, *Acts*, 158.

49. Thompson, *Acts*, 154.

50. Franklin, *Christ the Lord*, 101; Thompson, *Acts*, 156–57; Bock, *Acts*, 158, 165; Witherington, *Acts*, 179–80.

51. Walton, "Tale," 145.

52. Peterson, *Acts*, 166; Spencer, *Journeying*, 57; Thompson, *Acts*, 157–58.

53. See 1 Kgs 8:17–61. The temple is a "house for the name of Yahweh": 1 Kgs 5:3, 5; 8:17, 20; 1 Chr 22:7, 19; 2 Chr 2:1, 4; 6:7, 10. Throughout his prayer of dedication, Solomon speaks of people praying "toward this temple" or "toward this place": 1 Kgs 8:29, 30, 35, 38, 42, 44, 48; 2 Chr 6:20, 21, 26, 29, 32, 34, 38. Thompson, *Acts*, 158–59.

54. Thompson, *Acts*, 159; Franklin, *Christ the Lord*, 102; Walton, "Tale," 145; Ziesler, "Name," 28–41.

55. Thompson, *Acts*, 159.

which the manifestation of the divine name in the Temple had been a pointer.[56]

Likewise, Peterson explains,

> Preaching about the centrality of the exalted Christ in God's plans for Israel was a way of indicating that Jesus fulfils and replaces the temple and the whole structure of worship associated with it.[57]

If Jesus replaces the temple, this has important implications for the existing temple leadership. Luke turns to this matter in 4:1–22, which depicts a power struggle between the temple leadership, on the one hand, and Jesus and the apostles, on the other.[58] Feeling threatened, the temple leaders arrest Peter and John (4:2–3), yet they are powerless to stop the apostles from preaching (4:19–20), or the people from believing (4:4, 21–22).[59] Peter then announces to the temple leaders that Jesus is "the stone you builders rejected, which has become the cornerstone" (4:11). This is an allusion to Psalm 118:22, which refers to the temple, and thus the claim is unmistakable: "Christ is now the cornerstone of the new temple."[60] Whereas the temple used to be the place where the name of God was found, and where humanity could be united with God, now it is replaced by Jesus: "There is no other name under heaven given to mankind by which we must be saved" (4:12).[61] It is in Jesus, not the temple leadership, that this authority now resides.[62] Thus, "there is now no need for the old temple system and its leadership, as both have come to an end for the true people of God."[63] Indeed, the situation is yet more serious for the temple leadership: not only has their role come to an end, but in rejecting Christ (4:13–18), they themselves are cut off from the people of God (3:22–23).[64]

In 4:23—5:42, Luke demonstrates that in this new era, it is believers who are the true people of God, and it is the apostles (not the temple authorities)

---

56. Franklin, *Christ the Lord*, 100 (see also 100–102).

57. Peterson, *Engaging*, 139.

58. The three groups mentioned in 4:1 (the priests, the temple guard, and the Sadducees) "all had close connections with the temple and had a vested interest in what went on in its precincts." Witherington, *Acts*, 189.

59. Witherington, *Acts*, 190.

60. Beale, *Temple*, 216.

61. Walton, "Tale," 145.

62. Thompson, *Acts*, 161.

63. Thompson, *Acts*, 161.

64. Peterson, *Acts*, 186; Bock, *Acts*, 184.

who are the leaders of God's people.[65] In 4:23, a sharp distinction is made between those worshiping at the temple (especially the temple authorities) and the believers, when Luke writes that Peter and John return "to their own people." In the prayer that follows, it is this latter group which is identified as the true people of God (they are the Isaianic suffering servant), whereas the temple leadership is identified with those who oppose God (4:24–30; cf. Ps 2).[66] Moreover, the locus of God's presence is no longer the temple, but instead it is where the true people of God gather: "When they prayed, the place where they were meeting was shaken. And they were all filled with the Holy Spirit" (4:31).[67] This is reinforced in 4:32—5:42, with a series of miracles *outside* the temple. Walton notes that "God acts outside the Temple. . . . God's presence and activity is not tied to the Temple."[68]

Just as the believers are the new people of God and the new "place" where God dwells, so too the apostles are depicted as the true leaders of this people: they teach with authority (4:33; 5:20, 25, 28, 42), oversee the distribution of resources (4:34–35), enact discipline (5:1–11), perform miraculous signs (5:12–16), and appoint people to roles within the church (6:1–7).[69] At the same time the powerlessness of the "old guard" (the temple leadership) is comically portrayed: they imprison the apostles, and are baffled to find a locked and guarded empty jail (5:22–24), not realizing that the miraculously freed apostles are already preaching once again in the very place that the temple authorities are supposed to control—the temple (5:25)! Thus the apostles here "emerge as leaders of a renewed Israel, whose ministry is profoundly threatening to the old order."[70] The temple leadership, by contrast, is portrayed as people who have not received the Holy Spirit (5:32), and who fight against God (5:39).[71]

Luke brings to a climax the dual themes of the replacement of the temple leadership and of the temple in his account of Stephen's speech and martyrdom in 6:8—7:60. Regarding the temple leadership, their fate is sealed here. Stephen depicts them as standing in a long line of people who have rejected God's purposes and messengers.[72] Although they have accused Stephen of being "against Moses" (6:11), in reality, they are the ones who are against

---

65. Thompson, *Acts*, 162.
66. Thompson, *Acts*, 161–62.
67. Walton, "Tale," 145.
68. Walton, "Tale," 146–47.
69. Thompson, *Acts*, 162–63.
70. Peterson, *Acts*, 186.
71. Witherington, *Acts*, 232; Bock, *Acts*, 244.
72. Thompson, *Acts*, 168; Peterson, *Acts*, 264–65.

Moses, since they have rejected the one to whom Moses and the law pointed (7:51–53; cf. 7:27, 35, 39).[73] They prove the truth of Stephen's accusation when they respond with murderous rage (7:54, 57–58).

Regarding the temple itself, Stephen's extended survey of God's dealings with his people highlights the fact that God's presence has never been limited to the temple, nor even to Israel.[74] Rather, he was with Abraham in Mesopotamia (7:2), Joseph in Egypt (7:9), and Moses at the burning bush (7:30–33). In response to the accusation that he has spoken against the holy "place" (τόπος, *topos*), Stephen points to a series of "places" (the term "place," τόπος, *topos* appears in 7:7, 30, 33) which are not the temple but where God nevertheless manifested his presence.[75] Further, Stephen points out that even once the temple was built, God was not limited to it (7:48–50; cf. Isa 66:1–2). In this way, Stephen relativizes the temple, showing that it has never been the exclusive location for God's presence.[76]

Importantly, Stephen is not merely relativizing the temple. He is also announcing its *obsolescence* in this new era of salvation history.[77] If Stephen's speech provides a "map of divine space,"[78] then it is a map which ultimately leads not to the temple but rather to Christ, who is shown to be the final and ultimate "place" for accessing God's presence.[79] In a spectacular climax to Acts 2–7, Stephen looks up to heaven and sees "the glory of God, and Jesus standing at the right hand of God" (7:55). Thus the same glory of God that once appeared to Abraham (7:2), and was strongly associated with the temple in the mind of Stephen's hearers, is now identified with Jesus.[80] Next, Stephen points *not* to the temple, but to Jesus: "Look, . . . I see heaven open and the Son of Man standing at the right hand of God" (7:56).[81] Bruce explains the significance:

> The presence of the Son of Man at God's right hand meant that for his people a way for access to God had been opened up more immediate and heart-satisfying than the temple ritual could provide.[82]

73. Thompson, *Acts*, 167–68.
74. Thompson, *Acts*, 168.
75. Thompson, *Acts*, 168–69.
76. Bock, *Acts*, 307; Thompson, *Acts*, 165, 167, 169.
77. Schreiner, *Magnifying*, 633–34; Beale, *Temple*, 217–23.
78. Spencer, *Acts*, 70.
79. Sleeman, *Geography*, 165.
80. Thompson, *Acts*, 170.
81. Thompson, *Acts*, 170; Peterson, *Engaging*, 142.
82. Bruce, *Acts*, 157.

Bruce goes on: because "the hour of fulfillment" has arrived, from now on "there is no place for" the temple.[83] Jesus is the "new temple, which supplants earlier provisional arrangements."[84] This is demonstrated in Stephen's final words. Whereas the temple was once the place to which prayer was directed, where God's presence was accessed and where forgiveness of sins was obtained, now Jesus is that "place": Stephen directs his prayer to Jesus (7:59), and he looks to Jesus to bring both access to God's presence (7:59) and forgiveness of sins (7:60).[85] Thus Jesus fulfills and replaces the temple, performing "the functions which the temple was designed to perform."[86] He is "the culmination and fulfillment of the various locations for meeting God throughout Israel's history" and the one which "the temple anticipated."[87] The temple had a "preliminary role for God's people," a role which it no longer needs to perform.[88]

In conclusion, Luke's overarching purpose in Acts 2–7 with regard to the temple is to show that Jesus *fulfills and replaces* it, and that this means the end of the old temple system and its leadership. The isolated texts which have been cited by IM proponents as evidence of ongoing temple usage, when studied in their context, are actually part of a powerful argument on Luke's part that the temple is now obsolete, and that believers should instead look exclusively to Christ and the apostolic church for everything that the temple once provided.

iii. What does the text teach about worship and forms?

Let us now explore what Acts 2–7 teaches about worship and forms. Four points emerge.

---

83. Bruce, *Acts*, 157.

84. Perrin, *Jesus*, 64.

85. Walton, "Tale," 145–46; Thompson, *Acts*, 170–71.

86. Walton, "Tale," 144. See also Peterson, *Acts*, 266–67.

87. Thompson, *Acts*, 172.

88. Franklin, *Christ the Lord*, 107. Additional confirmation that a dramatic salvation-historical shift has taken place lies in the fact that throughout Acts, believers do not refer to the temple as a "holy place" (in contrast to non-believing Jews who do refer to it as such: 6:13; 21:28). Walton, "Tale," 136. For alternative views of Stephen's attitude to the temple, see Barrett, "Attitudes," 350–52; Walton, "Tale," 138–43; Sylva, "Meaning," 261–75.

1. Jesus Replaces Old Covenant Worship Forms

First, Acts 2–7 depicts a dramatic shift in the nature of worship. In proclaiming the end of the temple system, Luke does not announce its replacement with new or different outward forms. Instead, he shows that *Jesus* now performs the functions formerly belonging to the temple. Thus in the new covenant era, worship is no longer tied to divinely prescribed "outward forms, locations and ceremonials."[89] Instead of going to a *place* (the temple) to access God's presence and obtain forgiveness, believers now turn to a *person*, Jesus. Luke highlights this in his account of the lame man's experience (3:1–10), in Peter's preaching (3:12–26; 4:8–12; 5:29–32), and in Stephen's example (7:55–60). Thus worship is no longer tied to the use of certain God-given outward forms; rather, the defining characteristic of worship is now *faith in Jesus* (3:16, 19–20; 4:12; 5:31–32; 6:5; 7:55–60).[90] Now that the one to whom those outward forms pointed has come, those forms are obsolete.[91]

2. True Worship is God-Given

Second, notwithstanding this fundamental change in the nature of worship, worship is still God-given. Just as God once made worship possible through the giving of the temple and prescribed rituals, he now makes it possible by providing Jesus. And even though God no longer makes the same detailed form prescriptions as he did in the OT, he still sets the terms on which people engage him: through faith in Jesus.[92] The continuing operation of this foundational principle that true worship is God-given can be seen in observing the distinct roles played by God and his people in Acts 2–7. God plays the active role, sending and anointing Jesus (4:12, 27–28; 7:52), glorifying him (3:13, 15; 4:10; 5:30), and sending the Spirit (4:8, 31; 5:32), in order that all the blessings promised in the OT might be fulfilled (2:43; 3:18, 20–26; 4:11–12, 30; 5:12, 31; 7:59–60). By contrast, God's people play the role of *receivers* of that which is given by God, responding in faith and repentance to Jesus (3:16, 19; 4:4). They do not initiate this change in worship.

Thus though the cult is fulfilled, and the age in which these outward forms are prescribed has passed, worship still begins upon God's initiative,

---

89. Peterson, *Engaging*, 100 (see also 198, 219).
90. See Peterson, *Engaging*, 136, 144, 169–79, 187, 237–38.
91. See further Peterson, *Engaging*, 23, 80–282; Peterson, "Worship," 859–63; Carson, "Worship," 37–38.
92. Peterson, *Engaging*, 20, 26–27, 33, 73.

takes place because God makes it possible, and is made available to people through an obedient response to what God has done.

3. OT forms have unique but time-limited functions and meanings

Third, it emerged in our analysis of Acts 2–7 above that the temple had a specific and important function in God's plans as a *pointer* to Christ. For a time, it was the God-given place where God's presence could be accessed and forgiveness obtained. But with the coming of Jesus, it emerged that the temple's function had been to anticipate and point to the one who would perform those roles perfectly. Now, with the coming of Christ, it is no longer necessary for the temple to perform this preparatory, anticipatory function. Thus the period during which the temple was required to perform its God-given functions was *time-limited*. Now, in the new covenant age, it no longer performs the functions given to it by God during the old covenant era.

4. Forms can function as obstacles to faith in Christ

Fourth, we see here that forms can function as obstacles to faith in Christ. In 7:48–50, Stephen appears to accuse his opponents of using the temple idolatrously. In 7:41, when recalling the calf-idol incident, Stephen says that the Israelites worshiped what their "hands had made" (ἔργοις τῶν χειρῶν αὐτῶν, *ergois tōn cheirōn autōn*). Then in 7:48, he uses the same language in reference to the temple to assert that God does not live in "handmade" (χειροποιήτοις, *cheiropoiētois*) houses. Pao has shown that every use of "handmade" (χειροποιήτοις, *cheiropoiētois*) in the LXX refers to idols.[93] Thus the charge here appears to be one of idolatry. It seems that in their attitude to the temple (7:48–50) and in their rejection of the one to whom it pointed (7:51–53), Stephen's opponents have turned the temple into an idol.[94] Kilgallen writes,

> As *Moses* was rejected and the people's worship became blasphemous thereby, so with Christ rejected, the Temple worship becomes a blasphemy.[95]

---

93. Pao, *Acts*, 195.
94. Walton, "Tale," 143; Thompson, *Acts*, 169.
95. Kilgallen, *Stephen*, 94.

We learn here that even good, God-given forms can be misused, with the result that false worship ensues. An ongoing clinging to the temple after the temple's time has come to an end has drastic spiritual consequences for the Jews. Importantly, *their misuse of the form results in their failing to worship Christ*. Franklin writes,

> Jerusalem rejected Jesus because she preferred the Temple, saw that as the fulfillment of God's promises to Abraham, and failed to realize the preparatory nature of her own institutions.[96]

Forms, then, should not be regarded as harmless. They can function as obstacles to faith in Christ. Thus Acts 2–7 contains important teachings concerning forms and worship.

c. Other references to temple worship

We now come to a discussion of other references to the temple and temple worship in Acts, and in the rest of the NT.

i. References to temple worship in the rest of Acts

A study of subsequent references to temple worship in Acts affirms the above conclusion that it is not Luke's purpose to encourage ongoing participation in temple worship for Jewish believers (nor, by analogy, to encourage believers from other faiths to use the worship forms of their pre-conversion faiths). Two texts in the remainder of Acts have been cited by IM proponents in connection with this biblical precedent argument and are discussed here.

The first is Acts 9:2, in which Saul seeks letters from the high priest to the synagogues in Damascus authorizing the extradition of any believers he might find there. According to Higgins, Paul's expectation of finding believers in the Damascus synagogues shows that Jewish believers not only continued in *temple* worship, but also continued in *synagogue* worship.[97] For Higgins, this further contributes to the picture that Jewish believers lived out their new faith "within the social and religious life of the Jewish people."[98]

There is no doubt that Acts affirms that believers were *physically present* in synagogues at certain points. Indeed, Paul states that before his

---

96. Franklin, *Christ the Lord*, 105.
97. Higgins, "Identity," 118, 122; Higgins, "Inside What?," 77–78.
98. Higgins, "Identity," 118.

conversion, he did indeed find believers in synagogues and persecute them (22:19; 26:11). As well, a number of other texts also describe incidents where believers are present at synagogues (9:20; 13:5; 14:1; 17:1–2, 10–12, 17; 18:4, 19, 26–27; 19:8). However, as with references to the temple, it is important here to note carefully what Luke does and does not say concerning the activities of Jewish believers at synagogues. Importantly, *Luke never states that believers participate in synagogue worship.* Any conclusion that they do so is based on speculation. Luke is not silent, however, concerning the activity of believers in synagogues: he repeatedly affirms that what they do in synagogues is *proclaim Christ*. This is what Paul does after his conversion when he arrives at the Damascus synagogues (9:20), and this is what Paul and the other believers do in synagogues in the other texts (13:5; 14:1; 17:1–2, 10–12, 17; 18:4, 19, 26–27; 19:8). In light of this, it is simply not possible to mount the case that Luke is seeking to persuade readers who are Jewish believers to participate in synagogue worship. If Luke's descriptions are intended to function as a guide for Jewish believers, they are not being encouraged to worship in the Jewish way, but rather to *proclaim Christ* in the synagogues.[99]

The second text cited by IM proponents in connection with the biblical precedent argument is 21:17–26.[100] Here, Paul participates in a purification rite at the temple. Unlike the other Acts texts discussed above, this text *does* depict a believer participating in an aspect of temple worship.[101] It is important to investigate, however, whether Luke's purpose here is to promote ongoing participation in temple worship. The evidence strongly suggests that it is not. It is clear from the narrative that Paul's reason for participating in this rite is not simply that the temple is the natural place for a Jewish believer like himself to express devotion to God. Rather, he is trying to deal with a potentially fractious division within the early church. Jewish believers in Jerusalem who are "zealous for the law" are concerned that Paul is teaching Jewish diaspora believers to abandon Jewish laws and customs (21:20–21). So James and the elders propose that Paul participate in the purification rite in order to prove the falseness of the accusation (21:24).[102] In context,

99. See Nikides, "Building," 91–94.

100. Higgins, "Identity," 118, 122; Higgins, "Inside What?," 78; Ridgway, "Insider," 83; Woodberry, "To the Muslims," 24; Roberts and Jameson, "Conversion," 203–4, 208.

101. Regarding exactly what ritual is envisioned in 21:23–24, see Witherington, *Acts*, 649.

102. It was false in that Paul did not actively encourage Jewish believers to abandon their laws or their customs. Rather, he asserted that these matters are not required for salvation. See Rom 14:1–15:13; 1 Cor 7:19; Gal 5:6; 6:15. Peterson, *Acts*, 585–86; Witherington, *Acts*, 648; Keener, *Acts*, 3:3126–28; Schreiner, *Magnifying*, 637.

then, this is a "conciliatory action"[103] on Paul's behalf in which he "accommodates concerns"[104] held by Jerusalem believers. Paul is neither practicing nor promoting regular participation in temple worship as an expression of personal piety, but rather participating in a one-off rite designed to appease the Jerusalem believers because, as Bock suggests, he is "committed to the unity of the Christian body."[105] Further, Marshall questions whether Luke presents Paul's action as exemplary. He writes,

> Nevertheless, the action ended in apparent disaster, and this raises the question whether Luke possibly regarded the incident as indicating that such an action for the sake of peace was the wrong thing for Paul to do.[106]

Likewise Blomberg concludes that Luke as narrator does not approve of the conciliatory plan, as evidenced by the fact that it "disastrously backfires."[107] Even if Marshall and Blomberg are wrong and Paul's action *is* intended to be exemplary, at most, Paul is an exemplar of sensitivity to the scruples of Jewish believers, not of ongoing regular participation in temple worship.[108]

Finally, when Paul's appearance at the temple leads to an opportunity to preach, what Paul preaches (like Peter and Stephen before him) is *Jesus as the one who fulfills and replaces the temple!* Jesus is the Lord who reigns from heaven (22:6–10). *His* "name" must be called upon for the forgiveness of sins (22:16). And, in a commission that was only possible because the temple age has ended, he appeared to Paul while he was in the temple and commanded him to "leave" and go "far away" to preach to the Gentiles (22:17–18, 21).[109] Thus with regard to Paul's actions in 21:26, when it is seen in context, it is clear that Luke's purpose here is not to encourage his readers to use the forms of their pre-conversion faith in their regular worship.[110]

A related question concerns the Jewish believers in Jerusalem, who are said to be "zealous for the law" (21:20). Does Luke intend that they become

---

103. Peterson, *Acts*, 587.
104. Keener, *Acts*, 3:3141.
105. Bock, *Acts*, 643–44.
106. Marshall, *Acts*, 342. Cf. Peterson, *Acts*, 587–88.
107. Blomberg, "Christian," 412–13.

108. Paul demonstrates this sensitivity by observing the purification requirements when entering the temple area (21:23–24, 26, 29; 24:18). Cf. the false accusations in 21:28; 24:6. Thompson, *Acts*, 189–91; Walton, "Tale," 137. Many understand this incident as an instance in which Paul applies the principle in 1 Cor 9:19–23. Witherington, *Acts*, 651.

109. Thompson, *Acts*, 191.
110. Thompson, *Acts*, 191.

role models for his Jewish readers? IM proponents have taken the description in 21:20 positively, seeing here evidence that "a large insider movement was taking place."[111] Yet we should not be too quick to assume that Luke's attitude to this group is a positive one. Peterson notes that the expression "zealous for the law" (21:20) implies that this group has been influenced by the Pharisaic position (15:5), a position already discredited (15:1–29).[112] In regard to the phrase "zealous for the law," Peterson adds, "It is unlikely that the Paul we know from his letters would have been happy with such a self-designation by Jewish Christians."[113] Ultimately, Luke does not offer an explicit evaluation of this group's zeal for the law. His purposes appear to lie elsewhere. The group's role in the narrative is simply to raise the problem which acts as a trigger for Paul's arrest. It is not possible to conclude from this brief reference to their existence that Luke wants to hold them out as models for ongoing participation in Jewish worship.

In conclusion, a study of other key references to the synagogue and temple worship in Acts confirms the above conclusion regarding Acts 2–7. Luke's intention is not to persuade his Jewish readers to participate in synagogue and temple worship. On the contrary, he is concerned to direct attention away from the temple, and onto Jesus who has fulfilled and replaced it.

ii. References to the temple and temple worship in the rest of the NT

The following analysis of key references to the temple and temple worship in the rest of the NT further confirms the above conclusions. Beginning with the gospels, scholars have identified both "positive" and "negative" material concerning the temple, and this has led to a range of theories about the attitude of the evangelists to the temple.[114] However, when we recognize that the gospels are set during a moment in history when a major salvation-historical transition is about to take place, this apparent tension is resolved. Regarding the so-called "positive" texts, Jesus participates in temple worship himself and, in his teaching, he assumes that his hearers do likewise.[115] However, this is not an endorsement of temple worship in the new covenant era. Rather, it reflects the fact that the events of Jesus' life and ministry occur before his death and resurrection and the inauguration of the new age. This is clear

---

111. Ridgway, "Insider," 83; Roberts and Jameson, "Conversion," 202–4.
112. Peterson, *Acts*, 585.
113. Peterson, *Acts*, 585. See also Seifrid, "Jesus," 53.
114. See Barrett, "Attitudes," 361; Perrin, *Jesus*, 59–62.
115. See, for example, Matt 5:23–24; 23:17, 19, 21; Luke 2:21–40, 49; 17:14; 18:9–14; 21:1–4.

from the so-called "negative" texts, where Jesus and the evangelists *anticipate* the temple's replacement and obsolescence. Jesus prophesies the destruction of the temple (Mat 24:1–2; Mk 13:1–2; Luke 21:5–6). He declares the imminent arrival of an era where worship will no longer be tied to the geographical location of the temple, but will instead be "in spirit and truth" (John 4:20–24). The tearing of the temple curtain at the moment of Jesus' death is a decisive moment which denotes the end of the temple era (Mat 27:51; Mark 15:38; Luke 23:45).[116] The notion that Jesus will replace the temple appears frequently.[117] In relation to Matthew 12:6, where Jesus declares "I tell you that something greater than the temple is here," Perrin writes,

> The statement implies not only that the current temple has in some sense been made redundant on his coming, but also that the functions typically predicated of that temple have now been either transcended or devolved onto Jesus himself.[118]

In Luke 20:9–18, Jesus identifies the existing temple leadership with those who oppose God, and identifies himself as the foundation of a new temple.[119] In John 1:14, Jesus is cast as a new tabernacle where God's glory dwells.[120] In John 2:18–22, Jesus' body is depicted as a new temple that will replace the existing one.[121] Thus though the gospels are set before the inauguration of the new covenant, they prepare for the temple to be superseded and affirm that Jesus is the one who will fulfill and replace it.[122]

Paul also affirms that the temple age has ended, and that Christ now replaces the temple. When Paul states that "God was pleased to have all his fullness dwell in him" (Col 1:19; cf. 2:9), he alludes to Ps 68:16 which speaks of Zion as the place that God is "pleased to dwell." Thus in Paul's thought, Christ now performs perfectly the function which the temple once performed.[123] Further, because Christ sends the Spirit to believers, the Christian community also performs this role as the dwelling place of God on earth.

---

116. Walton, "Tale," 136; Green, "Demise," 495–515; McKelvey, "Temple," 808.
117. Chilton, "Temple," 1159–66.
118. Perrin, *Jesus*, 60.
119. Luke 20:17 (quoting Ps 118:22). Perrin, *Jesus*, 62.
120. He "dwelled" or "tabernacled" (ἐσκήνωσεν, *eskēnōsen*) among us. Perrin, *Jesus*, 53.
121. Cf. Matt 26:61; 27:40; Mark 14:57–58; 15:29–30. Gurtner and Perrin, "Temple," 944–45.
122. Keener, *Acts*, 1:1032.
123. Comfort, "Temple," 925.

Thus on a number of occasions, Paul depicts Christ's body, the church, as the temple (1 Cor 3:16–17; 2 Cor 6:16; Eph 2:21).[124] Perrin writes,

> For Paul, the redemptive-historical shift has occurred in Christ and as a result those who are of Christ and filled with the Holy Spirit corporately make up the new locus of God's presence.[125]

Whereas once offerings were made at the temple, in the new era, the lives of Christians are the new "cultic offerings."[126] Thus a thoroughgoing replacement is evident in Paul's letters: Christ, with the Spirit-filled Christian community, takes the place of the temple.[127]

Paul also seems to hint that ongoing attachment to temple worship in the new covenant age is spiritually dangerous. In Galatians 4:21–31, Paul casts the "faith/works of the law" dichotomy in terms of "the present city of Jerusalem" (corresponding to "works") and the heavenly temple-city "that is above" (corresponding to "faith"). To identify with the former, he says, is to be enslaved and miss out on the heavenly inheritance.[128]

The replacement and obsolescence of temple worship are presented most forthrightly in Hebrews 7–10, where the writer shows that the cultic practices associated with temple worship are now obsolete because a new and better way has come. Regarding the priesthood, which was responsible for administering temple worship, the author writes that "the former regulation is set aside . . . and a better hope is introduced" (7:18–19). Peterson explains, "Now that the ultimate priestly liturgy has been performed, there is no place for the operation of any human priesthood in an earthly sanctuary."[129] Regarding the Mosaic covenant which established and regulated temple worship, the author announces that Christ has brought a new covenant (7:22), which renders the old covenant obsolete (8:7–13). Regarding the sanctuary itself, the author shows that because Christ has entered the true heavenly sanctuary (9:11–12; cf. 8:2; 9:24), this has brought to an end the need to enter the earthly sanctuary, which was only ever a "shadow" or "copy" (8:5; 9:24).[130] Regarding temple sacrifices, because Christ has now offered a sacrifice which is "once for all" (9:12),

---

124. Note that he uses the term ναός, *naos* ("sanctuary") not ἱερόν, *hieron* ("temple courts"). See McKelvey, "Temple," 809–10; Comfort, "Temple," 924.

125. Perrin, *Jesus*, 70.

126. Phil 2:17; 4:18; Rom 12:1. Perrin, *Jesus*, 69.

127. Chilton, "Temple," 1165–66.

128. Perrin, *Jesus*, 66.

129. Peterson, *Engaging*, 231.

130. McKelvey, "Temple," 810.

"no further sacrificial action is necessary *or appropriate.*"[131] This is crucial for our purposes. Ongoing participation in temple worship is not merely *unnecessary*, but it is actually *inappropriate* in light of the unique and unrepeatable character of Jesus' sacrifice (7:27; 9:24–28; 10:10, 12, 14).[132] To continue to participate in the offering of temple sacrifices aimed at bringing atonement for sin is *totally incompatible with faith in Christ*. The elements of temple worship functioned in an anticipatory way, as "a shadow of the good things that are coming" (10:1; cf. 8:5).[133] Thus they served their purpose in their day, but ongoing use is inappropriate now that the one they anticipated has come. Thus temple worship as the divinely-given system of approaching God has now been "set aside" (10:9),[134] because its ideal has been fulfilled and realized in Christ (10:5–14).[135]

Because of all this, the writer exhorts believers to separate themselves from temple worship. Just as Christ "suffered outside the city gate" (13:12) (that is, outside the gates of Jerusalem), so too believers must "go to him outside the camp, bearing the disgrace he bore" (13:13).[136] Although the meaning of the phrase "outside the camp" is debated, it most likely refers to the need to sever ties with Jewish worship institutions.[137] Cockerill writes,

> If, therefore, the hearers would enjoy the fulfillment that Christ brings, they must separate themselves from the worship of the community that lives by the Old Covenant as if Christ had not come. This separation will incur the wrath of their former community . . . , but they must "bear" the "reproach of Christ."[138]

Having gone "outside the camp" (13:13), believers must identify with "the city that is to come," rather than Jerusalem (13:14), and offer spiritual sacrifices, rather than those offered at the temple (13:15–16).[139]

Peter also affirms the replacement of the temple and the assimilation of its functions by Jesus and the Christian community. In 1 Peter 2:4–9, Christ is portrayed as the foundation of the new temple and as the high

---

131. Chilton, "Temple," 1165 (emphasis added).
132. Peterson, *Engaging*, 230.
133. Peterson, *Engaging*, 233.
134. Peterson, *Engaging*, 231.
135. Peterson, *Engaging*, 230.
136. The walls of Jerusalem were understood to parallel the sacred boundaries of the wilderness camp. Lane, *Hebrews 9–13*, 542.
137. Bruce, *Hebrews*, 381–82; Filson, *Yesterday*, 63–64; Lane, *Hebrews 9–13*, 545–46; Walker, *Jesus*, 217, 221.
138. Cockerill, *Hebrews*, 702–3.
139. Guthrie, *Hebrews*, 440–41.

priest that presides there; the Christian community is portrayed as the new temple ("living stones . . . being built into a spiritual house"), and the holy priesthood that presides there.[140] In 2:5, both "house" (οἶκος, *oikos*) and "sacrifices" (θυσίας, *thusias*) are modified with the adjective "spiritual" (πνευματικὰς, *pneumatikas*), implying a contrast between this new spiritual temple and the old physical one.[141] The force of the contrast is to highlight that the Christian community, *not the temple*, is the "place" where God now dwells on earth, where true worship now takes place, and where acceptable sacrifices are now made.[142]

In conclusion, the NT authors consistently affirm that the age of temple worship has come to an end, and that Christ and the Christian community now take over the functions that the temple once performed. No texts can be found in which the NT authors encourage ongoing participation in temple worship, or explore the parameters within which it might be acceptable or desirable in the new covenant era. On the contrary, some authors actually depict ongoing participation as inappropriate and spiritually dangerous. Most, however, ignore the old temple, their focus instead being turned to the new temple and the true worship that is offered there.

d. The implications of Acts 2–7 and related texts for the IM debate

i. Acts 2–7 is not a precedent for believers to use the worship forms of their pre-conversion faith

A key objective here has been to assess the IM claim that certain texts from Acts 2–7 are biblical precedents for believers today to use the forms of their pre-conversion faiths in worship. It is clear from the above analysis that this claim is flawed and must be rejected. As we saw in chapter 1 (chapter 1, §4.b.iii.), a text can only be characterized as a precedent if there is textual evidence that the author intends it to function in that way. No evidence was found in Acts 2–7 (or indeed in the rest of the NT) of an authorial intention to promote ongoing participation in temple worship, let alone worship at the sanctuaries of other faiths. On the contrary, as we saw, Luke's purposes in Acts 2–7 are actually to announce the end of the temple age and to persuade his readers to look to Jesus for all that the temple once

---

140. Perrin, *Jesus*, 56–57.
141. Jobes et al., *1 Peter*, 150.
142. Jobes et al., *1 Peter*, 148, 150.

provided. Thus Luke's actual literary and theological purposes are strongly at odds with the IM claim.

As discussed above (see chapter 4, §2.b.ii.), there is no consensus in biblical scholarship regarding the question of Luke's attitude to the temple. Some do in fact agree with IM proponents that Luke has a positive view of the temple's ongoing significance.[143] However, it is important to note that *those who do so reject the notion that the NT documents speak consistently.* They suggest that Luke's "positive" view of the temple was in conflict with the more "negative" views of the other NT writers,[144] or even that Luke's work itself is internally contradictory with regard to the temple.[145] By contrast, if we accept the view that Luke is presenting Jesus as the fulfillment and replacement of the temple, we are not confronted with the problem of contradiction within Acts or within the NT generally, since this understanding is consistent with the teaching of the other NT authors (see chapter 4, §2.c.ii. above).[146]

In characterizing the temple references in Acts 2–7 as precedents, IM proponents have made two hermeneutical errors. First, they have failed to investigate authorial intent in the texts they cite.[147] Each time the argument is presented by IM proponents, there is no evidence of a broader inquiry into Luke's intended message or literary purposes. Rather, isolated texts are cited and the implications for the IM debate are immediately drawn. The result is that a foreign agenda has been imposed on the texts, one that is contradictory to Luke's purposes.

The second error relates to a failure to engage with important salvation-historical issues surrounding temple worship.[148] As we have seen, temple worship was, for a time, the God-given means by which his people accessed his presence and obtained forgiveness. But with the inauguration of the new age, it no longer performs these functions. A definitive salvation-historical transition has occurred. God's people no longer go to the temple to access God's presence and obtain forgiveness, because both are

---

143. Sylva, "Meaning," 261–75; Hurtado, *Lord*, 195–96; Chance, *Jerusalem*, 35–45.

144. Hurtado, *Lord*, 195–96; Chance, *Jerusalem*, 35–45.

145. Barrett, "Attitudes," 364.

146. Another interpretation that avoids finding inconsistency in the NT is that Luke is simply describing a salvation-historically unique transition period in which believers took some time to appreciate the implications of Christ's death and so withdraw from temple worship. Witherington, *Acts*, 163, 173.

147. For a discussion of this hermeneutical error, see Fee and Stuart, *How to Read*, 29–30; Vanhoozer, *Meaning*, 260–63.

148. For a discussion of this hermeneutical error, see Liefeld, *Interpreting*, 58; Doriani, *Biblical Application*, 86–87; Johnson, *Acts*, 5–13; Garner, "High Stakes," 270–72.

now found in Christ. A key problem with the writings of IM proponents in relation to Acts 2–7 is that, although they make the claim that Jewish believers continued to participate in temple worship, *they fail to discuss the theologically significant implications of such participation in light of the salvation-historical transition that has just occurred.* As we saw above, texts such as Hebrews 7–10 make it clear that new covenant believers must not perform the old temple rituals while ascribing to them their original OT meanings. So, for example, a believer must not depend upon the temple rituals designed to bring atonement for sin *in order to secure atonement for sin*, because to do so would undermine complete dependence on Christ's finished work. If the original OT meanings attached to the temple rituals are out of bounds to new covenant believers, then any claim that believers rightly continued to practice these rituals needs to be accompanied by an explanation of what new meanings they ascribed to them. Yet this matter is left unexplored and unexplained by IM proponents.[149] At the same time, it is significant that no NT writer ever explores the possibility of giving new meanings to the old temple rituals. Rather, as we have seen, the consistent NT emphasis is that these rituals have been fulfilled and replaced, and so are now obsolete. Thus Acts 2–7 does not provide a precedent for the use by believers of forms from their pre-conversion faith. To claim this text as a precedent in this way is to misuse it.

2. *Other implications for the IM debate*

Although Acts 2–7 does not establish a precedent for form-borrowing, and does not actually discuss forms other than those prescribed in the OT, it does teach a number of important principles regarding worship and forms, and we now consider the implications of these for the IM debate.

First, in Acts 2–7, Luke is concerned to direct the focus of his readers away from the temple and onto Christ. Thus Luke is concerned with equipping his readers to engage in true new-covenant worship. This once again reinforces the importance of evaluating the helpfulness or otherwise of a form through the lens of a biblical theology of worship. Luke's primary concern in this text is not contextualization. Rather, it is true worship. Therefore a crucial focus of the contextualization process needs to be a careful consideration of the impact of a given form on true, God-given worship.

Second, it is clear in Acts 2–7 that the essence of true worship in the new covenant age is responding to Christ in faith and repentance. An

---

149. IM proponents Higgins, Jameson, and Talman do, however, comment on this matter in relation to the book of Hebrews. See Higgins et al., "Myths," 52.

implication is that form-selectors need to ensure that their priority is the same as Luke's—that is, to ensure that believers are responding to Christ in faith and repentance. Discussions concerning whether to use a particular form need to be focused upon this scriptural priority. Other matters, such as whether the form is culturally familiar, need to be recognized as of secondary importance. As discussed above in chapter 2, some tests proposed by IM proponents seem to prioritize such secondary matters over this primary one (see chapter 2, §2.c.ii.2., §3.c.ii.2., and §4.c.ii.2.). Thus when considering using Muslim forms, form-selectors need to ask, and give priority to the matter of, *whether the form will facilitate or hinder dependence on Christ.*

Third, Acts 2–7 and related texts highlight that true worship is *responsive* in nature: God has taken the initiative to make worship of himself possible through Christ. What is needed from his people is a response of faith and repentance. Form-selectors must guard against any practice which might compromise or confuse the principle that Christian worship is fundamentally responsive in nature. BMBs should investigate what impact the use of Muslim forms is likely to have on their capacity to preserve the *responsive* character of true worship. This will be especially important if the forms in question have been previously associated in their thinking or practice with human initiative in worship or merit-accumulation through worship.

Finally, we saw in our analysis that forms can function as obstacles to faith in Christ (chapter 4, §2.b.iii.4. and§2.c.ii. above). A form can be used in such a way that worshipers either fail to grasp who Christ is (as with the Jews in Acts 7:48–50), or fail to take hold of what he has already done (Galatians 4:21–31; Hebrews 7–10), with the result that they fail to depend on him. Form-selectors need to be aware of the potential for forms to function in this way, and to carefully consider the likely impact of using the forms of other faiths. This will require consideration and investigation of worshipers' motivations and beliefs concerning given forms.

The "biblical compatibility" test advanced by some IM proponents (see chapter 1, §3.a.vi. above) focuses attention on the nature of the form. If a form is deemed "good" or "positive"[150] it is considered acceptable for contextualized use. However, the fact that even the good, God-given form of the temple could be used in such a way as to function as an obstacle to true worship demonstrates that form-selectors need to go beyond simply assessing the inherent nature of the form. Good or neutral forms can be used in such a way as to produce false worship. Form-selectors need therefore to ask what worshipers *believe* about certain forms, and what their motivations

---

150. Talman, "Old Testament," 49–57. Cf. Lewis's comments in Brogden, "Inside Out," 35.

might be in using them. As they seek forms which will best facilitate faith in Christ, form-selectors need to be attuned to the potential for forms to compromise or undermine such faith. Ultimately, the use of a form needs to be an *expression* of dependence on Christ, not a *substitution* for it.

Thus though Acts 2–7 cannot be applied as a precedent for believers to use forms from their pre-conversion faiths, the text does contain a number of important implications for the IM debate.

3. Acts 15

Acts 15 is both the second NT appropriation text and at the same time the first NT resistance text, since it has been claimed by both IM proponents and IM critics as a text supporting their respective positions. Acts 15 describes the church addressing the question of Gentile inclusion in the people of God. A dispute arises, originating in Antioch, concerning whether Gentile believers must be circumcised and obey the law of Moses (15:1–5). A council is convened in Jerusalem to debate the issue (15:6–21). A decision is reached that Gentile believers do not need to be circumcised or obey the Mosaic law, but that they should abide by four prohibitions. This decision is recorded in a letter addressed to Gentile believers (15:22–29), which is then delivered to the church in Antioch (15:30–35).[151]

a. The relevance of the text to the research problem

We begin our analysis with a consideration of the text's relevance to the research problem. IM proponents and IM critics claim that Acts 15 is relevant to the IM debate for different reasons, and these are now considered in turn.

i. Acts 15 as an appropriation text

IM proponents claim that Acts 15 is relevant both because it establishes that Gentile believers do not need to adopt Jewish forms, and also because it depicts Jewish believers continuing to use Jewish forms.[152] According to

---

151. On the historical debate concerning how Acts 15 relates to Gal 2:1–10, see Marguerat, "Paul," 106–7, 109–10; Witherington, *Acts*, 440–49; Peterson, *Acts*, 418–19; Bock, *Acts*, 487–93; Bauckham, "James and the Gentiles," 155; Bauckham, "James and the Jerusalem Church," 468–70.

152. Lewis, "Integrity," 43, 45; Roberts and Jameson, "Conversion," 203–4; Higgins, "Acts 15," 37.

IM proponents, a principle emerges here that believers are not required to take on the religious forms of another group (for example, that of a missionary), but are instead free to use the religious forms of their birth community.¹⁵³ Therefore, they conclude, BMBs do not need to adopt "Christian" forms to express their new faith in Christ, but can instead continue to use Muslim forms.¹⁵⁴

Regarding the claim concerning Gentile believers, it is important to note that IM proponents do not suggest that this text *explicitly* affirms the use by Gentile believers of Gentile worship forms. Rather, the claim seems to be that because the text rejects the imposition of foreign (here Jewish) forms on Gentile believers, the *implication* is that the Gentile believers are free to continue to use the forms of their pre-conversion faiths.¹⁵⁵ Whether or not this implication is a valid one is considered below (see chapter 4, §3.a.i.). At this point, it is sufficient to note that Acts 15 does not actually deal with the use of the forms of other faiths (that is, Gentile religious forms) by God's people (here, Gentile believers). While the text does explicitly affirm that Gentile believers do not need to obey the law of Moses, there is no explicit corresponding affirmation that they are free to use Gentile religious forms.¹⁵⁶

Regarding the second claim by IM proponents, namely that the text depicts Jewish believers using Jewish forms, this is accurate. It is certainly a reasonable inference that the believing Pharisees, who are insisting that the Gentiles obey the law of Moses (15:5), are in fact continuing to obey the law themselves. Thus the believing Pharisees are Jewish believers who use Jewish forms. However, it is less clear whether the other Jewish believers involved in the debate (such as Peter, Paul, Barnabas, and James) use Jewish forms. The text is silent on this matter (15:6–21). Nevertheless, the IM proponents' claim is correct in that the text does depict at least some Jewish believers who use Jewish forms. As discussed above (see chapter 4, §2.a.i.), although not technically from "another faith," Jewish forms can be considered as such for our purposes.

In summary then, this text does not depict Gentile believers using Gentile forms, but it does depict some Jewish believers using Jewish forms.

---

153. Lewis, "Honoring," 18; Dutch, "Should Muslims," 18; Talman, "Old Testament," 55; Talman, "Acts 15," 254–55.

154. Lewis, "Honoring," 18; Lewis, "Promoting," 76; Talman, "Acts 15," 251–52.

155. Lewis, "Integrity," 43–44; Brown, "Contextualization," 128.

156. Coleman, *Analysis*, 158–59; Farrokh, "New Testament Record," 230.

ii. Acts 15 as a resistance text

IM critics claim that Acts 15 is relevant because the practices which are *prohibited* in 15:20-21 and 15:28-29 are pagan religious practices, and so the text warns new believers against using the forms of their pre-conversion faiths.[157]

At issue here is whether the matters prohibited are in fact pagan religious practices which believing Gentiles might have used as part of their pagan worship before they came to faith. As the following discussion demonstrates, the evidence indicates that they are. In this section, I am simply establishing that the practices could be found in pagan religion at the time. Whether they are prohibited in Acts 15 *because* they are pagan religious practices or for another reason (such as to encourage sensitivity to Jews), is discussed below (chapter 4, §3.b.i.2.).

The first prohibition concerns abstaining from "the defilements caused by idols" (τῶν ἀλισγημάτων τῶν εἰδώλων, *tōn alisgēmatōn tōn eidōlōn*) (15:20) or "food sacrificed to idols" (εἰδωλοθύτων, *eidōlothutōn*) (15:29). This is probably a reference to the defilement caused by eating meat sacrificed to idols.[158] Thus a pagan cultic form is clearly in view.

The second prohibition concerns "sexual immorality" (πορνεία, *porneia*) (5:20, 29). If James wanted to simply prohibit sexual infidelity in one's own or a neighbor's home, the most appropriate term would have been μοιχεια, *moicheia*.[159] The term πορνεία, *porneia* by contrast, could have "a cultic dimension."[160] Given, as we shall see, that the other prohibited practices also have cultic associations, πορνεία, *porneia* here is likely a reference to "so called sacred prostitution . . ., the sort of thing that sometimes accompanied, or at least was believed to accompany, the pagan rites and feasts in pagan temples."[161]

The third prohibition concerns eating "the meat of strangled things" (τοῦ πνικτοῦ, *tou pniktou*) (5:20, 29).[162] Bock suggests that the reference to strangling is probably "a description of what happens with sacrifices or

---

157. Brogden, "Inside Out," 34; Corwin, "Humble Appeal," 10; Tennent, "Followers," 105-6.

158. Witherington, *Acts*, 460-63; Witherington, "Not So," 237-54; Peterson, *Acts*, 433, 438.

159. Cf. Matt 5:27-30. Witherington, *Acts*, 463; Steffeck, "Observations," 135.

160. See Rev 2:21; 14:8; 17:2, 4; 18:3 and 19:2. Silva, "πορνεύω," 109-11; Bock, *Acts*, 505.

161. Witherington, *Acts*, 463. See also Peterson, *Acts*, 434; Witherington, "Not So," 249.

162. Silva, "πνίγω," 823-25.

meals among Gentiles. The result of this form of death is that blood often is not drained from the animal."[163] The Magical Papyri describes pagan priests choking the sacrifice in an attempt to transfer its life-breath into the idol.[164] Thus once again, what seems to be in view here is a pagan cultic form.

The fourth prohibition concerns "blood" (τοῦ αἵματος, *tou haimatos*) (5:20, 29). While this could be a general prohibition on the consumption of blood in any circumstances,[165] in light of the cultic focus of the first three prohibitions, it seems likely that what is in view here is consuming blood in association with pagan sacrifice.[166] In this regard, Witherington points to evidence that pagan priests tasted the blood of sacrificed animals as part of the sacrificial ritual.[167]

In conclusion, all four prohibited practices are probably associated with pagan worship, and so the prohibitions most likely deal with the use of the forms of other faiths by God's people.

The next question, then, is whether what is in view here is Gentile believers using these forms *to worship the true God through Jesus*, or merely to worship the pagan gods of their pre-conversion faiths. There is no explicit indication in 15:20-21 or 15:28-29 regarding which of these is in view. James does not explain whether he is prohibiting the use of the forms to worship the true God, or to worship a false one. Rather, he issues a blanket prohibition, and so prohibits both of these potential uses. Thus the text is relevant as a resistance text.

b. The meaning of the text for the original audience

i. Is there evidence in the text that the author is seeking to persuade readers to use or resist the forms of their pre-conversion faith?

Let us now explore the meaning of Acts 15 for the original audience. Once again, IM proponents and IM critics have identified different meanings from this text, and so their respective arguments must be considered in turn.

---

163. Bock, *Acts*, 505. See also Peterson, *Acts*, 434.
164. Witherington, *Acts*, 464.
165. Peterson, *Acts*, 434.
166. Steffeck, "Observations," 135.
167. Witherington, *Acts*, 464, citing R. Ogilvie, *The Romans and Their Gods in the Age of Augustus* (New York: Norton, 1969), 49-51.

1. Acts 15 as an Appropriation Text

Acts 15 is one of the most frequently cited texts by IM proponents.[168] They claim that it establishes a principle that believers do not need to adopt the forms of another group, but are instead free to use those of their pre-conversion faith.[169] In accordance with the methodology set out in chapter 1, the key to evaluating this claim is authorial intent. Is there evidence in the text that Luke intends to communicate this principle? As the following analysis shows, there is not. Rather, his purposes lie elsewhere.

As noted above, Acts 15 does not explicitly affirm the ongoing use of Gentile forms by Gentile believers. The Council attests that Gentile believers do not need to adopt Jewish forms, but this is not the same as declaring that they are free to continue to use the pagan forms of their pre-conversion faiths.[170] On what basis, then, do IM proponents conclude that Acts 15 teaches that Gentiles can use Gentile forms? The conclusion seems to derive from IM proponents' understanding of what is at issue in Acts 15. According to IM proponents, the Jerusalem Council sought to answer the following question: do Gentiles need to adopt Jewish traditions and culture in order to be saved, or are they free to retain their own traditions and culture? For example, Lewis articulates the issue as follows:

> Did the message of Jesus Christ only have the power to save those who also accepted the religious framework in which Christ himself was incarnated, or *could the gospel save those in an alien context as well?*[171]

Similarly, Talman frames the issue as turning upon whether Jewish proselytism was to be required of Gentile believers, or whether they were free to remain Gentiles.[172]

---

168. See the list of articles provided by Coleman in which IM proponents cite Acts 15: Coleman, *Analysis*, 136n2. More recent additions to this list include: Morton and Talman, "Jerusalem Council"; Talman, "Acts 15"; Roberts and Jameson, "Conversion."

169. Lewis, "Honoring," 18; Lewis, "Integrity," 43–44; Massey, "Amazing Diversity," 8, 10; Ridgway, "Insider," 85; Dutch, "Should Muslims," 18; Talman, "Old Testament," 55; Talman, "Acts 15," 254–55; Travis, "Must all Muslims," 411; Roberts and Jameson, "Conversion," 203–4; Brown, "Contextualization," 127–28; Woodberry, "To the Muslims," 25–27. A second argument that IM proponents make from Acts 15, which is beyond the scope of this book, is that the text models a *process* for evaluating developments in the field that can be used today. See Talman, "Acts 15," 249, 255, 259; Woodberry, "To the Muslims," 25–27; Winter, "Third," 329; Higgins, "Acts 15," 30–31; Higgins, "Biblical Basis," 217–18, 222–23.

170. See Coleman, *Analysis*, 158.

171. Lewis, "Integrity," 43. Cf. Lewis, "Honoring," 18.

172. Talman, "Old Testament," 55; Talman, "Acts 15," 250.

It is not IM proponents alone who define the problem in Acts 15 in this way. Writing on the topic of contextualization generally, Ott, Strauss, and Tennent write,

> The apostles and elders of the church came together to determine whether Jesus's followers must first become culturally, ethnically, and religiously Jews, or whether they could be authentic followers of Christ *and remain part of their native cultures*.[173]

Likewise, Flemming maintains what is at issue in Acts 15 is the following:

> whether Gentile believers had to become culturally Jewish as a condition of their salvation and as part of their obedience to Christ, or *whether they could be accepted in all their "Gentile-ness."*[174]

Two key features of this view of Acts 15 need to be noted here. First, proponents maintain that the matter being debated is not merely whether Gentile believers must conform to Jewish forms, but also *whether they are free to retain their Gentile forms*. Second, they characterise Jewish forms such as circumcision and the Mosaic law primarily as *cultural* phenomena (downplaying the possibility that they have a unique biblical-theological significance). Kraft is most explicit in this respect:

> When the Judaizers insisted that Gentiles needed to be circumcised, they were in effect demanding that the Gentiles submit to "cultural conversion."[175]

Because IM proponents articulate the issue in this way, it follows that they are able to characterise the Council's decision as upholding the right of Gentile believers to use Gentile forms. Thus Brown sees Acts 15 as establishing "that Gentile believers should follow the customs of their own culture."[176] Similarly, Lewis concludes that the Council's decision upholds "the power of the gospel to save believers *who retained their Gentile culture and identity*."[177]

---

173. Ott et al., *Encountering*, 273 (emphasis added).

174. Flemming, *Contextualization*, 45 (emphasis added). See also Hesselgrave and Rommen, *Contextualization*, 10–11.

175. Kraft, *Christianity in Culture* (1979), 340–41. See also Whiteman, "Function," 50. IM proponent Higgins, however, distances himself from this primarily cultural view of OT forms. Higgins, "Acts 15," 30.

176. Brown, "Contextualization," 128. See also Talman, "Acts 15," 255; Ridgway, "Insider," 85.

177. Lewis, "Integrity," 43. See also Lewis, "Honoring," 18.

If this articulation by IM proponents (and others) of the issue under debate in Acts 15 were correct, then their inference that the Council decision affirms the ongoing use of Gentile forms by Gentiles might be valid. However, it is not correct, and so the inference is unwarranted. A careful consideration of Luke's literary and theological purposes, both throughout Acts and in the text of Acts 15 itself, reveals that the matter under debate here is *not whether Gentile believers can continue to use Gentile forms, but rather whether or not the Mosaic law is mandatory in the new covenant era.* Luke's concern is to announce a unique, salvation-historical transition, and to explain its implications, *not* to enunciate a general principle regarding the desirability of using the forms of one's birth community. That this is in fact the actual issue under debate in Acts 15 will now be demonstrated in two stages: first, by surveying the literary context of Acts 15, and second, by analyzing the text itself.

i. The literary context

Throughout Acts, a key concern of Luke's is to explore the following question:

> What is the relationship between the law of Moses and the people of God now, in the inaugurated kingdom after Jesus' ascension?[178]

Luke frequently raises the question of the role of the law. For example, he often records the accusation of Jewish opponents that believers are against the Mosaic law (6:11, 13-14; 18:13; 21:21, 28). The consistent theme emerging from the defenses is that Christians are not opposed to the law; rather, they follow the one to whom the law pointed. Peter (3:22-23), Stephen (7:53), and Paul (24:14; 25:8, 10; 26:22; 28:17) all articulate this same position.[179] Nevertheless, Luke repeatedly demonstrates that with the inauguration of the new covenant, a salvation-historical transition has taken place, and this has enormous implications for the law.[180] The direct authority for the people of God is now found in the teaching of the apostles (2:42), not the teaching of Moses

---

178. Thompson, *Acts*, 176. There is debate regarding what Luke's view of the law in Acts actually is. The view advanced here is that Luke shows that the law has been fulfilled. For a presentation of the alternate view (that Luke believes that the law has ongoing validity), see Jervell, *Luke*, 133-51; Jervell and Dunn, *Theology of Acts*, 54-61. For critiques of Jervell's view, see Schreiner, *Questions*, 171-79; Schreiner, *Law*, 225-26; Thompson, *Acts*, 176; Blomberg, "Law," 53-56; Blomberg, "Christian," 398; Seifrid, "Jesus," 39-40.

179. Thompson, *Acts*, 178.

180. Schreiner, *Questions*, 174-75.

(6:14; 15:21; 21:21, 28).[181] Further, as discussed above in our analysis of Acts 2–7 (chapter 4, §2.b.ii. and §2.b.iii), key institutions established under, and regulated by, the Mosaic law are now fulfilled and replaced by Jesus and the apostles: Jesus fulfills and replaces the temple and the associated sacrificial system, and the apostles replace the temple leadership.

A key concern of Luke in Acts then is to show that the law has been fulfilled, and to explore the implications of this.[182] Nowhere is this focus more apparent than in 10:10–16, where Peter is commanded to eat non-kosher food. In this text, the food laws are presented not merely as being *fulfilled* but also as *abrogated*. Significantly, it is Peter, *a Jew*, and not simply Cornelius, *a Gentile*, who is commanded to eat food which was forbidden to be eaten under Mosaic law. Thus Luke is not here establishing a principle that Jews should retain Jewish customs, while Gentiles can retain Gentile customs. Rather, Luke is announcing that a salvation-historical shift has taken place: from now on, *neither Jew nor Gentile* needs to abide by Mosaic food laws because they have been abrogated in the new covenant age.[183] Schreiner writes,

> The import of the vision cannot be limited to the Gentile mission.... The food laws are now abolished. A new era of redemptive history has arrived.... The law, then, is no longer required to belong to the people of God.[184]

We have seen that the question of the place of the Mosaic law in the new covenant age is a crucial one for Luke throughout Acts.[185] When seeking to identify what is at issue in Acts 15, it is important to acknowledge that in the preceding chapters, Luke has been concerned to demonstrate that the law is fulfilled in Jesus, and to explore the implications of this for believers. This strongly favors the understanding that Acts 15 is concerned with this same thematic question of the law's ongoing validity, and not with the different question of the permissibility of using Gentile religious forms. As we shall now see, the text of Acts 15 itself also supports this understanding.

---

181. Thompson, *Acts*, 178–79.
182. See Schreiner, *Law*, 226.
183. Thompson, *Acts*, 182; Blomberg, "Christian," 404.
184. Schreiner, *Questions*, 177. See also Schreiner, *Law*, 229; Thompson, *Acts*, 182; Seifrid, "Jesus," 43; Blomberg, "Christian," 404.
185. See further Thompson, *Acts*, 175–81; Witherington, "Not So," 207; Bock, *Acts*, 214–15; Peterson, *Acts*, 205.

ii. Acts 15

Luke makes it clear in 15:1–5 that the specific issue under debate is whether salvation depends upon obedience to the law of Moses. That *salvation* is at stake here (and not merely social identity)[186] is clear from 15:1, where Judaizers catalyze the debate by teaching that "unless you are circumcised . . . you cannot be saved."[187] That obedience to the *whole Mosaic law* is in view (and not just the practice of circumcision as an identity marker) is clear from 15:5, where some believing Pharisees declare that "the Gentiles must be circumcised and required to obey the law of Moses."[188]

It is important to recognize the background to the Judaizers' demand for law-observance in 15:1 and 15:5. According to the Mosaic law, Gentiles could become proselytes of Judaism and so be counted among the people of God.[189] Thus the Judaizers' demands are no mere ethnocentric insistence upon "cultural conversion,"[190] but rather an understandable application of the Mosaic law to the current situation. Schnabel comments,

> obeying the law was the *sine qua non* of belonging to God's people since the time of Moses . . ., the position of the Judean Christians is logically consistent.[191]

If Jesus had not inaugurated a new age, these believing Pharisees would have been justified in making their demands. However, Jesus has inaugurated a new age, and Luke's very purpose in Acts 15 is to highlight the implications.

Circumcision and the law are, therefore, God-given forms with unique theological meanings. As such, to characterize them as mere cultural phenomena is to seriously misunderstand what is at issue in Acts 15. In this regard, Wiarda writes,

> to suggest that the Mosaic law was purely a cultural *product* would run counter to the perspective of the Acts narrative.. . . Circumcision was the means of becoming a Jew, certainly. But it was also the required way for a Gentile to receive the blessings

---

186. *Contra* Butticaz, "Acts 15," 120–21.

187. Thompson, *Acts*, 183.

188. Thompson, *Acts*, 183; Peterson, *Acts*, 419; Witherington, *Acts*, 453; Bock, *Acts*, 487, 501; Blomberg, "Christian," 407; Seifrid, "Jesus," 46; Schnabel, *Acts*, 629.

189. Gen 17:10–14, 23–27; 34:14–16 and Exod 12:43–45, 48. Peterson, *Acts*, 421; Scobie, *Ways*, 579. Male converts would be circumcised and then the entire family would commit to live in obedience to the law. Peterson, *Acts*, 421; Blomberg, "Christian," 407.

190. *Contra* Kraft, *Christianity in Culture* (1979), 340–41.

191. Schnabel, *Acts*, 629. Cf. Bock, *Acts*, 495.

promised within the covenant relationship.... Those who gathered at the Jerusalem Council had to wrestle with something other than simply the pressures of culture and ethnocentrism.[192]

The issue raised in 15:1–5 is therefore not primarily a *cultural* one: can Gentile believers retain their own cultural practices or must they adopt Jewish ones? Rather, it is *theological*: do the scriptural requirements for the people of God (circumcision and obedience to the law) continue to be mandatory in the new covenant age?

In 15:6–19, Luke answers this theological question resoundingly in the negative. In the speeches of both Peter (15:7–11) and James (15:13–19), Luke communicates that Christ radically transforms the application of the law in the new covenant era. Peter, in rebutting the claim of the believing Pharisees, does not frame his argument in terms of the importance of believers retaining their own cultural forms and traditions, as one might expect if that were the topic under consideration. Rather, he argues that a salvation-historical transition has taken place. He begins in 15:7 by referring to the Cornelius event as a decisive and one-off "choice" that God made to extend salvation to the Gentiles. Then in 15:8, he recounts how God gave the Holy Spirit to the Gentiles, a gift which, in the theology of Acts, heralds "the arrival of the new era of promise."[193] Then in 15:9, Peter says of the Gentile believers that God "purified their hearts by faith." The term Peter uses here for "purified" (καθαρίζω, *katharizō*) is one strongly associated with Mosaic purity rituals.[194] Thus a *new era* has arrived: the purity that was once exclusively available through observance of the law is now accessed by faith.[195] Butticaz summarizes: "The soteriological function of the Law has thus reached its term."[196] Thus Peter's argument is that law-observance is not required *because* a salvation-historical transition has occurred: "God has moved on in his dealings with humanity, and it is sinful to demand obedience to the old way."[197]

It is important to grasp here that Peter is not merely asserting that Gentiles do not need to adopt Jewish laws. Rather, he goes much further, declaring that Christ's fulfillment and transformation of the law applies *to both Jew and Gentile*. Thus in 15:9, Peter affirms: "He did not discriminate

---

192. Wiarda, "Jerusalem," 234–35.

193. See 2:4; 10:44–47; 11:15–17. Bock, *Acts*, 500.

194. See Lev 11–18; Deut 14. Bauckham, "James and the Jerusalem Church," 125–26.

195. Peterson, *Acts*, 425; Beale, *Temple*, 232–33.

196. Butticaz, "Acts 15," 126.

197. Peterson, *Acts*, 426. See also Schreiner, *Questions*, 178.

between us and them"—both Jew and Gentile are purified by faith. In 15:10 he characterizes the law as "a yoke that neither we nor our ancestors have been able to bear." Then in 15:11, the yoke of the law is set in stark opposition to salvation through grace.[198] Most significantly, it is both Jews and Gentiles who are saved through grace (15:11). Thus, as Thompson concludes, "the implication of this is that circumcision is not even required for Jews, let alone Gentiles."[199] Likewise, Wiarda writes,

> Though this message highlights the implications of Christ's coming for the Gentiles, it is grounded in the assumption that his mission has created a new situation with respect to the law that applies equally to all people.[200]

Seifrid notes that the emphasis in 15:11 is, somewhat surprisingly, on the fact that *Jewish* believers are saved by grace. He concludes,

> According to Luke then, the dynamics of evangelistic success force the believing community to face the insights which are inherent to the Cornelius episode. . . . The basic considerations which determined the decision regarding the Gentiles in Acts 15, *apply to Jewish believers as well*, since there is no distinction between them and the Gentiles.[201]

Thus the issue that Peter addresses in 15:7-11 is *not* whether Gentiles can continue to use Gentile forms, but rather whether the law continues to be mandatory in the new age. His astonishing claim is that *neither Jew nor Gentile* is required to obey it.

In 15:12-19, James addresses the same issue and draws the same conclusion. Like Peter, he justifies his conclusion that law-observance is not required by arguing that a salvation-historical epoch-change has just taken place. He begins by characterizing the reports of conversion of Gentiles as evidence that God has taken from the Gentiles "a people [λαός, laos] for his name" (15:14). In the LXX, λαός, laos is ordinarily used of the Israelites to distinguish them from the Gentiles.[202] However, the prophets had anticipated a day when the nations would be joined together with Israel into

---

198. A strong adversative "but" (ἀλλὰ, alla) marks this contrast. Thompson, *Acts*, 183.

199. Thompson, *Acts*, 183. See also Blomberg, "Law," 64. Marshall writes: "What Peter disputed was the need to obey the law in order to be *saved*; whether Jews kept it for other reasons was a secondary matter." Marshall, *Acts*, 250.

200. Wiarda, "Jerusalem," 248.

201. Seifrid, "Jesus," 45 (emphasis added).

202. Deut 26:18-19; 32:8-9; Ps 135:12. Strong, "Jerusalem," 202; Bock, *Acts*, 502-3.

a unified λαός, *laos* of God: "Many nations will be joined with the LORD in that day and will become my people (λαός, *laos*)" (Zech 2:11). In 15:14, James alludes to this prophetic hope, and so declares that this day has arrived and a new salvation-historical era has dawned.[203] Once again, epoch-change is in view here. The implications of James's statement in 15:14 for the law are significant. If Gentiles converted outside the law are the people of God, then the age of the unfulfilled law is over.

In 15:15-18, James cites Amos 9:11-12 to justify his interpretation of events in 15:14. James chooses this text "because of the salvation-historical perspective it gives."[204] The text anticipates a time when "David's fallen tent" will be rebuilt (15:16; Amos 9:11), and Gentiles will be included amongst God's people (15:17; Amos 9:12).[205] According to James, this new era has now arrived: Christ is the Davidic king who is rebuilding the Davidic kingdom, and Gentiles like Cornelius are being included in his kingdom.[206] Thus when James concludes in 15:19 that Gentiles should not be required to obey that law, this is based on his argument in 15:14-18 that a decisive salvation-historical transition has occurred. A new era has dawned in which faith in Jesus (not circumcision) is the mark of God's people (cf. 15:11).

We have seen that there is no evidence in Acts 15 nor in its literary context that Luke's intention is to persuade readers to use the forms of their pre-conversion faith. The view that Acts 15 does establish such a principle is based on the erroneous understanding that the issue under debate in Acts 15 is whether Gentiles can continue to use Gentile forms. This is not the issue under debate. Rather, at issue is whether the law continues to be mandatory in the new covenant era. Luke's message is that "a new era of salvation history has dawned, and the law was no longer obligatory. . . . Circumcision as the entrance rite into the covenant had passed away."[207] The problem in Acts 15 is not ethnocentricity, but rather salvation history. The Judaizers' problem is not that they are "culturally bound,"[208] but rather that they are

203. Strong, "Jerusalem," 202. See also Bock, *Acts*, 503; Peterson, *Acts*, 429-30; Tannehill, *Acts*, 186-87; Blomberg, "Christian," 408.

204. Peterson, *Acts*, 430.

205. The LXX, which James cites, differs from the MT (which speaks only of the inclusion of Edomites, not all Gentiles). See Strong, "Jerusalem," 202; Bauckham, "James and the Gentiles," 178. There is debate concerning whether "David's fallen tent" is a reference to the temple or to the Davidic kingdom. See Schnabel, *Acts*, 638-40; Bauckham, "James and the Jerusalem Church," 453-56.

206. Bock, *Acts*, 503; Schreiner, *Questions*, 178; Beale, *Temple*, 233-34; Butticaz, "Acts 15," 123.

207. Schreiner, *Questions*, 178. On the importance of reading Acts 15 through the lens of salvation history, see Blomberg, "Law," 70-72.

208. Flemming, *Contextualization*, 45.

chronologically bound: they have not grasped that an epoch-change has occurred. Garner writes,

> While cultures surely felt a jolt at this critical historical point, this is not a period merely of cultural upheaval. It is foremost a period of *theological* upheaval in which the OT worship forms are replaced by the substance of those forms—Jesus Christ himself. The apostles faced the challenge of guiding the church to move from these spiritual typological forms (OT) to understanding and applying their antitypical realities (NT). . . . The reason the apostles handled things in Acts 15 the way they did . . . was *not* cultural neutrality. Rather they acted because of the epochal transition that Jesus Christ the son of God inaugurated.[209]

In conclusion then, while 15:1–19 *does* establish that law-observance is unnecessary, it does *not* provide permission to believers to use the forms of their pre-conversion faiths.

2. Acts 15 as a Resistance Text

IM critics cite the four prohibitions in 15:20–21 and 15:28–29 as evidence that Acts 15 cautions against the use by new believers of the forms of their pre-conversion faith.[210] Once again, in order to evaluate this claim, we need to inquire as to authorial intent, asking whether there is evidence in the text that Luke seeks to communicate such a caution. We have already seen that the four prohibited practices could be associated with pagan temple worship, and can therefore be characterized as the forms of other faiths (chapter 4, §3.a.ii.). The next stage in evaluating the claim made by IM critics is to ask *why* the prohibitions are imposed, and what Luke seeks to communicate to his readers by recording them.

A range of explanations has been offered regarding the purpose of the prohibitions, and there is nothing approaching a consensus on this matter.[211] No doubt one reason for such a diversity of opinions is the simple fact that James does not explain why the prohibitions are imposed (15:20–21; 15:28–29). However, when the various explanations are evaluated in light of the evidence concerning Luke's literary and theological purposes (from both Acts 15 and Acts more broadly), it becomes clear that not all are equally satisfactory. What follows is an analysis of the five most common

---

209. Garner, "High Stakes," 262–63.

210. Brogden, "Inside Out," 34; Corwin, "Humble Appeal," 10; Tennent, "Followers," 105–6.

211. Proctor, "Proselytes," 482.

explanations. As we will see, while there are problems with the first four, the fifth—that the prohibitions are aimed at urging Gentile believers not to participate in pagan idolatrous worship—is the most plausible.

i. An application of the laws in Leviticus 17–18

According to the first explanation, the prohibitions are based on Leviticus 17:8—18:18, which establishes a code for ritual purity for "resident aliens" (non-Israelites living in the land of Israel). According to this view, James does not require Gentile believers to obey the whole Mosaic law, but instead only those parts which Moses demanded of resident aliens.[212]

Although this view enjoys considerable support, there are a number of problems with it. First, the parallel between the rules in Leviticus 17–18 and the four prohibitions is not exact.[213] There is no clear equivalent in Leviticus 17–18 of the prohibition in Acts 15:20, 28 concerning "the meat of strangled things" (πνικτός, *pniktos*) (although the Acts prohibition could conceivably be related to the prohibition on consuming blood in Lev 17:10).[214] As well, the term "food sacrificed to idols" (εἰδωλοθύτων, *eidōlothutōn*) (Acts 15:29) does not appear in Leviticus 17–18 at all (although, again, the Acts prohibition could be connected to the prohibitions on certain sacrifices in Lev 17:5–7).[215]

Second, there are many other Mosaic laws for resident aliens living in the land of Israel which James does *not* apply in Acts 15.[216] Proponents of this view have offered no satisfactory explanation as to why these four rules are chosen and others are not.[217] In this regard, it is worth noting

---

212. Bauckham points to the repeated use of the phrase "in your/their midst" in Leviticus (17:8, 10, 12, 13 and 18:26) in establishing that these laws were especially for foreigners living in the land. Bauckham, "James and the Jerusalem Church," 459–80. See also Bauckham, "James and the Gentiles," 172–79; Jervell, *Luke*, 144.

213. Butticaz, "Acts 15," 127.

214. The term πνικτός, *pniktos* does not appear in the LXX at all. Wilson, *Luke*, 88–94; Peterson, *Acts*, 435; Thompson, *Acts*, 184; Proctor, "Proselytes," 475; Bock, *Acts*, 506; Blomberg, "Christian," 409; Steffeck, "Observations," 136.

215. Witherington, *Acts*, 465; Bock, *Acts*, 506; Blomberg, "Christian," 409.

216. Cf. Exod 23:12; Lev 16:29; 17:15–16; 20:2; 22:10, 18; 24:22; 25:47; Num 15:30; Deut 16:11, 14; 26:11. Blomberg, "Christian," 409; Thompson, *Acts*, 184; Peterson, *Acts*, 435.

217. Bauckham's explanation is that the laws that are not applied are all cultic, and because the NT church saw itself as the new temple of God, it would not have imposed cultic laws on Gentiles. Bauckham, "James and the Jerusalem Church," 461. However, there is nothing in the text of Acts to support the notion that the apostles made a distinction between cultic and non-cultic laws.

Bauckham's own concession that there is "no known Jewish parallel to the selection of precisely these four commandments from the Law of Moses as those which are binding on Gentiles."[218]

Third, the Leviticus 17–18 rules are directed to those living in the land of Israel, whereas the letter in Acts 15 is addressed to Gentiles living in the diaspora (15:23). Thus the geographical and theological settings are very different. The laws in Leviticus 17–18 are aimed at preserving the sanctity of the promised land (Lev 18:24–30); yet there are no indications in Acts 15 that the apostolic decree was aimed at preserving the purity of any specific geographical region.[219]

Fourth, this view is at odds with the theology of Acts 15, and indeed of the book as a whole, concerning the place of the law in the new covenant era. As we have seen, Luke's consistent message throughout Acts is that the time of the law, and of the institutions established by it, has come to an end. In 15:10–11, Peter argues that the yoke of the law should not be placed on the Gentiles. In 15:19, James concludes that the law should not be imposed on them. Does he really then proceed in 15:20 to impose certain Mosaic laws on the Gentiles? Further, in 15:24, the apostles expressly distance themselves from the Judaizers who are demanding law-observance (15:1, 5).[220] As Blomberg notes, "It seems incredible to imagine that the provisions of the Decree would implicitly affirm that party's claim."[221] As well, "the legitimating authority for the Apostolic Decree is not the Torah, but the Holy Spirit and the Apostles."[222] James introduces his decision, not by citing and applying the Mosaic law, but rather with the words, "It is my judgment" (15:19), and "We should write to them" (15:20). Then in the letter, the prohibitions are introduced with the words, "It seemed good to the Holy Spirit and to us" (15:28). Later, the decree is referred to as "the decisions reached by the apostles and elders" (16:4; cf. 21:25).[223] It is not the Mosaic law, then, that is being imposed here, *but a decision of the apostles legitimated by the Holy Spirit*.[224] Thus there are several problems with the first explanation.

---

218. Bauckham, "James and the Gentiles," 174.

219. Butticaz, "Acts 15," 127. See also Witherington, *Acts*, 464–65; Thompson, *Acts*, 184; Pao, *Acts*, 241–42; Peterson, *Acts*, 435.

220. Seifrid, "Jesus," 47.

221. Blomberg, "Christian," 408.

222. Butticaz, "Acts 15," 127.

223. Butticaz, "Acts 15," 127.

224. Marguerat, "Paul," 111.

ii. An application of the Noahic commands

According to the second explanation, the prohibitions are based on the so-called Noahic commands. According to Rabbinic tradition, seven commands were given to Noah as he emerged from the ark (Gen 9:3-6), and these commands were for all humanity, not just Israel. Noticing a partial similarity between these Noahic commands and the four prohibitions in Acts 15, some have proposed that the latter are based on the former, and thus that the Acts 15 prohibitions are aimed at providing a "summary outline of the righteousness that God expects from humanity."[225]

This explanation is unconvincing. First, it is anachronistic, since there is no evidence that this rabbinic belief existed during NT times. The earliest attestation comes from the second century AD.[226] Second, the parallel between the seven commands and the four prohibitions is not close.[227] According to rabbinic tradition, the seven Noahic commands prohibited idolatry, blasphemy, murder, incest, stealing, perverting justice, and eating flesh containing blood. James's prohibitions roughly parallel the first, third, fourth, and seventh of these. Nevertheless, incest is not the same as πορνεία, *porneia* and flesh containing blood is not the same as εἰδωλοθύτων, *eidōlothuton*. Both πορνεία, *porneia* and εἰδωλοθύτων, *eidōlothuton* have strong associations with pagan idolatry, whereas incest and blood-containing flesh do not. Third, as Barrett notes, "there is nothing in the text of Acts to call Noah to mind."[228] And fourth, the Noahic commands were regarded as applying to Gentiles living in the land of Israel, whereas Acts 15 is addressed to Gentiles in the diaspora. Once again, this is a different geographical and theological setting.[229]

iii. A concern with basic morality

According to the third explanation, the prohibitions are not based on any specific scriptural texts, but are simply imposed out of a broad concern for basic morality.[230] Proponents of this explanation understand the command

---

225. Proctor, "Proselytes," 477. The main proponent of this view is Bockmuehl: see Bockmuehl, "Noachide," 80-93.
226. Proctor, "Proselytes," 476; Witherington, *Acts*, 464; Bauckham, "James and the Gentiles," 174. For Bockmuehl's response, see Bockmuehl, "Noachide," 85-86.
227. Witherington, *Acts*, 464; Peterson, *Acts*, 434; Steffeck, "Observations," 136.
228. Barrett, *Acts*, 734.
229. Witherington, *Acts*, 464.
230. Barrett, *Acts*, 730-36.

to abstain from "blood" as a reference to murder. They base their view on the Western text which omits "the meat of strangled things" (πνικτός, *pniktos*) and also adds a negative form of the Golden Rule ("Do not do to others what you would not have them do to you").[231] Thus according to this view, the decree is moral, not cultic, in emphasis. It is aimed at prohibiting the cardinal sins of idolatry, sexual immorality and murder.

This explanation suffers from three significant problems. First, it is based on the Western text, which most agree is "a later understanding after the original setting had been lost."[232] When it is accepted that πνικτός, *pniktos* is original, and that the Golden Rule in the Western text was almost certainly a scribal addition, it becomes clear that the prohibitions are actually primarily cultic, not moral, in their focus.[233] Second, there are no good reasons for reading "blood" as a reference to murder. Given the cultic associations of the first three prohibitions, it is much more likely that a cultic consumption of blood is in view here too.[234] Third, if the purpose is to establish a minimal moral standard, why are only these four laws singled out? Are other moral violations, such as stealing and lying, considered less serious?[235] No adequate explanation for this has been offered. Thus there are problems with the third explanation.

iv. Enabling witness to, and table fellowship with, Jews

According to the fourth explanation, the prohibitions are ad hoc recommendations aimed at ensuring that Gentile believers do not cause unnecessary offence to either unbelieving or believing Jews.[236] Thus the practices most offensive to Jewish sensibilities are prohibited,[237] making it possible for believing Gentiles to engage in both witness to unbelieving Jews,[238] and to have table fellowship with believing Jews.[239]

---

231. Wedderburn, "Apostolic," 369.

232. Strong, "Jerusalem," 203. See also Wedderburn, "Apostolic," 369.

233. Wedderburn, "Apostolic," 369.

234. See chapter 4, §3.a.ii. above and Schreiner, *Questions*, 182.

235. Thompson, *Acts*, 185; Seifrid, "Jesus," 50.

236. Blomberg, "Law," 66; Blomberg, "Christian," 408–10; Schreiner, *Magnifying*, 638; Schreiner, *Questions*, 183–84; Seifrid, "Jesus," 44, 47; Peterson, *Acts*, 440.

237. According to some rabbinic texts, compromise by Jews was impossible on three matters: idolatry, the shedding of blood, and incest. Barrett, *Acts*, 734–35. See also Schreiner, *Questions*, 184.

238. Seifrid, "Jesus," 47; Blomberg, "Law," 66.

239. Schreiner, *Questions*, 184; Seifrid, "Jesus," 47; Flemming, *Contextualization*, 47.

This explanation is also problematic. First, proponents of this view characterize the prohibitions as merely non-binding, occasional recommendations.[240] Thus they are presented merely as what "seemed good" (15:28) and as something that the believers would "do well" to abide by (15:29). Peterson suggests that the word "requirement" in 15:28 "should not be read as a legal obligation, but as a moral appeal."[241] They are occasional since they only apply in Antioch, Syria and Cilicia (15:23) where the problem arose. Thus according to this view, the Gentiles have freedom with regard to these matters, yet are being urged here "to exercise their liberty with wisdom, restraint and love" for the sake of Jews.[242] While it is true that the prohibitions are not presented as new law, proponents of this view have nevertheless mischaracterized the authority and application of the decree. The prohibitions have authoritative force: the word for "requirements" in 15:28, ἐπάναγκες, *epanagkes*, literally means "necessary things." As well, the decree is later referred to as a "decision" (δόγματα, *dogmata*; literally a "rule, regulation") (16:4) of the apostles and elders. Proponents of this view downplay Luke's emphasis on the authority of the apostles in the new covenant era, an emphasis present both in Acts 15 (15:2, 4, 6, 22–23, 28) and throughout the book.[243] Further, the prohibitions apply not only to Gentiles in Antioch, Syria and Cilicia, but to *all* Gentiles (15:19; 16:4; 21:25).

Second, there are no indications in the text that James's concern is social. As Schnabel notes,

> James does not ask the Gentile believers to "respect" the Jewish believers, nor does he ask the Jewish believers not to "force" themselves on the Gentile believers. Had this "ethos" been James's main concern, he would have had other linguistic means to make this point.[244]

Third, proponents of this view fail to give adequate weight to the possibility that the prohibitions are imposed *for the spiritual benefit of believing Gentiles*, and not merely for the sake of promoting harmony with Jews. In light of the strong NT stance against sexual immorality on the grounds that it is inherently sinful (and not merely offensive to those with special sensitivities),[245] it is not possible to maintain that the aim of this prohibition

---

240. Schreiner, *Questions*, 184; Peterson, *Acts*, 439.

241. Peterson, *Acts*, 440.

242. Peterson, *Acts*, 440. See also Schreiner, *Questions*, 184.

243. For example, see 1:2, 8, 21–26; 2:37, 42; 4:33, 35, 37; 5:2, 12, 38–39. Thompson, *Acts*, 178–86; Wilson, *Luke*, 107.

244. Schnabel, *Acts*, 644.

245. Matt 15:19; Mark 7:21; 1 Cor 5:1, 6:13, 18, 10:18; Gal 5:19; Eph 5:3; Col 3:5; 1

is simply to ensure that Gentiles do not offend Jews. Clearly the prohibition applies even where there is no possibility of causing such offence.[246]

Fourth, to the extent that this explanation is concerned with the relationship between believers, it fails to take seriously Luke's repeated assertions in Acts that believing Jews are also no longer under the law. According to proponents of this explanation, believing Jews continue in the new covenant age to abide by food laws, creating a problem for table fellowship with believing Gentiles. Thus the prohibitions are seen as the solution to this problem.[247] Yet Acts 10–11 makes it clear that the food laws are abrogated for Jews as well as Gentiles. As well, Peter affirms the end of the law (15:9–11). While there are some believing Jews who fail to grasp this important theological reality (cf. 21:20–24), given Luke's concern throughout Acts to announce the end of the law, it is highly unlikely that his primary message here is that the Gentiles must respect the right of believing Jews to continue to obey the law.[248]

Fifth, as Wilson has demonstrated, the prohibitions are actually inadequate for establishing table fellowship between Gentiles and law-observing Jews, since "they do not even guarantee that no forbidden meat or wine (for example, pork or wine from libations) is used."[249]

In summary, then, the prohibitions may, in their implementation, have gone some way in facilitating social relations between Gentile believers and law-abiding Jews. However, this view is unsatisfactory as an explanation of their chief purpose.

v. Preventing ongoing participation in idolatry

The fifth and final explanation is the most plausible. According to this view, the problem being addressed is not primarily related to law, morality or social harmony, but rather worship: Gentile believers must be aware of the spiritual dangers *for them* associated with pagan worship. The primary

---

Thess 4:3; Rev 9:21.

246. Coleman, *Analysis*, 155n95; Schnabel, *Acts*, 644. Because of this, many proponents of this "social" view actually combine it with the fifth view. See Bock, *Acts*, 513; Steffeck, "Observations," 137–38; Peterson, *Acts*, 446.

247. Strong, "Jerusalem," 202.

248. According to Butticaz, the Jewish believers continue to obey the law, not as a "ritual code of purity," but now simply as a "cultural custom." Yet he offers no textual support for this conclusion. Butticaz, "Acts 15," 131. See also Marguerat, "Paul," 115–17.

249. Wilson, *Gentiles*, 189.

purpose of the prohibitions is to help Gentile believers understand that they "must separate themselves entirely from pagan worship."[250]

Witherington, a leading advocate of this view, proposes that 15:20 and 15:29 relate to attendance by Gentile believers at pagan temple feasts.[251] He supports this claim by showing that each of the prohibited practices is associated with pagan temple feasts. Regarding the first prohibition, concerning "food sacrificed to idols" (εἰδωλοθύτων, eidōlothutōn) (15:29), the association with pagan temple feasts is plain and uncontentious.[252]

Regarding the second prohibition, as discussed above (see chapter 4, §3.a.ii.), Witherington points out that the term used in 15:20 and 15:29 for sexual immorality, πορνεία, porneia, often has cultic associations. He suggests that if sexual infidelity occurring in homes was in view, μοιχεια, moicheia would have been the more appropriate term.[253] Given that πορνεία, porneia appears in 15:20 and 15:29 alongside other cultic terms, it is probably a reference here to cultic prostitution.

Regarding the third and fourth prohibitions, as discussed above (chapter 4, §3.a.ii.), Witherington adduces evidence that the choking and strangling of sacrifices, and the tasting of sacrificial blood, took place at pagan feasts.[254]

Having established that all four prohibitions are associated with pagan temple feasts, Witherington then argues that all four should be viewed together and a common setting for them identified. He points out that the only setting where all four of these activities could be found together was the pagan temple feast.[255]

---

250. Proctor, "Proselytes," 473. See also Wedderburn, "Apostolic," 385. Beale is another proponent of this view, although he combines it with the Leviticus 17–18 view. See Beale, *Temple*, 233, 239–41. Likewise Bock, Steffeck and Peterson are proponents of this view, although they combine it with the table fellowship view. See Bock, *Acts*, 513; Steffeck, "Observations," 137–38; Peterson, *Acts*, 446.

251. Witherington, *Acts*, 460–67.

252. Witherington, "Not So," 240 (see generally 237–54). See also Schnabel, *Acts*, 642.

253. Witherington, *Acts*, 463.

254. Witherington, *Acts*, 464. For a discussion of πνικτός, *pniktos* as referring to a particular method of pagan sacrifice whereby the animal was choked, see Wedderburn, "Apostolic," 385–88; Proctor, "Proselytes," 473–74.

255. Witherington, *Acts*, 464 (see generally 460–64). See also Witherington, "Not So," 249. Witherington cites 2 Maccabees 6:4–5 to show that Jews believed that pagans combined these elements of idol meat and sexual immorality in their worship. Witherington, *Acts*, 461–62. Further, Steffeck cites the pseudo-Clementine writings and Origen to demonstrate that, in the thinking of early Christians, when these two prohibited items were linked together, pagan temple worship was in view. Steffeck, "Observations," 139.

Additional arguments in favor of this view include the following. First, there is no indication, as some have claimed, that James shifts from discussing soteriological matters in 15:19, to purely social and cultural matters in 15:20.[256] Rather, the soteriological problem raised in 15:1 and 15:5 (what is required for salvation) continues to be the subject of discussion in 15:20. Thus, although Gentiles are not under the law (15:19), in order to be saved they must nevertheless turn from pagan idolatry (15:20).[257]

Second, as Pao has demonstrated, "a powerful polemic against the idols of the nations plays a significant role in the narrative of Acts."[258] Thus this view fits well with Luke's overall literary and theological purposes.

Third, of all the explanations put forward for the prohibitions, this view "probably lies closer to the original context."[259] It is unclear whether the Gentile recipients of the letter would have had sufficient knowledge of the OT to be able to recognize allusions to Noahic or Levitical rules. Yet given their background in pagan worship, they would certainly have been quick to notice that all of the prohibited practices are pagan temple practices. The letter was therefore "issued in a social context where the most natural way to read it would be to see it as a prohibition of attending such feasts and all that they entailed."[260]

Fourth, although some suggest that 15:21, where James refers to the Mosaic law being preached in every city on every Sabbath, supports other explanations better than this one,[261] in reality, 15:21 poses no problem for this explanation. When we recognize that a key emphasis in Acts 15 is the problem of the law being imposed as a burden (15:1, 5, 10, 19), it makes sense to understand 15:21 as an additional reference to this same problem, that of the law being imposed on the Gentiles. Thompson explains,

> Thus James essentially states, 'We should not make it difficult for the Gentiles turning to God . . . (we should of course, urge them to repent from their pagan idolatry), . . . for it is made difficult enough in the synagogues every Sabbath.[262]

---

256. Butticaz, "Acts 15," 128–29.

257. Thompson, *Acts*, 187.

258. See 8:4–24; 12:20–23; 13:4–12; 14:15–17; 17:24–31; 19:11–20, 26. See Pao, *Acts*, 181–212.

259. Strong, "Jerusalem," 203.

260. Witherington, *Acts*, 461.

261. Peterson, *Acts*, 435; Blomberg, "Law," 66; Woodberry, "To the Muslims," 27.

262. Thompson, *Acts*, 187. For an alternative interpretation of 15:21 that is nevertheless consistent with this view of the purpose of the prohibitions, see Witherington, *Acts*, 463.

Thus the purpose of the prohibitions is to urge Gentiles to "flee idolatry and immorality and the temple context where such things are thought to be prevalent."[263] The prohibitions appear to be particularly targeted at "participation in idol feasts and their attendant activities."[264] The decree calls for "a clean break with the pagan past."[265] So, taken as a whole, Acts 15 "applies the way for pagan idolatrous Gentiles to be saved: faith (in the Lord Jesus) and repentance (turning from idolatry)."[266] There is therefore strong evidence in the text of Acts that Luke is concerned to persuade Gentile readers to resist the use of pagan worship forms, that is, the forms of their pre-conversion faith.

ii. What does the text teach about worship and forms?

What follows is a summary of what Acts 15 teaches about worship and forms. Four points are identified.

1. New covenant worship is characterized by faith in Jesus, not outward forms

First, Acts 15 affirms that a dramatic shift in the nature of worship has taken place. The Judaizers' claim regarding the necessity of circumcision and law-observance (15:1, 5) is definitively rejected (15:19, 24, 28). But the Council does not propose new outward forms to replace these now-obsolete Mosaic ones. Thus in the new covenant, *worship is no longer characterized by outward forms*. Rather, the defining feature is faith in Jesus (15:9).

2. True worship is God-given

Second, notwithstanding this enormous change in the nature of worship, true worship is still something that is God-given: God makes worship of himself possible, and prescribes its terms.[267] Just as God once required engagement with himself to include circumcision and the Mosaic law, he has now determined that the requirement is faith in Christ (15:9). Just as purity

---

263. Witherington, *Acts*, 466. Cf. Strong, "Jerusalem," 203.
264. Witherington, "Not So," 252.
265. Witherington, "Not So," 250.
266. Thompson, *Acts*, 187.
267. Peterson, *Engaging*, 20, 26–27, 33, 73.

was once obtained through rituals he prescribed, now he has established a new way: by faith in Jesus, through grace (15:9, 11).

Indeed, a striking feature of Acts 15 is the emphasis on God as the exclusive agent responsible for the bringing about of this new situation whereby Gentiles (and Jews!) are saved apart from the law. The conversion of many Gentiles is something God has done (15:4; cf. 15:12). According to Peter, God took the initiative at every stage of the process: he made a choice to save the Gentiles (15:7), he sent the Spirit as proof of his decision (15:8), he made no distinction between Jew and Gentile (15:9), and he purified their hearts by faith (15:9). James likewise declares that this new situation has come about purely because of a decision and act of God (15:14). Thus it is God and God alone who has brought about this seismic shift in the nature of how humanity engages with him. The apostles simply observe and relate what God has done.

Therefore even though the age of detailed prescribed outward forms has passed, worship is still something that God makes possible and its terms are still set by him. The human role is to understand what God has done and to engage with him accordingly.

3. OT FORMS HAVE UNIQUE BUT TIME-LIMITED MEANINGS IN SALVATION HISTORY

Third, in Scripture, OT forms have unique, theological meanings, such that they cannot be characterized simply as Jewish cultural norms. For example, circumcision functioned as the sign of covenant membership, and was required by God of both Jew and Gentile who wished to be part of the people of God.[268] Circumcision's primary significance in Scripture lies therefore in its unique theological meaning, not in its status as a Jewish cultural norm. However, with the inauguration of the new covenant, many OT forms are now fulfilled and obsolete and so *no longer have these special, theological meanings*. Thus in Acts 10–11 we discover that the food laws are abrogated, and in Acts 15, that the law requiring circumcision is abrogated as well. If, when interpreting a NT text dealing with OT forms, we fail to take this into account, there is a danger that we will misunderstand and misapply the text.[269] In this regard, Garner helpfully observes,

---

268. Gen 17:10–14, 23–27; Exod 12:43–45, 48. Cf. Exod 4:24–26; Josh 5:2–7.

269. As we will see below (chapter 4, §3.d.iii.), a number of IM proponents make this hermeneutical mistake.

Old Covenant Jewish practices had been divinely given, possessing real spiritual significance, a significance culminating in the once-for-all work of Jesus Christ. Now OT faith in its old forms truly had come to an end; it attained fulfillment in Jesus Christ, the son of God. Thus because of Christ, to return to Judaism in its Old Covenant forms was eschatologically retrogressive, and to obey the covenant God through the Old Covenant spiritual signs was no longer necessary.[270]

4. Forms from new believers' pre-conversion faith pose special spiritual dangers to them, particularly the danger of unwanted meanings

Fourth, the prohibitions in Acts 15 highlight the fact that forms from new believers' pre-conversion faith actually pose special spiritual dangers to those new believers. In Acts 15, nothing less than salvation is at stake (15:1, 15:5). While James dismisses the Judaizers' claim that the Gentiles must be circumcised in order to be saved, he does make it clear that all traces of the false worship practices associated with their previous pagan faith must be eradicated. He imposes a strong prohibition: the verb used in 15:20 and 15:29 for "abstain" (ἀπέχω, *apechō*) means "to avoid contact with" or "to keep away from."[271] Thus even contact with these forms might be problematic. What is needed is complete separation. James and the apostles do not entertain the possibility that Gentile believers might reinterpret and reuse these pagan forms for Christian worship. On the contrary, they issue an all-encompassing prohibition: the forms are not to be used for any purpose.

In our study of OT resistance texts, we saw that a risk inherent in the use by God's people of the forms of other faiths is that foreign meanings associated with those forms—meanings alien to the principles of true worship—might remain, and so risk the distortion or corruption of true worship. There is no doubt that the meanings attached to the forms prohibited in Acts 15 are alien to the principles of true worship. Two examples are briefly discussed here to demonstrate this.

First, regarding the prohibition concerning πνικτός, *pniktos* (15:20, 29), the magical papyri attest to a belief that by strangling sacrificial animals, pagan priests could transfer the animals' life breath or spiritual vitality into

---

270. Garner, "High Stakes," 263.
271. Bock, *Acts*, 505.

the idol.²⁷² Clearly such beliefs concerning human capacity to manipulate the divine, and to worship through the medium of an idol, are contrary to the principles of true worship.²⁷³

Second, when pagan worshipers participated in temple feasts (a participation which might include using all the forms prohibited by Acts 15), they did so "in order to secure the good will of a god."²⁷⁴ Once again, this is contrary to the principles of true worship (that is, engagement with God), where worship is a *response* to divine favor and blessing that is bestowed purely by grace.²⁷⁵

Thus the meanings attached to these pagan worship forms were contrary to the principles of true worship. Had Gentile believers attempted to use these forms in their worship of God through Jesus, they would have run the risk of importing unhelpful meanings that could corrupt true worship. We cannot conclude with certainty that this is what James and the apostles had in mind when they issued the prohibitions, since they prohibit use of the forms *under any circumstances*, without explanation. Indeed, such was the spiritual danger associated with use of (or even contact with) these forms, that James and the apostles chose in this instance to make the prohibition a blanket one.

Finally, the example of the Judaizers and their attitude to circumcision (15:1, 5) provides further evidence of the danger of believers retaining forms that they used before they came to Christ because of the meanings associated with them. According to their pre-Christian worship, the meaning of circumcision for these Judaizers was that use of the form was essential for covenant membership, and thus salvation. The mistake which the Judaizers make in 15:1, 5 is to carry this pre-Christian meaning into new covenant worship. The result is disastrous: they have compromised the very message of the gospel itself (15:9, 11; cf. Gal 1:6-9; 2:15-16). So, just as pagan forms pose special spiritual dangers to pagan background believers, so too, for Jews who fail to grasp that OT forms are fulfilled in Christ, Jewish forms pose similar dangers to Jewish believers.

---

272. Witherington, *Acts*, 464.

273. See Exod 20:4-6, 23; 34:17; Deut 12:1-4, 29-31; Isa 40:18-20; 41:6-7; 44:9-20; Acts 8:4-24; 12:20-23; 13:4-12; 14:15-17; 17:24-31; 19:11-20, 26.

274. Witherington, "Not So," 243, see generally, 242-46.

275. See, for example, Exod 19:4-6; Deut 12:5-28; Acts 5:9-11; Eph 2:8-10. See further Block, *For the Glory*, 23; Carson, "Worship," 25-26.

c. Other NT references to circumcision, the law and the prohibitions

We now turn to a discussion of other references to circumcision, the law, and the prohibitions in the rest of the NT. Space does not permit a detailed discussion here, especially given that the role of the law in the new covenant is a substantial and debated issue in its own right.[276] Nevertheless, the following brief summary demonstrates that the above analysis of Acts 15 is consistent with broader NT teaching.

Regarding the law, notwithstanding the variety of views on this topic, it is generally agreed that (in some sense) the law is not abolished, but is instead fulfilled,[277] and that this fulfillment involves the abrogation of certain laws: food previously prohibited can now be eaten (Mark 7:19), and physical circumcision is no longer required (Gal 5:6; 6:15).[278]

Importantly, the *reason* for these changes is not because of a need for people to retain the forms of their birth communities and be free from foreign ones. Rather, it is because a salvation-historical transition has occurred. Thus the change to the food laws is presented in Mark 7:14–23 as a salvation-historical transition: that which was once declared by God to be unclean (Lev 11:1–47; Deut 14:1–22) is now declared by Jesus to be clean (cf. Acts 10:15). This text is not a permission for Gentiles to eat non-kosher food on the grounds that Jewish food laws are not part of their cultural heritage. Rather it is a declaration that *all* believers, Jew and Gentile alike, are free to eat all food because a salvation-historical shift regarding the law has occurred.[279] Likewise the change with regard to circumcision is also because a salvation-historical transition has occurred (Gal 2:15–16; 5:16–26), a transition which was in fact anticipated in the time of Abraham (Gal 3:6–19). Importantly, in the new covenant, neither Jew nor Gentile is required to be circumcised.[280] Thus the principle here is not that believers should retain the customs of their birth culture. Rather,

---

276. See Strickland, *Five Views*.

277. Matt 5:17–20; Rom 8:4; 13:8, 10; 1 Cor 9:21; Gal 5:14; 6:2.

278. See chapter 2, §2.c.i. above. Kruse, "Law," 629–36; Strickland, *Five Views*; Schreiner, *Law*; Blomberg, "Law," 71–72.

279. IM proponents Roberts and Jameson claim that "Jesus did not tell his Jewish disciples to abandon their Jewish roots," however, it appears from Mark 7:14–23, which was spoken to Jews only, that he did in fact do so. Roberts and Jameson, "Conversion," 201.

280. Jewish believers are like people who were once under the supervision of "guardians" (παιδαγωγὸς, *paidagōgos*) (that is, the law), but have now reached adulthood and so the guardians are no longer needed: Gal 3:23—4:7. Cf. Rom 2:17—3:31; 1 Cor 7:19; Phil 3:3–7; Col 2:11–12. Kruse, "Law," 635; Schreiner, "Circumcision," 137–39.

a salvation-historical transition regarding the law has occurred, such that circumcision is no longer mandatory for *anyone*.

Concerning other NT references to the prohibitions, again, space does not permit a thorough examination of relevant texts, and so we limit ourselves to the following three points. First, there are no other NT references outside Acts relating to prohibitions concerning "the meat of strangled things" (πνικτός, *pniktos*) and "blood" (αἷμα, *haima*). Second, regarding other NT references to "meat sacrificed to idols" (εἰδωλοθύτων, *eidōlothutōn*), a consistent teaching emerges: if it is known to be idol food, believers are to abstain from eating it.[281] Third, regarding other NT references to "sexual immorality" (πορνεία, *porneia*), this is always prohibited.[282] Further, while the term πορνεία, *porneia* can refer to sexual sin that is not associated with pagan cults,[283] wherever πορνεία, *porneia* is used in conjunction with εἰδωλοθύτων, *eidōlothutōn*, cultic sexual activity is in view.[284] This strengthens the above conclusion that Acts 15 (where idol meat and sexual immorality are also grouped together) is concerned with the pagan idol feast.[285] Thus wherever references to εἰδωλοθύτων, *eidōlothutōn* and πορνεία, *porneia* are grouped together, the message of the NT authors is the same: pagan background believers must stay away from using pagan forms at pagan temples. A "clean break with the pagan past" is required.[286]

d. The implications of Acts 15 and related texts for the IM debate

We now consider the implications of our analysis of Acts 15 and related texts for the IM debate.

---

281. 1 Cor 8:1—11:1 (see the analysis in chapter 5 below); Rev 2:14 and 2:20.

282. Matt 19:9; Mark 7:21; 1 Cor 5:1; 6:13, 18; 10:8; Gal 5:19; Eph 5:3; Col 3:5; 1 Thess 4:3; Rev 2:14, 20; 9:21.

283. See Matt 19:9; 1 Cor 5:1.

284. See 1 Cor 10:7–8; Rev 2:14, 20. The phrase "Satan's throne" in Rev 2:13 is probably a reference to a famous pagan temple in Pergamum. Witherington, "Not So," 250; Witherington, *Acts*, 466.

285. Witherington, "Not So," 246–47; Witherington, *Acts*, 466; Thompson, *Acts*, 186.

286. Witherington, "Not So," 250. See also Witherington, *Acts*, 466.

i. Acts 15 does not establish a principle that believers should retain the worship forms of their birth community

A key objective in our analysis of Acts 15 has been to evaluate the IM claim that Acts 15 establishes a principle that believers should not have foreign worship forms imposed upon them, but are instead free to retain the forms of their birth community (see chapter 4, §3.a.i. above). As the above analysis makes clear, this claim is based on a misunderstanding of Acts 15 and must therefore be rejected. By incorrectly identifying the issue in Acts 15 as concerning the right of Gentile believers to remain inside their Gentile culture and retain its forms, IM proponents have drawn out of the text a principle that Luke never intended to communicate. The real issue under debate concerns the role of the law in the new covenant age. Luke's concern is actually to announce a unique, unrepeatable salvation-historical transition and spell out its implications for all believers. Acts 15 *does* establish that Gentiles do not need to obey the law. But it does not establish that they are free to use the forms of their pre-conversion faiths.

A key problem with the IM argument is that it is based on the misconception that the Jews remain under the law. As we have seen, IM proponents claim that Acts 15 upholds the rights of Jews to retain Jewish forms, and of Gentiles to retain Gentile forms.[287] Lewis writes,

> In the first century there were in existence at least two radically different religions based on Jesus Christ. There was the Jewish version, breathing life into the laws of Moses and Jewish ritual holy days, and there was the Greco-Roman version, turning their philosophy-loving hearts into theology-loving hearts that explored the nuances of the Trinity and the Incarnation.[288]

On this point, Higgins even goes so far as to describe the believing Pharisees in 15:5 as an example of "a movement to Jesus among the Pharisees."[289] Yet as we have seen, in both Acts and the rest of the NT, it is not only Gentiles, *but Jews also*, who are now free from the law. Both groups are saved by faith in Christ through grace (15:9, 11). Further, regarding the believing Pharisees of 15:1, 5, *they are not presented by Luke as models to be imitated.*

---

287. Lewis, "Honoring," 18; Lewis, "Integrity," 43–44; Massey, "Amazing Diversity," 8, 10; Ridgway, "Insider," 85; Dutch, "Should Muslims," 18; Talman, "Old Testament," 55; Talman, "Acts 15," 254–55; Travis, "Must all Muslims," 411; Roberts and Jameson, "Conversion," 203–4; Brown, "Contextualization," 127–28; Woodberry, "To the Muslims," 25–27.

288. Lewis, "Integrity," 45. Cf. Brown, "Contextualization," 128.

289. Higgins, "Acts 15," 37. See also Roberts and Jameson, "Conversion," 204.

On the contrary, their position is totally rejected and discredited. Paul and Barnabas engage in "sharp dispute and debate" with them (15:2). Peter accuses them of "testing God" (πειράζετε τὸν θεόν, *peirazete ton theon*) (15:10), that is, hindering his purpose.[290] And in 15:24, the apostles go to great lengths to distance themselves from them: "Some went out from us without our authorization and disturbed you, troubling your minds by what they said."[291] Thus the view that Acts 15 envisages Jewish believers using Jewish forms, and Gentile believers using Gentile forms, is based on a misreading of the text. Acts 15 does not justify the use by believers of the forms of their pre-conversion faith.

ii. Acts 15 does warn of the dangers associated with believers using the forms of their pre-conversion faith

The second objective of our analysis has been to evaluate the claim by IM critics that the prohibitions in Acts 15 function as a warning to believers against using the forms of their pre-conversion faith. Before drawing a conclusion on this matter, two preliminary points need to be stated.

First, the different explanations for the purpose of the prohibitions carry different implications for the IM debate. Coleman explores this point. He notes that if the moral view is preferred, then the prohibitions themselves remain binding. However, if the table fellowship view is preferred, then Acts 15 calls believers to choose forms that maintain harmony between believers, and do not damage one's witness in the unbelieving community. If the pagan idolatry view is preferred, then Acts 15 calls believers to withdraw from participation in the worship of other religions.[292] Given that there is no consensus on the purpose of the prohibitions, it is worth heeding Coleman's caution against overly dogmatic conclusions. Nevertheless, on the basis of the arguments above that the fifth explanation is the most plausible (in light of the text of Acts 15 itself, Luke's literary and theological purposes in Acts generally, and the rest of the NT), we will now proceed to identify the implications of this explanation.

---

290. Peterson, *Acts*, 426. The verb used here for "test" (πειράζω, *peirazō*) is used elsewhere for serious acts of opposition to God's purposes. See Exod 17:2; Deut 6:16; Ps 95:9 (LXX). In Acts, it is used by Peter to denounce Sapphira, who agreed to "test the Spirit of the Lord" (πειράσαι τὸ πνεῦμα Κυρίου, *peirasai to pneuma Kuriou*) (5:9). Peterson, *Acts*, 426.

291. Blomberg, "Christian," 408.

292. Coleman, *Analysis*, 157–58.

Second, it is important to recognize that the pagan forms prohibited in Acts 15 are different to the Muslim forms advocated by IM proponents for use in contextualized worship. Thus it would be simplistic to conclude that because certain pagan forms are prohibited for pagan background believers in Acts 15, a "rule" exists that Muslim background believers must not use Muslim forms. Nevertheless, important *principles* do emerge, and their implications for the IM debate need to be considered.

Acts 15 sounds a warning to BMBs who are contemplating using Muslim forms, especially in the mosque setting. When James and the apostles consider the matter of the use by pagan background believers of pagan forms—particularly, it would appear, in the temple setting—they issue a blanket prohibition. They do not entertain the possibility that believers might continue to attend pagan temple feasts but reinterpret the forms. Instead, they call for complete separation and a decisive cutting of ties with temple worship. As Proctor writes,

> The priority for new Christian converts is to keep clear of other religious ties—especially tangible participation in other religions. . . . Constraint may be ended; but caution is still required. "When in doubt, don't get involved," may still apply in this matter.[293]

The approach taken by James and the apostles is markedly different to that advocated by IM proponents, whereby BMBs continue to attend mosque worship, using and reinterpreting Muslim forms. Undoubtedly, differences can be identified between pagan and Muslim forms, and between the temple feast and mosque worship. Yet both represent formalized, structured, communal attempts to engage in non-Christ-centered worship.[294] Thus Acts 15 does at the very least caution form-selectors to consider the dangers associated with using Muslim forms, especially in the context of participation in mosque worship.[295]

---

293. Proctor, "Proselytes," 478. Cf. Farrokh, "Insider Movements," 236.

294. On this issue, see Tennent, "Followers," 105-7.

295. Farrokh argues that Acts 15 (and other texts in Acts) "promotes religious discontinuity for new Gentile believers." See Farrokh, "Insider Movements," 238 (see generally 227-40).

iii. Other implications for the IM debate

A number of general principles regarding worship and forms emerged in our analysis, and these principles are relevant to the IM debate. Four implications are identified here.

First, Acts 15 highlights the fact that new covenant worship is characterized by faith in Jesus, not outward forms. Thus new covenant worshipers are not faced with the task, as their OT counterparts were, of identifying the "correct," God-given forms, and then using them. Rather, new covenant worshipers have great freedom in the selection of outward forms. For example, there is great freedom with respect to matters such as prayer (timing, wording, and posture) and gathering for corporate worship (location, architecture, liturgy, and gathering times). But this freedom needs to be exercised with the nature of new covenant worship in mind—that is, worship that is by faith in Jesus, through grace. A key test of a form's appropriateness, therefore, is whether using it facilitates worship that is by faith in Jesus and through grace, or somehow inhibits or confuses it.

Despite the great diversity in world Islam,[296] it is probably true to say that most BMBs will have come out of a background where they believed as Muslims that particular outward forms (such as the *sholat*, *zakat*, and fasting) were divinely prescribed and so essential to make worship effective. Thus a crucial task for most BMBs will be to transition from depending on the use of particular forms to make their worship effective, to depending on Christ and experiencing the accompanying freedom with regard to the choice of outward forms. It may be that use by BMBs of the Muslim forms previously thought to be necessary to constitute worship would hinder this process. For example, a BMB might try to use a modified *sholat* ritual to pray, only to discover that use of this form reinforces the mindset that performance of this ritual is necessary in order to engage in true worship or to win God's favor, thus undermining the dependence on Christ that is the essence of true worship. In such circumstances, an alternative prayer form would need to be sought.

Second, Acts 15 reinforces the proposition that true worship is God-given and that the human role in worship is *responsive* in nature: God's people simply *respond* in faith and repentance to what he has done. It is crucial for this dynamic to be preserved in the contextualization process. Form-selectors should seek out forms that reinforce this fundamental principle, and avoid those that compromise or confuse it. Given this, if BMBs find that particular Muslim forms have associations with human initiative

---

296. See Greer, "Review," 204.

in worship, or merit-accumulation as the goal of worship, then it may well be wise to avoid those forms.

Third, we saw in our analysis of Acts 15 that OT forms have unique, theological meanings, and that they cease to have these meanings in the new covenant age. This must be taken into account when articulating principles concerning contextualization on the basis of NT texts such as Acts 15 which deal with these OT forms. NT texts such as these are written to announce that a salvation-historical shift has occurred: the law has been fulfilled, and this is the reason that Jewish forms are no longer required. They are *not* written to teach principles about the desirability or permissibility of different ethnic groups retaining their own cultural norms.

Many IM proponents interpreting Acts 15 have erred here, adopting a cultural paradigm for interpretation rather than a salvation-historical one.[297] They mischaracterize circumcision and law-observance as merely "Jewish culture"[298] and so misunderstand Acts 15, wrongly concluding that it establishes the neutrality of *all* cultural and religious forms.[299] In fact, Luke's argument is only that *OT forms* no longer function in accordance with the specific theological meanings which God had previously given them, an argument which simply cannot be extended to forms of other faiths.

Finally, our analysis of Acts 15 also raised the possibility that the forms from a believers' pre-conversion faith might pose special spiritual dangers to those believers, precisely because of the history of usage in false worship. This point raises further doubts about the helpfulness of two "tests" for form-selection often advocated by IM proponents. The first is the "biblical compatibility" test (see chapter 1, §3.a.vi. above), according to which Muslims can retain Muslim forms that are "compatible with the Bible" (that is, forms which are not prohibited in Scripture or inherently immoral).[300] Yet James and the apostles in Acts 15 do not apply this test. If they had, they might have decided that since the meat of strangled animals was not prohibited in Scripture or inherently immoral, the form could be retained. Yet in reality they prohibited this form, most likely *because of*

---

297. Garner, "High Stakes," 261.

298. Brown, "Contextualization," 128.

299. For examples of this hermeneutical error in the interpretation of Acts 15, see Kraft, *Christianity in Culture* (1979), 340–41; Whiteman, "Function," 50; Lewis, "Honoring," 18; Lewis, "Integrity," 43; Talman, "Old Testament," 55; Talman, "Acts 15," 251–56; Massey, "Amazing Diversity," 8, 10; Ridgway, "Insider," 85; Roberts and Jameson, "Conversion," 202–4; Brown, "Contextualization," 128. For critiques, see Garner, "High Stakes," 260–64; Wiarda, "Jerusalem," 233–36.

300. Talman, "Acts 15," 258, 260. See also Lewis's comments in Brogden, "Inside Out," 35; Talman, "Old Testament," 49–57.

its association with false worship. Thus the biblical compatibility test, by itself, is inadequate. A particular Muslim form might not be prohibited by the Bible or inherently immoral, and yet still be unhelpful because of its associations with non-Christian worship.

The second test is Kraft's allegiance test (see chapter 1, §3.c.i. above). Kraft proposes that almost any form can be used to express allegiance to the true God, provided an appropriate Christian meaning is given to it, and so he encourages worshipers to use the forms of their birth communities, rather than adopting foreign, Christian forms. Again, the approach of James and the apostles is radically different. They do not encourage the Gentiles to continue using pagan forms so long as their allegiance is to Christ. Rather, because of the associations of these forms with false worship, they issue an all-encompassing prohibition on their use. They do not simply call the Gentiles to turn from idolatry, but they also equip them to do so by prohibiting the use of forms associated with idolatry. Kraft's approach is problematic because it does not deal with the dangers posed by forms based on their associations with false (that is, non-Christ-centric) worship.

Ultimately, any test used in the selection of forms needs to account for the potential for forms to influence the way a worshiper engages with God. For this reason, a much better test, and one that gives adequate weight to Luke's concerns as they have emerged in our analysis, is to ask whether a particular form is likely to be *helpful* in facilitating true worship, that is, worship that is by faith in Christ, through grace. Forms borrowed from the formalized, structured, communal systems of other faiths must be carefully analyzed in this regard.

Thus Acts 15 contains a number of important implications for the IM debate.

4. First Corinthians 8–10

As explained above (chapter 4, §1.), 1 Corinthians 8–10 is analyzed as both an appropriation text and a resistance text in this book. To avoid unnecessary duplication, the full analysis of this text can be found in chapter 5.

5. Conclusion

In this chapter, two NT appropriation texts have been studied (with the second also doubling as a NT resistance text). What has emerged in the analysis demonstrates a remarkable consistency, not only between the two texts studied in this chapter, but also between these texts and the OT appropriation texts analyzed in chapter 2. Just as we saw in chapter 2 that the OT appropriation texts could not be characterized as biblical precedents for believers to use the forms of other faiths, so too we have seen in this chapter that the NT appropriation texts cannot be characterized in that way. Moreover, the NT appropriation texts also teach a theology of worship and forms which has remarkably similar emphases to what emerged in our study of OT texts in chapters 2 and 3. In particular, a foundational theme that has once again emerged is that God provides a way for his people to engage him in worship, and so form-selectors must seek forms which help them to engage with him in this divinely given way. We now turn to an analysis of NT resistance texts.

5

New Testament Resistance Texts

1. Introduction

IN THIS CHAPTER, WE study 1 Corinthians 8–10 (which is both the third NT appropriation text and the second NT resistance text) and Colossians 2 (the third NT resistance text). The goal, as in previous chapters, is to identify the attitude of the biblical authors to the use by believers of the forms of other faiths, and then to draw implications for the IM debate.

2. Acts 15

As explained above (chapter 4, §1.), Acts 15 is analyzed as both an appropriation text and a resistance text in this book. To avoid unnecessary duplication, the full analysis of this text is presented above in chapter 4.

3. First Corinthians 8–10

First Corinthians 8–10 (like Acts 15) is an important text for the IM debate because it has been advanced by both IM proponents and IM critics as a text which supports their respective positions. In 1 Corinthians 8–10, Paul discusses idol food. He begins by exhorting his readers to refrain from eating it if doing so would cause the "weak" to stumble (8:1–13). He then illustrates the principle of giving up one's rights for the sake of others by citing examples from his own life (9:1–23). Next he provides a series of warnings concerning the danger of missing out on salvation (9:24—10:13), after which he calls on the Corinthians to avoid participation in idolatry, lest they miss out (10:14–22). He concludes the unit by discussing certain specific scenarios involving idol food (10:23—11:1).[1]

---

1. On the unity and provenance of 8:1—11:1, see Schmithals, *Gnosticism*, 92; Cheung, *Idol Food*, 82–85; Willis, "Corinthians," 103–4.

a. The relevance of the text to the research problem

The relevance of the text to the research problem, and to the IM debate more generally, is plain and not contentious. Although they draw different conclusions from Paul's teaching in this text, both IM proponents[2] and IM critics[3] claim that 1 Corinthians 8-10 is relevant to the IM debate because it discusses the use by believers of the forms of other faiths, specifically idol food and temple feasts. This claim is undoubtedly correct. The text is concerned throughout with the eating of "idol food" (εἰδωλοθύτων, *eidōlothutōn*) (8:1, 4, 7, 10; 10:19).[4] The term εἰδωλοθύτων, *eidōlothutōn* refers to food which had been offered to a god as part of a pagan cultic ritual, and then either eaten immediately (at the god's temple or in the private home of a worshiper), or taken to the market to be sold.[5] In light of our broad definition of the term "form" in chapter 1, idol food is clearly the form of another faith, and eating it is *using* the form of another faith.

A temple feast (which is probably in view in 8:10 and 10:14-22) is also the form of another faith. A temple feast involved the eating of idol food in a dining hall attached to a temple, in circumstances where the relevant god was viewed as the patron of the occasion.[6] Whether such feasts were *primarily* religious or social in nature is much debated (see chapter 5, §3.b.i.1. below). For now it is sufficient to note that even those feasts with a strong social focus nevertheless incorporated pagan rituals.[7] Thus temple feasts are undoubtedly the form of another faith.

Further, at issue throughout 1 Corinthians 8-10 is whether *believers* should use these forms, that is, whether they should eat idol food, and participate in temple feasts (see especially 8:1, 4, 9-13; 10:14—11:1). In light of our broad definition of worship as an all-of-life response that believers make to God (chapter 1, §4.d. above), it follows that what is at issue here is whether believers should use these forms in their all-of-life worship. In conclusion, 1 Corinthians 8-10 does indeed deal with the use of the forms of other faiths *by God's people* in their worship *as God's people*, and as such is relevant to our research problem.

---

2. Woodberry, "To the Muslims," 24-25; Higgins, "Acts 15," 37; Higgins, "Inside What?," 79; Lewis, "Integrity," 44, 48.

3. Coleman, *Analysis*, 159-62, 170-78; Tennent, "Followers," 107-8.

4. As well, in 10:28, the termἱερόθυτόν, *hierothuton* (the non-pejorative term for idol food used by pagans) is used.

5. Silva, "εἴδωλον," 98-102; Ciampa and Rosner, *Corinthians*, 373.

6. Ciampa and Rosner, *Corinthians*, 369.

7. Gooch, *Dangerous Food*, 15-26; Cheung, *Idol Food*, 27-38.

b. The meaning of the text for the original audience

i. Is there evidence in the text that the author is seeking to persuade readers to use or resist the forms of their pre-conversion faith?

IM proponents and IM critics make very different claims about the meaning and implications of 1 Corinthians 8–10.

IM proponents advance three arguments from this text. First, a number argue that Paul's approach of becoming all things to all people (9:22), coupled with his call for the Corinthians to imitate him (11:1), justifies the use by BMBs and missionaries of Muslim forms.[8] Indeed, Higgins, Jameson, and Talman describe the insider approach as "living out 1 Corinthians 9:19–23."[9]

Second, Lewis claims that in 1 Corinthians 8 and 10:23—11:1, Paul removes the Jerusalem Council's prohibition on eating idol food (Acts 15:29), and makes it "a matter of conscience."[10] Thus for Lewis, this text affirms the neutrality of the forms of other faiths:

> Paul makes it a matter of doing what least offends the conscience of the person you are eating with, noting that idols are nothing and therefore meat offered to them is not significant either. It seems clear that Paul does not consider it 'syncretistic' to adapt in this way.[11]

Third, Higgins also sees this text as affirming the neutrality of the forms of other faiths. He tentatively proposes that Paul's reference in 8:10 to a Corinthian believer eating in an idol's temple may be evidence of the existence of a Gentile insider movement within a pagan context. He writes,

> Paul's concern in the verse is not that the action was wrong in itself; in fact, he does not criticize the brother for the action. Rather, Paul's critique is based on the fact that it might encourage a weaker brother to eat in such a way, and again, defile his conscience. My point is that this text seems to refer to a Gentile believer who, without committing idolatry, is not only buying meat in the market or eating it in a private home, but is sitting at

---

8. Woodberry, "To the Muslims," 23–25; Lewis, "Integrity," 44, 48; Cumming, "Muslim," 26; Higgins, Jameson and Talman, "Myths," 48; Roberts and Jameson, "Conversion," 208–10; Caldwell, "Jesus in Samaria," 28; Richard, "All Things," 289; Woodberry, "Incarnational," 241; Travis and Woodberry, "When God's Kingdom," 28–29; Higgins, "Key," 160; Massey, "Amazing Diversity," 8.

9. Higgins et al., "Myths," 48.

10. Lewis, "Integrity," 44.

11. Lewis, "Integrity," 48n7.

table in the idol's temple. Further study is needed to determine what is in fact happening here. For now, I am only prepared to suggest that this is a possible example of a Gentile believer who is still "inside" part of their religious heritage.[12]

Turning to IM critics, they advance two main arguments from this text. First, while accepting that 1 Corinthians 9:19–22 does teach that believers must "enter into the experience and life-view of those they are seeking to reach," Tennent argues that the text does not go so far as to justify insider methodology.[13]

Second, Coleman argues that 1 Corinthians 8–10 actually *prohibits* participation by believers in religious meals in pagan temples. He concludes,

> Insider believers who participate in Muslim *religious* events with unbelieving Muslims, such as prayers at the mosque, cross a boundary delineated by Paul.[14]

In short, while IM proponents cite 1 Corinthians 8–10 to demonstrate that BMBs can use Muslim forms, IM critics cite the same text to argue that they cannot. In accordance with the methodology set out in chapter 1, the key to resolving this debate is to inquire as to authorial intent. At issue is whether Paul is seeking to persuade his readers to *use* the forms of their previous faith or to *resist* them.

However, before we can address this question directly, we must first survey the debate regarding the meaning of 1 Corinthians 8–10. Paul's argument is complex and nuanced, and has given rise to a number of very different understandings of his actual position on idol food. We will outline these different views now, identifying the view which has the best evidence to support it. Only then will we be in a position to draw conclusions regarding Paul's attitude to the use by the Corinthians of the forms of their pre-conversion faith.

1. What is Paul's argument in 1 Corinthians 8–10?

One reason for such a variety of opinion regarding Paul's position on idol food is that interpreters of 1 Corinthians 8–10 must engage in mirror reading in order to reconstruct the situation that led to Paul's letter. As Ciampa

---

12. Higgins, "Acts 15," 37. See also Higgins, "Inside What?," 79; Higgins, "Idol's Temple," 32; Higgins, "Biblical Basis," 221–22.
13. Tennent, "Followers," 108. Cf. Hwang, *Toward*, ch. 4.
14. Coleman, *Analysis*, 175 (see generally 170–78).

and Rosner note, this interpretative process is invariably subjective.[15] While there is general agreement that Paul is responding to a letter from the Corinthians in which they claim the right to eat idol food (8:1, 4),[16] there is disagreement on a number of matters: first, exactly what rights the Corinthians claimed in relation to idol food; second, when Paul is quoting the Corinthians and when he is asserting his own position; and third, whether the Corinthians were united against Paul in their position on idol food, or whether they were divided into two factions (the "knowledgeable" and the "weak") and were appealing to Paul to arbitrate.[17]

Another complicating factor is that idol food could potentially be consumed by Corinthian believers in a range of different circumstances: as part of a temple feast in a dining hall attached to a pagan temple, as part of a dinner party in the private home of a pagan neighbor, or when the Corinthian believers themselves purchased the food from the market (much, but not all, of the food available at the market had been previously offered to an idol).[18] Interpreters differ regarding which setting Paul has in mind in the major sections of 1 Corinthians 8–10.[19]

The main interpretative problem, however, concerns the apparent contradiction between 8:1–13 and 10:14–22.[20] In 8:4–6, Paul affirms the knowledge of the "knowledgeable" believers (that is, that idol food is not inherently bad, because the idol is nothing). The objection that he raises here against the "knowledgeable" eating idol food is not that doing so is inherently sinful, but rather that doing so might cause the "weak" (those without such knowledge) to stumble (8:7–13).Thus in 8:1–13, it seems that eating idol food by the "knowledgeable" is permissible, provided there are no "weak" Christians to witness it. However, in 10:14–22, any person who eats idol food is characterized as a participant with demons, and such eating is prohibited outright.[21] How is this apparent contradiction to be resolved? What follows is a description and evaluation of the four main views.[22]

15. Ciampa and Rosner, *Corinthians*, 368.

16. See Ciampa and Rosner, *Corinthians*, 368–69.

17. See Willis, *Idol*, 112; Willis, "Corinthians," 106–7; Ciampa and Rosner, *Corinthians*, 371; Flemming, *Contextualization*, 183–84; Hurd, *Origin*, 117–25, 143–48; Garland, *Corinthians*, 353–62; Gooch, *Dangerous Food*, 66; Cheung, *Idol Food*, 87–88.

18. Ciampa and Rosner, *Corinthians*, 369; Garland, *Corinthians*, 347; Willis, "Corinthians," 107–8.

19. Oh-Young, *1 Corinthians*, 154–57.

20. Fee, "Εἰδωλόθυτα," 172–74.

21. Gooch, *Dangerous Food*, 79.

22. Other views and variations on these views also exist. See further, Gooch, *Dangerous Food*, 79–83; Newton, *Deity*, 312–13.

According to the first view, often referred to as the traditional view, the apparent contradiction is resolved by envisaging different *settings* for the two texts, with 8:1-13 concerned primarily with eating marketplace idol food, and 10:14-22 concerned with eating idol food at idol temples. According to this view, Paul affirms, in both 8:1-13 and 10:23—11:1, the moral neutrality of marketplace idol food and the freedom of Christians to eat it, but urges them to forgo this freedom if eating will cause the "weak" to stumble. In 10:1-22, he prohibits participation in actual idol feasts at idol temples.[23]

In recent decades, "insuperable difficulties"[24] with this traditional view have been identified, such that today it has almost no support. Most importantly, the claim that 8:1-13 is primarily concerned with marketplace idol food is clearly wrong, since the only setting explicitly identified by Paul in 8:1-13 is that of an idol temple (8:10).[25] Further, if, as advocates of the traditional view maintain, 8:1-13 and 10:23—11:1 are addressing the same problem (the eating of marketplace idol food), then this creates a contradiction, since in 8:7-13, Paul passionately discourages eating it, whereas in 10:23-29, he permits eating it, except where the food's association with idols is made known.[26] Thus the traditional view is unsatisfactory.

The second view was first raised by Fee in 1977,[27] and has since gained widespread acceptance.[28] According to this view, the tension between 8:7-13 and 10:14-22 is resolved by understanding that these two texts represent the first and second parts of a two-stage argument against the eating of idol food in idol temples. Thus both texts have the same setting in mind: the idol temple. And Paul's ultimate goal is to prohibit outright the eating of idol food in this place. But he presents his case in two stages: first, the "knowledgeable" must not eat idol food there because of the spiritual harm they will do to the "weak" by drawing them into idolatry (8:7-13); and second, the "knowledgeable" must not eat idol food there because of the harm they

---

23. For presentations of this view, see Barrett, *Corinthians*, 188; Barrett, "Things," 40-59; Bruce, *Corinthians*, 78-102; Conzelmann, *Corinthians*, 146-80.

24. Fee, *Corinthians* (1987), 359.

25. Fee, *Corinthians* (1987), 359; Fisk, "Eating," 50-51.

26. Fee, *Corinthians* (1987), 359; Fisk, "Eating," 51.

27. Fee, "Food," 140-61; Fee, "Εἰδωλόθυτα," 172-97; Fee, *Corinthians* (1987), 357-491.

28. In the recently-published second edition of Fee's commentary, he notes that while his view was novel when he first presented it, it is now the "standard view." Fee, *Corinthians* (2014), 396n10. For other articulations of this view (or broadly similar variations of it), see Witherington, *Conflict*, 186-230; Garland, *Corinthians*, 347-504; Gooch, *Dangerous Food*, 83-84; Ciampa and Rosner, *Corinthians*, 369, 392-94, 475-76; Flemming, *Contextualization*, 185; Cheung, *Idol Food*, 82-162.

will do to themselves, since such an act amounts to idolatry.²⁹ According to this view, only in 10:23—11:1 does Paul deal with marketplace food that might have been offered to idols, where he affirms the freedom to eat except where the food's idolatrous origins are made known.³⁰

Proponents have put forward persuasive arguments in favor of this view. First, they rightly point out that, even though Paul advances different arguments in 8:7-13 and 10:14-22, his rhetorical goal in both texts is the same: to *dissuade* Corinthian Christians from eating idol food.³¹ Second, they note that although the arguments against eating in 8:7-13 and 10:14-22 are different, they are nevertheless compatible. Cheung writes,

> Abstention for the sake of the weak and abstention in order to avoid idolatry are not mutually exclusive arguments. On the contrary, they are mutually reinforcing in their prohibition of the consumption of idol food.³²

Notwithstanding the strength of these arguments, critics of Fee's view have identified various problems with it. First, according to this view, the Corinthians' "right/freedom" (ἐξουσία, *exousia*) to eat idol food in 8:7-13 is not a genuine one, but rather a right that they wrongly claim.³³ Yet an analysis of the text suggests that it is a genuine right. Paul calls it "this right of yours" (ἡ ἐξουσία ὑμῶν αὕτη, *hē exousia humōn hautē*) (8:9). If, as proponents of this view maintain, the practice is inherently sinful, surely Paul would qualify ἐξουσία, *exousia* here.³⁴ As well, the logic of 8:7 ("not everyone possesses this knowledge . . . ") only makes sense if the knowledge Paul refers to is true, and the eating of idol food *per se* is morally neutral.³⁵ Indeed, if the Corinthians' right to eat idol food is not a genuine one, it seems strange that Paul should devote so much space in chapter 9 to convincing the Corinthians of the need to voluntarily relinquish their rights for the sake of others. In giving examples from his own life in which he relinquishes his personal rights, Paul refers to genuine rights, not wrongly-claimed ones.³⁶

---

29. Fee, *Corinthians* (1987), 357-63.
30. Fee, *Corinthians* (1987), 359-60.
31. Cheung, *Idol Food*, 297.
32. Cheung, *Idol Food*, 96.
33. Fotopoulos, *Food*, 218; Garland, *Corinthians*, 359-60; Cheung, *Idol Food*, 89; Ciampa and Rosner, *Corinthians*, 375.
34. For example, he could have described it as "this right you claim to have" or "this so-called right" (cf. "so-called gods" [λεγόμενοι θεοὶ, *legomenoi theoi*] in 8:5). Naselli, "Idolatrous," 40. See also Fisk, "Eating," 60.
35. Fisk, "Eating," 60; Naselli, "Idolatrous," 38.
36. Fisk, "Eating," 59, 60; Kim, "*Imitatio Christi*," 215; Horrell, "Theological," 101.

Thus the Corinthians' right to eat idol meat is a genuine one, and so Fee's view needs, at the very least, some modification.[37]

A second objection raised by critics of Fee's view is that it is not plausible that Paul would begin discussing an idolatrous practice in 8:1, but defer his assessment of it as inherently idolatrous until 10:14–22.[38] For example, Fisk asks, "Could Paul really wait that long to challenge such serious sin?"[39] However, this objection to Fee's view is unpersuasive. What Fisk fails to acknowledge is that Paul *does* challenge the behavior of the "knowledgeable" in 8:1–13: it is a serious sin against the "weak" (whose stumbling they are causing), and ultimately against Christ himself; it is condemned as unloving behavior that has the potential to destroy fellow believers.

Further, though Paul's deferral of his evaluation of the practice as inherently idolatrous may seem odd to some, proponents of this view have drawn on the tools of rhetorical analysis to offer a range of plausible explanations as to why he might have done so. Fee suggests that Paul's "first concern" is with the attitude that lay behind the behavior of the "knowledgeable," and so he deals with this first (8:1–13), before moving on to correct their misunderstanding of the true nature of idolatry (10:14–22).[40] Cheung, by contrast, proposes that Paul, in his efforts to persuade the "knowledgeable," deliberately adopts a two-stage argument: "He first softens the Corinthians' resistance to the prohibition by appealing to their better nature" (8:1–13), but "saves his strongest argument for last" (10:14–22).[41] Gooch suggests, "Paul wishes not to lose his credibility with the Corinthians at the outset so offers a less offensive . . . reason for not eating in an idol's temple."[42] Finally, Garland writes,

> because the Corinthians did not yield to Paul's prior objection to idol food, he recognises that a lengthier, more subtle approach is demanded. . . . Consequently he employs indirect means.[43]

---

37. Fee argues that Paul's purpose in chapter 9 is not to illustrate the importance of relinquishing rights for the sake of others, but rather to defend his apostolic authority in the face of criticism arising from within the Corinthian church. Fee, *Corinthians* (1987), 9, 32, 363, 392–93, 399. For critiques of this aspect of Fee's view, see Ciampa and Rosner, *Corinthians*, 396; Fisk, "Eating," 59–60.

38. Horrell, "Theological," 99.

39. Fisk, "Eating," 54.

40. Fee, "Εἰδωλόθυτα," 197; Fee, *Corinthians* (1987), 363.

41. Cheung, *Idol Food*, 115–17.

42. Gooch, *Dangerous Food*, 84.

43. Garland, *Corinthians*, 361. See further Newton, *Deity*, 313; Ciampa and Rosner, *Corinthians*, 392–94; Witherington, *Conflict*, 195.

Thus this second objection to Fee's view is not strong.

The third view, originally put forward by Fisk,[44] posits that the apparent tension between 8:7–13 and 10:14–22 is resolved by recognizing that a range of different activities took place in pagan temples, some of which were primarily social, while others involved actual worship of pagan deities. Naselli writes,

> Paul's argument assumes two tiers of temple meals: 1) those not inherently idolatrous and objectively defiling (1 Cor 8:10); and, 2) those inherently idolatrous and objectively defiling (1 Cor 10:20–21).[45]

Similarly, Newton proposes that 8:7–13 and 10:14–22 deal with differing degrees of involvement in cultic activities: while 8:10 addresses mere eating, 10:14–22 is concerned with participation in the actual sacrificial offerings and then eating.[46]

Fisk and others advance the following arguments in support of this view. First, they adduce historical evidence to show that pagan temples had diverse functions: events held in temples fell on a spectrum ranging from primarily cultic and religious, to primarily social or business.[47] After surveying relevant historical and archaeological evidence, Naselli concludes that meals in idol temples "did not necessarily always begin with a formal demonic ceremony of sacrifice and prayer."[48]

Second, proponents of this view point out that what Paul condemns outright is "idolatry" (εἰδωλολάτραι, *eidōlolatrai*) (10:7, 14), not the eating of "idol food" (εἰδωλοθύτων, *eidōlothutōn*) (8:1, 4, 7, 10). Eating idol food may amount to idolatry, depending on the nature of the meal, but it is not an inherently idolatrous act.[49] Fisk writes,

---

44. Fisk, "Eating," 49–70. For other articulations of this view, see Naselli, "Idolatrous," 23–45; Horrell, "Theological," 83–114; Dickson, *Mission-Commitment*, 232–44.

45. Naselli, "Idolatrous," 38. Cf. Fisk, "Eating," 62.

46. Such participation involves making a sacrificial offering (10:20), drinking the cup of demons (10:21a), and partaking of the table of demons (10:21b). Newton, *Deity*, 24.

47. Fisk, "Eating," 62–63; Naselli, "Idolatrous," 30–35; Willis, *Idol*, 18–20, 41–42, 47–56; Newton, *Deity*, 198–99, 299, 304.

48. Naselli, "Idolatrous," 32–33. Naselli quotes Fotopoulos's finding that "it may have been possible to rent such temple dining rooms for private use not directly related to the cult." Fotopoulos, *Food*, 176.

49. Fisk, "Eating," 63–64; Naselli, "Idolatrous," 40–41.

Paul's intent was not to declare all temple meal attendance off limits; the *nature* of the meal, not its *location*, was the issue.[50]

There are two problems with this third view. First, critics of this view challenge the notion that Corinthian believers could have eaten in a pagan temple without participating in pagan religious rites. Gooch surveys archaeological and literary evidence[51] and concludes that the "dissociation of temples and meals involving religious rites was not likely."[52] Cheung, Garland, Newton, and Fotopoulos also survey the relevant historical and archaeological evidence and draw similar conclusions.[53] Thus the weight of contemporary scholarly opinion rejects the notion that Corinthian believers could have eaten in an idol temple without participating in idolatrous rites.

Second, proponents of this view characterize 8:1–13 as a *permission* for believers to eat at social temple events, provided no one is caused to stumble. For example, Fisk writes, "1 Cor 8:10 describes permissible temple attendance, while 10:19–22 clearly portrays what is off limits."[54] Yet this is a serious mischaracterization of 8:1–13. At no point in 8:1–13 does Paul give permission to the Corinthians to eat at a temple. On the contrary, his rhetorical purpose is to call them to refrain from doing so (8:13). To describe 8:1–13 as a permission is to make the same mistake that the "knowledgeable" Corinthians were making, and which Paul is critiquing here: that is, applying abstract theological knowledge without love and an awareness of context (8:1–3, 7–13). Paul does accept the truthfulness of the knowledge claimed by the Corinthians (that eating idol meat in isolation is not inherently idolatrous: 8:4–6), but he does not conclude on the basis of this knowledge that, provided the "weak" are not present, the "knowledgeable" can continue to eat at the temple. Rather he calls them to *abstain* because of the serious risk that they might cause the "weak" to stumble (8:7–13).

There are, therefore, problems with the first three views. The fourth and final view presented here, advanced by Ciampa and Rosner, is the most persuasive.[55] It is essentially a modification of (and improvement on) Fee's view. Like Fee, Ciampa and Rosner understand Paul to be providing consecutive arguments against the eating of idol meat: eating idol

---

50. Fisk, "Eating," 69 (emphasis added).
51. Gooch, *Dangerous Food*, 1–46.
52. Gooch, *Dangerous Food*, 81–82.
53. Cheung, *Idol Food*, 27–38, 93–95; Garland, *Corinthians*, 347–50; Newton, *Deity*, 255; Fotopoulos, *Food*, 65–70.
54. See, for example, Fisk, "Eating," 62.
55. Ciampa and Rosner, *Corinthians*, 367–499. See also Schreiner, *Corinthians*, 162–219.

meat is sinful, *both* because it might lead others into idolatry (8:7-13) and also because it can amount to a participation in idolatry (10:14-22).[56] But unlike Fee, Ciampa and Rosner consider Paul to be accepting that the right claimed by the "knowledgeable" to eat idol food is a genuine one based on true knowledge (8:4-6).[57] However, it is an "in theory"[58] right only. Once its exercise is conditioned "by factors the Corinthians have overlooked," the result will always be that the Corinthians abstain, both so as to avoid sinfully leading others into idolatry (8:7-13), and also so as to avoid committing idolatry themselves (10:14-22).[59]

In addition, whereas Fee understands Paul to be objecting primarily to eating idol food in the temple precincts, according to Ciampa and Rosner the problem is not confined to eating in the temple,[60] but instead extends to any eating in which there is an "association with idolatry."[61] Their evidence for this conclusion is persuasive: they point out that throughout 8:1—11:1, wherever there is a known link between the food and idolatry, Paul calls the Corinthians to abstain from eating.[62] Cheung makes the same point:

> Paul regards the eating of idol food, *with the awareness of their idolatrous origins*, as a sinful act.... Paul never explicitly says that it is acceptable to eat idol food, he only says that one may eat anything without inquiring into the possibility of its being previously offered to idols. If one is somehow informed of the idolatrous origins of the food, the only permissible action is to abstain.[63]

This point, made by both Ciampa and Rosner, and Cheung, is persuasive. No convincing rebuttal has been offered by proponents of the other three views. This fourth view is thus the best one, since it builds on the strengths of Fee's view, while avoiding its weaknesses (described above). Most importantly, it shows a healthy sensitivity to Paul's rhetorical purpose, recognizing that it is not to grant a limited permission to eat idol food, but rather to dissuade the Corinthians from eating idol food whenever and

---

56. Ciampa and Rosner, *Corinthians*, 369.
57. Ciampa and Rosner, *Corinthians*, 390.
58. Ciampa and Rosner, *Corinthians*, 390 (see also 377).
59. Ciampa and Rosner, *Corinthians*, 390 (see also 371, 388).
60. Ciampa and Rosner, *Corinthians*, 434-35.
61. Ciampa and Rosner, *Corinthians*, 369.
62. Ciampa and Rosner, *Corinthians*, 390, 487. See also Cheung, *Idol Food*, 108-9, 296-98; Schreiner, *Corinthians*, 163.
63. Cheung, *Idol Food*, 108-9.

wherever it is known to be idol food.[64] That this is indeed Paul's rhetorical purpose is further demonstrated below.

2. WHAT THEN IS PAUL'S ATTITUDE TO THE CORINTHIANS USING THE FORMS OF THEIR PRE-CONVERSION FAITH?

We are now in a position to investigate Paul's attitude to the question of whether the Corinthians should use the forms of their pre-conversion faith. As the following analysis makes clear, Paul's rhetorical goal in 1 Corinthians 8–10 is to persuade the Corinthians to *refrain* from using the forms of their previous faith. He views the forms as extremely spiritually dangerous, and he offers three arguments as to why Corinthian believers should abstain from using them: first, for the sake of the "weak"; second, for their own sake; and third, for the sake of unbelievers.

Paul presents his first argument in 8:1—9:23: the Corinthians should avoid eating idol food for the sake of the "weak," since eating risks drawing them into idolatry. The background appears to be that the Corinthians have written to Paul, asserting their right to eat idol food on the grounds that pagan gods are non-existent and thus idol food is not spiritually contaminated (8:4–6).[65] Paul accepts this point: there is nothing wrong with the food *per se* (8:8; cf. 10:25–27).[66] However, this legitimate right to eat idol food must not be exercised unlovingly (8:1–3, 9). By eating idol food, the "knowledgeable" might embolden the "weak" to do the same (8:10); yet, the "weak" would not eat it as mere food, "but as an act of participation in the worship of an idol," since this is the meaning which they attach to eating idol food (10:7).[67] In this way, the "knowledgeable," by acting on this knowledge in isolation, and ignoring the context in which they are applying it, would be agents of sin by causing the "weak" "to fall into sin" (8:13).[68]

The consequences would be disastrous for both groups. For the "weak," it would not simply be that their consciences are offended (as some have proposed).[69] Rather, they would be "destroyed" (8:11). The verb "destroy" (ἀπόλλυται, *apollutai*) is always used by Paul to refer to eternal, final destruction,[70] and so he is saying here that the "weak" would forfeit salva-

---

64. Ciampa and Rosner, *Corinthians*, 393; Cheung, *Idol Food*, 109.
65. Ciampa and Rosner, *Corinthians*, 385–86.
66. Ciampa and Rosner, *Corinthians*, 388, 478.
67. Ciampa and Rosner, *Corinthians*, 392.
68. Willis, *Idol*, 107.
69. See Garland, *Corinthians*, 358.
70. Garland, *Corinthians*, 389; Fee, *Corinthians* (1987), 387–88; Willis, *Idol*, 106.

tion.⁷¹ The "knowledgeable" would have been a "stumbling block" to them (8:9), a metaphor which, in the NT, *always* describes "an obstacle that keeps someone from finding their way to ultimate salvation."⁷² Garland concludes, "Paul is not afraid that they might offend the weak in some way but that they might cause them to fall away from their Christian faith."⁷³

The consequences for the "knowledgeable" would be equally dire. They are *contrasted* with the one who loves God and is known by him (8:3), suggesting that their spiritual condition is also imperiled. By acting as a stumbling block, they would be guilty of sinning, not only against the precious "weak" brother or sister "for whom Christ died" (8:11), but also against Christ himself (8:12). The actions of the "knowledgeable" are thus "condemned in the strongest possible way."⁷⁴

What then must the Corinthians do? They must be guided by love, not knowledge in isolation from context (8:1–3). They must build the "weak" up in faith (8:1), not in sin (8:10).⁷⁵ They must avoid *at all costs* anything which might cause a fellow believer to stumble—"Be careful" in 8:9 is a form of words reserved in the NT for the gravest of warnings.⁷⁶ And ultimately, they must imitate Paul himself, who is willing on these grounds to "never eat meat again" (8:13).⁷⁷ Thus Paul's rhetorical goal in 8:1–13 is not to affirm a limited right to eat idol meat. Rather, it is to persuade the Corinthians to *refrain from eating idol food*. Idol food is a spiritually dangerous form that should be avoided.⁷⁸

In 9:1–23, Paul strengthens his argument by showing that the principle in 8:13 (that Christians should forgo rights for the sake of the gospel) has broad application.⁷⁹ Paul explains that, although he has a right to material support from the Corinthians (9:1–14), he forgoes this right for the sake of

---

71. Schreiner, *Corinthians*, 178.

72. See Rom 9:32, 33; 14:13, 20; 1 Pet 2:8. Ciampa and Rosner, *Corinthians*, 391; Garland, *Corinthians*, 387.

73. Garland, *Corinthians*, 387.

74. Taylor, *Corinthians*, 209.

75. In a clever play on words, Paul asserts that love "builds up" (οἰκοδομεῖ, *oikodomei*) (8:1), but that the "weak" will be "emboldened/built up" (οἰκοδομηθήσεται, *oikodomēthēsetai*) to eat sinfully by the thoughtless behavior of the "knowledgeable" (8:10). Taylor, *Corinthians*, 208.

76. Ciampa and Rosner, *Corinthians*, 390.

77. 8:13 contains what Dodd calls a "paradigmatic 'I'"; it functions as a vehicle for Paul to model the behavior he expects the Corinthians to emulate. Cf. 11:1, where Paul explicitly calls the Corinthians to imitate him. Dodd, *Paul's Paradigmatic 'I'*, 99, 235.

78. Cheung, *Idol Food*, 130.

79. Dodd, *Paul's Paradigmatic 'I'*, 99, 235; Ciampa and Rosner, *Corinthians*, 396.

the gospel (9:12b, 15–18). In fact, he forgoes many rights and makes many accommodations so that he "might save some" (9:19–23). Renouncing rights for the gospel is the right thing for all believers to do in all situations.[80] In this, Paul's rhetorical goal is unchanged: he is seeking to persuade the Corinthians to forgo their right to eat idol food. As Cheung concludes, "Paul's aim is not to teach the Corinthians the nature of Christian freedom. The rhetorical purpose is rather this: 'Go and do likewise. Renounce (idol) food.'"[81]

First Corinthians 9:19–23 must be understood in this context. If this text is read *in isolation*, one might easily get the impression that Paul is seeking to persuade his readers to use the forms of other faiths (including their own pre-conversion faith). However, the following arguments show that such an impression is unlikely.

First, 9:19–23 is part of an argument *against* using the forms of other faiths. When we read 9:19–23 in its context (that is, as a supporting and illustrative argument for the principle in 8:13), it is apparent that "becoming all things to all people" (9:22) means *being willing to forgo rights to advance the gospel* (8:13, 9:1–18). And the specific right that Paul is calling the Corinthians to forgo is their right to use the forms of their pre-conversion faith (8:13).[82] Thus to conclude that 9:19–23 actually *encourages* the use by believers of the forms of other faiths is to draw a conclusion that is at odds with Paul's rhetorical purpose.

Second, Paul becomes "like" (ὡς, *hōs*) those he seeks to win, but he does not become exactly the same as them (9:20–21).[83] Thus the principle of becoming all things to all people is limited. Paul's accommodation is not a wholesale imitation.

Third, an additional limit is that Paul always remains "under Christ's law" (9:21). Thus in becoming like those he seeks to win, Paul does not join them in any behavior that would amount to false worship or any other sin.[84] As Witherington notes, "his accommodating behavior has clear limits. He does not say that he became an idolater to idolaters, or an adulterer to adulterers."[85] Likewise, Carson writes, "The principle of accommodation . . .

---

80. Garland, *Corinthians*, 399.
81. Cheung, *Idol Food*, 141.
82. Carson, "Pauline Inconsistency," 16; Garland, *Corinthians*, 41.
83. The exception being the "weak" (10:22).
84. Ciampa and Rosner, *Corinthians*, 428, 431; Flemming, *Contextualization*, 197; Witherington, *Conflict*, 211; Carson, "Pauline Inconsistency," 11–13.
85. Witherington, *Conflict*, 213–14.

has built-in limitations that spring from the gospel itself. . . . [It] is not a licence for unlimited flexibility."[86]

Thus Paul's intention in 9:19–23, when viewed in context, is not to persuade his readers to become like others *by using the forms of other faiths*. On the contrary, it is to persuade them to *refrain from* using such forms (even forms believed to be harmless) by calling them to be ready to give up their rights out of love for others.

Thus the first of Paul's three arguments against eating idol food, presented in 8:1—9:23, is that the Corinthians should refrain from eating it for the sake of the "weak." In 9:24—10:22, he presents his second argument: the Corinthians should also refrain from eating it for their own sake, since eating it in certain contexts amounts to idolatry.

He begins with a series of examples that show that those who fail to exercise discipline and self-restraint suffer loss. In 9:24–27, it is the positive example of an athlete who trains hard so as to "not be disqualified for the prize" (9:27). The reference to disqualification is "to God's potential eschatological judgment."[87] Then in 10:1–13, it is the negative example of the Israelites of the wilderness generation: they lacked self-restraint and were rejected by God as people unworthy of the promised land (10:5).[88] Even though the Israelites, like the Corinthians, had been "fully initiated into the redeemed community"[89] (10:1–4), they nevertheless experienced divine judgment because of their false worship (10:5–10). Thus with both the positive and negative examples, nothing less than salvation is at stake.[90] Paul's purpose in these examples is not to teach the Corinthians about athletics or even Israelite history: he wants them to abstain from idol feasts. The examples lay the foundation for Paul's main exhortation in 10:14–22: if the Corinthians want to avoid disqualification, divine judgment and rejection, they must exercise self-restraint by not participating in idol feasts.[91]

First Corinthians 10:14–22 begins with an urgent call: "flee from idolatry" (10:14). Paul goes on to explain that just as eating the Lord's Supper creates partnership with Christ and his people, so too eating idol food at a temple feast creates partnership with demons (10:15–20). Though idols do not represent actual gods (10:19), there is nevertheless

---

86. Carson, "Pauline Inconsistency," 12, 33.

87. Ciampa and Rosner, *Corinthians*, 442. See also Witherington, *Conflict*, 214.

88. Ciampa and Rosner, *Corinthians*, 433–35, 443; Witherington, *Conflict*, 218.

89. Ciampa and Rosner, *Corinthians*, 449; Garland, *Corinthians*, 446.

90. Garland, *Corinthians*, 446–47; Witherington, *Conflict*, 217–18.

91. Smit writes that the examples serve Paul's argument that "believers should abstain from sacrificial meals." Smit, "Rhetorical," 490.

a spiritual reality behind them in that they have been created at the instigation of demons posing as gods and those worshiping them worship those demons.[92]

On 10:20, Garland writes,

> Becoming "partners with demons" means that participants join in common enterprise with the work of demons. They are not just passive participants in a pagan ritual; they contribute to spreading demonic thralldom in the world.[93]

Because of this, it is impossible to have both partnership with Christ and his people through the Lord's Supper, and partnership with demons and false worshipers through an idol feast (10:21).[94] Should the Corinthians attempt to have both, they will bring God's judgment upon themselves (10:22). Thus Paul's second argument (presented in 9:24—10:22) is that the Corinthians must refrain from eating idol food, since doing so in certain contexts amounts to idolatry that arouses God's jealousy, resulting in judgment.

In 10:23—11:1, Paul presents his third and final argument: the Corinthians should also refrain from eating idol food for the sake of non-believers. Here Paul discusses marketplace food and dinner party invitations from pagan neighbors. He reaffirms that idol food is not in itself contaminated, with the result that food of an unknown origin (and which *might* therefore be idol food) can be eaten (10:25–27; cf. 8:4–6, 8).[95] However, if the food is publicly identified as idol food, the Corinthians must abstain from eating it, for the sake of the conscience of non-believing onlookers (10:28–29).[96] That the onlookers Paul has in mind are non-believers is clear from the term used by the hypothetical onlooker for idol food in 10:28: it is not the pejorative expression used by Christians (εἰδωλοθύτων, *eidōlothutōn*), but rather the positive one used by pagan worshipers (ἱερόθυτόν, *hierothuton*).[97] Why would the eating of idol food negatively impact the conscience of a non-believer? The reasons for this are discussed below (chapter 5, §3.b.ii.6.). For now, we simply note that Paul calls upon the Corinthians to curtail their freedoms by not eating.[98]

---

92. Ciampa and Rosner, *Corinthians*, 479 (see generally 473–74, 478). See also Witherington, *Conflict*, 225; Flemming, *Contextualization*, 188–89.

93. Garland, *Corinthians*, 437.

94. Witherington, *Conflict*, 226; Ciampa and Rosner, *Corinthians*, 482.

95. Ciampa and Rosner, *Corinthians*, 487; Garland, *Corinthians*, 486.

96. Garland, *Corinthians*, 492.

97. Ciampa and Rosner, *Corinthians*, 493.

98. Dodd, *Paul's Paradigmatic 'I'*, 101, 110; Fee, *Corinthians* (1987), 478; Ciampa

We have seen that throughout the unit, Paul's intent is to persuade the Corinthians to *resist* using certain forms from their pre-conversion faith (specifically, idol meat and temple feasts). These forms are extremely spiritually dangerous. Using them can amount to sin and can lead to false worship, which arouses divine wrath and judgment.

ii. What does the text teach about worship and forms?

We examine here what 1 Corinthians 8–10 teaches about worship and forms.

1. For new covenant worshipers, there is freedom with regard to outward forms

Whereas old covenant worship was characterized by the detailed prescription of outward forms (see chapters 2 and 3), this text makes it clear that for new covenant worshipers, there is now great freedom. The law prescribed outward forms in great detail, and yet Paul is "not under the law" (9:20). While he has freedom to temporarily place himself under it for the sake of evangelism or love for "weak" believers, he is not bound by it (9:20–22).[99] Instead, he is free to become "like" the various groups that he seeks to win (9:20–22).

This new covenant freedom with regard to the law (and thus to the forms prescribed by it) is also apparent from Paul's discussion of idol food. If the OT law had not been fulfilled by Jesus, then the eating of idol food would be directly prohibited and the issue in 1 Corinthians 8–10 would be easily resolved.[100] But since these laws have been fulfilled and no longer apply as direct prohibitions, Paul does not cite them when urging the Corinthians to refrain from eating idol food, citing instead other reasons for abstaining. In the new covenant, "Food does not bring us near to God; we are no worse if we do not eat, and no better if we do" (8:8). This means that the Corinthians have, at the very least, an in-principle or theoretical "freedom" (ἐξουσία, *exousia*) to eat idol (and any) food (8:9).[101] It also

---

and Rosner, *Corinthians*, 485–86.

99. Carson, "Pauline Inconsistency," 12; Witherington, *Conflict*, 212.

100. See, for example, Exod 34:15; Num 25:2; Lev 11:1–47.

101. *Contra* Cheung, *Idol Food*, 133–37. Of course, for reasons of love, it is a freedom that they should not exercise (8:1–13). But the point here is that there is at least a theoretical freedom in the new covenant since the OT laws concerning idol food are now fulfilled.

means that they have the freedom to eat marketplace food (which might have been offered to idols) without enquiring as to its origins (10:25). As Witherington notes, "this shows how far Paul had come since his days as a zealous Pharisee."[102] In the new covenant, idol food is not "inherently inconsumable due to what has been done to it."[103]

2. IN EXERCISING THIS FREEDOM, WORSHIPERS MUST BEWARE OF THE DANGERS ASSOCIATED WITH USING THE FORMS OF OTHER FAITHS

Though new covenant worshipers have genuine freedom in regard to outward forms, this freedom must be exercised with great care, since, as we have seen, the forms of other faiths have the potential to cause worship-related problems: for the "weak" (8:7–13), for the "knowledgeable" (10:14–22), and for unbelievers (10:25–29). New covenant worshipers must learn to curtail their freedoms so as to avoid these problems. They need to consider the impact of their form-selection on others and on themselves. As they do this, they should not simply be guided by "knowledge" (8:1–3) that a form is morally neutral (8:4–6, 8; 10:25–27). Rather, they must be guided by love which edifies (8:1–3) and which produces a willingness to forgo rights for the sake of the gospel (8:7—9:23).[104] Rather than making decisions based on the conviction that "I have the right to do anything" (10:23), they must understand that "not everything is beneficial" and "not everything is constructive" (10:23).[105] Thus alongside the great freedom that worshipers are given, they are also given great responsibility to choose forms wisely and lovingly, and must be ready to abstain from using a form that could lead to a fellow believer's false worship (8:7–13), unintended participation with demons (10:14–22), or a compromised testimony (10:25–29).

Paul's concluding exhortation once again emphasizes the need for form-selectors to consider the impact of their selections on others: "Do not cause anyone to stumble, whether Jews, Greeks, or the church of God" (10:32). Since "Jews" and "Greeks" refers to all non-believers, and "the church of God" refers to all believers, this is nothing less than a call for believers to consider the impact of their form-selections on *everyone*. This requires considerable awareness and conscientiousness, since different

---

102. Witherington, *Conflict*, 227.
103. Ciampa and Rosner, *Corinthians*, 488.
104. Witherington, *Conflict*, 196–97.
105. Ciampa and Rosner, *Corinthians*, 485–86.

groups (Jews, Greeks, the "weak," and the "knowledgeable") respond in different ways to different forms. For *Jews*, the eating of idol food by Corinthian believers would probably have caused them to stumble since it would give them "another reason (cf. 1:23) to denounce the church and so to avoid Christians" (they were, after all, strictly opposed to the eating of idol food).[106] The result would be that they would miss out on an opportunity to hear and receive the gospel. For *Greeks*, such eating could be interpreted as "a tacit affirmation of idolatrous beliefs thereby strengthening the 'Greek' in a form of 'piety' destined for destruction" (10:25-30).[107] For *the church of God*, as we have seen, such eating could lead to false worship (8:7-13).[108] Because the use by believers of the forms of their preconversion faith might cause a range of different groups to stumble (that is, to miss out on salvation), in selecting forms, believers must consider all these groups, and, motivated by love, refrain from using any forms that could cause members of any group to stumble.[109]

3. THE CONTEXT IN WHICH A FORM IS USED IMPACTS ITS MEANING

It emerges in this text that the context in which a form is used can render an otherwise harmless form harmful. Eating idol food is not an intrinsically idolatrous act (8:4-6, 8; 10:25-27). But when the eating takes place in particular contexts, the act can indeed amount to idolatry, both for the "weak" (8:7-13), and for the "knowledgeable" (10:14-22). As Flemming notes, "Context truly matters."[110] Importantly, in certain social and religious contexts (such as the pagan feast: 10:14-22), the context controls a form's meaning, such that participation amounts to idolatry, notwithstanding the attempt by the believer to attach a different, Christian meaning to the event. Flemming explains, "In this case the *form* (the ritual of eating at the pagan temple) and the *meaning* (idolatry and the activity of demons) are intertwined."[111] In relation to the Corinthians' claim that they can eat idol food, Garland points out, "Theoretically they are correct . . . , [but] life is not lived in the theoretical abstract, and eating food sacrificed to idols can lead

---

106. Dickson, *Mission-Commitment*, 255.
107. Dickson, *Mission-Commitment*, 255.
108. Dickson, *Mission-Commitment*, 255. Cf. Ciampa and Rosner, *Corinthians*, 497.
109. Garland, *Corinthians*, 489.
110. Flemming, *Contextualization*, 191. Cf. Ciampa and Rosner, *Corinthians*, 482; Fisk, "Eating," 70.
111. Flemming, *Contextualization*, 191.

to partnership with demons."[112] Likewise, Witherington notes that whether or not eating idol food amounts to idolatry depends upon where one eats, how one eats, and with whom one eats.[113] Thus a form which in isolation is "morally neutral," can, in certain contexts, become spiritually fatal.

4. A RISK INHERENT IN USING THE FORMS OF OTHER FAITHS IS THAT UNWANTED MEANINGS WILL BE IMPORTED

In 8:7-13 we see that where new believers use the forms of their pre-conversion faith, there is a risk that unwanted meanings will be imported, resulting in false worship. Eating idol food is not in and of itself an *inherently* idolatrous act (8:8). The food is not contaminated simply through being offered to idols. This is confirmed in 10:25-27, where Paul encourages the Corinthians to eat marketplace food (which may or may not be idol food) without enquiring as to its origins.[114]

However, when the "weak" eat food which they know has been offered to idols, they eat it as an act of worship honoring the god represented by the idol, and so commit idolatry (8:7).[115] This is because they are "still so accustomed to idols" (lit. "through intimate idol-experience until now":τῇ συνηθείᾳ ἕως ἄρτι τοῦ εἰδώλου, *tē sunētheia heōs arti tou eidōlou*) (8:7).[116] Fee comments on the meaning of this crucial phrase:

> Even though they know that the god does not exist, their former association with him or her as a god is still part of their experience of reality.... Their former way of life is woven into their consciousness and emotions in such a way that the old associations cannot be thus lightly disregarded.[117]

Therefore, when they eat idol food, they eat it "as (though it were) idol food" (ὡς εἰδωλόθυτον ἐσθίουσιν, *hōs eidōlothuton esthiousin*) (8:7b). Thus the problem is with "their state of mind when they eat."[118] Ciampa and Rosner describe this as subjective false worship, since it is the subjective thoughts

---

112. Garland, *Corinthians*, 385.
113. Witherington, *Conflict*, 187.
114. Fisk, "Eating," 63; Naselli, "Idolatrous," 33; Cheung, *Idol Food*, 155; Fee, *Corinthians* (1987), 480-81.
115. Garland, *Corinthians*, 380; Cheung, *Idol Food*, 128-29.
116. Ciampa and Rosner, *Corinthians*, 386; Gooch, *Dangerous Food*, 77-78.
117. Fee, *Corinthians* (1987), 379.
118. Garland, *Corinthians*, 380.

and beliefs of the worshiper that render the worship false.[119] Likewise, Fisk observes, in 8:7–13, "the ability of εἰδωλόθυτα, *eidōlothuta* to contaminate is determined solely by the belief system of the one eating."[120] Garland expands on this:

> For those with knowledge, the banquet may be only a social occasion, but it is not so for those with a weak conscience. Eating sanctified food had always been an act of worship that honored the god lurking behind the idol. Their minds are still infused with old conceptions that spring up involuntarily.[121]

Thus *the "weak" in 8:7 are not able to detach the pagan meaning from the pagan form.* The meaning which they previously attached to idol food before their conversion is the meaning they continue to attach to the form. So an unwanted meaning is imported into their worship as believers, with the result that their worship is corrupted, and they are defiled and destroyed (8:7, 11).[122]

Therefore the use of a morally neutral form can result in false worship, because a meaning attached to the form in believers' pre-conversion worship remains attached to it in their worship as believers. An implication of this is that the forms of believers' pre-conversion faith pose special spiritual dangers to those believers, precisely because of the associations that exist in their minds between the form and its original, non-Christian meaning. The reason that the "weak" are unable to separate the original non-Christian meaning from the (morally neutral) form is because they "are still so accustomed to idols" (8:7)—that is, because of their lengthy experience of using the form in idolatrous worship.[123] And so when they use the form, the old, pagan meaning remains, and false worship ensues (8:7, 9–12). Thus a given form might be completely harmless for one person (who has no history of using it as part of the worship of another faith and is unaware of the meanings attached to it in that worship), but spiritually fatal for another (who used it in his or her pre-conversion worship and is unable to detach the meaning from the form).

---

119. Ciampa and Rosner, *Corinthians*, 369.
120. Fisk, "Eating," 60.
121. Garland, *Corinthians*, 380.
122. Cheung, *Idol Food*, 129.
123. Ciampa and Rosner, *Corinthians*, 386.

5. Using the Forms of Other Faiths with Worshipers of That Faith Is Especially Problematic

First Corinthians 10:14–22 deals with a particular scenario in which believers not only use the forms of another faith, but also join with worshipers of that faith as they use those forms. Paul explains that this is an especially problematic practice. The Corinthians believe that they can participate in idol feasts, presumably on the grounds that idols represent non-existent gods, and thus that idol food eaten at the feasts is not spiritually contaminated (8:4–6; 10:19). But they are wrong, because they have failed to account for the fact that when this non-contaminated idol food is consumed *within the context of an idolatrous ritual*, such eating creates a partnership with demons and so is an inherently idolatrous act (10:20–22). Paul teaches that when someone participates in the corporate worship of a particular group, they enter into a spiritual fellowship with the other worshipers and with the object of their worship: this is true of Christian corporate worship (10:16–17), Jewish corporate worship (10:18), and pagan corporate worship (10:20).[124] Fisk observes,

> In each case, the worship of the group determines the nature of the act of the individual. Paul's urgent warning is that, by participating in a meal alongside pagans who are engaged in idol worship, Christians become guilty of idolatry by association; in fact, they become sharers in demon worship (10:20).[125]

Thus participation with false worshipers in their false worship can be objectively wrong, *regardless of what alternate meanings a believer might attempt to attach to the worship*. As Garland observes,

> some things are totally irreconcilable with life in Christ and remain absolutely wrong.... Being members of one body in Christ makes it impossible to be involved in idolatrous practices.[126]

Garland explains the important implication of this: "Presuming to have an advanced level of knowledge and no misgivings about an action does not make it acceptable."[127] Likewise, Ciampa and Rosner comment, "We are not innocent simply because we ourselves would not conceive [of our actions] as idolatry."[128] Ciampa and Rosner call this objective false worship since it

---

124. Garland, *Corinthians*, 477.
125. Fisk, "Eating," 64.
126. Garland, *Corinthians*, 392. Cf. Fee, *Corinthians* (1987), 475.
127. Garland, *Corinthians*, 392.
128. Ciampa and Rosner, *Corinthians*, 459.

occurs when people "participate in an activity that they consider innocent but which is in fact idolatrous."[129]

Thus with the phenomenon of objective false worship in 10:14–22, we see that the use of the forms of other faiths with worshipers of that faith might be sinful *even if the worshiper subjectively gives the form a new meaning*. We also see that forms which are, in isolation, not inherently sinful or idolatrous (such as idol food), can nevertheless become problematic when they are used in a particular context (here, the context of a pagan feast).

6. Using the forms of other faiths in the presence of non-believers can result in a compromised testimony

In 10:25–30, another problem associated with using the forms of other faiths emerges: that of a believer's testimony to non-believers being compromised. Paul discusses two specific scenarios here: purchasing and eating marketplace food, and eating at a dinner party hosted by an unbeliever. In both situations, it would not be clear to the believer whether the food has been previously offered to idols.[130] Paul explains that believers do not need to proactively enquire as to whether they are eating idol food (10:25–27). If they eat idol food without realizing it, no harm is done, since, as we have discussed, the food itself is not spiritually contaminated.

However, if the food is explicitly identified as idol food, then they must refrain from eating, for the sake of non-believing onlookers (10:28–29).[131] Paul is concerned that the Corinthians' testimony to non-believers will be compromised if they eat in this situation. Perhaps this is because eating might be interpreted by non-believing onlookers as participation in, or support of, idolatry.[132] Or perhaps it is because it might be interpreted as evidence that the believers are behaving hypocritically, and not in accordance with their convictions. After all, Corinthian pagans would probably be aware of Jewish and Christian scruples concerning idol food, and thus would probably expect Christians to abstain.[133] According to Garland, eating would be "a tacit recognition of the sanctity of pagan gods" which would

---

129. Ciampa and Rosner, *Corinthians*, 369.

130. Ciampa and Rosner, *Corinthians*, 487–93.

131. As discussed above (chapter 5, §3.b.i.2.), it is clear that the onlookers Paul has in mind here are non-believers, since the onlooker uses the pagan term for idol food (ἱερόθυτόν, *hierothuton*), rather than the pejorative term used by Christians (εἰδωλοθύτων, *eidōlothutōn*). Ciampa and Rosner, *Corinthians*, 493.

132. Ciampa and Rosner, *Corinthians*, 487, 493.

133. Ciampa and Rosner, *Corinthians*, 493.

"confirm rather than challenge the unbeliever's idolatrous convictions" and so "disable the basic Christian censure of pagan gods as false gods."[134] Ciampa and Rosner concur, suggesting,

> [Paul is concerned] to stress the undesirability of any behavior that would lead others to malign Christian teaching or practice.... If the other person's sense of moral judgment convinces them that the Christian is acting in a hypocritical or unethical manner and leads them to judge the Christian and think less of the gospel and its effects, the Christian is not promoting the gospel but hindering its success.[135]

What counts is not the fact that "knowledgeable" believers might construe their eating as harmless, but rather, how such eating is interpreted by non-believers.[136] Once again, we see that an action which might be harmless in isolation is rendered harmful by the context in which it takes place. By eating in this context, believers risk compromising their testimony to non-believers and so Paul urges them to abstain. Further, if they do abstain, they might actually create evangelistic opportunities. Dickson writes,

> The occasional withdrawal from pagan banquets hinted at in 10:28 would present a clear critique of paganism and would very likely lead to an opportunity for believers to explain the Christian position.[137]

7. Spiritually dangerous forms should be avoided

Paul's response to the spiritual dangers posed by idol food is to call on believers to abstain from eating it. An important point emerges here: if the use of a form is likely to lead to false worship or compromised testimony, the form should be avoided.

In response to the problem that the "weak" lack the liberating knowledge of the "knowledgeable" (8:7), Paul's approach is *not* to educate the "weak," but rather to exhort the "knowledgeable" to abstain from eating idol food (8:9–13). Garland writes,

> Paul assumes that [the "weak"] have been programmed to think in certain ways about sacrificed food, and he has no interest in

---

134. Garland, *Corinthians*, 497. Cf. Cheung, *Idol Food*, 157.
135. Ciampa and Rosner, *Corinthians*, 495.
136. Garland, *Corinthians*, 496.
137. Dickson, *Mission-Commitment*, 259.

deprogramming them. . . . He never urges them "to get with it" and never addresses the weak at all in this section or even implies that they are mistaken. . . . Paul's goal is to change the activity of the knowers.[138]

Where there is a risk that using the form of another faith will result in false worship, the form is to be avoided.

8. The goal is freedom from being bound to any forms

It also emerges in this text that the goal for new covenant worshipers is, like Paul, to be free from the need to use any particular forms. Although Paul is a Jew, he no longer considers himself one, as is evident from his statement, "To the Jews I became like a Jew" (9:20).[139] He has the freedom to become like a Jew in order to win Jews (9:20), but he is no longer permanently in that state. Likewise, he can become like a Greek to win the Greeks (9:21), but this is not his new permanent state. As Carson explains, Paul occupies "a third ground . . . and is prepared to move from that ground to become like a Jew or like a Gentile."[140] Likewise, Witherington writes, "Paul sees being a Christian as a third sort of thing, being neither simply Jewish nor simply Gentile."[141] Paul is not bound to any set of forms. As a new covenant Christian, he has freedom to move between groups and either use their forms or refrain from using their forms, depending on the impact of his form-selection on others and himself. Indeed, if he lacked this freedom (and so was bound to the forms of his birth culture), his capacity to win people would be severely constrained (9:19–23). Paul concludes the unit by calling upon believers to imitate his example (11:1).[142] Thus new covenant believers are not bound to use the forms of their birth culture, but instead have a freedom to choose whatever forms will best enable them to love others, avoid sin and idolatry, and promote the gospel.

c. Other references to idol food in the NT

There are just four other NT references to idol food, but a uniform picture emerges from these: Christians are to abstain from eating it. In Acts 15:29

---

138. Garland, *Corinthians*, 380–81, 384. Cf. Witherington, *Conflict*, 199.
139. Carson, "Pauline Inconsistency," 12.
140. Carson, "Pauline Inconsistency," 37.
141. Witherington, *Conflict*, 213.
142. Dodd, *Paul's Paradigmatic 'I'*, 100.

and 21:25, "idol food" (εἰδωλοθύτων, *eidōlothutōn*) is prohibited under the Apostolic Decree.[143] And in Revelation 2:14 and 2:19–20, one of the charges the reigning Lord Jesus brings against the churches in Pergamum and Thyatira is that they eat "idol food" (εἰδωλοθύτων, *eidōlothutōn*). Thus the rest of the NT is consistent with the above interpretation of 1 Corinthians 8–10: believers are to abstain from eating idol food.

d. The implications of 1 Corinthians 8–10 for the IM debate

A number of principles have emerged in our analysis of 1 Corinthians 8–10 that are of great relevance and importance to the IM debate.

i. First Corinthians 8–10 is not a precedent or a permission regarding the use the forms of other faiths

Many IM proponents have characterized 1 Corinthians 9:19–23 as a broad biblical permission for believers to use the forms of other faiths.[144] However, as we have seen, this text cannot be used in this way. It cannot be Paul's intention in 9:19–23 to promote the use by believers of the forms of other faiths, since 9:19–23 is a supporting argument for the claim in 8:7–13 that believers should *refrain* from using certain forms of other faiths. Rather than establishing believers' freedom to use forms of other faiths, the text actually establishes the need for believers to *give up their rights* (including the right to use the forms of other faiths) out of love for others. Not only that, but, as we saw above, 9:19–23 itself also identifies a series of limits to the principle of accommodation: believers are to become *like* those they seek to win, but not exactly the same as them; and believers always remain under the law of Christ, meaning that the principle of accommodation cannot be used to justify participation in false worship or other sin.[145]

A second argument that has been put forward from 1 Corinthians 8–10 is that of Higgins, who proposes that 8:10 might be a "possible example of a Gentile believer who is still 'inside' part of their religious heritage."[146] 8:10

---

143. *Contra* Higgins, "Idol's Temple," 30–31; Higgins, "Biblical Basis," 220–22.

144. Woodberry, "To the Muslims," 23–25; Lewis, "Integrity," 44, 48; Cumming, "Muslim," 26; Higgins, et al., "Myths," 48; Roberts and Jameson, "Conversion," 208–10; Caldwell, "Jesus in Samaria," 28; Richard, "All Things," 289; Woodberry, "Incarnational," 241; Travis and Woodberry, "When God's Kingdom," 28–29; Higgins, "Key," 160; Massey, "Amazing Diversity," 8.

145. See Hwang, *Toward*, ch. 4, "An Evaluation."

146. Higgins, "Acts 15," 37. See also Higgins, "Inside What?," 79; Higgins, "Biblical

may indeed refer to a real phenomenon that existed in Corinth whereby believers continued to participate in temple activities. However, as we saw above, Paul's rhetorical goal in the text is to dissuade such believers from doing so (notwithstanding the fact that their actions may not have been inherently idolatrous). Paul calls the "knowledgeable" to come out of the temple and abstain from eating idol meat. He does not issue any kind of a limited permission to continue to use the pagan forms, for example, when no "weak" believer is present. In response to Higgins, Ibrahim and Greenham write, "Paul's words of admonition . . . can hardly be construed as acquiescence in believers 'taking part in at least some of the religious events and practices of their birth religion.'"[147] Thus even though the text might bear witness to the existence of Corinthian insiders, Paul critiques their behavior, and so the text is not a precedent for believers remaining "inside" and using the forms of their pre-conversion faith.

A third IM proponent claim from this text is that of Lewis. She suggests that in 1 Corinthians 8 and 10:23–11:1, Paul makes the matter of eating idol food "a matter of conscience," advising believers to do "what least offends the conscience of the person you are eating with."[148] Thus for Lewis, this text affirms the neutrality of forms and the consequent freedom of BMBs to use Muslim forms. However, Lewis's claim is based on a mischaracterization of the problem in 8:7–13. As we saw above, the problem for the "weak" is not that they might suffer an offended conscience when they see the "knowledgeable" eating idol food. Rather, the problem is much more serious: they might be drawn into false worship, resulting in eternal ruin. Much more is at stake than an offended conscience. Paul does not therefore leave the decision to eat to the conscience of believers, but instead calls for abstinence. Lewis seems to treat Paul's teaching in 1 Corinthians 8 as essentially the same as his teaching in Romans 14.[149] However, the two texts address two different issues: 1 Corinthians 8–10 deals with idol food, whereas Romans 14 deals with food forbidden by Jewish food laws. Eating the former can amount to sin and idolatry, leading to spiritual ruin, and so is not merely a matter of conscience (1 Cor 8:7–13, 10:14–22, 32), whereas whether or not one eats the latter is a matter of indifference, and thus eating is a matter of conscience (Rom 14:1–4, 6, 14–18).[150]

Basis," 220–23.

147. Editorial comments by Ibrahim and Greenham in Higgins, "Biblical Basis," 225.

148. Lewis, "Integrity," 48n7. Cf. Higgins, "Idol's Temple," 32.

149. Lewis, "Integrity," 48n7.

150. Gooch, *Dangerous Food*; Cheung, *Idol Food*, 90–92; Garland, *Corinthians*, 360.

In conclusion, this text does not establish the neutrality of forms or the freedom of BMBs to use Muslim forms. First Corinthians 8–10 is neither a precedent nor a permission for believers to use the forms of other faiths.

ii. First Corinthians 8–10 is not a blanket prohibition on using the forms of other faiths, but it does warn of the dangers associated with such usage

First Corinthians 8–10 is not a blanket prohibition on the use by believers of the forms of other faiths. Paul certainly warns of the dangers associated with using the forms of other faiths, but he does not prohibit all possible uses of all forms of other faiths in all situations. Rather, Paul works within a framework whereby believers enjoy genuine freedom with regard to form-selection, but must exercise that freedom with an awareness of the dangers associated with particular forms, especially those of other faiths. This is further explored below.

iii. Other implications for the IM debate

Thus 1 Corinthians 8–10 does not establish a simple rule either permitting or prohibiting the use of the forms of other faiths. Rather, it equips form-selectors for their task through a profound theology of worship and forms. In what follows, we consider the implications of this for the IM debate.

1. THE RELATIONSHIP BETWEEN FORM AND MEANING

A foundational conviction of IM methodology is Kraft's assertion that form and meaning can be separated, so that new believers can use the forms of their pre-conversion faith but give new, Christian meanings to them (chapter 1, §3.c.i. above). First Corinthians 8–10 challenges Kraft's claim in two ways.

First, in 8:7–13, we are confronted with the problem of believers for whom form and meaning have not been (and possibly cannot be) separated, with the result that false worship ensues. Thus 8:7–13 raises the possibility that, though separating a particular form from its Muslim meaning might be possible for some, it might not be for others. Applied to the IM debate, the danger here is that some BMBs using Muslim forms might fail to separate form and meaning, and so retain the meaning they previously attached to the form before coming to faith, such that false worship ensues. For example, if, pre-conversion, they had performed the *sholat* prayer ritual as a method of accruing merit with God or cancelling sin, the danger is that they might continue to attach that meaning to the form post-conversion, so distorting true worship (which depends on Christ for those things). Thus 8:7–13 challenges Kraft's claim by highlighting the problem that even where it is theoretically possible to separate form and meaning, some may not be able to do so.

Second, 10:14–22 challenges Kraft's claim by showing that in certain situations (here it is the context of corporate worship), it may not even be *possible* to separate form and meaning. As we noted above, in the case of a pagan feast, the shared cultural understanding of the meaning determines the meaning for *all* participants. BMBs involved in form-selection need to be aware of the possibility that the same may hold for Muslim forms, particularly those associated with corporate worship.

Thus 1 Corinthians 8–10 exposes flaws in Kraft's hypothesis concerning form and meaning. By contrast, it affirms Hiebert's claim that form and meaning cannot always be easily separated.[151]

2. Form-Selectors Need to Consider the Impact of Forms on Worship

With 1 Corinthians 8–10, once again we see that in a text concerned with the use of the forms of other faiths, the author's major concern is worship, more so than contextualization. Paul's primary concern is not to identify how far the Corinthians can go in identifying with local culture; it is to equip them to avoid spiritually fatal false worship. Thus the priority for BMB form-selectors should not be that they select Muslim forms wherever possible. Rather, the priority should be that they select forms that facilitate true worship, and avoid forms that might draw them or others into false worship.

3. Form-Selectors Need to Be Aware of the Danger of the Importation of Unwanted Meanings

First Corinthians 8–10 highlights a series of problems that might arise if the forms of other faiths are used by believers. One of these is that of unwanted meanings being imported into the worship of believers, resulting in subjective false worship. BMB form-selectors need to be aware that if they choose a Muslim form, there is a danger that they will retain the

---

151. Hiebert, "Form," 106–10.

meaning that they previously attached to that form in their pre-conversion false worship, with the result that they engage in subjective false worship. Further, in light of Paul's insistence that the "knowledgeable" consider the effect of their form-selection on the "weak," BMBs need to recognize that even if they are satisfied that they can successfully discard the old Muslim meaning, they also need to be equally satisfied that *all* other BMBs with whom they interact will be able to do the same. If not, they risk becoming agents of false worship by causing the "weak" amongst them to stumble. And this is no small thing: to do so is to sin, both against the "weak" and ultimately against Christ himself.[152]

If BMBs evaluate the risk and decide that use of a Muslim form might lead to false worship (by themselves or others), they will avoid the problematic form if they wish to follow Paul's example. As we saw above, Paul's practical response to the problems associated with spiritually dangerous forms is to appeal to believers to avoid them. He does not attempt to reprogram the "weak" in their thinking about the form of idol food, rather he calls the "knowledgeable" to refrain from using it.

Like Acts 15, 1 Corinthians 8–10 thus highlights the fact that the forms of believers' pre-conversion faith pose special spiritual dangers because of the ongoing associations between the form and its old meaning. The implications of this principle in the IM context are significant. Whereas IM methodology encourages BMBs to use Muslim forms on the grounds of cultural familiarity, our analysis here raises the possibility that amongst believers of any religious background, BMBs might be the very ones who should *not* use Muslim forms. Muslim forms will pose special dangers to BMBs if the associations they have with those forms contradict or undermine the principles of true worship.

4. Form-selectors need to be aware of the special problems associated with participating in mosque worship

We saw above that, based on 10:14–22, there are special problems associated with the scenario whereby believers do not simply use the forms of other faiths, but also join with worshipers of that faith in their worship. We saw that in such a situation, the context might so control the meaning that believers are guilty of objective false worship, notwithstanding their attempts to subjectively give the form a new, Christian meaning.[153] BMBs need to be aware

---

152. Even though Paul's position on idol food is disputed (chapter 5, §3.b.i.1. above), this basic understanding of 8:7–13 is not in dispute.

153. Again, even though there are a range of different views regarding Paul's

of this possibility. Specifically, they need to consider whether these principles might apply to their participation in mosque worship. They need to understand that in this situation, an attempt to give their participation a Christian meaning will not necessarily be enough to forestall false worship.

IM proponents and critics have put forward various arguments concerning whether 10:14–22 prohibits BMB participation in mosque worship. IM critic Coleman argues that it does.[154] In making his case, Coleman writes,

> Even the most "liberal" or broadest interpretations of 1 Corinthians 8–10 only allow for participation at purely social functions conducted at a pagan temple.[155]

Greer responds that 10:14–22 does not prohibit BMB participation in mosque worship, on account of the differences between pagan and Muslim ceremonies. He writes,

> [Coleman] appears to make the error of "direct transferability," equating first century idolatrous worship with attendance at Muslim religious ceremonies. . . . What Coleman fails to recognize is that so many differences exist between first century Mediterranean world idol worship (along with dining at temples in Corinth) and Muslim religious ceremonies in the twenty-first century that these should not be equated.[156]

It is not possible to resolve this question on the basis of biblical analysis alone. What would also be needed is an analysis of mosque worship, and that is beyond the scope of this book. The goal here is simply to identify biblical principles that form-selectors must consider and then apply based on knowledge of their particular (mosque) context. With regard to this Greer-Coleman debate, Greer is right to suggest that differences between pagan temple worship and mosque worship *might* render 10:14–22 inapplicable. But these differences would need to be thoroughly investigated and articulated before such a conclusion could be confidently drawn. The important issue for BMBs to consider is whether the differences are sufficient to make the principle in 10:14–22 inapplicable. As they do so, they need to recognize that just as there are differences, so too there are similarities—in both cases what is in view is

---

argument in 1 Cor 8–10 (chapter 5, §3.b.i.1. above), this basic understanding of the meaning of 10:14–22 is agreed upon by proponents of all four major views outlined above.

154. See Coleman, *Analysis*, 170–78.
155. Coleman, *Analysis*, 175.
156. Greer, "Review," 207.

believers using the forms of other faiths, and joining with worshipers of that other faith as they use those forms in worship.

IM proponents cite certain differences between pagan and mosque worship, in support of the conclusion that 10:14–22 does not apply to mosque worship. First, they point out that there are no idols in mosques.[157] Yet in the NT, a physical idol is not needed for idolatry to occur. For example, in Colossians 3:5, Paul states that greed is idolatry. Indeed, the NT category of "idolatry" includes a great variety of types of false worship.[158] Therefore it cannot be concluded on the basis of the absence of physical idols in mosques alone that 10:14–22 does not apply here.

Second, Roberts writes that "not everything in Islam is demonic."[159] The reasoning here is that since participation in idol feasts in Corinth is prohibited on the grounds that it results in fellowship with demons (10:20–22), it follows that if mosque worship is not demonic, then 10:14–22 does not apply. Again, drawing a conclusion on this matter is not possible without first engaging in a study of mosque worship (both generally and in relation to specific local manifestations of it), and so is outside the scope of this book. Here we can simply affirm that this is another matter that BMBs should investigate when deciding whether to participate in mosque worship.[160] And 10:14–22 suggests that making this kind of an investigation might be difficult: the Corinthians did not *think* they were entering into fellowship with demons (10:19), but Paul revealed that they *were in fact doing so* without realizing it (10:20–21).

A further, related argument in support of the conclusion that 10:14–22 does not apply to mosque worship is that of IM proponent Higgins. He proposes that since communion with demons is the problem in 10:14–22, then what this text forbids is "the intentional and active attempt to commune (or connect) with a spiritual being other than God."[161] Thus according to Higgins, 10:14–22 is not an outright ban on participating in the rituals of other faiths (such as mosque worship), only a ban on participating with a subjective intention that is idolatrous.[162] Based on my analysis of 10:14–22 above, I propose that Higgins has drawn the wrong principle from the text. In participating in idol feasts, the "knowledgeable"

157. Higgins et al., "Myths," 50–51; Roberts, "Where We Agree," 546.

158. See Rosner, "Idolatry," 571; Curtis, "Idol," 381; Wright, *Mission*, 165–71. For a discussion of idolatry in the context of mission amongst Muslims, see Farah, "Adaptive," 174–76.

159. Roberts, "Where We Agree," 546.

160. For a discussion of this issue, see Fletcher, "Insider Movements," 190–91.

161. Higgins, "Idol's Temple," 35 (see also 33).

162. Higgins, "Idol's Temple," 35.

Corinthian believers are not *intending* to worship idols or demons. On the contrary, they think that their knowledge of the non-existence of the gods represented by the idols makes it safe for them to participate in idol feasts (10:19; cf. 8:4-6, 8). Yet Paul asserts that, regardless of their *intentions*, their behavior is *objectively idolatrous*. Thus the problem in 10:14-22 is not *subjective* false worship, but rather *objective* false worship. A subjective intention to worship only the true God is not enough to prevent participation in a temple feast from amounting to false worship (see chapter 5, §3.b.ii.5. above). Thus Higgins's argument is not persuasive.

Finally, some IM proponents claim that decisions about whether to participate in mosque worship should be left to the conscience of the believer. Woodberry writes,

> Paul teaches adaptability even to a pagan culture like Corinth as long as one is guided by conscience and by the desire to glorify God and see people be saved (1 Cor 10:23-33).[163]

Indeed, articles by IM proponents are replete with claims that "individual conscience should be determinative,"[164] that we must "leave it to the believer's conscience,"[165] and that "the issue is whether one's conscience is free and pure."[166] The following quotation from Wilbur Smith appears in the introduction to a section of *Understanding Insider Movements*: "How far should one go in identifying with another people? . . . Just as far as our conscience will allow us to go."[167] Certainly, believers must avoid doing anything that violates their consciences (Rom 14:5, 14). As well, the decision regarding whether to participate in mosque worship is undoubtedly one that BMBs themselves are responsible for making. But this is not the same as saying that the individual conscience alone determines the rightness or wrongness of believers' choices. As 10:14-22 demonstrates, participation in an activity can be false worship, even when, according to the believer's conscience, it is permissible. As BMBs make decisions about participation in mosque worship, they must recognize a need to go further than simply deferring to their consciences. Participating in mosque worship might amount to objective false worship, even if their consciences raise no objections.[168]

163. Woodberry, "Incarnational," 242.
164. Talman, "Muslim," 515.
165. Talman, "Muslim," 515.
166. Taylor, "Contextualization," 384.
167. Talman and Travis, *Understanding*, 391.

168. For an analysis of the application of 10:14-22 in a Korean-Confucian ancestor veneration context which engages with similar issues to those discussed here, see Oh-Young, *1 Corinthians*, 217-28.

5. Form-selectors need to be aware of the possibility of a compromised testimony

BMBs engaged in form-selection also need to be aware of the possibility that using a Muslim form in the presence of non-believers might result in a compromised testimony. As we saw above, in 10:25–29, Paul urges the Corinthians to refrain from eating idol meat identified as such in front of non-believers, because to do so might be interpreted by the non-believing onlookers in a way that hinders the gospel's advance. BMBs need to consider whether using Muslim forms in the presence of non-believing Muslims (or other non-believers) might have a similar effect. For example, might use of Muslim forms or participation in Muslim rituals by BMBs be interpreted by Muslim onlookers as an acceptance of the effectiveness of those forms and rituals? Might an opportunity to critique that which these Muslims are trusting in be lost? Might an opportunity to present the gospel be missed? Obviously the answers to these questions will depend upon the context. But 10:25–27 shows that these are important questions for BMBs to consider as they choose forms.

6. An appropriate test for form-selection

Our analysis of 1 Corinthians 8–10 supports the conclusion in previous chapters that the "biblical compatibility" test advocated by some IM proponents (see chapter 1, §3.a.vi.) is an unhelpful one, especially in light of the problem of subjective false worship. Whereas the "biblical compatibility" test focuses attention on the inherent nature of the form, 8:7–13 highlights the possibility that a form whose inherent nature is unobjectionable (such as idol meat which is not spiritually contaminated) can nevertheless be spiritually fatal because of the meaning attached to it. Likewise, certain Muslim forms might be unobjectionable in their inherent nature (such as the prostrations associated with the *sholat* form), but could equally be spiritually dangerous for BMBs because of the meanings associated with the form.

In 1 Corinthians 8–10, Paul rejects a focus on "knowledge" alone that a form is permissible (8:1–6, 8), or on perceived "rights" to use a form (8:9; 9:4–5, 12, 15, 18). Instead he encourages form-selectors to forgo these rights (8:7—9:23), and to seek that which edifies (8:1–3), which is beneficial and constructive (10:23), and which helps people to engage God in worship (10:24, 31–33). Paul's theology of forms is thus *purpose-oriented*: forms must be selected with the purpose of their use in mind. Forms are a means to an end; true worship is that end. A test that reflects Paul's approach then should not simply seek what is acceptable, but rather whatever *best* achieves the purpose of using the form.

The test proposed in this book (asking *whether a form will facilitate or hinder true worship*) is better than the "biblical compatibility" test because it accounts for the problem of subjective false worship, and also Paul's purpose-oriented theology of forms. BMBs should not merely seek forms that are permissible or inherently morally unobjectionable, but rather those which *best* facilitate true worship for all, so promoting God's glory (10:31–33).

7. Freedom from Being Bound to Use Certain Forms

Finally, we saw above that Paul set forth as an ideal for all believers his own radical approach to forms, whereby he was not bound to use any particular set of forms, but instead moved between groups, giving up freedoms to use forms that he might otherwise enjoy, for the sake of loving other believers and promoting the gospel. Form-selectors need to consider whether their choices will help them to understand, embrace and apply this new covenant freedom. BMBs who are considering using Muslim forms will need to ask whether doing so is consistent with this principle. Ultimately, form-selectors need to make decisions that foster their ability to become all things to all people, so that they might save some.

We have seen that a series of important implications for the IM debate arise from 1 Corinthians 8–10. We now examine our final NT resistance text.

4. Colossians 2:6–23

In Colossians 2:6–23, Paul confronts a false teaching (hereafter, "the philosophy": 2:8) that is threatening the Colossian church. He urges the Colossians to walk in Christ (2:6–7), describes all that Christ has already accomplished on their behalf (2:8–15), and critiques the practices advocated by the proponents of the philosophy (2:16–23).[169]

---

169. Most agree that 2:6–23 is a discreet textual unit. See Pao, *Colossians*, 149; Moo, *Colossians*, 176; Melick, *Colossians*, 249; McKnight, *Colossians*, 276.

a. The relevance of the text to the research problem

i. Does this text deal with the use of the forms of other faiths by God's people?

For this text to be relevant, it must deal with the use by God's people of the forms of other faiths. The following analysis demonstrates that it does.

1. THE FORMS OF OTHER FAITHS

It is clear from Paul's critique of the philosophy in 2:6–23 that its proponents (hereafter, "the errorists") are advocating a variety of practices (which are "forms" for our purposes).[170] They are promoting the observance of certain food and drink regulations and Jewish holy days (2:16). They are also arguing for certain ascetic practices, involving "false humility"[171] (2:18, 23), rigorous abstinence (2:21), and "harsh treatment of the body" (2:23).[172] They are also engaging in a practice which Paul describes as the "worship of angels" (θρησκεία τῶν ἀγγέλων, *thrēskeia tōn aggelōn*) (2:18). Whatever this contentious phrase refers to,[173] it seems to involve mystical visionary experiences (2:18). Some infer from Paul's statement concerning spiritual circumcision (2:11–13) that the errorists are also advocating physical circumcision,[174] although not all agree that this inference is warranted.[175] Thus the errorists are promoting certain forms. Since Paul in this text is critiquing them for doing so (see 2:8, 16, 18, 20–23), this is clearly a text that deals with the use of forms.

The next question is: are these forms those *of another faith*? To answer this question we need to engage with one of the most debated topics in Colossians scholarship, concerning the nature and origins of the philosophy. Many have attempted a reconstruction of the philosophy, based both on a mirror reading of Paul's polemic against it, and also on what is

---

170. See the definition of "form" (chapter 1, §4.d. above).

171. The Greek term used, ταπεινοφροσύνη, *tapeinophrosunē*, refers to self-denial or self-abasement, through fasting or other ascetic practices. Moo, *Colossians*, 50–51; Witherington, *Colossians*, 162.

172. Moo, *Colossians*, 51, 236; McKnight, *Colossians*, 276.

173. If τῶν ἀγγέλων, *tōn aggelōn* is taken as an objective genitive, then it is the worship of angels. But, if it is taken as a subjective genitive, then it could be worshiping like, or participating with, angels as they worship God. Gupta, *Colossians*, 101; Pao, *Colossians*, 189; Moo, *Colossians*, 226–27.

174. Pao, *Colossians*, 164; Gupta, *Colossians*, 93.

175. Moo, *Colossians*, 51–52.

known of the religious environment in Colossae at the time.[176] In doing so, scholars grapple with the fact that the philosophy seems to contain a mix of Jewish and non-Jewish elements. Some of the practices are distinctly Jewish in character, such as food laws (2:16, 21), Jewish holy days (2:16),[177] and (if we accept that circumcision was one of the practices) circumcision (2:11–13). And yet others are not so easily linked to Judaism, such as certain ascetic and visionary practices, and the worship of angels (2:18, 23).[178] Scholars have proposed a great variety of possibilities regarding the sources of the non-Jewish elements. These include Greek mystery religions,[179] local (Phrygian) folk religion,[180] astrology,[181] early Gnosticism,[182] and pagan Cynic philosophy.[183]

Based on this plethora of possible sources, a wide variety of reconstructions of the philosophy have been proposed. However, there are two that enjoy the most widespread support.[184] According to the first, Jewish mysticism is thought to be the dominant (for some, even the exclusive) influence lying behind the philosophy.[185] Proponents of this view argue that even the elements often thought to be non-Jewish[186] were in fact common practices in Jewish mystic communities. Specifically, they propose that the ascetic practices of 2:18 and 2:23 were cultic acts aimed at helping worshipers enter into visionary experiences where they could participate with angels in their worship of God.[187]

176. See Patzia, *Colossians*, 16.

177. The phrase "a religious festival, a New Moon celebration, or a Sabbath day" in 2:16 is a common way of referring to Jewish holy days in the OT. In addition, the shadow/reality language of 2:17 suggests that a contrast between old and new covenants is being made (cf. Heb 8:5; 10:1). Moo, *Colossians*, 25, 53.

178. Pao, *Colossians*, 26–27.

179. Argall, "Source," 6–20; Patzia, *Colossians*, 17; Barth and Blanke, *Colossians*, 10–16.

180. Arnold, *Colossian Syncretism*, 61–244.

181. Patzia, *Colossians*, 16; Lohse, *Colossians*, 98.

182. Lightfoot, *Colossians*, 73–113.

183. Martin, *Colossians*, 11–169.

184. Gupta, *Colossians*, 17.

185. Smith, *Heavenly*, 33, 38, 39–87, 143–45; Sappington, *Revelation*, 26–225; McKnight, *Colossians*, 29–34; Witherington, *Colossians*, 110.

186. That is, certain ascetic practices, visionary practices and the worship of angels: 2:18, 23.

187. McKnight, *Colossians*, 276. Dunn advances a variation of this view. He argues that all of the practices can be explained with reference to standard Jewish teaching at the time, as practiced in the local synagogues (and thus not as practiced by ascetic Jewish mystics). Dunn, *Colossians*, 23–34. For a critique of Dunn's view, see Pao, *Colossians*,

According to the second reconstruction, the philosophy was a syncretistic mix of Judaism and other religious traditions.[188] Arnold, for example, adduces historical evidence that fear of spiritual powers was common in Phrygia at the time, and that magic and ritual power were used for self-protection in Phrygian folk religions. He argues that the practices referred to in 2:18 and 2:23 are drawn from these local folk religions and are designed to ward off evil.[189] At the same time, he agrees that other aspects of the philosophy, such as the observance of Jewish holy days, derived from Judaism.[190]

Because of the limited nature of the evidence, choosing between these reconstructions is difficult.[191] Indeed, Barclay writes that the whole matter is "an unsolved, and insoluble, mystery."[192] However, for our purposes here, certainty regarding the origins of the forms of the philosophy is not essential. What is important is simply to establish that the forms are those of *other faiths*. That much at least is not in dispute. Regardless of which reconstruction is closer to the truth, it seems clear that the forms discussed in 2:6–23 are a combination of OT Jewish forms (which, as discussed above, can be treated as the forms of other faiths for our purposes: see chapter 4, §2.a.i.), and some extra-biblical forms practiced by some religious group (whether Jewish mystics, Phrygian folk religionists, or another group). Thus notwithstanding the different views on the origin of the philosophy, its forms were certainly borrowed from other faiths.

2. Used by God's people in their worship as believers

Finally, the text is concerned with the use of these forms *by believers in Christian worship*. Paul writes to the Colossian believers (1:2) out of a concern that the errorists might deceive them (2:4) and take them captive (2:8) by persuading them to use the forms in question (2:16, 18, 20). Thus at issue in this text is the use *by believers* of these forms.

28; Moo, *Colossians*, 55–56.

188. Moo writes that "a majority of scholars" adopt this position. Moo, *Colossians*, 57. See Beale, *Colossians and Philemon*, 12–16; Patzia, *Colossians*, 16–18; Lightfoot, *Colossians*, 73–113; DeMaris, *Colossian Controversy*, 41–145; Bradley, "Colossians," 17–36; Barth and Blanke, *Colossians*, 10–16; Wilson, *Colossians*, 219.

189. Arnold, *Colossian Syncretism*, 103–244.

190. Arnold, *Colossian Syncretism*, 150–54, 195–97, 226, 243–44. For a critique of Arnold, see Bevere, *Sharing*, 30–46.

191. Moo, *Colossians*, 49; Gupta, *Colossians*, 18; Pao, *Colossians*, 27.

192. Barclay, *Colossians*, 54.

As well, it seems that the errorists themselves are at least *professing* Christians. We can infer this from 2:19, where Paul claims that because of their preoccupation with ascetic practices and visionary experiences (2:18), the errorists "have lost connection with the head" (οὐ κρατῶν τὴν κεφαλήν, *ou kratōn tēn kephalēn*: lit. "not holding onto the head"). The sense here is that they were once connected to Christ, and that their losing of this connection is an unintended consequence of their focus on the practices, and indeed is a situation of which they are unaware.[193] Most infer from this verse that the errorists arose from within the Christian community.[194]

Further, there is no evidence in the text to suggest that the errorists are calling the Colossians to turn away from Christ. Certainly, Paul rejects their teaching as *implicitly* undermining the sufficiency of Christ (2:9–23), but it does not appear that they are making any *explicit* claims to this effect.[195] As Gupta notes, "If the philosophers came out against Christ explicitly, Paul's rhetoric would probably have been more condemnatory."[196] Rather, it seems that they are promoting these practices, not as an alternative to faith in Christ, but as a way for Christ-followers to obtain wisdom (2:3, 23) and spiritual fullness (2:10), and to restrain sinful inclinations (2:23). Thus in 2:6–23, Paul is not responding to a call by non-believers to join with them in their non-Christian worship, but rather, to a call by professing believers to join with them as they use the forms of other faiths in their worship as believers.

Thus 2:6–23 is indeed a text that deals with the use of the forms of other faiths by God's people, and is therefore relevant to our purposes.

b. The meaning of the text for the original audience

i. Is there evidence in the text that the author is seeking to persuade readers to resist the forms of other faiths?

There is abundant evidence in the text that Paul's purpose is to persuade the Colossians to avoid the forms advocated by the errorists, on the grounds that using them risks distorting true worship and bringing about their spiritual ruin. The essence of Paul's argument is that whatever the worshipers might seek to obtain by using the forms has in fact already been secured by Christ and is presently available to those who are in Christ. Therefore, using

---

193. Moo, *Colossians*, 47; McKnight, *Colossians*, 30.
194. Moo, *Colossians*, 230. Contra Dunn, *Colossians*, 185.
195. Moo, *Colossians*, 52–53, 60, 63.
196. Gupta, *Colossians*, 18–19.

the forms is not only unnecessary, but it is actually spiritually dangerous, since it undermines full dependence on Christ.

Despite the imprecision of engaging in mirror readings, in order to understand Paul's argument it will be helpful firstly to cautiously sketch an outline of the errorists' teaching to which he is responding. In light of Paul's frequent use of "wisdom" (1:9, 28; 2:3, 23; 3:16) and "fullness" (1:19, 25; 2:9, 10), it seems that the errorists are offering a way to obtain true wisdom, spiritual fulfillment, and spiritual maturity.[197] The errorists are offering solutions to two major spiritual problems faced by humanity: those of sin and malevolent spiritual beings.[198] Regarding sin, it seems that the errorists are promising victory over sin through adherence to strict calendrical and ascetic rules (2:16, 20–23).[199] Regarding spiritual beings, historical evidence suggests that people in first century Hellenistic society suffered a high degree of anxiety about the influence exerted by spiritual beings over their daily lives, and that they sought "some sort of effectual means for appeasing, worshipping, or manipulating these powers in order to obtain a degree of protection."[200] We can infer from Paul's focus in Colossians on the "dominion of darkness" (1:13), the spiritual powers (1:16; 2:15), and the "elemental spiritual forces of this world" (2:8, 20),[201] that the errorists are emphasizing the Colossians' vulnerability to malevolent spiritual beings, and at the same time promising that protection is available to those who use the relevant forms, particularly those involving mystical visions and the worship of angels (2:18).[202]

In response, Paul contends that spiritual maturity is obtained not by using the forms, but rather by continuing to "walk" (περιπατέω, peripateō) in Christ (2:6).[203] Περιπατέω, peripateō is used idiomatically here to refer to living in a certain way.[204] This way is thoroughly christocentric: it involves

---

197. Gupta, *Colossians*, 15–16, 87; Moo, *Colossians*, 193.

198. Moo, *Colossians*, 57.

199. Moo, *Colossians*, 69–70.

200. Wilson, *Hope*, 4.

201. "Elemental spiritual forces of this world" translates the Greek phrase τὰ στοιχεῖα τοῦ κόσμου, *ta stoicheia tou kosmou*. The meaning of this phrase is debated. It could be a reference to spiritual beings. But it might instead refer to "the elementary teachings of this world" or even "the physical components of this world." See Moo, *Colossians*, 50; Pao, *Colossians*, 160–61; McKnight, *Colossians*, 226–28; Witherington, *Colossians*, 155.

202. Moo, *Colossians*, 63–65; Gupta, *Colossians*, 16. Practitioners of Greek mystery religions sought protection from spiritual beings through mystical and visionary experiences. Wilson, *Hope*, 3–4.

203. Patzia, *Colossians*, 18; Moo, *Colossians*, 69–70.

204. Gupta, *Colossians*, 89.

being rooted in Christ, built up in Christ, strengthened in faith in Christ, and overflowing with thankfulness to Christ (2:7).[205] As Gupta notes, Paul's implicit concern in 2:6–7 is that the philosophy might undermine this God-ordained Christ-focused process of spiritual growth, with use of the forms functioning as a *substitute* for "walking" in Christ:

> Paul was fearful that some Colossian believers, having already come to new life in Christ, virtually set Christ aside to find completion or fullness through another means.[206]

What is implicit in 2:6–7 becomes explicit in 2:8—to accept the philosophy is to be "taken captive" (συλαγωγῶν, *sulagōgōn*), a vivid image taken from the world of slavery.[207] The philosophy is enslaving because it is "hollow" (a sharp contrast with the "fullness" that is available in Christ: 2:9–10; cf. 1:9, 25),[208] "deceptive" (since it does not deliver what it promises: 2:23), and, most importantly, because it is worldly in origin and does not depend on Christ (2:8). Here is the nub of the problem with the philosophy: by demanding certain practices as necessary for spiritual fulfillment, it distracts attention from Christ and undermines confidence in his sufficiency and supremacy.[209] Paul unpacks this in 2:9–15 by showing that whatever the errorists might be promising the Colossians if only they use the forms, Christ has in fact already secured for them.[210] If the errorists promise "fullness" (that is, spiritual maturity and a special experience of God's presence and blessing),[211] Paul declares that believers already have this fullness through their union with Christ (2:9–10).[212] Witherington comments, "Since Christ is where the whole fullness of God dwells, it follows that one need not and should not look elsewhere to experience God or to be filled with the divine presence."[213]

If the errorists promise protection from spiritual beings, Paul declares that Christ has authority over those beings (2:10b), indeed that he has already disarmed, defeated and humiliated them in his death (2:15). The

---

205. Gupta, *Colossians*, 89; Moo, *Colossians*, 175–76.
206. Gupta, *Colossians*, 89.
207. McKnight, *Colossians*, 224; Moo, *Colossians*, 185; Gupta, *Colossians*, 90.
208. Garland, *Colossians*, 145–46.
209. Pao, *Colossians*, 161; Moo, *Colossians*, 193.
210. Smith, *Heavenly*, 113–14.
211. Pao, *Colossians*, 163; Moo, *Colossians*, 195.
212. The perfect passive participle "filled" (πεπληρωμένοι, *peplērōmenoi*) expresses an ongoing state that began in the past. Witherington, *Colossians*, 156; Moo, *Colossians*, 195; Pao, *Colossians*, 163.
213. Witherington, *Colossians*, 156.

result is that believers have been set free from these beings and their rules (2:20). Thus believers already enjoy full protection in Christ, and have nothing to fear from malevolent spiritual beings.[214]

If the errorists promise a way to restrain sinful inclinations (see 2:23), Paul declares that believers have already experienced a spiritual circumcision which involved "the stripping off" (τῇ ἀπεκδύσει, *tē apekdusei*) of the sin-corrupted human disposition (2:11).[215] Thus Christ has already conquered the power of sin in believers' lives. Not only that, but he has also dealt with guilt for sin: those who are in Christ have new life and forgiveness of sins (2:13). The completeness of this forgiveness is underlined in 2:14: the "certificate of debt" (χειρόγραφον, *cheirographon*) which stands against us (probably a reference to the sin-debt humans owe to God) has been cancelled through being nailed to the cross (that is, it has been cancelled because of Christ's death) (2:14).[216]

Having demonstrated the complete sufficiency of Christ to provide all that the Colossians might be tempted to seek by using the forms (2:9–15), Paul proceeds to mount a direct attack on the philosophy and its insistence on the use of these forms (2:16–23). He gives four reasons as to why the Colossians should not use the forms.

First, those of the forms which are Jewish in origin are outdated.[217] Paul explains that the Jewish food and calendrical forms listed in 2:16 are a "shadow" of what was to come, whereas the "reality" is Christ (2:17).[218] The shadow/reality contrast was common in Greek philosophical tradition (especially Plato), with "shadow" referring to that which is not reality but has

---

214. Cf. 1:15–20. Patzia, *Colossians*, 18; Moo, *Colossians*, 63–65, 184.

215. Lit. "the body of the flesh" (τοῦ σώματος τῆς σαρκός, *tou sōmatos tēs sarkos*). Some understand the circumcision metaphor in 2:11 as a reference to Christian conversion, others as a reference to Christ's death. Either way, the sense is that Christ has already subdued the sinful human disposition and so in him, believers have access to victory over the power of sin. Moo, *Colossians*, 199–200, 207; Gupta, *Colossians*, 93–94; Deenick, *Righteous*, 130–38.

216. Witherington, *Colossians*, 158; Gupta, *Colossians*, 95–96; Moo, *Colossians*, 208–12; Pao, *Colossians*, 176–77. Many have noted a realized eschatology in Colossians, more so than in Paul's other letters. As Witherington writes, this can be explained with reference to Paul's polemical purpose here: "This emphasis is largely due to the rhetorical attempt to counter the errorists and show that believers already to a significant degree have now in Christ what they are looking for in the ascetic practices and experiences. Thus they need not go in a new direction to obtain such things." Witherington, *Colossians*, 167.

217. Gupta, *Colossians*, 97.

218. Lit. "body" (σῶμα, *sōma*). The term σῶμα, *sōma* is used metaphorically here, meaning "reality" or "substance." McKnight, *Colossians*, 271.

only an appearance of reality.[219] Yet here Paul replaces the ontological contrast with a temporal one, with "shadow" referring to the era of promise and "reality" referring to the present era of fulfillment inaugurated by Christ.[220] As a "shadow," the Jewish forms of 2:16 once provided "a preliminary glimpse of God's will for his people."[221] But they belonged to an earlier era that has now passed, and so the Colossian believers do not need to use them.[222]

Second, using the forms might be spiritually fatal. As a result of using the forms in 2:18, the errorists have "lost connection with the head" (2:19). McKnight comments, "The language is dramatic and might be connected to themes of apostasy, heresy and false prophets."[223] Although the forms in 2:18 are ostensibly aimed at producing humility,[224] the effect has been the very opposite: the errorists have been "puffed up" with pride (2:18), resulting in a failure to hold on to Christ (2:19a).[225] Because Christ is the only source of spiritual nourishment (2:19b), this is a spiritually fatal development.[226] Moo's summary highlights the dangers associated with using these forms:

> The false teachers were so preoccupied with their own program for spiritual fullness that they were separating themselves from the only true source of spiritual power: the Lord Jesus Christ.[227]

Third, using the forms might lead to enslavement to malevolent spiritual beings. Paul explains that the ascetic rules of 2:21 are sourced in the "elemental spiritual forces" (2:20)[228] and in "human commands and teachings" (2:22). With Christ's victory over malevolent spiritual beings (2:10, 15), believers are liberated from such beings and their rules, and so submission to them is not only unnecessary, but also thoroughly inappropriate (2:20–22).

---

219. Pao, *Colossians*, 186. Greek philosophers ordinarily use "shadow" (σκιὰ, *skia*) with either "reality" (πρᾶγμα, *pragma*) or "form" (εἰκών, *eikōn*), whereas Paul uses it with "body" (σῶμα, *sōma*). See further Pao, *Colossians*, 186.

220. Pao, *Colossians*, 186; McKnight, *Colossians*, 270; Moo, *Colossians*, 222–23.

221. McKnight, *Colossians*, 271.

222. Moo, *Colossians*, 223.

223. McKnight, *Colossians*, 278.

224. "False humility" (ταπεινοφροσύνῃ, *tapeinophrosunē*) has a semi-technical sense, referring to self-humbling or self-abasement by fasting or other ascetic practices. Witherington, *Colossians*, 162; Moo, *Colossians*, 50–51.

225. Gupta, *Colossians*, 100–101; Witherington, *Colossians*, 162.

226. McKnight, *Colossians*, 279.

227. Moo, *Colossians*, 60.

228. Again, we note here that not everyone takes "elemental spiritual forces" (τῶν στοιχείων τοῦ κόσμου, *tōn stoicheiōn tou kosmou*) as a reference to spiritual beings. Some take it as a reference to elementary teachings. Moo, *Colossians*, 50; Pao, *Colossians*, 160–61; McKnight, *Colossians*, 226–28; Witherington, *Colossians*, 155.

Indeed, if the Colossians submit to the rules, they are living as if they still belong to "the world" (2:20), and as if the spiritual beings still have control over their lives.[229] Smith concludes, "The Colossian philosophy was empty deceit, as it was giving the principalities and powers a means of enslaving the Colossian Christians again through asceticism and rituals."[230]

Fourth, the forms are ineffective.[231] We can infer from 2:23 that the aim of the ascetic rules in 2:20-23 is to restrain "the flesh" (σάρξ, *sarx*), that is, the sinful impulse. It seems that the errorists are claiming that temptation to sin can be overcome by subduing the body through ascetic practices.[232] But Paul declares that these practices "lack any value in restraining sensual indulgence" (2:23).[233] They are thus "incapable of accomplishing their design."[234]

Paul's clear and explicit purpose in 2:6-23 is therefore to persuade the Colossians to resist the call by the errorists to use the relevant forms. The Colossians do not need to use them, since Christ has already secured all that the forms are aimed at obtaining. Not only that, but if they do use them, there is a danger that their capacity to grasp the sufficiency and supremacy of Christ, and so completely depend on him, will be undermined. Instead of using these forms, the Colossians should simply continue to "walk" in Christ.

ii. What does the text teach about worship and forms?

What follows is a summary of what Colossians 2:6-23 teaches about worship and forms.

---

229. Garland, *Colossians*, 182-83; Arnold, *Colossian Syncretism*, 308. "The world" here refers to the fallen world over which the spiritual beings rule. Believers have been set free from this world. Moo, *Colossians*, 234. As Arnold points out, Paul's suggestion that the ascetic rules are somehow sourced in the "elemental spiritual forces" (2:20) is an "ironic twist," since the errorists appear to be holding out these rules as a means of gaining protection from these malevolent spiritual beings. Arnold, *Colossian Syncretism*, 308.

230. Smith, *Heavenly*, 132-33.

231. Pao, *Colossians*, 183-84.

232. Moo, *Colossians*, 242.

233. The Greek in 2:23 is difficult. The sense could be that the rules are incapable of restraining the sinful impulse. Alternatively, it could be that the rules do not lead to the legitimate satisfaction of the body, that is, they do not permit the legitimate enjoyment of God-given physical experiences. This former has the greater support. See Moo, *Colossians*, 238-40; McKnight, *Colossians*, 286-87.

234. McKnight, *Colossians*, 286.

1. True Worship is God-Given, Whereas False Worship is Human-Designed

A key principle in this text is that true worship is God-given. This is a text in which Paul addresses the matter of worship, that is, how humans engage with God. He upholds dependence on Christ as true worship and rejects the worship of the philosophy as false. Crucially, a key distinguishing factor between the two approaches is their respective origins.

The worship that Paul upholds as true is so *because* it is from God. In 2:6, it is something the Colossians "received" (παραλαμβάνω, *paralambanō*). Παραλαμβάνω, *paralambanō* is a technical term referring to the transmission of a tradition or teaching.[235] This notion is reinforced with the reference to "the faith" (τῇ πίστει, *tē pistei*) in 2:7.[236] Paul insists that those who passed on this tradition to the Colossians were commissioned by God to communicate a message about God-designed worship (1:7–8; 2:25, 27).[237] Further, the true worship described in 2:9–15 is initiated by God and given by him: God, through Christ, provides "fullness" (2:9–10), victory over the sinful disposition (2:11–13), new life and forgiveness of sins (2:13–14), and freedom from malevolent spiritual beings (2:15). Thus what makes the way of worship true, contends Paul, is that it is given by God and made possible by God.[238]

By contrast, the worship of the philosophy is false because it is worldly in origin. It depends on "human tradition" and "the elemental spiritual forces of this world," but not "on Christ" (2:8).[239] Regardless of whether "the elemental spiritual forces" (τὰ στοιχεῖα, *ta stoicheia*) refers to malevolent spiritual beings, or to the elementary teachings or principles of the world (see chapter 5, §4.b.i. above), either way, the point is clear: as a way of worship, the philosophy is false because it is not from God but is from some other, worldly, source.[240] Indeed, as Moo notes, "the real sting" in Paul's critique comes with the claim at the end of 2:8 that the philosophy does not depend on Christ.[241] Paul repeats

---

235. Garland, *Colossians*, 142.
236. Moo, *Colossians*, 68.
237. Moo, *Colossians*, 186–87.
238. Peterson, *Engaging*, 20, 26–27, 33, 73.
239. Many have commented on the strong contrast here between the divine tradition (2:6–7), and "human tradition" (2:8, 22). Moo, *Colossians*, 68, 177; Pao, *Colossians*, 155; Garland, *Colossians*, 141–42.
240. Regardless of whether the στοιχεῖα, *stoicheia* are spiritual beings or elementary teachings, they are "of this world" (τοῦ κόσμου, *tou kosmou*), and thus not of God. Garland, *Colossians*, 142–44.
241. Moo, *Colossians*, 193.

the claim that the worship of the philosophy is false because of its non-divine origin in 2:20–22, where the ascetic rules are once again linked with the "elemental spiritual forces" (2:20), and once again described as "based on merely human commands and teachings" (2:22).

Pao identifies in these texts a series of allusions to OT anti-idol polemic texts.[242] If Pao is right in drawing these connections, this reinforces the principle that it is the worldly origin of the philosophy that makes its way of worship false. Pao draws out the implications: "Paul is not simply accusing the false teachings of being merely human teachings, but that these teachings represent a false worship that cannot be tolerated."[243] Thus 2:6–23 teaches that true worship is God-given and based wholly on Christ, whereas false worship is not.

2. For New Covenant Worshipers, There Is Freedom with Regard to Outward Forms

This text affirms the principle that new covenant believers, unlike their old covenant counterparts, enjoy great freedom with regard to outward forms. The Colossians do not need to observe the OT food and calendrical regulations listed in 2:16, because they are a "shadow;" they stand in contrast to Christ, who is the "reality" (2:17).[244] Witherington explains, "These rules, while good in their day, are but shadows to be left behind now that the real substance that they foreshadowed has appeared—Christ."[245] Likewise, Beale writes, "The law's preparatory adumbrating function has come to an end, since the messianic "substance" to which it pointed has arrived."[246] Further, in 2:11–13, Paul treats the OT form of physical circumcision "as a pointer to the greater redemptive reality of Christ and his followers being 'circumcised' or 'cut off' from the old sinful world."[247] Because the

---

242. For example, Pao suggests that "hollow and deceptive philosophy" (2:8) alludes to Isa 44:9 and Zech 10:2; "depends on human tradition" (2:8) alludes to Isa 40:18–24; 41:4–7; 44:9–11; "rather than on Christ" (2:8) alludes to Deut 32:21 and Ps 96:5; "not performed by human hands" (2:11) alludes to 1 Sam 12:21; Isa 46:6–7, 57:13; and Jer 14:22; and "based on merely human commands and teachings" (2:22) alludes to Isa 29:13. Pao, *Colossians*, 174, 196.

243. Pao, *Colossians*, 160.

244. Moo, *Colossians*, 222; McKnight, *Colossians*, 269; Gupta, *Colossians*, 98, 106–7.

245. Witherington, *Colossians*, 160–61.

246. Beale, "Colossians," 862. See also Pao, *Colossians*, 199–200; Garland, *Colossians*, 173–75.

247. Beale, "Colossians," 862.

Colossians have a spiritual circumcision from Christ, they do not need the OT form of physical circumcision.[248]

New covenant believers are not only free not to use OT forms, but they are also free from the need to use forms sourced elsewhere. In 2:20, Paul insists that because the Colossians "died with Christ to the elemental spiritual forces of the world," they do not need to submit to the world's rules. In the phrase "died . . . to," the preposition translated "to" (ἀπὸ, *apo*) is normally rendered "from." Thus Paul is emphasizing the freedom that believers enjoy *from* the world and its rules.[249]

Thus new covenant worshipers are not bound to use OT forms, or forms sourced elsewhere. What makes worship true in the new covenant era is not the use of prescribed forms, but rather *a believer's connection to Christ*. It is those who are "in Christ" that enjoy all the things that false worshipers long to obtain through their worship: fullness (2:9–10), victory over sin's power (2:11–13), removal of guilt for sin (2:13–14), and protection from spiritual beings (2:15). That is why Paul calls the Colossians simply to keep "walking" in Christ (2:6–7), and at the same time to reject the philosophy (2:8), since it leads to believers losing their connection with Christ (2:19).

Thus new covenant worshipers enjoy great freedom with regard to outward forms. New covenant worship is not marked by the use of a system of prescribed forms, but rather by continuing dependence on Christ.

3. The Forms of Other Faiths Have the Potential to Distort True Worship

This text warns of the potential for the forms of other faiths to distort true worship. As we have seen, in Christ, God has already provided everything which the forms advocated by the errorists are aimed at securing. True worship, then, begins with recognizing this, and responding in full dependence on Christ. Paul is so insistent in his rejection of the forms promoted by the errorists because using them has the potential to undermine the capacity of believers to grasp Christ's sufficiency, an understanding fundamental to dependence on him and him alone.[250] As Pao writes, "The most critical deficiency of such regulations is that they distract one from the work of God in Christ."[251] Likewise, Arnold writes that Paul saw the philosophy as dangerous

---

248. Garland, *Colossians*, 146, 148–49, 157–58; Pao, *Colossians*, 178.

249. Moo, *Colossians*, 233; Harris, *Colossians*, 127.

250. Pao, *Colossians*, 175.

251. Pao, *Colossians*, 200 (also 181). See also Beale, *Colossians*, 148; McKnight, *Colossians*, 33, 224.

because "it demeaned the person of Christ and became a substitute for a vital relationship with the exalted Lord."[252] It is important to recognize that Paul is not rejecting all religious forms or rituals. As Gupta notes, such a conclusion would be problematic, given "how much he supports and regulates rituals elsewhere."[253] Rather, Paul is rejecting those forms or rituals that "become an inappropriate centre of faith"[254] and that "deprive Christ of the glory that belongs to him alone."[255] Colossians 2 warns that the forms of other faiths—if they are designed to obtain that which Christ has already secured—embody this dangerous potential. In this regard, it is worth noting here that the forms that Paul supports and regulates elsewhere (especially baptism and the Lord's Supper) are intentionally aimed at directing the worshiper's focus *upon Christ's work*, rather than distracting from it.[256] Building on his observation that 2:6–23 contains a series of allusions to OT anti-idol polemic texts (chapter 5, §4.b.ii.1. above), Pao concludes that the underlying problem with the philosophy is that, as with idolatry, it leads to worshipers putting their trust in something other than God—in this case, in their use of particular forms.[257] When this happens, worshipers' connection to Christ is severed (2:19), and so they are no longer able to engage in true worship.[258]

Thus we learn from Colossians 2 that the forms of other faiths have the potential to distort true worship.

4. A RISK INHERENT IN USING THE FORMS OF OTHER FAITHS IS THAT UNWANTED MEANINGS WILL BE IMPORTED

Colossians 2 highlights that a risk inherent in using the forms of other faiths is that unwanted meanings will be imported. Most think it highly unlikely that the errorists were *explicitly* teaching the insufficiency of Christ.[259] Rather, the insufficiency of Christ was *implicit* in their promotion of particular forms, since the meaning attached to those forms *assumed the insufficiency of Christ*. The following two examples will serve to illustrate this point.

---

252. Arnold, *Colossian Syncretism*, 227.
253. Gupta is referring to the importance of baptism and the Lord's Supper in Paul's letters. Gupta, *Colossians*, 113.
254. Smith, *Heavenly*, 113–14.
255. Pao, *Colossians*, 201. See also Gupta, *Colossians*, 113.
256. See further Meeks, *Urban Christians*, 140–62.
257. Pao, *Colossians*, 175.
258. McKnight, *Colossians*, 279; Moo, *Colossians*, 230.
259. See Moo, *Colossians*, 48, 52–53, 60, 63, 225; Gupta, *Colossians*, 18–19.

First, concerning the false humility, worship of angels and visionary experiences of 2:18, there are essentially two views regarding the background of this form. Some think a pagan form has been borrowed here, and that what is being described is the magical invocation of angels to ward off evil.[260] Others think that a form from Jewish mysticism has been borrowed, in which the ascetic practices are conceived of as a means of entering into a visionary experience which involves worshiping *with* angels.[261] Proponents of both theories are able to adduce historical evidence that these respective meanings were in fact attached to the form by adherents of the respective faiths.[262] Regardless of which theory is correct, what is important for our purposes is that *both* of these meanings undermine the principles of true worship and the sufficiency of Christ. Christ has triumphed over spiritual beings (2:10, 15), and so warding off evil is unnecessary. And in Christ, believers have complete access to the full presence of God (2:9–10), and so ascetic practices and visionary experiences aimed at entering into God's presence are similarly unnecessary. Both meanings are therefore anti-gospel meanings. Whichever was attached to the form by the errorists, the very serious end result was that they lost connection with Christ (2:19).

Second, concerning the ascetic practices of 2:23, these forms might have been borrowed from a number of different faiths. As Gupta notes, "These kinds of restrictive prohibitions were indicative of purity regulations in many ancient religions."[263] But the meaning attached to them in these different religions was essentially the same: the basic belief was that the sinful human disposition could somehow be restrained or overcome through denigrating the body and self-denial.[264] Again, this is a meaning which undermines the principles of true worship and the sufficiency of Christ. For believers, the sinful human disposition, or "flesh" (σάρξ, *sarx*), has already been removed through the spiritual circumcision of Christ,[265] and so to attempt to achieve this by other means is to fail to depend on what Christ has done.

Colossians 2 thus illustrates the danger that with the use of the forms of other faiths might come the importation of unwanted and worship-distorting meanings.

---

260. Arnold, *Colossian Syncretism*, 20, 92–93, 97–98, 231–32.

261. Smith, *Heavenly*; Moo, *Colossians*, 226; Witherington, *Colossians*, 161–62.

262. See Arnold, *Colossian Syncretism*, 8–102; Smith, *Heavenly*, 39–73; Witherington, *Colossians*, 162.

263. Gupta, *Colossians*, 102.

264. Gupta, *Colossians*, 92–93.

265. Moo, *Colossians*, 199–200, 207; Gupta, *Colossians*, 93–94.

c. The implications of Colossians 2 for the IM debate

We now turn to a consideration of the implications of our analysis of Colossians 2 for the IM debate. It is important to recognize that the situation in Colossians 2 is not an exact parallel to that of IM. With IM, BMBs deliberately and self-consciously attempt to give Muslim forms a new, Christian meaning.[266] There is no evidence in the text that the errorists were calling the Colossians to do the same. In light of this difference, we should not simply conclude that because Paul rejected the philosophy with its borrowed forms, so too IM methodology with its promotion of Muslim forms must also be rejected.

Nevertheless, Colossians 2 is still relevant to the IM debate because of the principles concerning worship and forms that emerge from it. It deals with a situation in which believers are being called to use the forms of other faiths in their worship as believers, and so helps form-selectors today to know what issues they should consider. Five implications are identified here.

First, in Colossians 2 we see once again that where the biblical authors deal with the question of believers using the forms of other faiths, of utmost concern to them is not contextualization but rather true worship. Paul's intent is to equip the Colossians to engage in true worship, and to protect against any corruption of true worship. Therefore form-selectors who are considering using Muslim forms for the sake of contextualization need to consider the likely impact of such usage on their capacity to engage in true worship. This is more important than whether or not a particular form is culturally familiar.

Second, Colossians 2 reinforces the foundational worship principle that true worship is God-given, whereas false worship has its origins in "the world." An implication for form-selectors is that forms should be assessed for suitability in light of this foundational principle. Forms which help worshipers to receive and use the God-given way to engage him should be used, and forms which have the potential to hinder, confuse, or distort this process should be avoided.

Third, Colossians 2 affirms that new covenant believers enjoy great freedom with regard to outward forms. The mark of true worship is not the use of certain prescribed forms, but rather being connected to Christ, which is expressed in complete dependence on him. Therefore IM proponents are right to emphasize the freedom that BMBs have to select worship forms.[267]

---

266. Uddin, "Contextualized," 269; Higgins, "Key," 156.

267. See, for example, Higgins et al., "Myths," 43; Woodberry, "Incarnational," 247–48; Talman, "Acts 15," 252.

Fourth, this freedom with regard to forms is a qualified one: it needs to be exercised with wisdom and an awareness of the impact of forms on worship. Importantly, Colossians 2 provides an example of a time when the forms of other faiths were distorting believers' true worship. As form-selectors consider whether or not to use Muslim forms, they need to be aware of this possibility. Of particular importance in this respect is the nature of Christian worship. Colossians 2 makes clear that everything that believers need to engage God in worship and enjoy his presence and blessing has already been secured by Christ, and is presently available to those who respond in faith, expressed in dependence and obedience. Christian worship is thus fundamentally *responsive* in nature: it is an ongoing process of receiving with thankfulness and dependence that which God gives in Christ. According to Colossians 2, to introduce notions of worship as a *means of* entering God's presence to worship, or of obtaining his protection or blessing, or of achieving spiritual progress, is to distort true worship.

Form-selectors need to be especially sensitive to this matter. If a Muslim form is designed to secure something which Christ has already secured, it should be recognized as having the potential to corrupt true worship. If a Muslim form has the potential to undermine worshipers' grasping of the sufficiency of Christ or distract from the completed work of Christ, this likewise should be acknowledged. If a Muslim form has the potential to function as a substitute for dependence on Christ, such that worshipers put their trust in their use of the form, once again, this needs to be taken into account.[268]

Fifth, and related, as form-selectors assess the potential impact of a form, they need to be particularly aware of the danger of unwanted, worship-distorting meanings being imported into their worship along with the borrowed form. Colossians 2 shows how this can happen, even at an implicit level. As we noted above, the errorists in Colossae were probably not *explicitly* teaching the insufficiency of Christ's work, but rather communicating that message *implicitly* by promoting forms which assumed Christ's insufficiency. This suggests that forms can communicate an implicit, non-verbal message which contradicts and undermines that which the worshiper verbally confesses. Because the messages communicated by forms are non-verbal and implicit, the danger is that they will have an impact on worshipers of which the worshipers themselves have no awareness. Thus, in the IM context, BMBs might verbally affirm the sufficiency of Christ, but the repeated use of a form that assumes Christ's insufficiency in the original context—for example, Muslim ritual prayers—might eventually result in a shift in locus of their trust:

---

268. Cf. Green, "Guidelines," 246–47.

from Christ to their use of the form. The goal, of course, would be for the BMB to discard the meaning originally attached to the form, to the extent that that meaning assumed the insufficiency of Christ. But if BMBs do choose to use a Muslim form, they need to be aware, not only of the potential for the original meaning to remain attached and so undermine their dependence on Christ, but also of the fact that this process might occur even while they continue to verbally affirm Christ's sufficiency.

In discussing the contemporary meaning of Colossians 2, Gupta suggests that this text is not opposed to forms and rituals *per se*, but rather to those which import unhelpful meanings into Christian worship.[269] He encourages form-selectors to ask, "What is the meaning behind the ritual? Does it affirm the proper worldview? Does it point to Christ?"[270] As form-selectors consider using Muslim forms, it would certainly be a useful process to analyze the relevant Muslim forms by asking questions such as these proposed by Gupta.

Indeed, if the danger in Colossians 2 is that the use of borrowed forms might result in the importation of meanings that *undermine* the sufficiency of Christ, then it follows that it would be helpful for form-selectors to intentionally seek out forms that *affirm* the sufficiency of Christ. What is needed is forms that reinforce the completeness of Christ's work and that invite worshipers to respond in thankful dependence. In light of the priority of true worship over contextualization (discussed above), forms which affirm the sufficiency of Christ should be preferred over other forms, regardless of whether they are Muslim forms or otherwise. The primary criterion in form-selection should be a form's potential to facilitate dependence on Christ, not its cultural familiarity to the worshiper.[271] Glaser helpfully explains the importance of a Christ-focused test:

> Colossians tells the Christians how to discern which ideas from the other religions they can use, and which they must reject. The test is Christ: Do the new ideas help us to appreciate his greatness? Do they recognize the total sufficiency of his incarnation, death and resurrection?[272]

Thus Colossians 2 contains a number of important implications for the IM debate.

---

269. Gupta, *Colossians*, 111–14.
270. Gupta, *Colossians*, 113–14.
271. See the Appendix for a discussion of how this principle might be applied in a particular context.
272. Glaser, *Bible*, 164.

5. Conclusion

In this chapter, two NT resistance texts have been studied (with the first also doubling as a NT appropriation text). Once again, a remarkable consistency has emerged, both between the texts studied in this chapter, and between the texts in this chapter and the OT resistance texts studied in chapter 3. As with the OT resistance texts, the NT resistance texts cannot be characterized as blanket prohibitions on the use by new covenant believers of the forms of other faiths. They do contain, however, strong warnings concerning the dangers of such use. As well, the theology of worship and forms that has emerged in this chapter is thoroughly consistent with that identified in chapters 2–4. Once again, a central theme has been that since God makes worship of himself possible, his people must seek forms that help them to use that God-given way.

6

Conclusion

A SIGNIFICANT DEBATE EXISTS regarding whether the use by BMBs of Muslim forms amounts to contextualization or syncretism. My goal in this book has been to develop a scripturally-grounded method for distinguishing contextualization from syncretism with regard to the use of the forms of other faiths. In chapter 1, I identified the need for this study, with a survey of the debate. In particular, I noted the existence of two types of biblical texts: those that may appear to encourage the use by God's people of the forms of other faiths (appropriation texts), and those that may appear to discourage it (resistance texts). In chapters 2–5, I analyzed a series of representative appropriation and resistance texts from the OT and the NT, drawing implications for the IM debate. Now in this final chapter, I will synthesize the results of the analysis in chapters 2–5 and summarize the implications of this for the IM debate and for the task of distinguishing contextualization from syncretism in contextualized form-selection.

1. Synthesis and implications

a. The Bible neither permits outright nor prohibits outright the use of the forms of other faiths

The analysis in chapters 2–5 demonstrates that the question of whether believers should use the forms of other faiths cannot simply be resolved by identifying a general overarching biblical permission or prohibition, because appropriation texts cannot be taken as establishing precedents, and neither can resistance texts be taken to be blanket prohibitions.

The analysis of all six appropriation texts shows that these texts are not precedents giving biblical permission to BMBs today to use Muslim forms. In the case of all six texts, no intent can be found on the part of the biblical author to establish a precedent by which believers are encouraged to use the forms of other faiths.[1] On the contrary, the actual authorial intention in the text often contradicts the notion that readers should themselves initiate the borrowing of such forms. For example, in Genesis 17, Exodus 12–13, and 1 Chronicles 28, the author's purpose is not to persuade the Israelites to borrow Canaanite forms, but rather to persuade them to only use the *specific forms that God prescribes* for specific purposes, since prescribing forms was, at that stage in salvation history, God's exclusive prerogative.[2] Further, in Acts 2–7, Luke's purpose is not to persuade Jewish background believers to use the Jerusalem temple, but rather to announce the end of the temple system.[3] In Acts 15 and 1 Corinthians 8–10, the author's purpose is not to persuade pagan background believers to use pagan forms, but to avoid using them.[4] Thus the appropriation texts do not establish precedents for using the forms of other faiths.

At the same time, an analysis of the six resistance texts shows that, while the authors do undoubtedly seek to dissuade the reader from using particular forms of other faiths in particular contexts, none of these texts can be characterized as a blanket prohibition on the use by God's people of the forms of other faiths today. In each case, the use of the *particular* forms in question is resisted because of its potential to corrupt and distort true worship. In Exodus 32–34 and Hosea 8, the use of a bull-idol is resisted; in Deuteronomy 12 it is the use of Canaanite shrines and rituals; in Acts 15 and 1 Corinthians 8–10, it is the use of forms associated with temple worship, such as idol food; and in Colossians 2, it is circumcision and ascetic practices.[5] Yet while all these texts do indeed warn of the dangers associated with using particular forms of other faiths, none of these warnings is expressed in the form of a general prohibition on *all possible uses of all forms* of other faiths.

b. The Bible asserts a NT freedom to choose forms and equips believers to do so

New covenant believers enjoy considerable freedom when it comes to selecting forms. Whereas forms are prescribed in considerable detail in the OT, especially regarding worship at the central cult,[6] in the NT, Jesus is

1. See chapter 2, §2.b.i., §3.b.i., §4.b.i.; chapter 4, §2.b.i, §3.b.i.; chapter 5, §3.b.i.
2. See chapter 2, §2.b.ii., §3.b.ii., §4.b.ii.
3. See chapter 4, §2.b.ii.
4. See chapter 4, §3.b.i.; chapter 5, §3.b.i.
5. See chapter 3, §2.b.i., §3.b.i., §4.b.i.; chapter 4, §3.b.i.2.; chapter 5, §3.b.i., §4.b.i.
6. See chapter 2, §2.b.iii.2., §3.b.iii.2., §4.b.iii.2.; chapter 3, §2.b.i.2, §3.b.i.3., §4.b.i.3.

presented as fulfilling and replacing many of these outward forms, such as the temple (Acts 2–7)[7] and circumcision (Acts 15 and Colossians 2).[8] Jesus ushers in a new era in which worship is focused on him, with the result that there now exists a far greater freedom with regard to outward forms.[9] This does not mean, however, that all forms are equally good or helpful choices. The biblical authors stress that forms have the potential to significantly shape beliefs and dependencies, and in particular, that poorly chosen forms have the potential to distort or corrupt worship. While the biblical authors do not generally issue blanket permissions or prohibitions regarding forms, they do equip new covenant believers to make wise choices as they exercise their freedom in selecting forms. And so, in 1 Corinthians 8–10, for example, Paul both affirms the fact that form-selectors enjoy considerable freedom, while simultaneously highlighting the dangers associated with certain forms and calling for restraint.[10]

c. The most important factor in determining a form's usefulness is its impact on worship, *not* contextualization

A crucial finding in this research is that for the biblical authors, the key concern in the form-selection process is not contextualization (that is, how God's message is to be related and applied to a particular context), but rather worship (that is, how God's people are to engage with him). All ten texts studied in this book have been selected because each deals with the use by God's people of the forms of other faiths. Though these texts represent different salvation-historical eras and different literary genres, and have been used to support opposing arguments in the IM debate, a remarkably consistent picture emerges regarding the concerns of the biblical authors. *In each text, the author's primary concern is to equip God's people to engage in true worship, or to help them avoid false worship, or both.* In Genesis 17, Exodus 12–13, 1 Chronicles 28, and Deuteronomy 12, the authors do this by setting out God's positive prescriptions for true old-covenant worship.[11] In Exodus 32–34, Deuteronomy 12, and Hosea 8, they do so through a series of warnings and prohibitions concerning false worship.[12] In Acts 2–7, Acts 15, and Colossians 2, the authors

---

7. See chapter 4, §2.b.ii.
8. See chapter 4, §3.a.i., §3.b.ii.1.; chapter 5, §4.b.ii.2.
9. See chapter 2, §2.c.i., §3.c.i., §4.c.i.; chapter 3, §2.c.i., §3.c.i., §4.c.i.; chapter 4, §2.b.iii, §3.b.iii, chapter 5, §3.b.ii, §4.b.ii.
10. See chapter 5, §3.b.ii.
11. See chapter 2, §2.b.ii., §3.b.ii., §4.b.ii.
12. See chapter 3, §2.b.i., §3.b.i., §4.b.i.

do so by identifying Jesus as the fulfillment of OT worship institutions and calling believers to depend exclusively on him in faith.[13] And in Acts 15, 1 Corinthians 8–10, and Colossians 2, they do so by calling believers to avoid forms that have the potential to corrupt this complete dependence on Jesus, which is the mark of new-covenant worship.[14]

The primary concern of the authors in all 10 texts is worship. It is not contextualization: the focus is not upon the need for believers to be culturally relevant or to prioritize certain forms on the grounds that they are local or culturally familiar ones. This is not to say that such matters are unimportant. Nevertheless, it is significant that contextualization is not the chief concern of the biblical authors in *any* of these texts which treat the use by God's people of the forms of other faiths. Rather, their purpose is to ensure that God's people are engaging with God in the way he makes possible, and on the terms that he sets.

Importantly, then, if form-selectors today wish to reflect the concerns of the biblical authors, and indeed of God who inspired them, they too must prioritize the matter of worship. Because of this, I propose that as BMBs and cross-cultural missionaries engage in the process of selecting contextualized forms, they give greatest weight to the impact a given form is likely to have on true worship, asking: *Will this form facilitate or hinder believers in their capacity to engage God in true worship?*

d. The biblical authors equip form-selectors to choose forms that facilitate worship through a theology of worship and forms

Once we recognize that facilitating true worship is the chief concern in these texts, it becomes clear that the texts richly equip form-selectors to choose appropriate forms through providing a profound theology of forms and worship. In order to choose a form wisely, form-selectors need to understand both the purpose and function of forms, and also the nature of worship. These texts have much to teach on both of these important matters, and in so doing, they equip form-selectors for their task.

What follows is a summary of the theology of forms and worship that emerges from the ten texts, with an explanation of the implications for form-selectors. The appendix provides an example of how these principles might be used by BMBs as they engage in contextualized form-selections.

---

13. See chapter 4, §2.b.ii., §2.b.iii., §3.a.i., §3.b.ii.; chapter 5, §4.b.
14. See chapter 4, §3.b.i.2., chapter 5, §3.b.i.2., §4.b.

i. True worship is God-given

Nine of the ten texts affirm the foundational principle that true worship is God-given: God makes engagement with himself possible, and God sets the terms on which we engage him.[15] In the old covenant era, the focus of worship was the centralized cult. In the new covenant era, it is Christ. Engagement with God is now made possible through the finished work of Christ, and the terms which God sets are faith in Christ, expressed in continued dependence on, and obedience to, him.[16] Form-selectors need to understand this foundational principle, and seek out forms that facilitate worshipers' capacity to understand and apply it.

ii. False worship is human-designed and human-initiated

The corollary is also true: false worship is human-designed and human-initiated. It originates with people, is at their initiative, and is on their terms. It seeks to earn or secure the right to engage God in worship, and to receive his blessing and favor through the worship. It invariably involves a rejection of the God-given way of worship. For example, in Exodus 32, the Israelites reject the God-given way to worship and, at their own initiative, seek to secure God's protection through the construction of the bull-idol.[17] Likewise, in Deuteronomy 12, what distinguishes an acceptable worship place from an unacceptable one is whether it is chosen by Yahweh or by people.[18] And in Colossians 2, true worship is received from God, whereas false worship depends on human tradition.[19] Form-selectors need to understand the difference between human-designed and God-given worship, and be wary of any forms that might promote patterns of thought in which the form is used to secure God's favor, or to secure that which Christ has already made available.

iii. The function of forms is to facilitate an acceptable worship-response

The biblical authors present an understanding of the function of worship forms which is radically different to understandings held by adherents of

15. See chapter 2, §2.b.iii.1., §3.b.iii.1., §4.b.iii.1.; chapter 3, §2.b.ii.1., §3.b.ii.1., §4.b.ii.1.; chapter 4, §2.b.iii.2., §3.b.ii.2., §1.b.iii.1.; chapter 5, §4.b.ii.1.

16. See chapter 2, §2.c.i., §3.b.iv., §3.c.i., §4.c.i.; chapter 3, §2.c.i., §3.c.i., §4.c.i.; chapter 4, §2.b.iii.1., §3.b.ii.1., chapter 5, §3.b.ii.1., §4.b.ii.2.

17. See chapter 3, §2.b.i.2.

18. See chapter 3, §3.b.i.3, §3.b.ii.2.

19. See chapter 5, §4.b.ii.1.

other faiths at the time. For such adherents, forms ordinarily had an instrumental or transactional function: use of the form was believed to cause the desired result to come to pass.[20] By contrast, according to the biblical authors, forms are a means by which God's people express their faith-response to God's prior action of making worship possible or conferring blessing. For example, in Genesis 17 and Exodus 12–13, the God-given forms are not a means of securing God's blessing or favor, but rather are a means of taking hold of that which God graciously gives.[21] Thus the function of forms in the Bible is to facilitate an acceptable worship-response. Form-selectors must adopt a biblical understanding of the function of forms, and seek out forms that reinforce the notion that worship is a receiving, by faith, of a privilege granted by God.

iv. Forms have the potential to shape beliefs and dependencies

A number of texts highlight the power and potential of forms to shape beliefs and dependencies. Because of this, the process of form-selection is a serious and important one. For example, in Exodus 12–13 and 1 Chronicles 28, the authors leave nothing to chance, giving prescriptions concerning the Passover and temple design that are remarkably detailed, with each detail being richly imbued with appropriate meaning.[22] Conversely, in Deuteronomy 12, Moses, recognizing the power of Canaanite forms to unhelpfully shape beliefs and dependencies, takes the extreme step of calling for their total eradication and forbids the Israelites even to learn about their usage in Canaanite worship.[23] Form-selectors need to be aware of the power of forms and their potential impact on worshipers.

v. Certain forms of other faiths have the potential to corrupt true worship

All six resistance texts show that certain forms of other faiths have the potential to corrupt true worship. For example, in Hosea 8, use of the Bethel calf-idol has caused the Israelites to engage with Yahweh as if he were a Canaanite fertility god.[24] In 1 Corinthians 8, eating idol food causes

---

20. See chapter 3, §2.b.ii.3., §3.b.ii.3., §4.b.ii.3.; chapter 4, §3.b.ii.4.; chapter 5, §4.b.ii.4.
21. See chapter 2, §2.b.iii.3., §3.b.iii.3.
22. See chapter 2, §3.b.iii.4., §4.b.iii.3.
23. See chapter 3, §3.b.ii.3.
24. See chapter 3, §4.b.ii., §4.c.ii.2.

a "weak" believer to re-engage with the god represented by the idol, and so stumble.[25] In all six texts, the authors are concerned to alert readers to the danger of foreign-form-induced false worship, to highlight its serious spiritual consequences, and to equip readers to avoid it. If BMBs are considering using Muslim forms, they need to be aware of this danger and consider whether the form in question has this potential.

vi. A specific risk inherent in the forms of other faiths is that unwanted, worship-distorting meanings could be imported

All six resistance texts highlight the fact that when the forms of other faiths are used by God's people, there is a danger that the meanings attached to those forms by adherents of those other faiths will remain attached to the forms. If those meanings contradict or undermine the principles of true, God-given worship, the result is that the worship of God's people is corrupted and distorted.[26] For example, when Aaron makes a bull-idol in Exodus 32, the form of the idol is not borrowed in isolation from the meanings commonly attached to it in ANE idol worship. Rather, those meanings (especially the belief that a deity can be accessed and controlled through creation of the idol) are imported into Israel's worship along with the form.[27] Likewise, the meanings attached to the ascetic practices in Colossians 2 (specifically the notion that the sinful human disposition can be overcome through self-denial and self-denigration) contradict the principles of true worship, undermining the sufficiency of Christ. Paul resists the use of these forms in order to prevent the importation of the associated worship-distorting meanings.[28]

In all six resistance texts, the authors treat this problem of the importation of worship-distorting meanings as very serious indeed, indicating that the resulting false worship leads to divine wrath and judgment. Further, in the case of the three NT resistance texts (Acts 15, 1 Corinthians 8–10, and Colossians 2), the forms resisted include those of *new believers' pre-conversion faith*. These texts therefore emphasize that the forms of believers' pre-conversion faith pose special spiritual dangers to those

---

25. See chapter 5, §3.b.i.2., §3.b.ii.4.

26. See chapter 3, §2.b.ii.3., §3.b.ii.3., §4.b.ii.3.; chapter 4, §3.b.ii.4.; chapter 5, §3.b.ii.4., §4.b.ii.4.

27. See chapter 3, §2.b.ii.3.

28. See chapter 5, §4.b.ii.4.

believers, because of the associations in their minds between the form and its original, non-Christian meaning.[29]

Form-selectors therefore need to be alert to the possibility of unwanted meanings being imported, and of the special dangers associated with BMBs using Muslim worship forms. BMBs considering using Muslim forms must investigate the meanings attached to the forms, and consider whether those meanings contradict or support the principles of true worship in Christ.

vii. Form and meaning cannot always be easily separated

Almost all the texts cast doubt on Kraft's claim that forms (including the forms of other faiths) are "neutral vehicles" which can be re-invested with new meanings and used by believers. Instead, they affirm Hiebert's position that form and meaning cannot always be easily separated.[30]

In some texts, the link between form and meaning is intrinsic: in Genesis 17, a promise relating to offspring (meaning) is signified by a mark on the male reproductive organ (form);[31] in Exodus 12–13, a dramatic and sudden rescue (meaning) is remembered with a series of symbols of haste (form).[32] In these cases, the meaning is clearly built into the form, and thus the link between the two is extremely strong.

In other texts, even though the link is not intrinsic, it is nevertheless so well established in the minds of worshipers that they are unable to discard the old meaning, with the result that false worship ensues: the Israelites in Exodus 32–34 and Hosea 8 are unable to detach deity manipulation (meaning) from the use of a bull-idol (form),[33] and the "weak" believer in 1 Corinthians 8 is unable to eat idol food (form) without forging a worshipful connection with the god represented by the idol (meaning).[34]

Form-selectors therefore need to be aware that the task of discarding a meaning previously attached to a form in Muslim worship may be difficult, or even impossible. The strength of the connection between a given form and its meaning in Muslim worship should be carefully evaluated.

---

29. See chapter 4, §3.b.ii.4., chapter 5, 3.b.ii.4., §4.b.ii.3., §4.b.ii.4.

30. See chapter 1, §3.c., chapter 2, §2.c.ii.2., §3.c.ii.2., §4.c.ii.2.; chapter 3, §2.c.ii.2., §4.c.ii.2.; chapter 4, §3.d.iii.; chapter 5,§3.d.iii.1.

31. See chapter 2, §2.b.iii.4.

32. See chapter 2, §3.b.iii.4.

33. See chapter 3, §2.b.ii.3., §4.b.ii.3.

34. See chapter 5, 3.b.ii.4.

viii. Morally neutral forms can cause false worship

Because the link between form and meaning cannot always be broken, it follows that forms which are "morally neutral" or "not inherently evil" can nevertheless cause false worship, because of the meanings attached to them. In Deuteronomy 12, the morally neutral form of an altar must be destroyed because of its potential to cause false worship;[35] in 1 Corinthians 8–10, idol food which is not spiritually contaminated must nevertheless be avoided;[36] and in Colossians 2, forms which were given by God himself in a previous salvation-historical era (circumcision, foods, and calendrical forms) are causing believers to lose connection with Christ.[37] Form-selectors must go beyond merely satisfying themselves that a form is morally neutral, and instead investigate the meaning associated with the form and its likely impact on worship.

ix. Using the forms of other faiths with worshipers of that faith is especially problematic

Because the context in which a form is used impacts the meaning of the form for *all* involved, the use by a believer of the form of another faith *with worshipers of that faith* might amount to objective false worship, notwithstanding the believer's attempt to subjectively give the form a Christian meaning. For example, in 1 Corinthians 10, believers who participate in idol feasts are guilty of idolatry, even though they believe that since the gods that the idols represent do not exist, their participation is harmless.[38] BMBs who are considering participating in mosque or other communal Muslim worship need to consider whether such participation might amount to objective false worship of this nature.

x. Using the forms of other faiths before non-believers can result in a compromised testimony

If believers use the forms of other faiths in the presence of non-believers, there is a danger that doing so will compromise their testimony. For example, in 1 Corinthians 10, Paul suggests that if, in the presence of non-believers,

---

35. See chapter 3, §3.b.ii.2.
36. See chapter 5, §3.b.i.2., §3.b.ii.
37. See chapter 5, §4.b.i., §4.b.ii.3, §4.b.ii.4.
38. See chapter 5, §3.b.ii.5., §3.d.iii.4.

believers eat food that has been identified as idol food, doing so might hinder the gospel's advance. He therefore urges believers to abstain from eating in such circumstances.[39] Form-selectors also need to consider this possibility. It will be especially important to consider what message BMBs might communicate to onlooking Muslims when they use Muslim forms.

xi. Form-selectors need to consider the impact of using a form on themselves and everyone around them

Form-selectors need to consider the impact of their selections on three different groups: first, fellow believers (lest they be led into false worship: 1 Corinthians 8);[40] second, themselves (lest they engage in false worship: all six resistance texts);[41] and third, non-believers (lest they lose their opportunity to have an encounter with the gospel: 1 Corinthians 10).[42] Form-selectors need to be aware of the impact of forms on themselves and others, and avoid any that might cause anyone to stumble.

xii. Spiritually dangerous forms are best avoided

Forms that have the *potential* to corrupt true worship are best avoided. For example, in Deuteronomy 12, Moses calls the Israelites to eradicate, not reinterpret, the spiritually dangerous Canaanite forms;[43] in Acts 15, James prohibits Gentile believers from using various forms associated with pagan temple worship;[44] and in 1 Corinthians 8–10, Paul encourages Corinthian believers to refrain from eating idol food, even though he accepts that the food is not in itself spiritually contaminated.[45] If form-selectors have analyzed a form, and identified a significant potential for it somehow to hinder or corrupt the capacity of any believer to engage in true worship, then it may be that they would best exercise their freedom to reject it and seek an alternative.

---

39. See chapter 5, §3.b.ii.6., §3.d.iii.5.
40. See chapter 5, §3.b.i.2., §3.b.ii., §3.d.iii.3.
41. See chapter 3, §2.c.ii., §3.c.ii., §4.c.ii.; chapter 4, §3.d.ii., §3.d.iii.; chapter 5, §3.d.ii., §3.d.iii, §4.c.
42. See chapter 5, §3.b.ii.6.
43. See chapter 3, §3.b.i.1., §3.c.ii.
44. See chapter 4, §3.b.i.2., §3.d.ii.
45. See chapter 5, §3.b.i.2., 3.b.ii.

xiii. The goal for all believers is freedom to choose the most appropriate forms

Not only do believers have substantial freedom with regard to the selection of forms (chapter 5, §4.c. above), but more than this, they are not bound to any one set of forms. Instead, they are free to choose those that best support their worship and witness in their context. For example, in 1 Corinthians 9, Paul asserts his freedom to move between different groups and use different forms, all for the sake of promoting the gospel.[46] Form-selectors need to be aware of this broad goal in their choice of forms, and recognize that they are not limited to using the forms of their pre-conversion faith.

xiv. The best forms are those that reinforce the sufficiency of Christ

Finally, the best forms are those that affirm and reinforce the sufficiency of Christ's work, and which facilitate believers in making a response of thankful dependence. For example, in Colossians 2, forms which are designed to obtain that which Christ has already secured are rejected.[47] By contrast, forms prescribed or encouraged by NT authors (especially baptism and the Lord's Supper) are ones which explicitly point to Christ's finished work and facilitate a response of thankful dependence in believers.[48] Not only should form-selectors avoid forms with the potential to corrupt true worship, they should also actively seek out those forms which best help believers to understand and embrace the sufficiency of Christ.

2. How is contextualization to be distinguished from syncretism?

Based on the above synthesis, I am now able to propose a method for distinguishing contextualization from syncretism with regard to the use of the forms of other faiths.[49] As discussed above, a crucial finding in this research is the fact that in all ten texts where the forms of other faiths are used, what is at stake is true worship. In light of this, I propose that, when it comes to using the forms of other faiths, the key to distinguishing contextualization

46. See chapter 5, §3.b.ii.8, §3.d.iii.7.
47. See chapter 5, §4.b.i., §4.b.ii.3.
48. See chapter 5, §4.b.ii.3.
49. I am employing the terms in accordance with traditional evangelical usage, whereby "contextualization" refers to the permissible mixing of biblical faith and other elements, and "syncretism" refers to impermissible mixing (see chapter 1, §3.b.).

from syncretism lies in the *impact on worship* of any given form. This potential impact needs to be thoroughly evaluated. If using a Muslim form leads to false worship (that is, if it somehow undermines or compromises a continuing Christ-dependence in the form-user or in others), then syncretism could be present. If it does not, then the use of the form could be characterized as an appropriate contextualization. Further, in determining the impact of a form on worship, form-selectors need to consider the criteria described above (chapter 6, §1.d.) concerning forms and worship.

As we saw in chapter 1 (chapter 1, §3.b.iii.), missiologists have advanced two different types of approaches for distinguishing contextualization from syncretism: structuralist, on the one hand, and outcome-focused on the other. The approach I am proposing here is outcome-focused. A structuralist approach focuses attention on the nature of the form used. The form itself is assessed, and if it is deemed good, permissible or at least neutral, then using it is characterized as appropriate contextualization. But if the form is deemed bad or impermissible, then using it is considered to be syncretistic. The biblical data studied in this book does not support a structuralist approach. As we have seen, in the new covenant era, there is an essential freedom with regard to forms. Forms, simply by virtue of their use by other faiths, are neither permitted nor prohibited outright. Rather, using such forms becomes a problem if it leads to a corruption or distortion of God-given worship. What matters, therefore, is the *outcome* of form-usage, permitting us to conclude that the NT teaching on forms supports an outcome-focused approach, not a structuralist one.

I am not the first to propose adopting an outcome-focused approach (see chapter 1, §3.b.iii.). Rather, the contribution of this research is, first, to provide biblical support for adopting such an approach; second, to suggest that the outcome that needs to be considered is the impact on worship; and third, to provide criteria for that evaluation (chapter 6, §1.d.).

3. A way forward?

As we saw in chapter 1 (chapter 1, §3.a.), even though the IM debate has been going for over 20 years, the debate remains a polarized one, and no consensus has been reached on whether the use of Muslim forms in IM can be embraced as contextualization or rejected as syncretistic. I propose that this lack of progress in the debate can be attributed, at least partly, to various methodological and hermeneutical errors on the part of participants as they have constructed their arguments. In what follows, some key claims made in the IM debate are evaluated in light of the findings in this book. It is hoped that this evaluation will both explain the lack of progress to date, and also demonstrate the possibility of progress if the methods and findings of this research are applied.

a. Poston: IM is syncretistic in its very essence

On the basis of the injunction in Deuteronomy 12 to eradicate Canaanite forms, IM critic Poston argues that "the importation of non-Christian religious practices into a Christian context is never to be tolerated,"[50] and so concludes that IM is "syncretistic in its very essence."[51] As we saw in chapter 3 (chapter 3, §3.c.), the main error here is to directly apply Deuteronomy 12 without first considering relevant redemptive-historical developments affecting the contemporary application of Mosaic law. Because of this, Poston draws a structuralist conclusion: the fact that Muslim forms are used is by itself sufficient to render the practice syncretistic. No evaluation of the impact of using the forms is deemed necessary. Yet as we have seen, a structuralist approach does not reflect the new covenant position regarding forms. Due attention to the salvation-historical setting of these texts leads to a different conclusion.[52]

A compounding problem with Poston's analysis is that he neither acknowledges nor engages with appropriation texts. Had he done so, he would have had to account for the presence of texts in which the forms of other faiths are used, and he would not have been able to draw the structuralist conclusion that he draws.

b. Davis, Peterson, and others: the biblical precedent argument

Davis, Peterson, and others claim that texts which depict the use of the forms of other faiths by God's people function as precedents which justify the use of such forms (including Muslim forms) today.[53] As we saw in our analysis of all six appropriation texts,[54] the main error of this argument concerns the matter of authorial intent. No textual evidence of an

---

50. Poston, "You Must Not," 245 (see also 248).

51. Poston, "You Must Not," 252.

52. In fact, Poston is one of a number of IM critics who adopt a structuralist approach to assess IM, and conclude that it is syncretistic simply by virtue of the fact that Muslim forms are used. See Nikides, "Response," 100; Morton, *Insider*, ch. 11.

53. See Ott er al., *Encountering*, 271; Davis, *Poles Apart*, 131–34, 141; Talman, "Old Testament," 51, 55–56; Petersen, "Investigation," 117–18, 127.

54. See chapter 2, §2.b.i., §3.b.i., §4.b.i.; chapter 4, §2.b.i., §3.b.i.1.; chapter 5, §3.b.i.

authorial intent to establish such a precedent can be found, and so the claim amounts to a misuse of the texts.

This argument also fails to show sensitivity to the salvation-historical setting of the texts. As we saw in chapters 2 and 3,[55] during the OT era, form-selection was a divine prerogative. Therefore the OT authors could not have had the intention of equipping their readers to select their own forms. Since a *"text cannot mean what it never meant,"*[56] the OT "divine appropriation" texts cannot be claimed as precedents for God's people today to use the forms of other faiths. To make such a claim is to impose NT freedoms upon OT texts. This same error is evident in the following question posed by Davis. In relation to Yahweh's appropriation of foreign forms in OT appropriation texts, he asks,,

> If Yahweh did it, why are His servants (missionaries) so reluctant to follow suit?[57]

Davis's argument is, on the surface, convincing. Yet if these texts were never intended to set precedents for God's people in the process of form-selection, then a reluctance to "follow suit" is entirely appropriate. It may be that the use of certain forms of other faiths is appropriate for other reasons, but it cannot be justified on the basis of the biblical precedent argument.

A compounding problem is that most proponents of the biblical precedent argument construct their case based on an unbalanced and unrepresentative selection of texts, citing only appropriation texts and ignoring resistance texts.[58] As a result, their writings give the impression that the biblical authors have an unqualified positive stance towards the use by believers of the forms of other faiths. Yet as we have seen, resistance texts warn of the dangers associated with using such forms. To the extent that proponents of this argument fail to sound these warnings, their contributions are unbalanced. Davis, for example, concludes his articulation of the biblical precedent argument with the claim that "the church has nothing to lose by testing some of the radical innovations suggested."[59] Yet when we listen to the warnings in the resistance texts, it becomes clear that believers do in fact have much to lose if the forms of other faiths are used in such a way that false worship ensues.

---

55. See chapter 2, §2.b.iii.2., §3.b.iii.2., §4.b.iii.2.; chapter 3, §2.b.i.2., §2.b.ii., §3.b.i.3., §3.b.ii., §4.b.i.3.

56. Fee and Stuart, *How to Read*, 30 (emphasis original).

57. Davis, *Poles Apart*, 134.

58. See chapter 1, §3.a.viii.1. An exception is Talman (see Talman, "Old Testament," 49–52).

59. Davis, *Poles Apart*, 141.

c. Talman and others: the "biblical compatibility" test

Like Davis, Peterson and others, IM proponent Talman advances the biblical precedent argument. However, unlike these other proponents of the biblical precedent argument, Talman does acknowledge the existence of both resistance and appropriation texts. Yet his proposal for resolving the apparent tension between the two sets of texts is problematic. He suggests that the Bible describes a process in which the positive forms of other religions are appropriated by God's people, while the negative ones are rejected.[60] He calls believers today to imitate this process, and so advocates a "biblical compatibility" test for contextualized form-selection, in which positive and neutral Islamic forms are appropriated, but negative ones are rejected or reinterpreted.[61]

Because Talman calls for an evaluation of the nature of the form, his approach is also a structuralist one. Yet, as we saw in chapters 2 and 3,[62] in the OT era, forms are divinely prescribed, and so what distinguishes OT appropriation and resistance texts is not whether the relevant forms are positive or negative, but rather whether they are selected by God or by his people. In all the OT appropriation texts, it is *God himself* who selects the forms, and this is what makes the appropriation acceptable. On the other hand, in all the OT resistance texts, it is *God's people* who are attempting to appropriate the foreign forms, and for this reason the appropriation is resisted. The intention of the author is not to equip the Israelites for the task of form-selection, since that is not the Israelites' responsibility. These texts do not therefore provide the basis for a "biblical compatibility" test in which forms must be evaluated as positive or negative. Talman's conclusion that they do so is based on a reading that fails to take into account the salvation-historical setting of the texts.

In addition, in calling form-selectors today to evaluate forms as positive or negative, Talman unhelpfully distracts from the chief concern of the biblical authors: not the *nature* of the form, but its *impact* on worship. Specifically, Talman's test leaves a door open for the use of forms that, notwithstanding their moral neutrality, could nevertheless negatively impact believers' capacity to engage in true worship (for example, because of unhelpful meanings subjectively attached to the forms).

60. Talman, "Old Testament," 49–52.
61. Talman, "Old Testament," 55–56. For other presentations of the test, see Higgins, "Key," 156; Brown, "Biblical Muslims," 70–73. Rebecca Lewis in Brogden, "Inside Out," 35.
62. See chapter 2, §2.b.iii.2., §3.b.iii.2., §4.b.iii.2.; chapter 3, §2.b.i.2., §2.b.ii., §3.b.i.3., §3.b.ii., §4.b.i.3., §5.

d. Kraft: the allegiance test

Kraft calls for believers to use local cultural and religious forms, suggesting that, provided a form can be used to express allegiance to the true God, that form is an appropriate one.[63] Kraft's approach is outcome-focused: he claims that syncretism occurs not simply because a borrowed religious form is used, but rather because of the way it is used.[64] In this respect, Kraft's approach is supported by the texts studied in this book.

Kraft's error, however, is to identify allegiance as the key issue in assessing a form's impact. As we have seen, in all ten texts concerned with the use of the forms of other faiths, the key issue is the matter of *how* people engage with God (worship), not simply with *whom* they are attempting to engage (allegiance). In fact, a focus on allegiance unhelpfully distracts attention from this matter, and has even the potential to create a false sense of security. After all, all six resistance texts show that worship can be directed *to the true God* and yet nevertheless be false worship. Correct allegiance is therefore no guarantee of acceptable worship. Worship that is in Jesus' name, and yet which depends on human effort or performance of ritual rather than Christ's finished work, is false worship.

e. A way forward: a focus on the impact of forms on worship

We have seen that a number of key claims in the IM debate have been made on the basis of methodological and hermeneutical errors which have led to unhelpful assumptions and the use of categories which do not reflect the concerns of the biblical authors. This may explain the lack of progress in the IM debate.

The approach that I am proposing here has been developed inductively from an analysis of the biblical texts, allowing the texts themselves to determine the appropriate categories for thinking about the use of the forms of other faiths. When we analyze the texts on their own terms, seeking to identify the concern of the biblical authors, a remarkable unity and consistency emerges. In all ten texts, the concern of the authors is to promote true worship and guard against false worship. The apparent tension between appropriation texts and resistance texts turns out to be no tension at all. Both sets of texts affirm that true worship is God-given. Both reject human initiation in worship. Both affirm that God is passionately concerned to ensure that his people engage in true worship and avoid false worship. Both affirm the importance and potential influence of worship forms, and thus the importance of making wise form-selections. Both affirm that there

---

63. See chapter 1, §3.c.i.
64. Kraft, "Dynamic Equivalent," 115; Kraft, *Christianity in Culture* (1979), 93.

can be a strong link between forms and the meaning attached to them, such that forms cannot always be separated from their meanings. Both affirm that forms should be used to receive by faith God's gracious provision, and not to attempt to earn merit with God or to manipulate him. Thus a remarkably consistent picture emerges from all ten texts.

It is hoped that these insights will help to bring about progress in the IM debate. Until now, most participants in the IM debate (and from both sides of the debate) have adopted a structuralist approach to distinguishing contextualization from syncretism, leading to a stalemate. It is hoped that the use of an outcome-focused approach will open the way for greater agreement. Until now, a category often used in the debate has been that of the permissibility ("Can believers use Muslim forms?").[65] It is hoped that the use of the category of worship ("What impact do these forms have on worship?") will prove to be a more fruitful alternative. Until now, appropriation and resistance texts have often been cited simply as proofs that Muslim forms either can or cannot be used. It is hoped both sets of texts might rather be seen as having the potential to equip form-selectors to make wise choices that facilitate true, God-given worship.

4. Areas for further study

As discussed in chapter 1 (chapter 1, §3.b.iii.), Hiebert's critical contextualization model for form-selection appropriately calls on believers to perform both an identification and exegesis of relevant Scripture, and a study of the form in question to ascertain its meaning and function. My focus has been on the identification and exegesis of Scripture. Also needed are studies which investigate the meaning and function of Muslim forms in Islam.[66] Given that particular forms might have different meanings and functions in different settings, context-specific studies are also required.[67]

In light of the conclusion in this book that form-selectors need to consider the impact of forms on worship, it follows that it would be especially helpful to conduct field studies of IM communities aimed at investigating the impact of using Muslim forms on Christian worship. Some field studies of IM communities have been made,[68] but none yet which specifically investigates

---

65. The approaches summarized above (chapter 6, §3.) use this category. More generally, it is clear from the questions often posed by participants in the debate that the category of permissibility is being used. For example, Schmidt asks, "How much syncretism is allowed?" and Racey asks, "How far is too far?" Schmidt, "How Much," 26; Racey, "How Far," 304.

66. See Schlorff, "Translational Model," 305–28.

67. See Farah, "Complexity," 89.

68. See the three field studies reported in Farrokh, "Umma," 71–80. See also

the impact of using Muslim forms on worship, and which uses the criteria described above (chapter 6, §1.d.) to evaluate this impact.

More generally, field studies identifying the specific challenges that BMBs face in understanding and embracing a biblical understanding of worship would be very helpful. An example of such a study is Don Little's recent survey of people involved in discipling BMBs. One of his findings is particularly relevant here:

> [Respondents] described how difficult it is for BMBs to grasp the spiritual nature of the Christian life. The reason that this is so hard is that in most Muslim communities, pleasing God is tied to religious rituals.... In contrast, the Christian life is about relationships—with God and with people—not about religious deeds. It is precisely because this is so different from Islamic thinking and practice that new believers often have such a hard time understanding the practice of Christian faith.[69]

More studies like Little's are needed to help form-selectors understand the specific discipleship challenges facing BMBs, and so enable wise application of the biblical principles identified in this book.

Finally, based on the biblical warnings identified in this study concerning the dangers associated with using the forms of other faiths, it may be that some BMBs choose not to use Muslim forms. However, forms traditionally used by Christians may also carry unhelpful meanings for BMBs. For example, for many Muslims, the symbol of the cross is associated with the crusades and imperialism.[70] Therefore, there is an ongoing need to identify and develop forms which BMBs can use in contextualized worship: forms which take into account *both* the biblical teaching and *also* the needs of the specific BMB community.

Prenger, *Muslim*, ch. 3–5.
  69. Little, *Effective*, 174.
  70. See chapter 1, §3.a.i.

Appendix

IN THE BOOK, I identified biblical principles for form-selectors to take into account as they consider whether to use the forms of their pre-conversion faith. These principles could not be applied to any particular context, since such an application would require an understanding of the meaning of particular forms for the relevant BMBs in that context, and field research aimed at gathering that kind of information was beyond the scope of my research. However, the following imaginary discussion[1] is offered as an example of how the biblical principles might possibly be applied in practice. It is not presented here to advocate one particular outcome (after all, in different contexts, different meanings may be attached to the relevant forms so that different outcomes would be appropriate), but rather to suggest a process in which the principles identified in the book might be applied in a ministry context.

The dialogue below imagines the following scenario:

> Six months ago, four unmarried Muslim men came to faith, and started a small house-church. Today they are discussing whether to continue to use a contextualized version of the *sholat* prayer ritual when they pray. They have read and discussed the ten biblical texts analyzed in the book, and have come to the same understanding of the meaning of those texts as presented in the book.

This is a fictional conversation, but it is based on my own ministry experiences and specifically on conversations I have had with Muslims and BMBs in the context in which I live and serve.

---

1. My model for using this form is Brian Tabb's hypothetical conversation in Tabb, *Suffering*, 199–214.

Imaginary Discussion between 4 BMBs

Yusuf. Brothers, we have read and discussed what Allah says in the Holy Books about using the forms of other faiths. Now it is time to talk about what this means for us. Should we keep using Muslim forms?

Arif. There are a lot of Muslim forms. We could be here a long time!

Yusuf. Let's take them one by one. Today, we'll discuss the *sholat* form. Since we became followers of Isa, we've been using the *sholat* form to pray.

Arif. Although we did replace some phrases with prayers from the *Zabur*.[2]

Yusuf. True. So what do you think: should we keep doing this? Is this modified *sholat* form the best one for us to use when we pray?

Zeky. It's interesting that you ask the question that way—what is the "best form"?—because that is a new way of thinking about it for me. Until now, I thought about it more in terms of right or wrong, acceptable or unacceptable.

Arif. Yes, me too. And so I thought that since it's not wrong to use the *sholat*—after all, there's nothing wrong with doing prostrations and recitations—then we should use it because that is what we're used to. But now I have a new way of thinking about forms. Forms are not an end in themselves, but a means to an end. And that end is engaging Allah in true worship.

Zeky. Exactly. And so we're not just looking for forms that are acceptable, but for the form that *best* helps us to achieve that end.

Arif. So the question is: what form for praying best helps us to worship? As we learned, true worship is made possible by Isa Al Masih, and we engage Allah in worship when we depend completely on what Isa has done for us in faith. So to put the question another way: does the *sholat* form help us to do that or not?

Yusuf. Before we can answer that question, we need to think about the meaning of the *sholat* form for us. We saw some examples in the Holy Books where new believers used the forms from their old worship, and the old meaning crept into their worship, causing false worship.

---

2. "Psalms."

ARIF. So the question is: what was the meaning of *sholat* for us before we came to faith?

YUSUF. Yes, exactly.

ZEKY. My imam always preached that the reason we perform *sholat* is to cancel sin. He said if I sinned 5 times in a given day, but did *sholat* 5 times that day, then I would have a clean slate for that day. He was very clear: if our final account is positive, we go to heaven. If negative, to hell.

YUSUF. So you performed *sholat* to cancel sin.

ZEKY. That's right.

ARIF. I was taught that the day I die, there will be a chasm between me and heaven. If I want to enter heaven, I will need to cross a bridge which is as thin as a human hair and as sharp as a sword. But every time I *sholat*, I added another human hair's width to my bridge.

YUSUF. So you performed *sholat* to build your bridge to heaven?

ARIF. Yes. And when I skipped doing it, I felt anxious.

YUSUF. Brother Yana, how about you?

YANA. I performed *sholat* to get *pahala*.[3] I thought that when I did it, Allah would bless me.

YUSUF. That was the same for me too. I did it hoping that Allah would bless me with money or good health or protect me from bad fortune.

ZEKY. Actually, I had that hope as well. I thought my life would go better if I did it.

YUSUF. Ok. Are these meanings compatible with the way of worship given to us by Isa?

ZEKY. No. Isa cancels sin by dying in our place. I can't—and don't need to—cancel sin by performing *sholat*.

ARIF. That's right. Isa is preparing a room for us in heaven, and has prepared the way there. I don't need to build my own bridge to get there.

---

3. "Merit with God."

YANA. Yes. In Isa, we already have every spiritual blessing. I can't earn more by performing *sholat*. And I don't need to.

YUSUF. So all of our old meanings are in tension with the way of worship given to us by Isa.

YANA. So we have to stop using *sholat*?

YUSUF. Not necessarily. It depends how using it affects us now. This is the question we need to ask now: if we keep using the *sholat* form, is there a chance that our old motivations will creep in? Is there a chance we'll depend on our performance of *sholat* to get what we should depend fully on Isa for?

ARIF. You know, I hadn't really thought about this until today. But as I look back over the last 6 months, I think that sometimes the old patterns of thought have resurfaced as we've performed *sholat* together in our gatherings.

ZEKY. Me too. You remember when I confessed that struggle with sin I was having about a month ago.

YUSUF. You were very courageous to do so.

ARIF. Yes, you were.

ZEKY. Well, as I felt the shame of that sin before Allah, I remember looking forward to our next gathering here so I could work off the guilt and shame through performing *sholat*. What I should have done at that point was receive forgiveness from Isa as a gracious gift. I think the old mindset of cancelling sin through religious ritual stopped me from depending fully on what Isa did on the cross.

YANA. But was it the *sholat* form that caused you to think that way, or just years of believing that you were the one responsible for cancelling your sin?

ZEKY. It's hard to say. It feels like the two are all meshed together in my head. After thirty years of performing *sholat*, there are some very ingrained patterns. But our discussion of the Holy Books today has helped me to see that a crucial part of the journey we are on now as followers of Isa is learning to depend completely on Isa and what he did, and at the same time learning to turn away from false dependencies. For me, the *sholat* form is so tied up with false dependencies—with depending on my performance of *sholat*—that I think it is not the best form for me to use now.

Arif. Yes, same for me. We saw when we read the Holy Books that a form is dangerous if it was previously used to secure what Isa Al Masih has secured already and gives to us graciously and freely. That's what the *sholat* form was, and maybe partly still is, for me—something I used to secure what I now know is only available as a gift from Isa.

Yana. I don't think it has that effect on me. I am able to use it to express my dependence on Isa. What's more, I like using it because it's what I'm accustomed to, and because it gives me a link with my heritage. By retaining forms like the *sholat*, it says something important for me—it says that people from our ethnic group can be followers of Isa.

Yusuf. That is important. And so is the matter of depending fully on Isa. In the end, we want to be using forms that remind us of the sufficiency of what Isa has done, not forms that undermine that, even subtly. Mmm. This requires Allah's wisdom. I wonder if we might be able to find a solution by breaking the *sholat* form down into smaller parts. Brothers Arif and Zeky, are there aspects of the *sholat* form that particularly reinforce old patterns of thought for you?

Arif. Well, for me, praying in Arabic—a language that I don't understand—makes it hard for me to relate to Allah through prayer. Another thing is the chanting or repeating of phrases. Saying the same phrase many times has strong connotations of accruing merit for me.

Zeky. Yes, same for me. My mind would switch off. I didn't actually think of it as relating to Allah at all. Just something I had to do the right number of times to get the desired effect.

Yusuf. What about the prostrations?

Arif. I think I could continue to do those without the same problem. To me, the prostrations just show respect and awe for Allah. And I think that is a good thing.

Yusuf. How about for you, brother Zeky?

Zeky. I might need to think about this more. Right now, it feels like the "whole package" has associations that are unhelpful for me. I need to learn to bring my sin to Isa and receive his gracious forgiveness, but my instinct is still to look to *sholat* as a way to work it off. I have realized today that using *sholat* these last 6 months has not helped me in this journey.

YANA. If that is the case, I am happy for us to look for another way to pray together for now. I don't need to use the *sholat* to please God, and I don't want our prayer times to stop you maturing in Al Masih, brother.

ZEKY. Thank you brother. The grace of Isa is strong in you.

YUSUF. I propose that we pray now, and keep praying and reflecting through the week, and then discuss this again next time we gather.

ARIF. Yes, but if we are going to pray right now, we will need to know what form to use!

YUSUF. How about I just lead us in a simple prayer for today? *(The brothers kneel together and raise their palms)*

O Lord, you are the gracious and merciful one. You have provided a way for us to enter your presence to worship—through the death and resurrection of Isa Al Masih. Please help us to depend fully on that way you have provided—to depend fully on Isa Al Masih. And please give us your wisdom as we decide together what forms best help us to do that. In the name of Isa Al Masih we pray, Amen.

Bibliography

Abdo, Ahmad. "A BMB's Identity is in Christ, Not Islam." In *Muslim Conversions to Christ: A Critique of Insider Movements in Islamic Contexts*, edited by Ayman S. Ibrahim and Ant Greenham, 435–36. New York: Peter Lang, 2018.

Aberbach, Moses, and Leivy Smoler. "Aaron, Jeroboam and the Golden Calves." *Journal of Biblical Literature* 86 (1967) 129–40.

Achtemeier, E. *Minor Prophets I*. Understanding the Bible Commentary Series. Grand Rapids: Baker, 2012.

Akin, David L. "The Insider Movement and Life in a Local Body of Believers: An Impossible Union from the Start." In *Muslim Conversions to Christ: A Critique of Insider Movements in Islamic Contexts*, edited by A.yman S. Ibrahim and Ant Greenham, 451–53. New York: Peter Lang, 2018.

Alexander, T. Desmond. "The Passover Sacrifice." In *Sacrifice in the Bible*, edited by R. T. Beckwith and M. J. Selman, 1–24. Grand Rapids: Paternoster, 1995.

———. *From Paradise to the Promised Land: An Introduction to the Pentateuch*. Grand Rapids: Baker, 2002.

Alexander, T. Desmond, and Brian. S. Rosner, eds. *New Dictionary of Biblical Theology*. Downers Grove, IL: InterVarsity, 2000.

Allen, Leslie C. "צחק." In *NIDOTTE* 3:796–97.

Andersen, Francis I. "A Lexicographical Note on Exodus xxxii 18." *Vetus Testamentum* 16 (1966) 108–11.

Andersen, Francis I., and David Noel Freedman. *Hosea: A New Translation with Introduction and Commentary*. Anchor Yale Bible Commentaries. Garden City, NY: Doubleday, 1980.

Archer, G. L. "Contextualization: Some Implications from Life and Witness in the Old Testament." In *New Horizons in World Mission*, edited by David J. Hesselgrave, 199–216. Grand Rapids: Baker, 1980.

Argall, R. A. "The Source of a Religious Error in Colossae." *Calvin Theological Journal* 22 (1987) 6–20.

Armerding, C. E. "Festivals and Feasts." In *DOTP* 300–13.

Arnold, Bill T. *Genesis*. New Cambridge Bible Commentary. Cambridge: Cambridge University Press, 2009.

Arnold, Clinton E. *The Colossian Syncretism: The Interface Between Christianity and Folk Belief at Colossae*. Grand Rapids: Baker, 1996.

Ashford, B. R. "A Theologically Driven Missiology for a Great Commission Resurgence." In *The Great Commission Resurgence: Fulfilling God's Mandate in Our Time*, edited by Chuck Lawless and Adam Greenway, 177–207. Nashville: B&H, 2010.

Averbeck, R. E. "Tabernacle." In *DOTP* 807–27.

Ayub, Edward. "Observations and Reactions to Christians involved in a New Approach to Mission." *St Francis Magazine* 5 (2009) 21–40.

Azumah, John. "Islam and Contextualisation: The Insider Movements in Islam." In *Islam and Christianity on the Edge: Talking Points in Christian-Muslim Relations into the 21st Century*, edited by John Azumah and Peter Riddell, 7–24. Brunswick East: Acorn, 2013.

Baden, Joel S. *J, E, and the Redaction of the Pentateuch*. Tübingen: Mohr Siebeck, 2009.

Baeq, D. S. "Contextualizing Religious Form and Meaning: A Missiological Interpretation of Namaan's Petitions (2 Kings 5:15–19)." *International Journal of Frontier Missiology* 27 (2010) 197–207.

Bailey, L. R. "The Golden Calf." *Hebrew Union College Annual* 42 (1971) 97–115.

Baird, Robert D. *Category Formation and the History of Religions*. The Hague: Mouton, 1971.

Barclay, John M. G. *Colossians and Philemon*. London: Bloomsbury Academic, 2004.

Barnett, Jens. "Refusing to Choose: Multiple Belonging among Arab Followers of Christ." In *Longing for Community: Church, Ummah, or Somewhere in Between?*, edited by David Greenlee, 19–28. Pasadena: William Carey, 2013.

Barré, M. L. "Treaties in the ANE." In *ABD* 6:653–56.

Barrett, C. K. "Attitudes to the Temple in the Acts of the Apostles." In *Templum Amicitiae: Essays on the Second Temple Presented to Ernst Bammel*, edited by W. Horbury, 345–67. JSNTSup 48. Sheffield: Sheffield Academic, 1991.

———. *A Critical and Exegetical Commentary on the Acts of the Apostles: Introduction and Commentary on Acts XV-XXVIII*. International Critical Commentary. Edinburgh: T. & T. Clark, 1998.

———. *The First Epistle to the Corinthians*. Black's New Testament Commentaries. New York: Hendrickson, 1968.

———. "Things Sacrificed To Idols." In *Essays on Paul*, edited by C. K. Barrett, 40–59. New York: SPCK, 1982.

Barrett Fisher, M. "A Practical Look at Discipleship and the Qur'an." In *Muslim Conversions to Christ: A Critique of Insider Movements in Islamic Context*, edited by Ayman S. Ibrahim and Ant Greenham, 345–62. New York: Peter Lang, 2018.

Barth, Marcus, and Helmut Blanke. *Colossians*. Translated by Astrid B. Beck. The Anchor Yale Bible Commentaries. New Haven, CT: Yale University Press, 2005.

Bauckham, Richard. "James and the Gentiles: Acts 15:13–21." In *History, Literature, and Society in the Book of Acts*, edited by Ben Witherington, 154–84. Cambridge: Cambridge University Press, 1996.

———. "James and the Jerusalem Church." In *The Book of Acts in its Palestinian Setting, vol 4: The Book of Acts in its Palestinian Setting*, edited by Richard Bauckham, 415–80. Grand Rapids: Eerdmans, 1995.

———. "The Parting of the Ways: What Happened and Why." *Studia Theologica* 47 (1993) 135–51.

Beale, G. K. "Colossians." In *Commentary on the New Testament Use of the Old Testament*, edited by G. K. Beale and D. A. Carson, 841–70. Grand Rapids: Baker, 2007.

———. *Colossians and Philemon*. Baker Exegetical Commentary on the New Testament. Grand Rapids: Baker, 2019.

———. *The Temple and the Church's Mission: A Biblical Theology of the Dwelling Place of God*. Downers Grove, IL: InterVarsity, 2004.

———. *We Become What We Worship: A Biblical Theology of Idolatry*. Downers Grove, IL: IVP Academic, 2008.
Beeby, H. D. *Grace Abounding: A Commentary on the Book of Hosea*. Grand Rapids: Lightning Source, 1989.
Bellinger, W. H. *Leviticus, Numbers*. Understanding the Bible Commentary Series. Grand Rapids: Baker, 2012.
Best, Harold M. *Unceasing Worship: Biblical Perspectives on Worship and the Arts*. Downers Grove, IL: InterVarsity, 2003.
Bevere, Allan R. *Sharing in the Inheritance: Identity and the Moral Life in Colossians*. London: Bloomsbury, 2003.
Biddle, Mark E. *Deuteronomy*. Smyth & Helwys Bible Commentary. Macon, GA: Smyth & Helwys, 2003.
Bill and Jane [pseud.]. "Pointing the Way: The Translator's Role in Contextualization." *International Journal of Frontier Missiology* 7 (1990) 85–94.
Binger, Tilde. *Asherah: Goddesses in Ugarit, Israel and the Old Testament*. Sheffield: Sheffield Academic, 1997.
Birch, Bruce C. *Hosea, Joel, and Amos*. Westminster Bible Companion. Louisville: Westminster John Knox, 1997.
Block, Daniel I. *Deuteronomy*. The NIV Application Commentary. Grand Rapids: Zondervan, 2012.
———. *For the Glory of God: Recovering a Biblical Theology of Worship*. Grand Rapids: Baker, 2014.
———. *How I Love Your Torah, O LORD!: Studies in the Book of Deuteronomy*. Eugene, OR: Cascade, 2011.
———. "Other Religions in Old Testament Theology." In *Biblical Faith and Other Religions: An Evangelical Assessment*, edited by David W. Baker, 43–78. Grand Rapids: Kregel, 2004.
Blomberg, Craig L. "The Christian and the Law of Moses." In *Witness to the Gospel: The Theology of Acts*, edited by I. H. Marshall and D. Peterson, 397–416. Grand Rapids: Eerdmans, 1998.
———. *The Historical Reliability of John's Gospel: Issues and Commentary*. Downers Grove, IL: InterVarsity, 2001.
———. "Implications of Globalization for Biblical Understanding." In *The Globalization of Theological Education*, edited by Alice Frazer Evans et al., 213–46. Maryknoll, NY: Orbis, 1993.
———. "The Law in Luke-Acts." *Journal for the Study of the New Testament* 22 (1984) 53–80.
Bock, Darrell L. *Acts*. Baker Exegetical Commentary on the New Testament. Grand Rapids: Baker, 2007.
Bockmuehl, Markus. "The Noachide Commandments and New Testament Ethics." *Revue Biblique* 102 (1995) 72–101.
Bokser, B. M. "Unleavened Bread and Passover, Feasts of." In *ABD* 6:755–65.
Borgen, P. "Paul Preaches Circumcision and Pleases Men." In *Paul and Paulinism: Essays in Honour of C. K. Barrett*, edited by S. G. Wilson and M. D. Hooker, 85–102. London: SPCK, 1982.
Bosman, Hendrick L. "פֶּסַח." In *NIDOTTE* 3:642–44.
Bourne, Phil. "Summary of the Contextualization Debate." *St Francis Magazine* 5 (2009) 58–80.

Bradley, J. "The Religious Life-Setting of the Epistle to the Colossians." *Studia Biblica et Theologica* 2 (1972) 17–36.
Braun, Roddy. *1 Chronicles*. Word Biblical Commentary. Waco, TX: Nelson, 1986.
Brichto, Herbert C. "The Worship of the Golden Calf: A Literary Analysis of a Fable on Idolatry." *Hebrew Union College Annual* 54 (1983) 1–44.
Brogden, Dick. "Inside Out: Probing Presuppositions among Insider Movements." *International Journal of Frontier Missiology* 27 (2010) 33–40.
Brown, Rick. "Biblical Muslims." *International Journal of Frontier Missiology* 24 (2007) 65–74.
———. "Brother Jacob and Master Isaac: How One Insider Movement Began." *International Journal of Frontier Missiology* 24 (2007) 41–42.
———. "Contextualization without Syncretism." *International Journal of Frontier Missiology* 23 (2006) 127–33.
Bruce, F. F. *1 and 2 Corinthians*. New Century Bible Commentary. Grand Rapids: Eerdmans, 1971.
———. *The Book of Acts*. New International Commentary on the New Testament. Grand Rapids: Eerdmans, 1988.
———. *The Epistle to the Hebrews*. New International Commentary on the New Testament. Grand Rapids: Eerdmans, 1990.
Bruckner, James. K. *Exodus*. Understanding the Bible Commentary Series. Grand Rapids: Baker, 2012.
Brueggemann, Walter. *Deuteronomy*. Abingdon Old Testament Commentaries. Nashville: Abingdon, 2011.
———. *Genesis*. Interpretation. Atlanta: John Knox, 1982.
Burrows, M. "Theological Ideals, Cross-Cultural Realities: Syncretism and Hybridity in Christian Culture Crossings." In *Traditional Ritual as Christian Worship: Dangerous Syncretism or Necessary* Hybridity, edited by William R. Burrows and R Daniel Shaw, 20–37. Maryknoll, NY: Orbis, 2018.
Burrows, William R., and R. Daniel Shaw. "Prologue." In *Traditional Ritual as Christian Worship: Dangerous Syncretism or Necessary Hybridity*, edited by William R. Burrows and R Daniel Shaw, xix–xxiv. Maryknoll, NY: Orbis, 2018.
Butticaz, Simon. "Acts 15 or the 'Return of the Repressed'? The Church and the Law in Acts." In *Torah in the New Testament: Papers Delivered at the Manchester-Lausanne Seminar of June* 2008, edited by Michael Tait and Peter Oakes, 118–32. London: T. & T. Clark, 2009.
Cairns, Ian. *Word and Presence: A Commentary on the Book of Deuteronomy*. International Theological Commentary. Grand Rapids: Eerdmans, 1992.
Caldwell, S. "Jesus in Samaria: A Paradigm For Church Planting among Muslims." *International Journal of Frontier Missiology* 17 (2000) 25–31.
Carson, D. A. *Biblical Interpretation and the Church: The Problem of Contextualization*. Nashville: Nelson, 1984.
———. "Church and Mission: Reflections on Contextualization and the Third Horizon." In *The Church in the Bible and the World: An International* Study, edited by D. A. Carson, 213–57. Exeter: Paternoster, 1987.
———. "Current Issues in Biblical Theology: A New Testament Perspective." *Bulletin for Biblical Research* 5 (1995) 17–41.
———. *Exegetical Fallacies*. 2nd ed. Grand Rapids: Baker, 1996.

———. *Jesus the Son of God: A Christological Title Often Overlooked, Sometimes Misunderstood, and Currently Disputed*. Wheaton: Crossway, 2012.

———. "The Limits of Dynamic Equivalence in Bible Translation." *Evangelical Review of Theology* 9 (1985) 200–213.

———. "Pauline Inconsistency: Reflections on 1 Corinthians 9:19–23 and Galatians 2:11–14." *Churchman* 100 (1986) 6–45.

———. "Worship under the Word." In *Worship by the* Book, edited by D. A. Carson et al., 11–62. Grand Rapids: Zondervan, 2010.

Carson, D. A., et al. *Justification and Variegated Nomism*. 2 vols. Grand Rapids: Baker Academic, 2001, 2004.

Chance, J. Bradley. *Jerusalem, the Temple, and the New Age in Luke-Acts*. Macon, GA: Mercer University Press, 1988.

Cheung, Alex. *Idol Food in Corinth: Jewish Background and Pauline Legacy*. Sheffield: Sheffield Academic, 1999.

Childs, Brevard S. *Exodus: A Commentary*. Old Testament Library. London: SCM, 1974.

Chilton, B. "Temple." In *DLNT* 1159–66.

Christensen, Duane L. *Deuteronomy 1:1—21:9 (revised)*. Word Biblical Commentary 1–11. Nashville: Thomas Nelson, 2001.

Ciampa, Roy E., and Brian S. Rosner. *The First Letter to the Corinthians*. Pillar New Testament Commentary. Grand Rapids: Eerdmans, 2010.

Clark, Andrew C. "The Role of the Apostles." In *Witness to the Gospel: The Theology of Acts*, edited by I. Howard Marshall and David Peterson, 169–90. Grand Rapids: Eerdmans, 1998.

Clowney, E. P. "Presbyterian Worship." In *Worship: Adoration and* Action, edited by D. A. Carson, 110–22. Eugene, OR: Wipf & Stock, 2002.

Cockerill, Gareth Lee. *The Epistle to the Hebrews*. New International Commentary on the New Testament. Grand Rapids: Eerdmans, 2012.

Coleman, Doug. "Doug Coleman Responds to Bradford Greer's Critique." *International Journal of Frontier Missiology* 29 (2012) 47–53.

———. *A Theological Analysis of the Insider Movement Paradigm from Four Perspectives: Theology of Religions, Revelation, Soteriology and Ecclesiology*. Pasadena: William Carey, 2011.

Comfort, P. W. "Temple." In *DPL* 923–25.

Conn, Harvie M. *Eternal Word and Changing Worlds: Theology, Anthropology and Mission in Trialogue*. Grand Rapids: Zondervan, 1984.

———. "Normativity, Relevance and Relativism." In *Inerrancy and Hermeneutic: A Tradition, a Challenge, a Debate*, edited by Harvie M. Conn, 185–209. Grand Rapids: Baker, 1988.

Connor, John H. "When Culture Leaves Contextualized Christianity Behind." *Missiology* 19 (1991) 21–29.

Conzelmann, Hans. *1 Corinthians*. Hermeneia: A Critical & Historical Commentary on the Bible 1. Philadelphia: Fortress, 1975.

Corniche, Salaam. "Islam's Alleged Allergic Reaction to Christ and Christianity: Truth or Fiction." *St Francis Magazine* 10 (2014) 10–15.

Corwin, Gary. "A Humble Appeal to C5/Insider Movement Muslim Ministry Advocates to Consider Ten Questions, with Responses from Brother Yusuf, Rick Brown, Kevin Higgins, Rebecca Lewis and John Travis." *International Journal of Frontier Missiology* 24 (2007) 5–20.

———. "Insider Movements and Outsider Missiology." *Evangelical Missions Quarterly* 42 (2006) 10–11.
———. "Telling the Difference." *Evangelical Missions Quarterly* 40 (2004) 282–83.
Craigie, Peter C. *The Book of Deuteronomy*. New International Commentary on the Old Testament. Grand Rapids: Eerdmans, 1976.
Cumming, Joseph. "Muslim Followers of Jesus?" In *Understanding Insider Movements: Disciples of Jesus within Diverse Religious Communities*, edited by Harley Talman and John Jay Travis, 25–30. Pasadena: William Carey, 2015.
Currid, John D. *Against the Gods: The Polemical Theology of the Old Testament*. Wheaton: Crossway, 2013.
Curtis, E. M. "Idol, Idolatry." In *ABD* 3:376–81.
Davies, W. D. *The Gospel and the Land: Early Christianity and Jewish Territorial Doctrine*. Berkeley: University of California Press, 1974.
Davis, John R. *Poles Apart? Contextualizing the Gospel*. Bangkok: Kanok Bannasan, 1993.
Day, J. "Canaan, Religion of." In *ABD* 1:831–37.
De Vaux, Roland. *Ancient Israel: Its Life and Instructions*. Translated by John McHugh. Grand Rapids: Eerdmans, 1997.
De Vries, Simon J. *1 and 2 Chronicles*. Forms of the Old Testament Literature. Grand Rapids: Eerdmans, 1989.
Dearman, J. Andrew. *The Book of Hosea*. New International Commentary on the Old Testament. Grand Rapids: Eerdmans, 2010.
Decker, Frank. "When Christian Does Not Translate." *Mission Frontiers* Sept-Oct (2005) 8.
Deem, Ariella. "The Goddess Anath and Some Biblical Hebrew Cruces " *Journal of Semitic Studies* 23 (1978) 25–30.
Deenick, Karl. *Righteous By Promise: A Biblical Theology of Circumcision*. Downers Grove, IL: IVP Academic, 2018.
DeLapp, Nevada Levi *Theophanic "Type-Scenes" in the Pentateuch*. London: T. & T. Clark, 2018.
DeMaris, Richard. *The Colossian Controversy: Wisdom in Dispute at Colossae*. Sheffield: JSOT, 1994.
Dick, Michael B. "Prophetic Parodies of Making the Cult Image." In *Born in Heaven, Made on Earth*, edited by Michael B. Dick, 1–53. Winona Lake, IN: Eisenbrauns, 1999.
Dickson, J. P. *Mission-Commitment in Ancient Judaism and in the Pauline Communities: The Shape, Extent and Background of Early Christian Mission*. Tubingen: Mohr Siebeck, 2003.
Dixon, R. L. "Moving on From the C1-C6 Spectrum." *St Francis Magazine* 5 (2009) 3–19.
Dodd, Brian. *Paul's Paradigmatic 'I': Personal Example as Literary Strategy*. Sheffield: Sheffield Academic, 1999.
Doriani, Daniel M. *Putting the Truth to Work: The Theory and Practice of Biblical Application*. Phillipsburg: P & R, 2001.
Droogers, André. "Syncretism: the Problem of Definition, the Definition of the Problem." In *Dialogue and Syncretism: An Interdisciplinary Approach*, edited by Jerald Gort et al., 7–25. Grand Rapids: Eerdmans, 1989.

Dumbrell, William J. *Covenant and Creation: An Old Testament Covenantal Theology*. Carlisle: Paternoster, 1984.
Dunn, James D. G. *The Epistles to the Colossians and to Philemon*. The New International Greek Testament Commentary. Grand Rapids: Eerdmans, 2014.
———. *The New Perspective on Paul*. Grand Rapids: Eerdmans, 2008.
Durham, John I. *Exodus*. Word Biblical Commentary. Waco, TX: Word, 1987.
Dutch, Bernard. "Should Muslims Become 'Christians'?" *International Journal of Frontier Missiology* 17 (2000) 15–24.
Duvall, J. Scott, and J. Daniel Hays. *Grasping God's Word: A Hands-on Approach to Reading, Interpreting, and Applying the Bible*. Grand Rapids: Zondervan, 2001.
Edelman, R. "To 'Annôt Exodus xxxii 18." *Vetus Testamentum* 16 (1966) 355.
Eidevall, Goran. *Grapes in the Desert: Metaphors, Models, and Themes in Hosea 4–14*. Stockholm: Almqvist & Wiksell, 1996.
Eissfeldt, O. "Lade Und Stierbild." *Zeitschrift für die alttestamentliche Wissenschaft* 58 (1940–1941) 190–215.
Enns, Peter. *Exodus*. NIV Application Commentary. Grand Rapids: Zondervan, 2000.
Espiritu, Daniel L. "Ethnohermeneutics or Oikohermeneutics? Questioning the Necessity of Caldwell's Hermeneutics." *Journal of Asian Mission* 3 (2001) 267–81.
Fadi, Al. "Biblical Salvation in Islam? The Pitfalls of Using the Qur'an as a Bridge to the Gospel." In *Muslim Conversions to Christ: A Critique of Insider Movements in Islamic Contexts*, edited by Ayman S. Ibrahim and Ant Greenham, 159–77. New York: Peter Lang, 2018.
Farah, Warrick. "Adaptive Missiological Engagement within Islamic Contexts." *International Journal of Frontier Missiology* 35 (2018) 171–78.
———. "The Complexity of Insiderness." *International Journal of Frontier Missiology* 32 (2015) 85–91.
Farah, Warrick, and Kylie Meeker. "The W-Spectrum: Worker Paradigms in Muslim Contexts." *Evangelical Missions Quarterly* 51 (2015) 366–75.
Farbridge, M. H. *Studies in Biblical and Semitic Symbolism*. Repr. Milton Park: Taylor & Francis, 1970.
Farrokh, F. "Let's Leave Shahada to Real Muslims." *Evangelical Missions Quarterly* 51 (2015) 402–10.
———. "The New Testament Record: No Signs of Zeus Insiders, Artemis Insiders, or Unknown-God Insiders." In *Muslim Conversions to Christ: A Critique of Insider Movements in Islamic Contexts*, edited by Ayman S. Ibrahim and Ant Greenham, 227–46. New York: Peter Lang, 2018.
———. "Will the Umma Veto SITO? Assessing the Impact of Theological Deviation on Social Acceptability in Muslim Communities." *International Journal of Frontier Missiology* 32 (2015) 69–80.
Fee, Gordon D. "2 Corinthians VI.14–VII.1 and Food Offered to Idols." *New Testament Studies* 23 (1977) 140–61.
———. "Εἰδωλόθυτα Once Again: An Interpretation of 1 Corinthians 8–10." *Biblica* 61 (1980) 172–97.
———. *The First Epistle to the Corinthians*. New International Commentary on the New Testament. Grand Rapids: Eerdmans, 1987.
———. *The First Epistle to the Corinthians, Revised Edition*. New International Commentary on the New Testament. Grand Rapids: Eerdmans, 2014.

———. *Gospel and Spirit: Issues in New Testament Hermeneutics*. Peabody, MA: Hendrickson, 1991.

Fee, Gordon D., and Douglas Stuart. *How to Read the Bible for All Its Worth*. Grand Rapids: Zondervan, 2003.

Filson, Floyd V. *"Yesterday": A Study of Hebrews in the Light of Chapter 13*. London: SCM, 1967.

Finegan, Jack. *Myth and Mystery: An Introduction to the Pagan Religions of the Biblical World*. Grand Rapids: Baker, 1997.

Firth, David G. "Worship as Community Creation: Deuteronomy's Vision of Worship." In *In Praise of Worship: An Exploration of Text and Practice*, edited by David J. Cohen et al., 3–18. Eugene, OR: Pickwick, 2010.

Fisk, B. N. "Eating Meat Offered to Idols: Corinthian Behavior and Pauline Response in 1 Corinthians 8–10 (A Response to Gordon Fee)." *Trinity Journal* 10 (1989) 49–70.

Fitzmyer, Joseph A. *Acts of the Apostles: A New Translation with Introduction and Commentary*. Anchor Yale Bible Commentaries. New York: Doubleday, 1998.

Flemming, Dean. *Contextualization in the New Testament: Patterns for Theology and Mission*. Leicester: Apollos, 2005.

Fletcher, Joshua. "Insider Movements: Sociologically and Theologically Incoherent." In *Muslim Conversions to Christ: A Critique of Insider Movements in Islamic Contexts*, edited by Ayman S. Ibrahim and Ant Greenham, 179–208. New York: Peter Lang, 2018.

Fotopoulos, John. *Food Offered to Idols in Roman Corinth: A Social-rhetorical Reconsideration of 1 Corinthians 8:1—11:1*. Tubingen: Mohr Siebeck, 2003.

Frame, John M. *The Doctrine of the Knowledge of God*. Phillipsburg: P&R, 1987.

———. *Worship in Spirit and Truth*. Phillipsburg: P&R, 1996.

Frank, Audrey. *Covered Glory: The Face of Honor and Shame in the Muslim World*. Eugene, OR: Harvest House, 2019.

Franklin, Eric. *Christ the Lord: A Study in the Purpose and Theology of Luke-Acts*. London: SPCK, 1975.

Fretheim, Terence. E. *Exodus*. Interpretation. Louisville: John Knox, 1991.

———. "אֱלֹהִים." In *NIDOTTE* 1:405–6.

Friedman, R. E. "Tabernacle." In *ABD* 6:292–300.

Frost, Michael, and S. Alan Hirsch. *The Shaping of Things to Come: Innovation and Mission for the 21st-century Church*. Grand Rapids: Baker, 2003.

Garland, David E. *Colossians, Philemon*. NIV Application Commentary. Grand Rapids: Zondervan Academic, 2009.

———. *First Corinthians*. Baker Exegetical Commentary on the New Testament. Grand Rapids: Baker, 2003.

Garner, David B. "High Stakes: Insider Movement Hermeneutics and the Gospel." *Themelios* 37 (2012) 249–74.

Garrett, Duane A. *Hosea, Joel: An Exegetical and Theological Exposition of Holy Scripture*. New American Commentary. Nashville: B&H, 1997.

Gentry, Peter J., and Stephen J. Wellum. *Kingdom through Covenant: A Biblical-Theological Understanding of the Covenants*. 2nd ed. Wheaton: Crossway, 2018.

Gilliland, Dean S. "New Testament Contextualization: Continuity and Particularity in Paul's Theology." In *The Word Among Us: Contextualizing Theology for Mission Today*, edited by Dean S. Gilliland, 52–73. Dallas: Word, 1989.

———, ed. *The Word Among Us: Contextualizing Theology for Mission Today.* Dallas: Word, 1989.

Glaser, Ida. *The Bible and Other Faiths: Christian Responsibility in a World of Religions.* Cumbria: Global Christian Library, 2005.

Glasser, Arthur F. "Old Testament Contextualization: Revelation and Its Environment." In *The Word Among Us: Contextualizing Theology for Mission* Today, edited by Dean S. Gilliland, 32–51. Dallas: Word, 1989.

Goldsworthy, Graeme. "Gospel and Kingdom." In *The Goldsworthy* Trilogy, edited by Graeme Goldsworthy, 1–148. Cumbria: Paternoster, 2000.

———. "Relationship of Old Testament and New Testament." In *NDBT* 81–88.

Gooch, Peter D. *Dangerous Food: 1 Corinthians 8–10 in Its Context.* Waterloo: Wilfrid Laurier University Press, 2006.

Gordon, Cyrus H., and Gary A. Rendsburg. *The Bible and the Ancient Near East.* 4th ed. New York: W. W. Norton, 1997.

Gordon, Robert P. "טוב." In *NIDOTTE* 2:353–57.

Gore, R. J. *Covenantal Worship: Reconsidering the Puritan Regulative Principle.* Phillipsburg: P&R, 2002.

Gort, Gerald. "Syncretism and Dialogue: Christian Historical and Earlier Ecumenical Perception." *Mission Studies* 6 (1989) 9–22.

Grafas, Basil. "A View from the Bridge: Insider Movement Critics Speak Out." *St Francis Magazine* 6 (2010) 934–38.

Gray, George Buchanan. *Sacrifice in the Old Testament: Its Theory and Practice.* Oxford: Clarendon, 1925.

Green, Denis. "Guidelines from Hebrews for Contextualization." In *Muslims and Christians on the Emmaus* Road, edited by J. Dudley Woodberry, 233–50. Monravia: MARC, 1989.

Green, Joel B. "The Demise of the Temple as 'Culture Center' in Luke-Acts: An Exploration of the Rending of the Temple Veil." *Revue Biblique* 101 (1994) 495–515.

Green, Tim. "Conversion in the Light of Identity Theories." In *Longing for Community: Church, Ummah, or Somewhere in Between?*, edited by David Greenlee, 41–52. Pasadena: William Carey, 2013.

———. "Identity Issues for Ex-Muslim Christians, With Particular Reference to Marriage." *St Francis Magazine* 8 (2012).

Greenham, Ant. "Communal Solidarity versus Brotherhood in the New Testament." In *Muslim Conversions to Christ: A Critique of Insider Movements in Islamic* Contexts, edited by Ayman S. Ibrahim and Ant Greenham, 247–64. New York: Peter Lang, 2018.

Greenlee, David. "Living Out an 'In-Christ' Identity: Research and Reflections Related to Muslims Who Have Come to Faith in Jesus Christ." *International Journal of Frontier Missiology* 30 (2013) 5–12.

Greer, Bradford. "Book Review of A Theological Analysis of the Insider Movement Paradigm from Four Perspectives: Theology of Religions, Revelation, Soteriology and Ecclesiology, by Doug Coleman." *International Journal of Frontier Missiology* 28 (2011) 204–9.

Greidanus, Sidney. *Preaching Christ from Genesis: Foundations for Expository Sermons.* Grand Rapids: Eerdmans, 2007.

Grisanti, Michael A. "תעב." In *NIDOTTE* 4:314–18.

Gupta, Nijay K. *Colossians*. Smyth & Helwys Bible Commentary. Macon, GA: Smyth & Helwys, 2013.

Gurtner, Daniel M. and Nicholas Perrin. "Temple." In *DJG* 939–47.

Guthrie, George H. *Hebrews*. NIV Application Commentary. Grand Rapids: Zondervan, 2009.

Hahn, Ferdinand. *The Worship of the Early Church*. Volume 12. Philadelphia: Fortress, 1973.

Hahn, Scott W. *The Kingdom of God as Liturgical Empire: A Theological Commentary on 1–2 Chronicles*. Grand Rapids: Baker, 2012.

Haleblian, Krikor. "The Problem of Contextualization." *Missiology* 11 (1983) 95–111.

Hall, R. G. "Circumcision." In *ABD* 1:1025–31.

Hamilton, Victor P. *The Book of Genesis, Chapters 1–17*. New International Commentary on the Old Testament. Grand Rapids: Eerdmans, 1990.

———. *Exodus: An Exegetical Commentary*. Grand Rapids: Baker, 2011.

Haran, Menahem. "Seething a Kid in Its Mother's Milk." *Journal of Jewish Studies* 30 (1979) 23–35.

———. *Temples and Temple-service in Ancient Israel: An Inquiry Into Biblical Cult Phenomena and the Historical Setting of the Priestly School*. Oxford: Oxford University Press, 1978.

Harman, A. *Deuteronomy: The Commands of a Covenant God*. Fearn: Christian Focus, 2001.

Harriman, David. "Epilogue: Force Majeure: Ethics and Encounters in an Era of Extreme Contextualization." In *Muslim Conversions to Christ: A Critique of Insider Movements in Islamic* Contexts, edited by Ayman S. Ibrahim and Ant Greenham, 455–500. New York: Peter Lang, 2018.

Harris, Murray J. *Colossians and Philemon*. Exegetical Guide to the Greek New Testament. Grand Rapids: Eerdmans, 1991.

Harrison, William H. *In Praise of Mixed Religion: The Syncretism Solution in a Multifaith World*. Montreal: MQUP, 2014.

Hartley, John E. *Genesis*. Understanding the Bible Commentary Series. Grand Rapids: Baker, 2012.

Hattori, Yoshiaki. "Theology of Worship in the Old Testament." In *Worship: Adoration and* Action, edited by D. A. Carson, 21–50. Eugene, OR: Wipf & Stock, 2002.

Head, P. M. "The Temple in Luke's Gospel." In *Heaven on Earth: The Temple in Biblical Theology*, edited by T. Desmond Alexander and Simon Gathercole, 101–19. Carlisle: Paternoster, 2004.

Heider, George C. *Cult of Molek: A Reassessment*. Sheffield: JSOT, 1985.

Hesselgrave, David J. *Communicating Christ Cross-culturally: An Introduction to Missionary Communication*. Grand Rapids: Zondervan, 1991.

———. "Great Commission Contextualization." *International Journal of Frontier Missiology* 12 (1995) 115–19.

———. *Paradigms in Conflict: 10 Key Questions in Christian Missions Today*. Grand Rapids: Kregel, 2005.

———. "Syncretism: Mission and Missionary Induced?" In *Contextualization and Syncretism: Navigating Cultural Currents*, edited by Gailyn Van Rheenen, 71–98. Pasadena: William Carey, 2006.

———. "Traditional Religions, New Religions, and the Communication of the Christian Faith." In *Encountering New Religious Movements: A Holistic Evangelical*

Approach, edited by Irving Hexham et al., 137–58. Grand Rapids: Kregel Academic, 2004.

Hesselgrave, David J., and Edward Rommen. *Contextualization: Meanings, Methods and Models*. Grand Rapids: Baker, 1989.

Hiebert, Paul G. *Anthropological Insights for Missionaries*. Grand Rapids: Baker, 1985.

———. *Anthropological Reflections on Missiological Issues*. Grand Rapids: Baker, 1994.

———. "Critical Contextualization." *International Bulletin of Missionary Research* 11 (1987) 104–11.

———. "Critical Contextualization." *Missiology: An International Review* 12 (1984) 287–96.

———. "Form and Meaning in the Contextualization of the Gospel." In *The Word Among Us: Contextualizing Theology for Mission Today*, edited by Dean S. Gilliland, 101–20. Dallas: Word, 1989.

———. "Syncretism and Social Paradigms." In *Contextualization and Syncretism: Navigating Cultural Currents*, edited by Gailyn Van Rheenen, 31–48. Pasadena: William Carey, 2006.

———. *Transforming Worldviews: An Anthropological Understanding of How People Change*. Grand Rapids: Baker, 2008.

Hiebert, Paul G., et al. *Understanding Folk Religion: A Christian Response to Popular Beliefs and Practices*. Grand Rapids: Baker, 1999.

Higgins, Kevin. "Acts 15 and Insider Movements Among Muslims: Questions, Process, and Conclusions." *International Journal of Frontier Missiology* 24 (2007) 29–40.

———. "At Table in the Idol's Temple? Local Theology, Idolatry, and Identification in 1 Corinthians 8–10." *International Journal of Frontier Missiology* 31 (2014) 27–36.

———. "The Biblical Basis for Insider Movements." In *Muslim Conversions to Christ: A Critique of Insider Movements in Islamic Contexts*, edited by Ayman S. Ibrahim and Ant Greenham, 209–226. New York: Peter Lang, 2018.

———. "Discipling the Nations and the Insider Movement Conversation." *Mission Frontiers* 33 (2011) 26–27.

———. "Identity, Integrity and Insider Movements: A Brief Paper Inspired by Timothy C. Tennent's Critique of C-5 Thinking." *International Journal of Frontier Missiology* 23 (2006) 117–23.

———. "Inside What? Church, Culture, Religion and Insider Movements in Biblical Perspective." *St Francis Magazine* 5 (2009) 74–91.

———. "The Key to Insider Movements: The 'Devoted's' of Acts." *International Journal of Frontier Missiology* 21 (2004) 155–65.

Higgins, Kevin, et al. "Myths and Misunderstandings about Insider Movements." In *Understanding Insider Movements: Disciples of Jesus within Diverse Religious Communities*, edited by Harley Talman and John Jay Travis, 41–54. Pasadena: William Carey, 2015.

Hill, Andrew E. *1 and 2 Chronicles*. NIV Application Commentary. Grand Rapids: Zondervan, 2010.

Hirsch, E. D. *The Aims of Interpretation*. Volume 2429. Chicago: University of Chicago Press, 1976.

———. "Meaning and Significance Reinterpreted." *Critical Inquiry* 11 (1984) 202–24.

———. *Validity in Interpretation*. New Haven, CT: Yale University Press, 1967.

Hoerth, Alfred J., et al. *Peoples of the Old Testament World*. Grand Rapids: Baker, 1998.

Hooker, Paul K. *First and Second Chronicles*. Westminster Bible Companion. Louisville: Westminster John Knox, 2001.
Hornung, Erik. *Conceptions of God in Ancient Egypt*. Ithaca: Cornell University Press, 1982.
Horrell, David. "Theological Principle or Christological Praxis? Pauline Ethics in 1 Corinthians 8:1—11:1." *Journal for the Study of the New Testament* 67 (1997) 83–114.
Horton, Michael. *The Christian Faith: A Systematic Theology for Pilgrims On the Way*. Grand Rapids: Zondervan, 2011.
House, Paul R. *Old Testament Theology*. Downers Grove, IL: InterVarsity, 1998.
Hubbard, D. A. "Foreword." In *The Word Among Us: Contextualizing Theology for Mission Today*, edited by Dean S. Gilliland, vii–viii. Dallas: Word, 1989.
Hundley, M. "To Be or Not To Be: A Reexamination of Name Language in Deuteronomy and the Deuteronomic History." *Vetus Testamentum* 59 (2009) 533–55.
Hunt, J. H. "Idols, Idolatry, Teraphim, Household Gods." In *DOTP* 437–41.
Hurd, John C. *The Origin of 1 Corinthians*. London: SPCK, 1965.
Hurowitz, Victor. *I Have Built You an Exalted House: Temple Building in the Bible in Light of Mesopotamian and North-West Semitic Writings*. Sheffield: Sheffield Academic, 1992.
Hurtado, Larry W. *Lord Jesus Christ: Devotion to Jesus in Earliest Christianity*. Grand Rapids: Eerdmans, 2003.
Hurvitz, Avi. *A Linguistic Study of the Relationship between the Priestly Source and the Book of Ezekiel: A New Approach to an Old Problem*. Paris: Gabalda, 1982.
Hwang, Jerry. *Hosea*. Zondervan Exegetical Commentary on the Old Testament. Grand Rapids: Zondervan, forthcoming.
Hwang, Wonjoo. *Toward a Healthier Contextualization among Muslims: A Biblical Theological Evaluation of the Insider Movement and Its Lessons*. Eugene, OR: Wipf & Stock, 2019.
Hyatt, J. P. *Commentary on Exodus*. New Century Bible Commentary. London: Oliphants, 1971.
Ibrahim, Ayman S. "Who Makes the Qur'an Valid and Valuable for Insiders? Critical Reflections on Harley Talman's Views on the Qur'an." In *Muslim Conversions to Christ: A Critique of Insider Movements in Islamic* Contexts, edited by Ayman S. Ibrahim and Ant Greenham, 139–57. New York: Peter Lang, 2018.
Ibrahim, Ayman S., and Ant Greenham, eds. *Muslim Conversions to Christ: A Critique of Insider Movements in Islamic Contexts*. New York: Peter Lang, 2018.
Imbach, S. R. "Syncretism." In *EDT* 1062–63.
Iskander, Weam. "Question Marks on Contextualization!" In *Muslim Conversions to Christ: A Critique of Insider Movements in Islamic* Contexts, edited by Ayman S. Ibrahim and Ant Greenham, 431–34. New York: Peter Lang, 2018.
Jacob, Edmond. *Theology of the Old Testament*. London: Hodder & Stoughton, 1958.
Janzen, J. Gerald. *Exodus*. Westminster Bible Companion. Louisville: Westminster John Knox, 1997.
Japhet, Sara. *I and II Chronicles: A Commentary*. Old Testament Library. Louisville: Presbyterian, 1993.
Jaz, Abu. "The Cultural Insider, Theological Outsider (CITO)." *International Journal of Frontier Missiology* 32 (2015) 61–67.

Jennings, Nelson. "Suburban Evangelical Individualism: Syncretism or Contextualization." In *Contextualization and Syncretism: Navigating Cultural Currents*, edited by Gailyn Van Rheenen, 159–78. Pasadena: William Carey, 2006.

Jervell, Jacob. *Luke and the People of God: A New Look at Luke-Acts*. Minneapolis: Augsburg, 1972.

Jervell, Jacob, and James D. G. Dunn. *The Theology of the Acts of the Apostles*. Cambridge: Cambridge University Press, 1996.

Jobes, Karen H., et al. *1 Peter*. Baker Exegetical Commentary on the New Testament. Grand Rapids: Baker, 2005.

Johnson, Dennis E. *The Message of Acts in the History of Redemption*. Phillipsburg: P&R, 1997.

Johnson, G. L. W., and G. P. Waters, eds. *By Faith Alone: Answering the Challenges to the Doctrine of Justification*. Wheaton: Crossway, 2006.

Jonker, Louis C. *1 and 2 Chronicles*. Understanding the Bible Commentary Series. Grand Rapids: Baker 2013.

Kato, Byang H. "The Gospel, Cultural Context, and Religious Syncretism." In *Let the Earth Hear His Voice*, edited by J. D. Douglas, 1216–28. Minneapolis: World Wide, 1975.

Keel, Othmar. *The Symbolism of the Biblical World: Ancient Near Eastern Iconography and the Book of Psalms*. New York: Seabury, 1978.

Keener, Craig S. *Acts: An Exegetical Commentary: Volume 1: Introduction and 1:1—2:47*. Grand Rapids: Baker, 2012.

———. *Acts: An Exegetical Commentary: Volume 2: 3:1—14:28*. Grand Rapids: Baker, 2013.

———. *Acts: An Exegetical Commentary: Volume 3: 15:1—23:35*. Grand Rapids: Baker, 2014.

Keller, Timothy. *Gospel Contextualization: Center Church: Part Three*. Grand Rapids: Zondervan, 2013.

Key, A. F. "Traces of the Worship of the Moon God Sin among the Early Israelites." *Journal of Biblical Literature* 84 (1965) 20–26.

Kilgallen, John. *The Stephen Speech: A Literary and Redactional Study of Acts 7:2–53*. Rome: Biblical Institute, 1976.

Kim, Seyoon. "*Imitatio Christi* (1 Corinthians 11:1) How Paul Imitates Jesus Christ in Dealing with Idol Food (1 Corinthians 8–10)." *Bulletin for Biblical Research* 13 (2003) 193–226.

Kitchen, K. A. "Calf, Golden." In *NBD* 158–59.

———. *On the Reliability of the Old Testament*. Grand Rapids: Eerdmans, 2003.

Klein, Ralph W. *1 Chronicles: A Commentary*. Hermeneia: A Critical and Historical Commentary on the Bible. Minneapolis: Fortress, 2006.

Klein, William W., et al. *Introduction to Biblical Interpretation*. Nashville: Thomas Nelson, 2004.

Klink, Edward W., and Darian R. Lockett. *Understanding Biblical Theology: A Comparison of Theory and Practice*. Grand Rapids: Zondervan, 2012.

Knoppers, Gary N. *First Chronicles*. Anchor Yale Bible Commentaries 12. New York: Doubleday, 2004.

Köstenberger, Andreas J., and Richard D. Patterson. *Invitation to Biblical Interpretation: Exploring the Hermeneutical Triad of History, Literature, and Theology*. Grand Rapids: Kregel Academic, 2011.

Kraft, Charles. H. *Anthropology for Christian Witness*. Maryknoll, NY: Orbis, 1996.
———. *Christianity in Culture: A Study in Dynamic Biblical Theologizing in Cross-cultural Perspective*. Maryknoll, NY: Orbis, 1979.
———. *Christianity in Culture: A Study in Dynamic Biblical Theologizing in Cross-cultural Perspective*. 25th Anniversary Edition. Maryknoll, NY: Orbis, 2005.
———. "Communicating the Gospel God's Way." *Ashland Theological Bulletin* 12 (1979) 3–60.
———. *Communication Theory for Christian Witness*. Maryknoll, NY: Orbis, 1991.
———. "Contextualizing Communication." In *The Word Among Us: Contextualizing Theology for Mission Today*, edited by Dean S. Gilliland, 121–40. Dallas: Word, 1989.
———. "Distinctive Religious Barriers to Outside Penetration." In *Media in Islamic Culture*, edited by C. R. Schumaker, 65–76. Wheaton: Evangelical Literature Overseas, 1974.
———. "Dynamic-Equivalent Churches in Muslim Society." In *The Gospel and Islam: A 1978 Compendium*, edited by D. M. McCurry, 114–28. Monrovia: Missions Advanced Research and Communication Center, 1979.
———. "Is Christianity a Religion or a Faith?" In *Appropriate* Christianity, edited by Charles H. Kraft, 83–97. Pasadena: William Carey, 2005.
———. "Meaning Equivalence Contextualization." In *Appropriate* Christianity, edited by Charles H. Kraft, 155–68. Pasadena: William Carey, 2005.
———. "Psychological Stress Factors among Muslims." In *Media in Islamic Culture*, edited by C. R. Schumaker, 137–44. Wheaton: Evangelical Literature Overseas, 1974.
———. "Toward a Christian Ethnotheology." In *God, Man and Church Growth: A Festschrift in Honor of Donald Anderson McGavran*, edited by A. R. Tippett, 109–26. Grand Rapids: Eerdmans, 1973.
———. *Worldview for Christian Witness*. Pasadena: William Carey, 2008.
Kraft, Kathryn Ann. *Searching for Heaven in the Real World: A Sociological Discussion of Conversion in the Arab World*. Oxford: Wipf & Stock, 2013.
Kraus, H. J. *Worship in Israel: A Cultic History of the Old Testament*. Oxford: Basil Blackwell, 1966.
Kruse, C. G. "Law." In *NDBT* 629–36.
Kuhn, Mike. "*Tawḥīd*: Implications for Discipleship in the Muslim Context." In *Muslim Conversions to Christ: A Critique of Insider Movements in Islamic* Contexts, edited by Ayman S. Ibrahim and Ant Greenham, 327–44. New York: Peter Lang, 2018.
Labuschagne, C. J. "'You Shall Not Boil a Kid in Its Mother's Milk': A New Proposal for the Origin of the Prohibition." In *The Scriptures and the Scrolls: Studies in Honour of A. S. Van Der Woude on the Occasion of His 65th* Birthday, edited by F. Garcia Martínez et al., 6–17. Leiden: Brill, 1992.
Lane, William L. *Hebrews 9–13*. Word Biblical Commentary. Dallas: Word, 1991.
Larkin, William J. *Culture and Biblical Hermeneutics: Interpreting and Applying the Authoritative Word in a Relativistic Age*. Grand Rapids: Baker, 1988.
———. *Culture and Biblical Hermeneutics: Interpreting and Applying the Authoritative Word in a Relativistic Age*. Eugene, OR: Wipf & Stock, 2003.
Lewis, Rebecca. "Promoting Movements to Christ within Natural Communities." *International Journal of Frontier Missiology* 24 (2007) 75–76.

———. "Insider Movements: Honoring God-Given Identity and Community." *International Journal of Frontier Missiology* 26 (2009) 33–36.

———. "The Integrity of the Gospel and Insider Movements." *International Journal of Frontier Missiology* 27 (2010) 41–48.

Liefeld, Walter. L. *Interpreting the Book of Acts* Guides to New Testament Exegesis. Grand Rapids: Baker, 1995.

Lightfoot, J. B. *St. Paul's Epistles to the Colossians and to Philemon.* London: Macmillan, 1875.

Lilley, J. P. U. "Understanding the Herem." *Tyndale Bulletin* 44 (1993) 169–77.

Lim, Bo H., and Daniel Castelo. *Hosea.* Two Horizons Old Testament Commentary. Grand Rapids: Eerdmans, 2015.

Lingel, Joshua, et al. *Chrislam: How Missionaries are Promoting an Islamized Gospel.* Garden Grove: i2 Ministries, 2011.

Lingenfelter, Sherwood. *Transforming Culture: A Challenge for Christian Mission.* Grand Rapids: Baker, 1998.

Lipiński, Edward. "Cult Prostitution in Ancient Israel?" *Biblical Archaeology Review* 40 (2014) 48–56.

Little, Don. *Effective Discipling in Muslim Communities: Scripture, History and Seasoned Practices.* Downers Grove, IL: InterVarsity, 2015.

Lods, Adolphe. "Images and Idols, Hebrew and Canaanite." *ERE* VII:138–42.

Lohse, E. *Colossians and Philemon: A Commentary on the Epistles to the Colossians and to Philemon.* Translated by W. R. Poehlmann and R. J. Karris. Hermeneia: A Critical & Historical Commentary on the Bible. Philadelphia: Fortress, 1971.

Longman, Tremper. *How to Read Exodus.* Downers Grove, IL: InterVarsity, 2010.

———. *Immanuel in our Place: Seeing Christ in Israel's Worship.* Phillipsburg: P&R, 2001.

Lowe, Donald. "'Son of God' in Muslim Idiom Translations of Scripture." In *Muslim Conversions to Christ: A Critique of Insider Movements in Islamic* Contexts, edited by Ayman S. Ibrahim and Ant Greenham, 299–326. New York: Peter Lang, 2018.

Lu, Jeffrey S. "עֵגֶל." In *NIDOTTE* 3:320–21.

Luc, Alex T. "חטא." In *NIDOTTE* 2:87–93.

Lundbom, Jack R. *Deuteronomy: A Commentary.* Grand Rapids: Eerdmans, 2013.

Machinist, Peter. "The Question of Distinctiveness in Ancient Israel." In *Essential Papers on Israel and the Ancient Near East*, edited by Frederick E. Greenspahn, 420–42. New York: New York University Press, 1991.

Mackay, John L. *Exodus.* Fearn: Mentor, 2001.

Mann, Thomas W. *Deuteronomy.* Westminster Bible Companion. Louisville: Westminster John Knox, 1995.

Margalit, Baruch. "The Meaning and Significance of Asherah." *Vetus Testamentum* 40 (1990) 264–97.

Marguerat, Daniel. "Paul and the Torah in the Acts of the Apostles." In *Torah in the New Testament: Papers Delivered at the Manchester-Lausanne Seminar of June* 2008, edited by Michael Tait and Peter Oakes, 97–117. London: T. & T. Clark, 2009.

Marshall, I. Howard. *The Acts of the Apostles: An Introduction and Commentary.* Tyndale New Testament Commentaries. Grand Rapids: Inter-Varsity, 1980.

Martin, Troy W. *By Philosophy and Empty Deceit: Colossians as Response to a Cynic Critique.* Sheffield: Bloomsbury, 1996.

Massey, Joshua. "God's Amazing Diversity in Drawing Muslims to Christ." *International Journal of Frontier Missiology* 17 (2000) 5–14.

———. "His Ways are not Our Ways." *Evangelical Missions Quarterly* 35 (1999) 188–97.

———. "Misunderstanding C5: His Ways are not Our Orthodoxy." *Evangelical Missions Quarterly* 40 (2004) 296–304.

———. "Planting the Church in Underground Muslim Contexts." *International Journal of Frontier Missiology* 13 (1996) 139–53.

Mathews, Kenneth A. *Genesis 11:27—50:26.* New American Commentary. Nashville: Broadman & Holman, 2005.

McComiskey, Thomas Edward. "Hosea." In *The Minor Prophets: An Exegetical and Expository* Commentary, edited by Thomas Edward McComiskey, 1–238. Grand Rapids: Baker, 2008.

McConville, J. Gordon. *Deuteronomy.* Apollos Old Testament Commentary. Downers Grove, IL: Apollos, 2002.

———. *Exploring the Old Testament: A Guide to the Prophets.* London: Society for Promoting Christian Knowledge, 2002.

———. *Grace in the End: A Study in Deuteronomic Theology.* Grand Rapids: Zondervan, 1993.

———. *Law and Theology in Deuteronomy.* Sheffield: JSOT, 1984.

McConville, J. G., and J. G. Millar. *Time and Place in Deuteronomy.* Sheffield: Sheffield Academic, 1994.

McCurry, Don. "A Time for New Beginnings." In *The Gospel and Islam: A 1978* Compendium, edited by Don McCurry, 13–21. Monrovia: MARC, 1979.

McDermott, Gerald R. *Can Evangelicals Learn from World Religions? Jesus, Revelation and Religious Traditions.* Downers Grove, IL: InterVarsity, 2000.

McEvenue, Sean. E. *The Narrative Style of the Priestly Writer.* Rome: Biblical Institute, 1971.

McGavran, Donald A. "The Biblical Base from Which Adjustments are Made." In *Christopaganism or Indigenous Christianity,* edited by Tetsunao Yamamori and Charles R. Taber, 35–56. Pasadena: William Carey, 1975.

———. *Bridges of God: A Study in the Strategy of Missions.* Eugene, OR: World Dominion, 2005.

McGavran, Donald A., and C. Peter Wagner. *Understanding Church Growth.* Grand Rapids: Eerdmans, 1990.

McKelvey, R. J. "Temple." In *NDBT* 806–11.

McKenzie, Steven L. *I and II Chronicles.* Abingdon Old Testament Commentaries. Nashville: Abingdon, 2004.

McKnight, Scot. *The Letter to the Colossians.* New International Commentary on the New Testament. Grand Rapids: Eerdmans, 2018.

Meeks, Wayne A. *The First Urban Christians: The Social World of the Apostle Paul.* 2nd ed. New Haven, CT: Yale University Press, 2003.

Melick, Richard R. *Philippians, Colossians, Philemon.* New American Commentary. Nashville: Broadman, 1991.

Mendenhall, George E. "Covenant Forms in Israelite Tradition." *Biblical Archeologist* 17 (1954) 50–76.

Merrill, Eugene H. *Deuteronomy: An Exegetical and Theological Exposition of Holy Scripture.* New American Commentary. Nashville: B & H, 1994.

———. "דֶּרֶךְ." In *NIDOTTE* 1:989–93.

Meyers, Carol. "Temple, Jerusalem." In *ABD* 6:350–69.
Millar, J. Gary. "Land." In *NDBT* 623–27.
Miller, Duane Alexander. "Word Games in Asia Minor." In *Muslim Conversions to Christ: A Critique of Insider Movements in Islamic* Contexts, edited by Ayman S. Ibrahim and Ant Greenham, 283–98. New York: Peter Lang, 2018.
Moberly, R. W. L. *At the Mountain of God: Story and Theology in Exodus 32–34*. Sheffield: Bloomsbury, 1983.
———. "בטח." In *NIDOTTE* 1:644–49.
Monson, J. "The New 'Ain Dara Temple: Closest Solomonic Parallel." *Biblical Archeology Review* 26 (2000) 20–35.
Monson, John. "Solomon's Temple." In *DOTHB* 929–35.
Moo, Douglas J. "The Law of Christ as the Fulfillment of the Law of Moses: A Modified Lutheran View." In *Five Views on Law and Gospel*, edited by W. G. Strickland, 319–76. Grand Rapids: Zondervan, 1996.
———. *The Letters to the Colossians and to Philemon*. Pillar New Testament Commentary. Grand Rapids: Eerdmans, 2008.
Moorhead, John. "Cooking a Kid in Its Mother's Milk: Patristic Exegesis of An Old Testament Command." *Augustinianum* 37 (1997) 261–71.
Moreau, A. Scott. "Contextualization: From an Adapted Message to an Adapted Life." In *The Changing Face of World* Missions, edited by Michael Pocock et al., 321–48. Grand Rapids: Baker, 2005.
———. "Contextualization, Syncretism, and Spiritual Warfare: Identifying the Issues." In *Contextualization and Syncretism: Navigating Cultural* Currents, edited by Gailyn Van Rheenen, 47–70. Pasadena: William Carey, 2006.
———. *Contextualization in World Missions: Mapping and Assessing Evangelical Models*. Grand Rapids: Kregel Academic, 2012.
———. "Syncretism." In *EDWM* 924–25.
Moreau, A. Scott, et al. *Introducing World Missions: A Biblical, Historical, and Practical Survey*. Grand Rapids: Baker, 2004.
Morton, Jeff. *Insider Movements: Biblically Incredible or Incredibly Brilliant?* Eugene, OR: Wipf & Stock, 2012.
Morton, Jeff, and Harley Talman. "Does the Jerusalem Council of Acts 15 Support Insider Movement Practices?" *Evangelical Review of Theology* 37 (2013) 308–20.
Motyer, J. A. "Circumcision." In *NBD* 204–5.
Mullins, M. R. "Syncretistic Movements." In *DAC* 809–10.
Munayer, Salim. *Hosea*. Asia Bible Commentary Series. Manila: Asia Theological Association, 2010.
Naselli, Andrew David. "Was It Always Idolatrous for Corinthian Christians to Eat εἰδωλόθυτα in an Idol's Temple? (1 Cor 8–10)." *Southeastern Theological Review* 9.1 (2018) 23–45.
Naudé, Jacobus A. "חרם." In *NIDOTTE* 2:276–77.
Nelson, Richard D. "Herem and the Deuteronomic Social Conscience." In *Deuteronomy and Deuteronomic Literature: Festschrift C. H. W. Brekelmans*, edited by Marc Vervenne and Johan Lust, 39–54. Leuven: Leuven University Press, 1997.
Newton, Derek. *Deity and Diet: The Dilemma of Sacrificial Food at Corinth*. Sheffield: Sheffield Academic, 1998.
Nicholls, Bruce J. *Contextualization: A Theology of Gospel and Culture*. Repr. Downers Grove, IL: IVP, 2003.

Nicholson, Ernest W. *God and His People: Covenant and Theology in the Old Testament*. Oxford: Clarendon, 1988.

Nida, Eugene A., and Charles R. Taber. *The Theory and Practice of Translation*. Leiden: Brill, 1969.

Niehaus, Jeffrey J. *Ancient Near Eastern Themes in Biblical Theology*. Grand Rapids: Kregel Academic, 2008.

Nikides, Bill. "Building a Missiological Foundation: Modality and Sodality." In *Muslim Conversions to Christ: A Critique of Insider Movements in Islamic* Contexts, edited by Ayman S. Ibrahim and Ant Greenham, 81–104. New York: Peter Lang, 2018.

———. "Lost in Translation: Insider Movements and Biblical Interpretation." In *Chrislam: How Missionaries are Promoting an Islamized Gospel*, edited by Joshua Lingel et al. Garden Grove: i2 Ministries, 2011.

———. "A Response to Kevin Higgins' 'Inside What? Church, Culture, Religion, and Insider Movements in Biblical Perspective." *St Francis Magazine* 2 (2009) 92–113.

Nogalski, James D. *The Book of the Twelve: Hosea-Jonah*. Smyth & Helwys Bible Commentary. Macon, GA: Smyth & Helwys, 2011.

O'Mathúna, Donald P. "Divination, Magic." In *DOTP* 193–97.

Oden, R. A. "The Persistence of Canaanite Religion." *Biblical Archeologist* 39 (1976) 31–36.

Oh-Young, Kwon. *1 Corinthians 1–4: Reconstructing Its Social and Rhetorical Situation and Re-Reading It Cross-Culturally for Korean-Confucian Christians Today*. Eugene, OR: Wipf & Stock, 2010.

Olyan, Saul M. *Asherah and the Cult of Yahweh in Israel*. Atlanta: Scholars, 1988.

Oppenheim, A. Leo. *Ancient Mesopotamia: Portrait of a Dead Civilization*. Chicago: University of Chicago Press, 2013.

Osborne, Grant R. *The Hermeneutical Spiral: A Comprehensive Introduction to Biblical Interpretation*. 2nd ed. Downers Grove, IL: IVP Academic, 2006.

Oswalt, John N. "The Golden Calves and the Egyptian Concept of Deity." *Evangelical Quarterly* 45 (1973) 13–20.

Ott, Craig, et al. *Encountering Theology of Mission: Biblical Foundations, Historical Developments, and Contemporary Issues*. Grand Rapids: Baker Academic, 2010.

Owens, Larry. "Syncretism and the Scriptures." *Evangelical Missions Quarterly* 43 (2007) 74–80.

Pannenberg, Wolfhart. *Basic Questions in Theology*. Volume 2. London: SCM, 1970.

Pao, David W. *Acts and the Isaianic New Exodus*. Tübingen: Mohr Siebeck, 2000.

———. *Colossians and Philemon*. Zondervan Exegetical Commentary on the New Testament. Grand Rapids: Zondervan Academic, 2012.

Parshall, Phil. *Beyond the Mosque: Christians Within Muslim Community*. Grand Rapids: Baker, 1985.

———. "DANGER! New Directions in Contextualization." *Evangelical Missions Quarterly* 34 (1998) 404–6, 409–10.

———. *Muslim Evangelism: Contemporary Approaches to Contextualization*. 2nd ed. Waynesboro: Gabriel, 2003.

———. *New Paths in Muslim Evangelism: Evangelical Approaches to Contextualization*. Grand Rapids: Baker, 1980.

Patterson, Paige. "Essential Inside Information on the Insider Movement." In *Muslim Conversions to Christ: A Critique of Insider Movements in Islamic* Contexts, edited by Aymam S. Ibrahim and Ant Greenham, 365–73. New York: Peter Lang, 2018.

Patzia, Arthur G. *Ephesians, Colossians, Philemon.* Understanding the Bible Commentary Series. Grand Rapids: Baker, 2011.
PCA Study Committee on Insider Movements. "A Call to Faithful Witness: A Report of the Ad Interim Study Committee on Insider Movements to the Forty-Second General Assembly of the Presbyterian Church of America."
Perrin, Nicholas. *Jesus the Temple.* Grand Rapids: Baker, 2010.
Petersen, Brian K. "A Brief Investigation of Old Testament Precursors to the Pauline Missiological Model of Cultural Adaptation." *International Journal of Frontier Missiology* 24 (2007) 117–29.
———. "The Possibility of a 'Hindu Christ-Follower': Hans Staffner's Proposal for the Dual Identity of Disciples of Christ within High Caste Hindu Communities." *International Journal of Frontier Missiology* 24 (2007) 87–97.
Peterson, David G. *The Acts of the Apostles.* The Pillar New Testament Commentary. Grand Rapids: Eerdmans, 2009.
———. *Engaging with God: A Biblical Theology of Worship.* Downers Grove, IL: InterVarsity, 1992.
———. "Worship." In *NDBT* 855–63.
Plastaras, James. *The God of Exodus: The Theology of the Exodus Narratives.* Milwaukee: Bruce, 1966.
Pocock, Michael, et al. *The Changing Face of World Missions: Engaging Contemporary Issues and Trends.* Grand Rapids: Baker, 2005.
Poston, Larry. "'You Must Not Worship in Their Way . . . ' When Contextualization Becomes Syncretism." In *Contextualization and Syncretism: Navigating Cultural Currents*, edited by Gailyn Van Rheenen, 243–63. Pasadena: William Carey, 2006.
Poythress, Vern S. *Interpreting Eden: A Guide to Faithfully Reading and Understanding Genesis 1–3.* Wheaton: Crossway, 2019.
Pratt, Richard. L. *1 and 2 Chronicles.* Fearn: Mentor, 1998.
Prenger, Jan Hendrik. *Muslim Insider Christ Followers.* Pasadena: William Carey, 2017.
Pritchard, James B. *The Ancient Near East in Pictures: Relating to the Old Testament.* Princeton: Princeton University Press, 1954.
———. *Ancient Near Eastern Texts Relating to the Old Testament.* 3rd ed. Princeton: Princeton University Press, 1969.
Proctor, John. "Proselytes and Pressure Cookers: The Meaning and Application of Acts 15:20." *International Review of Mission* 85 (2006) 469–83.
Propp, William H. C. *Exodus 1–18.* Anchor Yale Bible Commentaries 2. New York: Doubleday, 1998.
Provan, Iain W. *1 and 2 Kings.* Understanding the Bible Commentary Series. Grand Rapids: Baker, 2012.
Racey, David. "Contextualization: How Far is Too Far?" *Evangelical Missions Quarterly* 32 (1996) 304–10.
Rayburn, Robert G. *O Come, Let Us Worship: Corporate Worship in the Evangelical Church.* Eugene, OR: Wipf & Stock, 2010.
Rendsburg, Gary A. "Hebrew Philological Notes (II)." *Hebrew Studies* 42 (2001) 187–95.
Rendtorff, Rolf. *The Problem of the Process of Transmission in the Pentateuch.* Sheffield: SAP, 1990.
Richard, H. L. "Religious Syncretism as a Syncretistic Concept: The Inadequacy of the 'World Religions' Paradigm in Cross-Cultural Encounter." *International Journal of Frontier Missiology* 31 (2014) 209–15.

———. "All Things are Yours." In *Understanding Insider Movements: Disciples of Jesus within Diverse Religious Communities*, edited by Harley Talman and John J. Travis, 289–92. Pasadena: William Carey, 2015.

Ridgway, John. "Insider Movements in the Gospels and Acts." *International Journal of Frontier Missiology* 24 (2007) 77–86.

Ritchie, Daniel F. N. *The Regulative Principle of Worship: Explained and Applied*. Orlando: Xulon, 2007.

Roberts, Michael. "Where We Agree . . . and Don't?" In *Understanding Insider Movements: Disciples of Jesus within Diverse Religious Communities*, edited by Harley Talman and John J. Travis, 545–48. Pasadena: William Carey, 2015.

Roberts, Michael, and Richard Jameson. "Conversion in the New Testament." In *Understanding Insider Movements: Disciples of Jesus within Diverse Religious Communities*, edited by Harley Talman and John J. Travis, 199–212. Pasadena: William Carey, 2015.

Rommen, Edward, and Harold Netland, eds. *Christianity and the Religions: A Biblical Theology of World Religions*. Pasadena: William Carey, 1995.

Rosner, Brian S. "Biblical Theology." In *NDBT* 3–10.

———. "Idolatry." In *NDBT* 569–75.

Ross, Allen P. *Recalling the Hope of Glory: Biblical Worship from the Garden to the New Creation*. Grand Rapids: Kregel, 2006.

Rowley, H. H. *Worship in Ancient Israel: Its Forms and Meaning*. Eugene, OR: SPCK, 1976.

Rudman, Dominic. "When Gods go Hungry: Mesopotamian Rite Clarifies Puzzling Prophecy." *Bible Review* 18 (2002) 30–39.

Ryken, Philip Graham, and R. Kent Hughes. *Exodus: Saved for God's Glory*. Wheaton: Crossway, 2005.

Sailhamer, John H. *The Pentateuch As Narrative: A Biblical-Theological Commentary*. Grand Rapids: Zondervan, 1992.

Sanavi, Mohammad. "The Insider Movement and Iranian Muslims." In *Muslim Conversions to Christ: A Critique of Insider Movements in Islamic Contexts*, edited by Ayman S. Ibrahim and Ant Greenham, 441–46. New York: Peter Lang, 2018.

Sappington, Thomas J. *Revelation and Redemption at Colossae*. London: Bloomsbury, 1991.

Sarna, Nahum M. *Genesis*. JPS Torah Commentary. Philadelphia: Jewish Publication Society, 1989.

Sasson, Jack M. "Bovine Symbolism in the Exodus Narrative." *Vetus Testamentum* 18 (1968) 380–87.

———. "Circumcision in the Ancient Near East." *Journal of Biblical Literature* 85 (1966) 473–76.

———. "The Worship of The Golden Calf." In *Orient and Occident: Essays Presented to Cyrus H. Gordon on the Occasion of his Sixty-Fifth Birthday*, edited by Harry A. Hoffner and Cyrus H. Gordon, 151–59. Kevelaer: Verlag Butzon & Bercker, 1973.

Satterthwaite, P. E. "Biblical History." In *NDBT* 43–51.

Schaper, Robert N. *In His Presence: Appreciating your Worship Tradition*. Nashville: Nelson, 1984.

Schineller, Peter. "Inculturation and Syncretism: What is the Real Issue?" *International Bulletin of Missionary Research* 16 (1992) 50.

Schlorff, Sam. "The Translational Model for Mission in a Resistant Muslim Society: A Critique and an Alternative." *Missiology* 28 (2000) 305–28.

Schmidt, L. D. "How Much Syncretism is Allowed?" *Evangelical Missions Quarterly* 49 (2013) 26–33.

Schmidtke, Sabine. "Introduction." In *The Oxford Handbook of Islamic Theology*, edited by Sabine Schmidtke, 1–23. Oxford: Oxford University Press, 2016.

Schmithals, Walter. *Gnosticism in Corinth*. Nashville: Abingdon, 1971.

Schnabel, Eckhard. *Acts*. Zondervan Exegetical Commentary on the New Testament. Grand Rapids: Zondervan, 2016.

Schreiner, Thomas R. *1 Corinthians: An Introduction and Commentary*. Tyndale New Testament Commentary. Downers Grove, IL: InterVarsity, 2018.

———. *40 Questions about Christians and Biblical Law*. Grand Rapids: Kregel Academic, 2010.

———. "Circumcision." *DPHL* 137–39.

———. *The Law and Its Fulfillment: A Pauline Theology of Law*. Grand Rapids: Baker, 1993.

———. *New Testament Theology: Magnifying God in Christ*. Grand Rapids: Baker, 2008.

Schreiter, Robert J. "Defining Syncretism: An Interim Report." *International Bulletin of Missionary Research* 17 (1993) 50–53.

Scobie, Charles H. H. *The Ways of our God: An Approach to Biblical Theology*. Grand Rapids: Eerdmans, 2003.

Scurlock, J. A. "Magic (ANE)." In *ABD* 4:464–68.

Segal, J. B. *The Hebrew Passover: From the Earliest Times to A.D. 70*. Oxford: Oxford University Press, 1963.

Seifrid, Mark A. "Jesus and the Law in Acts." *Journal for the Study of the New Testament* 30 (1987) 39–57.

Shaw, R. Daniel. "The Dynamics of Ritual and Ceremony: Transforming Traditional Rites to their Intended Purpose." In *Traditional Ritual as Christian Worship: Dangerous Syncretism or Necessary* Hybridity, edited by R. Daniel Shaw and William R. Burrows, 1–19. Maryknoll, NY: Orbis, 2018.

Silva, Moisés. "εἴδωλον." In *NIDNTTE* 2:98–102.

———. "πορνεύω." In *NIDNTTE* 4:109–11.

———. "πνίγω." In *NIDNTTE* 3:823–25.

Simnowitz, Adam. "Appendix: Do Muslim Idiom Translations Islamize the Bible? A Glimpse Behind the Veil." In *Muslim Conversions to Christ: A Critique of Insider Movements in Islamic Contexts*, edited by Ayman S. Ibrahim and Ant Greenham, 501–23. New York: Peter Lang, 2018.

Simundson, Daniel J. *Hosea, Joel, Amos, Obadiah, Jonah, Micah*. Abingdon Old Testament Commentaries. Nashville: Abingdon, 2011.

Sleeman, Matthew. *Geography and the Ascension Narrative in Acts*. Cambridge: Cambridge University Press, 2009.

Smit, Joop F. M. "The Rhetorical Disposition of First Corinthians 8:7—9:27." *Catholic Biblical Quarterly* 59 (1997) 476–91.

Smith, Gary V. *Hosea, Amos, Micah*. NIV Application Commentary. Grand Rapids: Zondervan, 2011.

Smith, Ian. *Heavenly Perspective: A Study of the Apostle Paul's Response to a Jewish Mystical Movement at Colossae*. London: Bloomsbury, 2006.

Smith, Jay. "An Assessment of the Insider's Principle Paradigms." *St Francis Magazine* 5 (2009) 20–51.

Soggin, J. Alberto. *Israel in the Biblical Period: Institutions, Festivals, Ceremonies, Rituals.* Translated by John Bowden. Edinburgh: T. & T. Clark, 2001.

Soulen, Richard N., and R. Kendall Soulen. *Handbook of Biblical Criticism.* Louisville: Westminster John Knox, 2001.

Spencer, F. Scott. *Acts.* Sheffield: Sheffield Academic, 1997.

———. *Journeying Through Acts: A Literary-Cultural Reading.* Peabody, MA: Hendrickson, 2004.

Spencer, J. R. "Golden Calf." In *ABD* 2:1065–69.

Sprinkle, J. M. "Sexuality, Sexual Ethics." In *DOTP* 741–53.

Stackert, Jeffrey. *A Prophet Like Moses: Prophecy, Law, and Israelite Religion.* Oxford: Oxford University Press, 2014.

Steffeck, E. "Some Observations on the Apostolic Decree in Acts 15:20, 29 (and 21:25)." In *Torah in the New Testament: Papers Delivered at the Manchester-Lausanne Seminar of June* 2008, edited by Michael Tait and Peter Oakes, 133–42. London: T. & T. Clark, 2009.

Stewart, R. A. "Passover." In *NBD* 871–73.

Strange, Daniel. *"For Their Rock is Not as Our Rock": An Evangelical Theology of Religions.* Nottingham: InterVarsity, 2013.

Strauss, Steve. "The Role of Context in Shaping Theology." In *Contextualization and Syncretism: Navigating Cultural Currents*, edited by Gailyn Van Rheenen, 99–128. Pasadena: William Carey, 2006.

Strickland, Wayne G., ed. *Five Views on Law and Gospel.* Grand Rapids: Zondervan, 1996.

Strong, D. K. "The Jerusalem Council: Some Implications for Contextualization." In *Mission in Acts: Ancient Narratives in Contemporary* Context, edited by Robert L. Gallagher and Paul Hertig, 196–208. Maryknoll, NY: Orbis, 2004.

Stuart, Douglas. *Exodus.* New American Commentary. Nashville: Broadman & Holman, 2006.

———. *Hosea-Jonah.* Word Biblical Commentary. Waco, TX: Word, 1987.

Sumithra, Sunand. "Syncretism, Secularization and Renewal." In *The Church in the Bible and the World: An International* Study, edited by D. A. Carson, 258–74. Eugene, OR: Wipf & Stock, 1987.

Sylva, Dennis D. "The Meaning and Function of Acts 7:46–50." *Journal for Biblical Literature* 106 (1987) 261–75.

Tabb, Brian J. *Suffering in Ancient Worldview: Luke, Seneca and 4 Maccabees in Dialogue.* London: Bloomsbury, 2017.

Talman, Harley. "Acts 15: An Inside Look." In *Understanding Insider Movements: Disciples of Jesus within Diverse Religious* Communities, edited by Harley Talman and John Jay Travis, 249–62. Pasadena: William Carey, 2015.

———. "Islam, Once a Hopeless Frontier, Now? Comprehensive Contextualization." *International Journal of Frontier Missiology* 21 (2004) 6–12.

———. "Muslim Followers of Jesus and the Muslim Confession of Faith." In *Understanding Insider Movements: Disciples of Jesus within Diverse Religious* Communities, edited by Harley Talman and John Jay Travis, 501–16. Pasadena: William Carey, 2015.

———. "The Old Testament and Insider Movements." *International Journal of Frontier Missiology* 30 (2013) 39–58.
Talman, Harley, and John J. Travis eds. *Understanding Insider Movements: Disciples of Jesus within Diverse Religious Communities.* Pasadena: William Carey, 2015.
Talmon, S. "The Gezer Calendar and the Seasonal Cycle of Ancient Canaan." *Journal of the American Oriental Society* 83 (1963) 177–87.
Tanchanpongs, Natee. "Developing a Palate for Authentic Theology." In *Local Theology for the Global Church: Principles for an Evangelical Approach to* Contextualization, edited by Matthew Cook et al., 109–23. Pasadena: William Carey, 2010.
Tannehill, Robert C. *The Narrative Unity of Luke-Acts: The Acts of the Apostles.* Volume 2. Minneapolis: Fortress, 1990.
Tappeiner, Daniel A. "A Response To Caldwell's Trumpet Call to Ethnohermeneutics." *Journal of Asian Mission* 1 (1999) 223–32.
Taylor, David. "Contextualization, Syncretism, and the Demonic in Indigenous Movements." In *Understanding Insider Movements: Disciples of Jesus within Diverse Religious Communities,* edited by Harley Talman and John Jay Travis, 375–84. Pasadena: William Carey, 2015.
Taylor, Mark. *1 Corinthians: An Exegetical and Theological Exposition of Holy Scripture.* New American Commentary. Nashville: B&H, 2014.
Tennent, Timothy C. "Followers of Jesus (Isa) in Islamic Mosques: A Closer Examination of C-5 'High Spectrum' Contextualization." *International Journal of Frontier Missiology* 23 (2006) 101–15.
Thomas, David, and Roggema, Barbara, eds. *Christian-Muslim Relations. A Bibliographical History: Volume 1 (600–900).* Leiden: Brill, 2009.
Thompson, Alan J. *The Acts of the Risen Lord Jesus: Luke's Account of God's Unfolding Plan.* Downers Grove, IL: InterVarsity, 2011.
Thompson, J. A. *1, 2 Chronicles: An Exegetical and Theological Exposition of Holy Scripture.* New American Commentary. Nashville: B&H, 1994.
Tigay, Jeffrey H. *Deuteronomy.* JPS Torah Commentary. Philadelphia: The Jewish Publication Society, 1996.
Tillich, Paul, and Robert C. Kimball. *Theology of Culture.* New York: Oxford University Press, 1964.
Toews, Wesley I. *Monarchy and Religious Institution in Israel Under Jeroboam I.* Atlanta: Scholars, 1993.
Travis, John. "The C1 to C6 Spectrum." *Evangelical Missions Quarterly* 34 (1998) 407–8.
———. "Messianic Muslim Followers of Isa." *International Journal of Frontier Missiology* 17 (2000) 53–59.
———. "Must all Muslims Leave 'Islam' to Follow Jesus?" *Evangelical Missions Quarterly* 34 (1998) 411–15.
Travis, John, and Anna Travis. "Appropriate Approaches in Muslim Contexts." In *Appropriate Christianity,* edited by Charles H. Kraft, 397–414. Pasadena: William Carey, 2005.
———. "Contextualization Among Hindus, Muslims and Buddhists, A Focus on 'Insider Movements.'" *Mission Frontiers* 27 (2005) 12–15.
———. "Roles of 'Alongsiders' in Insider Movements: Contemporary Examples and Biblical Reflections." *International Journal of Frontier Missiology* 30 (2013) 161–69.

Travis, John, and J. Dudley Woodberry. "When God's Kingdom Grows Like Yeast: Frequently Asked Questions about Jesus Movements Within Muslim Communities." *Mission Frontiers* Jul–Aug (2010) 24–30.

Travis, John, et al. "Four responses to Timothy C. Tennent's Followers of Jesus (Isa) in Islamic Mosques: A Closer Examination of C-5 'High Spectrum' Contextualization." *International Journal of Frontier Missiology* 23 (2006) 124–26.

Tsumura, D. T. "Canaan, Canaanites." In *DOTHB* 126–27.

Uddin, Rafique. "Contextualized Worship and Witness." In *Muslims and Christians on the Emmaus Road*, edited by J. Dudley Woodberry, 267–73. Monrovia: MARC, 1989.

Van Dam, Cornelis. "Golden Calf." In *DOTP* 368–71.

———. "שׁחת." In *NIDOTTE* 4:92–93.

van der Toorn, Karel. "Prostitution (Cultic)." In *ABD* 5:510–13.

Van Pelt, M., et al., "רוּחַ." In *NIDOTTE* 3:1073–78.

Van Rheenen, Gailyn. "Syncretism and Contextualisation: The Church on a Journey Defining Itself." In *Contextualization and Syncretism: Navigating Cultural Currents*, edited by Gailyn Van Rheenen, 1–29. Pasadena: William Carey, 2006.

Van Seters, John. *Abraham in History and Tradition*. New Haven, CT: Yale University Press, 1974.

———. "The Place of the Yahwist in the History of Passover and Massot." *Zeitschrift für die alttestamentliche Wissenschaft* 95 (1983) 167–82.

VanGemeren, Willem A. "The Law is the Perfection of Righteousness in Christ: A Reformed Perspective." In *Five Views on Law and Gospel*, edited by Wayne G. Strickland, 13–58. Grand Rapids: Zondervan, 1996.

———. *New International Dictionary of Old Testament Theology and Exegesis*. 5 vols. Grand Rapids: Zondervan, 1997.

Vanhoozer, Kevin J. "Exegesis and Hermeneutics." In *NDBT* 52–63.

———. *Is There a Meaning in this Text?: The Bible, the Reader, and the Morality of Literary Knowledge*. Grand Rapids: Zondervan, 2009.

von Rad, Gerhard. *Genesis: A Commentary*. Translated by John H. Marks. Old Testament Library. Philadelphia: Westminster John Knox, 1972.

———. *Old Testament Theology: The Theology of Israel's Historical Traditions*. Louisville: Westminster John Knox, 2001.

———. *Studies in Deuteronomy*. Translated by David Stalker. London: SCM, 1953.

Walker, Christopher, and Michael Dick. *The Induction of the Cult Image in Ancient Mesopotamia*. Helsinki: Neo-Assyrian Text Corpus Project, 2001.

Walker, James. "Why the Church Cannot Accept Muhammad as a Prophet." In *Muslim Conversions to Christ: A Critique of Insider Movements in Islamic Contexts*, edited by Ayman S. Ibrahim and Ant Greenham, 105–21. New York: Peter Lang, 2018.

Walker, P. W. L. *Jesus and the Holy City: New Testament Perspectives on Jerusalem*. Grand Rapids: Eerdmans, 1996.

Walsh, Jerome T. *Old Testament Narrative: A Guide To Interpretation*. Louisville: Westminster John Knox, 2009.

Waltke, Bruce K., and Charles Yu. *An Old Testament Theology*. Grand Rapids: Zondervan, 2011.

Walton, John H. *Ancient Near Eastern Thought and the Old Testament: Introducing the Conceptual World of the Hebrew Bible*. Grand Rapids: Baker, 2006.

———. *Genesis*. NIV Application Commentary. Grand Rapids: Zondervan, 2001.

Walton, John H., et al. *The IVP Bible Background Commentary: Old Testament*. Downers Grove, IL: InterVarsity, 2000.
Walton, Steve. "A Tale of Two Perspectives? The Place of the Temple in Acts." In *Heaven on Earth: The Temple in Biblical* Theology, edited by T. Desmond Alexander and S. Gathercole, 135–49. Carlisle: Paternoster, 2004.
Wan, Enoch. "A Critique of Charles Kraft's Use/Misuse of Communication and Social Sciences in Biblical Interpretation and Missiological Formulation." In *Missiology and the Social Sciences: Contributions, Cautions, and* Conclusions, edited by Edward Rommen and Gary Corwin, 121–64. Pasadena: William Carey, 1996.
Waterman, L. D. "Do the Roots Affect the Fruits?" *International Journal of Frontier Missiology* 24 (2007) 57–63.
———. "God's Kingdom Advance is Stronger than Human Veto: A Response to Fred Farrokh's 'Will the Umma Veto SITO?.'" *International Journal of Frontier Missiology* 32 (2015) 82–83.
———. "Insider Movements: Current Issues in Discussion." *Evangelical Review of Theology* 37 (2013) 292–307.
Wedderburn, A. J. M. "The 'Apostolic Decree': Tradition and Redaction." *Novum Testamentum* 35 (1993) 362–89.
Weeks, Noel. *Admonition and Curse: The Ancient Near Eastern Treaty/Covenant Form as a Problem in Inter-Cultural Relationships*. London: T. & T. Clark, 2004.
———. "Problems with the Comparative Method in Old Testament Studies." *Journal for Biblical Literature* 62 (2019) 287–306.
Wellhausen, Julius. *Prolegomena to the History of Israel*. Repr. Cambridge: Cambridge University Press, 2013.
Wenham, Gordon J. *Genesis 16–50*. Word Biblical Commentary. Dallas: Word, 1994.
Wessels, Anton. "Biblical Presuppositions for and against Syncretism." In *Dialogue and Syncretism: An Interdisciplinary Approach*, edited by Jerald Gort et al., 52–65. Grand Rapids: Eerdmans, 1989.
Whelchel, James R. "Ethnohermeneutics: A Response." *Journal of Asian Mission* 2 (2000) 125–33.
Whitacre, Rodney A. *John*. IVP New Testament Commentary. Downers Grove, IL: InterVarsity, 2010.
Whiteman, Darrell L. "The Function of Appropriate Contextualization in Mission." In *Appropriate* Christianity, edited by Charles H. Kraft, 49–79. Pasadena: William Carey, 2005.
Whybray, R. N. "'*Annôt* in Exodus xxxii 18." *Vetus Testamentum* 17 (1967) 122.
———. *The Making of the Pentateuch: A Methodological Study*. Sheffield: SAP, 1987.
Wiarda, Timothy. "The Jerusalem Council and the Theological Task." *Journal of the Evangelical Theological Society* 46 (2003) 233–48.
William, J. S. "Inside/Outside: Getting To The Center Of The Muslim Contextualization Debates." *St Francis Magazine* 7 (2011) 58–95.
Williams, H. H. Drake. *Making Sense of the Bible: A Study of 10 Key Themes Traced Through the Scriptures*. Eugene, OR: Wipf & Stock, 2014.
Williams, Mark S. "Aspects of High-Spectrum Contextualization in Ministry to Muslims." *Journal of Asian Mission* 5 (2003) 75–91.
Williamson, Paul R. *Abraham, Israel and the Nations: The Patriarchal Promise and its Covenantal Development in Genesis*. London: Bloomsbury, 2001.
———. "Circumcision." In *DOTP* 122–25.

———. *Sealed with an Oath: Covenant in God's Unfolding Purpose*. Downers Grove, IL: InterVarsity, 2007.

Willis, Timothy M. "'Eat and Rejoice before the Lord': The Optimism of Worship in the Deuteronomic Code." In *Worship and the Hebrew Bible: Essays in Honor of John T. Willis*, edited by M. Patrick Graham et al., 276–94. London: Bloomsbury, 1999.

Willis, Wendell Lee. "1 Corinthians 8–10: A Retrospective After Twenty-Five Years." *Restoration Quarterly* 49 (2007) 103–12.

———. *Idol Meat in Corinth: The Pauline Argument in 1 Corinthians 8 and 10*. Eugene, OR: Wipf & Stock, 2004.

Wilson, Gerald H. "בַּיִת." In *NIDOTTE* 1:655–57.

Wilson, Ian. *Out of the Midst of the Fire: Divine Presence in Deuteronomy*. Atlanta: Scholars, 1995.

Wilson, Robert McL. *Colossians and Philemon*. International Critical Commentary. London: Bloomsbury Academic, 2005.

Wilson, S. G. *The Gentiles and the Gentile Mission in Luke-Acts*. Cambridge: Cambridge University Press, 2005.

———. *Luke and the Law*. Cambridge: Cambridge University Press, 1983.

Wilson, Walter T. *The Hope of Glory: Education and Exhortation in the Epistle to the Colossians*. Leiden: Brill, 1997.

Winter, Ralph. "A Third Reformation? Movements of the Holy Spirit Beyond Christendom." In *Understanding Insider Movements: Disciples of Jesus within Diverse Religious* Communities, edited by Harley Talman and John Jay Travis, 327–32. Pasadena: William Carey, 2015.

Witherington, Ben. *The Acts of the Apostles: A Socio-Rhetorical Commentary*. Grand Rapids: Eerdmans, 1998.

———. *Conflict and Community in Corinth: A Socio-Rhetorical Commentary on 1 and 2 Corinthians*. Grand Rapids: Eerdmans, 1995.

———. *The Letters to Philemon, the Colossians, and the Ephesians: A Socio-Rhetorical Commentary on the Captivity Epistles*. Grand Rapids: Eerdmans, 2007.

———. "Not So Idle Thoughts on *Eidolothuton*." *Tyndale Bulletin* 44 (1993) 237–54.

Wolfe, J. Henry. "Insider Movements: An Assessment of the Viability of Retaining Socio-Religious Insider Identity in High Religious Contexts." PhD diss., The Southern Baptist Theological Seminary, 2011.

Wolff, Hans Walter. *Hosea*. Hermeneia: A Critical and Historical Commentary on the Bible. Philadelphia: Fortress, 1974.

Woodberry, J. Dudley. "Contextualization Among Muslims: Reusing Common Pillars." *International Journal of Frontier Missiology* 13 (1996) 171–86.

———. "The Incarnational Model of Jesus, Paul, and the Jerusalem Council." In *Understanding Insider Movements: Disciples of Jesus within Diverse Religious* Communities, edited by Harley Talman and John Jay Travis, 241–47. Pasadena: William Carey, 2015.

———. "To the Muslims I became a Muslim?" *International Journal of Frontier Missiology* 24 (2007) 23–28.

Woodbridge, P. D. "Circumcision." In *NDBT* 411–14.

Wright, Christopher J. H. "The Authority of Scripture in an Age of Relativism: Old Testament Perspectives." In *The Gospel in the Modern World: A Tribute to John Stott*, edited by Martyn Eden and David F. Wells, 31–48. Downers Grove, IL: InterVarsity, 1991.

———. *Deuteronomy*. New International Biblical Commentary. Carlisle: Paternoster, 1996.

———. *Deuteronomy*. Understanding the Bible Commentary Series. Grand Rapids: Baker, 2012.

———. *God's People in God's Land: Family, Land, and Property in the Old Testament*. Grand Rapids: Eerdmans, 1990.

———. *The Mission of God: Unlocking the Bible's Grand Narrative*. Downers Grove, IL: InterVarsity, 2006.

Wright, G. Ernest. *The Old Testament Against Its Environment*. London: H. Regnery Company, 1950.

Wright, N. T. *Justification: God's Plan and Paul's Vision*. Downers Grove, IL: IVP Academic, 2009.

Wyatt, N. "Of Calves and Kings: The Canaanite Dimension in the Religion of Israel." *Scandinavian Journal of the Old Testament* 6 (1992) 68–91.

———. *Religious Texts from Ugarit*. 2nd ed. London: Continuum, 2002.

Youngblood, Ronald. "The Abrahamic Covenant: Conditional or Unconditional?" In *The Living and Active Word of God: Studies in Honor of Samuel J. Schultz*, edited by Morris Inch and Ronald Youngblood, 31–46. Winona Lake, IN: Eisenbrauns, 1983.

Zahniser, A. H. Mathias. *Symbol and Ceremony: Making Disciples across Cultures*. Monrovia: MARC, 1997.

Zehner, Edwin. "Orthodox Hybridities: Anti-Syncretism and Localization in the Evangelical Christianity of Thailand." *Anthropological Quarterly* 78 (2005) 585–617.

Zevit, Ziony. *The Religions of Ancient Israel: A Synthesis of Parallactic Approaches*. New York: Continuum, 2001.

Ziesler, John A. "The Name of Jesus in the Acts of the Apostles." *Journal for the Study of the New Testament* 4 (1974) 28–41.

www.ingramcontent.com/pod-product-compliance
Lightning Source LLC
Chambersburg PA
CBHW071151300426
44113CB00009B/1162